Economic and Political Change in Asia and Europe

Bernadette Andreosso-O'Callaghan
Frédéric Royall
Editors

Economic and Political Change in Asia and Europe

Social Movement Analyses

Springer

Editors
Bernadette Andreosso-O'Callaghan
Department of Economics
Kemmy Business School
University of Limerick
Ireland

Frédéric Royall
School of Language, Literature, Culture
and Communication
University of Limerick
Ireland

ISBN 978-94-007-4652-7 ISBN 978-94-007-4653-4 (eBook)
DOI 10.1007/978-94-007-4653-4
Springer Dordrecht Heidelberg New York London

Library of Congress Control Number: 2012945911

Printed on acid-free paper

Springer is part of Springer Science+Business Media (www.springer.com)

Acknowledgments

This work is a result of many months of fruitful cooperation between all of the authors of this book. This work started under the auspices of the ASEF (Asia-Europe Foundation) in 2009. We are therefore indebted to ASEF for its financial, administrative, and academic support throughout the timeline of the project. Financial assistance was also provided by the Centre for European Studies at the University of Limerick (Ireland). The editors thank all the book's contributors for their time and patience in this project. We are also grateful for the attention given by Mr. Frank O'Callaghan in proofreading the manuscript, Ms. Claire Ryan for editorial assistance, and Ms. Bernadette Deelen-Mans and Ms. Evelien Bakker of Springer.

Contents

Part III National Examples

Part IV Commentary

List of Figures

List of Tables

Appendices

Abbreviations

ABB	Alex Boncayo Brigade [Armed Partisan Unit]
ABVV/FGTB	Algemeen Belgisch Vakverbond/Fédération générale du travail de Belgique (Federation of Belgian Trade Unions]
AC	Agir Ensemble Contre le Chômage [Act Together Against Unemployment]
ACLVB/CGSLB	Algemene Centrale der Liberale Vakbonden van België/Centrale générale des syndicats libéraux de Belgique [Federation of Liberal Trade Unions of Belgium]
ACTION	Alliance of Citizens Towards Independence, Oneness and Nationalism
ACV/CSC	Algemeen christelijk vakverbond/Confédération des syndicats chrétiens [Confederation of Christian Trade Unions]
ANGVC	Association Nationale des Gens du Voyage Catholique [National Association of Catholic Travelers]
APEIS	Association pour l'Emploi, l'Information et la Solidarité des Chômeurs et Travailleurs Précaires [Association for Employment, Information and the Solidarity of the Unemployed and Precarious Workers]
ASEF	Asia-Europe Foundation
ASNIT	Association Sociale Nationale Internationale Tzigane [National International Social Tzigane Association]
ASSEDIC	Associations pour l'Emploi dans l'Industrie et le Commerce [Associations for Employment in Industry and Commerce]
ATOM	August Twenty-One Movement
ATTAC	Association pour la Taxation des Transactions pour l'Aide aux Citoyens (Association for the Taxation of Financial Transactions to Aid Citizens)
BAYAN	Bagong Alyansang Makabayan [New Nationalist Alliance]
BCC-CO	Basic Christian Community – Community Organization
BLA	Broad Legal Alliance
CAFA	Committee for Anti-Filipino Activities

CAP	Common Agricultural Policy
CCdC	Comité Central des Chômeurs [Central Committee of the Unemployed]
CCEJ	Citizens' Coalition for Economic Justice
CCP	Chinese Communist Party
CPP	Communist Party of the Philippines
CEC	Commission of the European Communities
CGT	Chômeur Confédération Générale du Travail – chômeur (General Confederation of Work – Unemployed)
CGTU	Confédération Générale du Travail Unitaire (Unitary General Confederation of Labor)
CL	Central Luzon
CNL	Christians for National Liberation
CoE	Council of Europe
CPAR	Congress for a People's Agrarian Reform
CRISP	Centre de Recherche et d'Information Socio-Politiques (Belgium)
CV	Coefficient of variation
DAL	Droit au Logement [The Right to Housing]
DGB	Deutscher Gewerkschaftsbund [Confederation of German Trade Unions]
EC	European Community
ECA	European Claimants' Association
ECCI	Executive Committee of the Communist International
ECGCI	European Contact Group on Church and Industry
EDSA	Epifanio de los Santos Avenue [a boulevard that goes through the city of Manila
EMU	European Monetary Union
ENU	European Network of the Unemployed
EP	European Parliament
ESF	European Social Forum
EU	European Union
FAO	Food Agriculture Organization
FNASAT	Fédération Nationale des associations solidaires d'action avec les Tsiganes et les Gens du voyage [National Federation of Associations in Solidarity with Tsiganes and Travelers]
FSS	Forum des Sans [Forum of the "Have-Nots"]
FWENU	First West European Network of Unemployed People
GC	General Command of the NPA
GDP	Gross Domestic Product
GONGO	Government Organized Non-Governmental Organization
HALDE	Haute Autorité de Lutte Contre les Discriminations et pour l'Égalité [High Authority for the Fight against Discrimination and for Equality]
HDI	Human Development Index
HMB	Hukbong Mapagpalaya ng Bayan [People's Liberation Army]
IBRD	International Bank for Reconstruction and Development
INOU	Irish National Organisation of the Unemployed

INSEE	Institut National de la Statistique et des Études Économiques [French National Institut of Statistics and Economic Studies]
JAJA	Justice for Aquino, Justice for All
KAGUMA	Kapisanan ng mga Gurong Makabayan [Association of Patriotic Teachers]
KASAMA	Katipunan ng mga Samahang Manggagawa [Federation of Labor Unions]
KM	Kabataang Makabayan [Patriotic Youth]
KMP	Kilusang Magbubukid ng Pilipinas [Peasant Movement of the Philippines]
LACC	Labor Advisory and Consultative Council
LCR	LigueCommunisteRévolutionnaire[FrenchCommunistRevolutionary League]
LEADS	League of Editors for a Democratic Society
LM	Lapiang Mangagawa [Filipino Workers' Party]
MAKIBAKA	Makabayang Kilusan ng Bagong Kababaihan [Free Movement of New Women]
MAN	Movement for the Advancement of Nationalism
MASAKA	Malayang Samahang Magsasaka [Free Association of Peasants]
MDP	Movement for a Democratic Philippines
MLG	Marxist-Leninist Group
MNCP	Mouvement National des Chômeurs et Précaires [National Mouvement of the Unemployed and Precarious People]
MoU	Memoranda of Understanding
MR	Manila-Rizal Committee
MSV	Mouvement des Sans Voix [Movement of the Speechless]
MTU	Migrants' Trade Union
NAC	National Administrative Council
ND	National Democratic
NDF	National Democratic Front
NEO	National Employment Office (Belgium)
NGO	Non-Governmental Organization
NHK	Japan Broadcasting Corporation
NPA	New People's Army
NPS	National Peasant Secretariat
NSM	New Social Movement
NSP	National Peasant Secretariat
NUFC	National United Front Commission
NUSP	National Union of Students of the Philippines
NUWM	National Unemployed Workers' Movement
OECD	Organization for Economic Cooperation and Development
OSCE	Organization for Security and Co-operation in Europe
PAPA	People's Assembly on the Pope's Arrival
PCF	Parti communiste français [French Communist Party]
PKI	Partai Komunis Indonesia [Indonesian Communist Party]

PKM	Pambansang Katipunan ng mga Magbubukid [PKM or National Association of Peasants]
PKP	Partido Komunista ng Pilipinas [Communist Party of the Philippines]
PO	People's Organization
Pop.Dem.	Popular Democrats
POS	Political Opportunity Structure
PPP	Purchasing Power Parity
PRC	People's Republic of China (PRC)
PS	Parti Socialiste [Socialist Party]
PSR	Philippine Society and Revolution
RILU	Red International of Labour Unions
SCAUP	Student Cultural Association of the University of the Philippines
SCM	Student Christian Movement
SKD	Samahang Demokratiko ng Kabataan [Union of Democratic Youth]
SNC	Syndicat National des Chômeurs [French Nation Trade Union of the Unemployed]
SP.A	Flemish Socialist Party
TAN	Transnational advocacy/activist networks
TOYM	Ten Outstanding Young Men (award)
TSM	Transnational social movements
TUC	Trade Union Congress
UFAT	Union Française des Associations Tsiganes [French Union of Tsiganes Associations]
UK	United Kingdom
UNDP	United Nations Development Program
UNIDO	United Democratic Opposition
UP	University of the Philippines
USA	United States of America
WENWUC	West European Network on Work and Unemployment and the Churches
WTO	World Trade Organization
WWII	World War Two
ZOTO	Zone One Tondo Organization

Chapter 1
Collective Action and Relatively Powerless People in Europe and Asia

Bernadette Andreosso-O'Callaghan and Frédéric Royall

1.1 Introduction

This book arose out of a workshop held at the University of Limerick (Ireland) in September 2010. The event brought together a number of scholars from various universities in Europe, Asia, and North America. The majority of the chapters in this book are based on the Limerick workshop papers, although Dominique Caouette's is a specially commissioned contribution.

The workshop's main objectives were (1) to compare and to contrast the research tools and dominant paradigms in social movement research, (2) to assess the ways relatively "powerless" people[1] mobilize in Asia and Europe, and (3) to investigate the ways the mobilizations of these people have been analyzed with respect to their relevant Asian and European social, political, economic, and cultural contexts. As such, the workshop participants focused on a number of interrelated issues:

- The status of relatively powerless people in Europe and in Asia
- The sociological profiles of the mobilized and an assessment of the personal factors which enable them to do so
- The issue of whether they have trajectories that are different from those of the rest of the population

[1] The notion of relatively powerless people draws on Michael Lipsky's work (1968). It refers in essence to people's weak volume of political resources and so to their dominated position in a "champ de pouvoir" – a domain of power relations (Mouchard 2010).

B. Andreosso-O'Callaghan (✉)
Department of Economics, Kemmy Business School, University of Limerick, Limerick, Ireland
e-mail: Bernadette.andreosso@ul.ie

F. Royall
School of Languages, Literature, Culture and Communication, University of Limerick, Limerick, Ireland
e-mail: Frederic.royall@ul.ie

B. Andreosso-O'Callaghan and F. Royall (eds.), *Economic and Political Change in Asia and Europe: Social Movement Analyses*, DOI 10.1007/978-94-007-4653-4_1,

- The extent to which organizations or people are able to act on their behalf
- The specific forms of engagement used in countries of these regions
- The political and institutional opportunities – or constraints – that relatively powerless people encounter in these regions
- The influences of social, political, economic, and cultural contexts
- The impact of collective action: internal to the group (to establish or to improve on a common identity), protest-oriented (to reach specific gains), and/or culturally oriented (to get the general public to see these people in a different light)

The comparative Europe-Asia dimension is one of the key and novel elements of this book. This approach stems from two observations: economic and political, one the one hand, and social, on the other. From political and economic standpoints, Asian countries are increasingly gaining in economic and political importance in the world. Their rise as economic powers is being nurtured, for a large part, by their espousing of economic *laissez-faire* principles born in Europe during the century of the enlightenment. Owing to their expanding economic size, these countries can no longer be ignored as major international economic and political forces. From a social point of view, major economic change in a number of Asian countries has also led to key social and political challenges. One such challenge is how to deal with the rising number of social movements that challenge the principles and outcomes of *laissez-faire* (neoliberal) policies. Social, political, and economic analysts and commentators are increasingly aware of these issues. Perhaps surprisingly, there is a limited (but growing) body of literature on Asian social movements. Also perhaps understandably, much of the research on Asian social movements has adopted research parameters based on or developed for European social and political contexts. This being the case, one of the key comparative elements of this book is to assess whether the analysis of the growing issue of social movements in Asia can be best conducted by using benchmarks founded on European social, political, economic, and cultural contexts or frames of reference. As such, the book deals with the social, political, economic, and cultural differences between Europe and Asia. The analyses focus attention on these differences and on the consequences or on the effects of national and transnational neoliberal policies on social conflict and on the dynamics of collective action in various countries of these regions. The following sections outline the discussions and debates covered in the book.

1.2 Social and Economic Backdrops

The early decades of economic integration in Europe were marked by sustained economic growth and by increasing levels of social inclusion.[2] During the same period of time, many Asian countries – and in particular South Korea, Taiwan,

[2] Unemployment rates in the Common Market of the 1960s and early 1970s were low (at 2% or lower)· whereas annual growth rates were still in excess of 4% in pre-1973 Common Market economies such as France.

Singapore, and Malaysia – were embarking on a process of rapid economic growth and development. In the European Common Market countries of that time and in a large part of Asia, economic growth was increasingly translated by rising standards of living and by a decrease in poverty levels. This was coupled with initial steps in a gradual democratization process in the region exemplified by the early establishment of democracies in Japan and India.

The oil shock of the early 1970s produced a seismic fracture, as it put an end to an era of favorable economic performance in Europe as well as in the United States. In response to this break, supply-side policies, grounded in neoclassical and neoliberal currents of thought, were enacted facilitating trade liberalization at the global level and exerting additional pressures on the low-skilled segments of the European labor markets. A new era of socioeconomic exclusion ensued, which was soon to be addressed at the European Community level by President of the Commission Jacques Delors's pledge for the creation of a "European social space."

1.3 Recession and Social Movements

It would appear that in the context of the financial and economic crisis of the late years of the 2000s and the early years of the 2010s, the panoply of detrimental effects, such as the closure of (mostly small) firms, job losses and cuts in wages, welfare benefits and public services, has – perhaps surprisingly – coincided with what some social commentators consider to be the relative passivity of the working and middle classes in many European countries. Yet, these are the segments of the population most affected by the crisis. Accordingly, this situation contrasts sharply with that of the 1930s (as analyzed in the chapter by Matt Perry of the University of Newcastle, United Kingdom), a period during which the combined effects of the Great Depression and colonial wars led to various social upheavals and collective actions such as the hunger marches in France and in England (see also Reiss and Perry 2011). Social commentators attribute several factors to the present inertia among large swathes of people most affected by worldwide social and economic upheavals. These analysts point to the decline of labor organizations, to the demise of class ideology, and to the perceived defeat of "anticapitalist" alternatives since the fall of the Berlin Wall.

Yet, the acceleration of the neoliberal agenda in European Union (EU) countries and its forced application in several Asian countries, notably since the 1997 Asian crisis, seem to have dovetailed with the emergence of some social movements connected with a crisis of democratic representation (Castells 1997). Conscious of the inability of the neoliberal state to fulfill its welfare obligations, many contemporary social movements are composed of (or tend to represent) dispossessed and marginalized people (Boo Teik 2010: 11–15), on the one hand, but also, on the other hand, of intellectuals and the middle class – as in the case of Thailand shortly after the International Monetary Fund (IMF) "rescue" of the country.

Beyond these developments and contrary to the viewpoint whereby apathy characterizes today's relatively powerless people, we question whether there is any direct correlation between economic downturns and periods of mobilization (McCarthy and Zald 1977: 1214–1215), and whether there is a positive correlation between social exclusion – a direct consequence of prolonged and recurrent economic downturns – and the rise of social movements (Frank and Fuentes 1990). There may well be a connection, but it seems that there is no automatic link between these phenomena. People become frustrated or deprived for a great number of reasons, and this does not necessarily imply that they will be or that they are always in a position to initiate collective action. People need to perceive their grievances subjectively and to interpret them collectively as unjustified deprivations (Baglioni et al. 2008: 325–327; Chabanet and Royall 2009). Although we accept that there may well be a perception that many people today – in Europe as elsewhere – are lethargic in the face of social and economic upheaval, as the Irish situation may show,[3] we note that this view may be incorrect simply because mobilization takes many expressive and nonexpressive forms.[4] Street demonstrations, protests, or strikes may be considered as expressive forms, but when people refuse to pay rent for public accommodation or when they release "peace" balloons in a public space, they can also show discontent in discreet ways at individual or even at collective levels. Similarly, when people commit suicide, this may also be a very unfortunate and individual way of expressing discontent (see the Chap. 14 by Michiaki Okuyama in this volume).

We also consider that many social commentators have focused for far too long on the various constraints that relatively powerless people must overcome in order to engage in collective action: sociological, cultural, financial, political, organizational, and so on. A vast body of research provides numerous examples around the world, both current and historical, of how these people overcome a host of obstacles. It is not the contributors to this book's intention to come back over this well-tread territory. Rather, we wish to consider the ways that scholars challenge the dominant paradigms with respect to the collective action of powerless people, how they describe the ways that powerless people initiate collective action across cultural, political, and social divides, and how they assess the outcome/impact of such activities.

Linked to these points is the fact that much of recent scholarship has focused on the mobilization of socially, economically, and politically excluded people such as the unemployed, prostitutes, homeless people, migrants, and so on (Giugni 2009; Froissard 2009; Mathieu 2001; Snow et al. 2005). But research is also increasingly addressing workplace conflicts of more or less "new" categories on the margins of traditional employer/employee relations (Denis 2005). These people have a marginal or precarious status in the world of work and often experience material insecurity or instability (Sinigaglia 2009). The collected essays in this volume seek to look at the situation of all these various categories of people.

[3] Following a 15-year period of sustained growth, the Irish economy contracted sharply in 2008 and the Irish government was compelled to seek the financial help of the European Central Bank, of the IMF. Very few public demonstrations took place in the country.

[4] According to Balme and Chabanet (2008: 28), a "mobilization" may refer to two forms of action. The first type corresponds to expressive and conflict-oriented forms of action, whereas the second type is characterized as being far more discreet and consensual.

1.4 Common Traits: Asia and Europe

Relatively powerless people in Europe and Asia probably have many things in common aside from their unenviable status. One shared trait may be that they often express themselves in the public domain and advance specific demands for inclusion, respect, and recognition (Boumaza and Hamman 2007; Shigetomi and Makino 2009). In general, studies on powerless people, whatever their location (East or West), seem to adopt one of the two following lines of inquiry. The first relates to the capability of these people to initiate collective action. Accordingly, studies show that these people use their own relevant social capital or of that of their organization's leaders, including organizational skills. Studies also show that powerless people come to depend on external factors such as favorable political or institutional opportunities. In such studies, the focus of analysis is not really the unlikelihood of the collective action of the powerless but rather the reasons why such events occur. Included in this line of inquiry are attempts to account for people's individual and collective reasons for participating in organizations that act on their behalf.

Another rival line of inquiry questions the validity of these types of approaches. Scholars have suggested that there are very few examples indeed whereby relatively powerless people have in fact mobilized. They claim that what normally happens is that specialists – professional activists or mobilization entrepreneurs as it were – mobilizes on their behalf. Accordingly, this second line of research questions the distinctiveness of many of today's collective actions – in Europe as in Asia – and insists that scholars should really focus on the sociological bases of relatively powerless people or of their organizations.

This book does not seek to resolve the debate. Elements of both schools of thought are apparent in the various chapters. The chapters highlight nonetheless that social movements pervade the different cultures and countries of the regions – East and West. They also show that social movements are embedded in collective and organized opposition to the ruling groups and oligarchies of countries subjected to a broadly similar neoliberal agenda.

1.5 Chapter Descriptions

The book is divided into three parts, each focusing on a specific theme. Part I deals with economic, political, and social globalization in Asia and Europe. Part II focuses on social movements in a comparative perspective. Part III presents case study examples drawn from European and Asian contexts. The final part/chapter presents a sociological overview of the merits of doing comparative work on social movements.

By way of introduction to Part I, the first chapter by Bernadette Andreosso-O'Callaghan of the University of Limerick (Ireland) [*Economic Change and Social Dynamics: Converging and Diverging Trends Across Different Economies*] provides a general comparative background that explains the different ingredients fostering social movements, such as income divergence. She sets the scene by proposing an economic analysis of socioeconomic convergence during the "golden" and "post-golden" ages in both regions of the world. The chapter reveals the clear and adverse circumstances that foment social mobilization, particularly in the case of the EU, a region where responses to adverse economic conditions in terms of food and energy were immediate. The quantitative analysis contrasts long-term economic growth, inequality, and poverty trends, and it depicts the various shocks produced by economic crises (oil, Asian, and current) as a fertile ground for social mobilization. Christian Lahusen's chapter (University of Siegen, Germany) is centered on the notion of social cohesion as dealt with in EU circles [*European Integration, Social Cohesion and Political Contentiousness*]. By analyzing the relationship between European integration, social cohesion, and the political contentiousness of Europe, the chapter discusses whether European integration fosters the "Europeanization" of collective action. It argues that segregations along core-periphery and class structures prevail, and that the "Europeanization" of political contentions and mobilizations will evolved more easily within the European core and the more privileged classes. Carsten Storm's chapter (University of Bochum, Germany) deals with the cultural and philosophical foundations of collective action, particularly in China, and with the neo-Confucianist and neoconservative attempts at establishing a Chinese way of being vis-à-vis that of the western world [*Images and Frameworks of Collective Action in China*]. This chapter is essential in that it clarifies the broad theoretical framework necessary for the appraisal and understanding of social movements in an Asian country such as China. As such, it provides interesting insights in the study of social movements in the broader cases of Asian countries.

The chapter by Didier Chabanet (European University Institute, Florence, Italy) questions the openness of EU institutions with respect to various interest groups [*European Governance and Democracy*]. These institutions may provide alternative forms of access to some actors that are underrepresented in national institutions. In this regard, he examines two areas of public policy and mobilization corresponding to the defense of the rights of migrants and unemployed people, the latter being pioneers of the so-called antiglobalization movement. The last chapter in Part I is by M. Bruna Zolin (University of Venice, Italy) [*Agricultural Markets and Food Riots: The European Union and Asia Compared*]. She shows the delicate situation of structural imbalances in world food markets that led to the 2008 food riots in a number of countries across the two regions (including Greece before the economic crisis of the first decade of the 2000s). The chapter highlights the impact of rising food prices on already at-risk segments of the population, and it explores policies implemented in the two regions so as to stabilize these key markets.

In Part II, the interface between marginalization and the transnationalization of social movements is tackled in Pascale Dufour's chapter (Université de Montréal, Canada) [*Marginalization and Transnationalizing Social Movements: How One Relates to the Other*]. The author aims to fill a gap in the literature by exploring this relationship through the example of the "No-Vox Movement." She questions whether the process of transnationalization is building solidarities and whether it is led by recognition beyond borders. Frédéric Royall's chapter (University of Limerick,

Ireland) looks at a little discussed facet of "Europeanization from below" [*Transnational Collective Action and the European Network of the Unemployed*]. His discussion is based on a review of developments within the European Network of the Unemployed (ENU) between the mid-1980s to the late 1990s. He reflects in particular on the significance of the ENU's evolution with respect to transnational collective action and the impact that the transnationalization processes had on the organization, its affiliates, and individual members.

The third part of the book encompasses a series of national examples of social movements in Asia and Europe. Drawing from historical evidence, Matt Perry's chapter (University of Newcastle, England) is a comparative analysis of the 1930s hunger marches in France and in England [*The "Comités des Chômeurs" (1921–41): A Historical Precedent of French Movements of the Unemployed*]. Next, Jean Faniel's chapter (CRISP, Brussels, Belgium) aims to explain the differences in mobilization intensity generated by three social policy reforms in Belgium (minimum subsistence income, greater controls of the unemployed, and early retirement reforms) [*Comparing Mobilizations Against Three Social Reforms in the 2000s in Belgium*]. He also explores the issue of the renewed protest against a prior reform at the outset of the 2008 crisis. By using a comprehensive data set on young unemployed individuals in the city of Geneva, Marco Giugni and Jasmine Lorenzini (University of Geneva, Switzerland) examine the relationship that exists between employment status, social capital, and political participation [*Employment Status and Political Participation: Does Exclusion Influence the Protest Behavior of the Young Unemployed?*]. In the next chapter, the case of France is explored by Anne-Cécile Renouard (Université de Strasbourg, France). She analyzes the specific case of the Gypsy community in this country [*Practical Uses of Administrative and Cultural Categories Across the Field of Pro-Gypsy Activities in France Today: Activist Constructions and Adaptations to Political Categorizations*].

The last three chapters in Part III deal with social movements in Asian countries. The chapter by Birgit Häse (Technische Universität Dresden, Germany) on collective action in China highlights social exclusion and collective action in China as they relate to nongovernmental organizations [*Challenges of Social Engagements: NGO Work in China*]. The case of Japan is appraised by Michiaki Okuyama (Nanzan University, Japan) through the specific angle of the suicide problem in this country [*The Suicide Problem in Contemporary Japanese Society: Its Economic and Social Backdrop and Religious Reactions*]. Although not referring to collective action per se, the chapter deals with the consequences of social and economic recession at the individual level – and their impact on the collective – and explores expressive forms of discontent. The author argues that the legacy of Japan's lost decade and the introduction of neoliberal economic policies increased precariousness in the country. Owing to a certain cultural tradition, suicide is seen as a means to internalize a collective problem at the individual level. Indeed, noble suicide or suicide to preserve honor is still seen as a suitable means to respond to economic and social pressures in this country. The last chapter in Part III is by Dominique Caouette (Université de Montréal, Canada) [*Constructing and Controlling People's Power from the Grassroots: Philippine Social Movement Activism in Historical Perspective*]. The chapter explains how the Philippine revolutionary movement led by the Communist Party of the Philippines has persisted over time by demonstrating how it has the defining elements of a social movement, namely, a great capacity and adaptability to respond to political opportunities in a way that ensures its survival despite national and international changes.

Lilian Mathieu's chapter (Centre National de la Recherche Scientifique and of the Centre Max Weber of the École Normale Supérieure de Lyon, France) concludes the book [*What Do Social Scientists Do When They Do Comparative Work?*]. He argues that many social movement scholars use comparative approaches. Indeed, some of the most important empirical and theoretical contributions in this field have been comparative. He argues that scholars often take for granted the methodological interest of comparison and so he asks what social scientists compare when they do comparative research. He considers that this question is often left unanswered. In other words, Mathieu argues that words/concepts such as "social movements," "protest," "activism," or even "the state" do not necessarily have the same meaning across social, cultural, and political settings. He does not suggest that comparison is of no use for social movement scholars but rather that these scholars need controlled and contextualized comparisons that look for "family resemblances" or that they must base their work on comprehensive theoretical frameworks. One such framework, argues Mathieu, is that provided by McAdam et al. (2001).

1.6 Conclusion

Economic change, without a commensurate political and governance change – in Asia but in Europe too – has brought about a number of unexpected economic and social consequences: increasing income disparity, unemployment, poverty, social inequality, rural-urban migration, harsh working conditions, etc. The levels of poverty and the incidence of social exclusion vary considerably from country to country in that social and economic inequality is often linked to specific local/national conditions. However, these issues present major challenges particularly for many developing Asian countries today, and very visible signs of discontent and/or of political contention are becoming increasingly common (Froissard 2009).

Developments in Asia are not without precedent as events in Europe over the past 20 years or so show quite clearly. But can developments in Europe, for example, serve as a model to explain what is taking place in Asia? In what respect are there similarities or differences between the two regions? To what extent do political, economic, or social systems influence the initiation of collective action? Are the collective actions of marginalized/disadvantaged people in Europe an indication of very specific cultural attributes of these societies?

As discussed above, the book brings together a number of scholars who discuss theoretical and case study examples drawn from a range of European and Asian contexts. The book seeks to be comparative in focus but also to help scholars to assess how groups of powerless people that come from extremely diverse social, political, cultural, and/or institutional frameworks succeed in coming together and initiating collective action. What emerges from the chapters is the recognition that there are key similarities across cultural and geographic boundaries. Today's economic crisis, the upheavals in traditional forms of participation, the weakening of social security systems, the widening gulf in social and economic inequality, and the desire of groups of relatively powerless people to act for themselves or to forge alliances with others and to challenge the *status quo* can be noted across Europe and Asia.

Another key point that emerges from this book is related to the issue of groups' autonomy. Whereas many academics never really challenge the capacity of the more "dominant" or the more "visible" groups to initiate collective action (women, environmentalists, the public sector, or industrial workers), people in precarious situations are rarely "visible" in the public domain because they are often absent or hidden from or do not participate in key economic, political, or social structures such as trade unions, political parties, and associations. When people in precarious situations participate collectively – in initiating collective action for example – it is usually expected that such activities are short-term and that their "protests" will die down in no time at all. In such circumstances, two key types of questions emerge from this book and can be summarized as follows.

The first series of questions are broad in nature. Are the social movements of the powerless that have emerged in Asia and in Europe really the same? Can the mainly "western" social movement paradigms generally explain developments in the East and the West given the vastly different cultural and philosophical foundations of collective action in the two regions as discussed and highlighted by Carsten Storm in his chapter in this volume? The upshot is that it may well be useful for social movement scholars to look at the ways the various social movement paradigms are used to investigate similar issues and, in doing so, to compare and contrast the situations in Europe and in Asia. In other words, and to take into consideration some of the criticism lodged against a number of the classical approaches to political participation, it may well be important that social movement scholars look more broadly at the ways that relatively powerless people give meaning to their actions in both East and West.

The second set of questions is narrow in focus. Do the poor, the marginalized, the people in precarious employment, and the "have-nots" in Europe and in Asia really initiate collective action or rather, in the main, do other collective actors (mobilization entrepreneurs) do so on their behalf? These mobilization entrepreneurs would be considered to be people who are not categorized as suffering from marginalization or from precariousness. The answers to these types of question can change the ways that scholars look at the relevant issues. On the one hand, scholars could focus on the resources that relatively powerless people mobilize (such as social capital), on the strategies that these people use, or on how they build identities. On the other hand, scholars could focus on the extent to which relatively powerless people depend (a) on specific political opportunities or social contexts in which they are embedded or (b) on the alliances that they are able to forge with more powerful allies. In such circumstances, it may well be that social movement scholars should no longer consider as relevant the fact that the internal characteristics of relatively powerless people's movements form obstacles to mobilization, and they may also need to reassess how they view political socialization in general in both the East and the West.

References

Baglioni, S., Baumarten, B., Chabanet, D., & Lahusen, C. (2008). Transcending marginalization: The mobilization of the unemployed in France, Germany, and Italy in a comparative perspective. *Mobilization, 13*(3), 323–335.

Balme, R., & Chabanet, D. (2008). *Collective action and European democracy*. New York: Rowman & Littlefield.

Boo Teik, K. (2010, April 9–10). *Social movements and the crisis of neoliberalism in Malaysia and Thailand*. Keynote Paper at the Workshop on social movements confronting neoliberalism: Comparative perspectives on social movements, theory and practice in Asia and Latin America, University of North Carolina, Chapel Hill.

Boumaza, M., & Hamman, P. (Eds.). (2007). *Sociologie des mouvements de précaires: Espaces mobilisés et répertoires d'action*. Paris: L'Harmattan.

Castells, M. (1997). *The power of identity*. Oxford: Blackwell.

Chabanet, D., & Royall, F. (2009). Economic recession and the mobilization of the unemployed: France and Ireland compared. *French Politics, 7*(3/4), 268–293.

Denis, J.-M. (Ed.). (2005). *Le Conflit en grève: Tendances et perspectives de la conflictualité contemporaine*. Paris: La Dispute.

Frank, A. G., & Fuentes, M. (1990). Civil democracy, social movements in world history. In S. Amin, G. Arrighi, A. G. Frank, & I. Wallerstein (Eds.), *Transforming the revolution: Social movements and the world-system*. New York: Monthly Review Press.

Froissard, C. (2009). The rise of migrant workers' collective action: Toward a new social contract in China. In K. E. Kuah-Pearce & G. Guiheux (Eds.), *Social movement in china and Hong Kong: The expansion of protest space*. Amsterdam: Amsterdam University Press.

Giugni, M. (Ed.). (2009). *The politics of unemployment in Europe: Policy responses and collective action*. Aldershot: Ashgate.

Lipsky, M. (1968). Protest as a political resource. *The American Political Science Review, 62*(4), 1144–1158.

Mathieu, L. (2001). *Mobilisations de prostituées*. Paris: Belin.

McAdam, D., Tarrow, S., & Tilly, C. (2001). *Dynamics of contention*. Cambridge: Cambridge University Press.

McCarthy, J., & Zald, M. (1977). Resource mobilization and social movements: A partial theory. *The American Journal of Sociology, 82*(6), 1212–1241.

Mouchard, D. (2010). Les mouvements sociaux, laboratoires de la démocratie. *La Vie des Idées*. http://www.laviedesidees.fr/Les-mouvements-sociaux.html. Last accessed 24 Nov 2010.

Reiss, M., & Perry, M. (Eds.). (2011). *Unemployment and protest: New perspectives on two centuries of contention*. Oxford: Oxford University Press.

Shigetomi, S., & Makino, K. (Eds.). (2009). *Protest and social movements in the developing world*. London: Edward Elgar.

Sinigaglia, J. (2009). The mobilization of intermittents in the entertainment sector in France. *French Politics, 7*(3–4), 294–315.

Snow, D., Soule, S., & Cress, D. (2005). Identifying the precipitants of homeless protest across 17 U.S. Cities, 1980 to 1990. *Social Forces, 83*(3), 1183–1210.

Part I
Economic, Political and Social Globalization in Asia and Europe

Chapter 2
Economic Change and Social Dynamics: Converging and Diverging Trends Across Different Economies

Bernadette Andreosso-O'Callaghan

2.1 Introduction

The theme of convergence has been at the core of much economic and political discourse worldwide since the Second World War (WWII). For example, in the case of some developing countries, although convergence was not explicitly mentioned in the *Final Communiqué* of the Asian-African Conference in Bandung in April 1955, the call by the participating countries for greater economic cooperation (Article A1), for the provision of technical assistance (Article A2), and for common actions to stabilize world commodity prices (Article A5) lays down implicitly the foundations for economic convergence between these countries.[1] In the case of Europe, convergence appears in the *Principles* of the 1957 Treaty of Rome (Article 2), where it is stated that:

> The Community shall have as its task [...] to promote throughout the Community a harmonious and balanced development of economic activities, [...], a high degree of convergence of economic performance, a high level of employment and of social protection, the raising of the standard of living and quality of life, and economic and social cohesion and solidarity among Member States.

Clearly, this early European view of (economic) convergence was seen as being intimately connected with issues such as harmonious development, social protection, quality of life, social cohesion, and solidarity. In particular, social harmony seemed, in the view of the then Commission, to go hand-in-hand with economic convergence. And yet, in spite of this early holistic view of the concept of convergence,

---

[1] The 27 (+ Vietnam North and South) participating countries in the Bandung Conference are referred to here as the "Bandung countries."

B. Andreosso-O'Callaghan (✉)
Department of Economics, Kemmy Business School, University of Limerick, Limerick, Ireland
e-mail: Bernadette.andreosso@ul.ie

B. Andreosso-O'Callaghan and F. Royall (eds.), *Economic and Political Change in Asia and Europe: Social Movement Analyses*, DOI 10.1007/978-94-007-4653-4_2,

the EU and international economics literature has essentially defined convergence on the basis of gross domestic product (GDP) per capita alone. A shift toward more people-centered convergence indicators started taking place in the 1990s when, on the basis of the work done by development economists such as ul Haq (1995) and Anand and Sen (1999), the United Nations Development Program (UNDP) started using composite indicators of development for its annual human development reports. These indicators include sociological and human development components, and they are particularly appropriate for studying socioeconomic development and convergence in the case of developing and emerging countries since they combine GDP per capita growth with social indicators such as health, life expectancy, and educational attainment.[2] In spite of these methodological breakthroughs, the literature on convergence has very much remained centered on economic indicators. This calls for the analysis of a wider concept of convergence in the case of different regions and countries, such as the one proposed in this chapter.

After WWII, economic change has enabled the emergence of new economic powers such as Japan, South Korea, and lately, China. Since these "emerged" and emerging countries have been catching up with the levels of development attained by rich countries, a certain degree of economic, and moreover socioeconomic, convergence has taken place. In the case of Europe and of other western countries, the economic history literature on *income* convergence across countries generally acknowledges the existence of two distinct chronological periods after the Second World War: the period spanning from the 1950s to the mid/late 1970s is seen as being the "golden age" in which both income convergence and distributional convergence took place. By contrast, the "post-golden age" period is characterized by distributional divergence and polarization, with, on average, rich countries getting richer, and with far less mobility across income groups within the different countries, than in the previous period (Epstein et al. 2007). A major structural break, i.e., the oil shocks of the early 1970s, is the critical juncture between these two different periods. The "post-golden age" period corresponds to a time period during which social movements have flourished, particularly in Europe; it is therefore as if (economic) divergence was associated with social unrest.

This chapter thus addresses two major issues: with the help of a simple analysis of macro socioeconomic performance indicators over a long period, one is to compare and contrast macro socioeconomic convergence in Asia and Europe, and the second is, by analyzing intracountry income distribution, to assess the degree of income disparity, the latter being a well-known ingredient of the dismantling of social cohesion. The analysis of the comparative analysis of socioeconomic indicators in a broad global context (Sect. 2.1) will shift to a discussion on growth, development, and poverty (Sect. 2.2) at the world level. The two ensuing sections will specifically focus on the European Union (EU) and Asia, respectively. Conclusive avenues will be suggested in a final section.

[2] Other indices have been devised, such as the Genuine Progress Index, or Index of economic well-being (for more on this, see Osberg and Sharp 2002).

Table 2.1 Major socioeconomic indicators by broad region of the world

	GDP/ Cap (1)	GDP/ Cap Growth (%) (2)	GFCF/ GDP (%) (3)	Manufacturing VA/ GDP (4)	Illiteracy rate (%) (5)	Child labor (%) (6)	Life expectancy (years) (7)
	(1999)	(1999/1960)	(1999)	(1999)	(1999)	(1999)	(1999)
East Asia and Pacific	3,823	513	29.3	32.8	14.0	8.7	68.9
South Asia	2,114	139.5	21.0	15.7	46.0	15.5	62.6
Middle East and North Africa	5,108	1.1[a]	21.7	14.2	35.8	4.7	68.0
Sub-Saharan Africa	1,600	17.5	17.0	15.8	39.4	29.3	46.8
Latin America	6,817	89.7	19.3	20.8	11.9	8.6	69.8
EMU-11	22,345	110.2[b]	20.6	19[c]	0.0	0.1	77.8

Source: World Development Indicators, CD Rom

Key: (1) and (2) GDP per capita in constant US dollars of 1995; (3), (4) (5), (6), and (7) are defined as above

[a]Growth between 1980 and 1999 only

[b]World GDP growth (instead of EU-11)

[c]Figure for 2001, extracted from EUROSTAT, Theme 4, Trade and Services, 2004

2.2 Growth, Structural Change, and Macro Socioeconomic Performance by Broad World Region

According to Maddison's long-term estimates of per capita GDP growth, Asia – excluding Japan – grew substantially less rapidly than Africa over the period 1500–1950, and the growth of per capita GDP in Africa between 1913 and 1950 was above world levels (Maddison 2001). The recurring incidence of African "lost decades" from the 1950s onward implies that the growth of the mean per capita incomes has been the highest in Asian countries and the lowest in African countries over the period 1960s–late 1990s. Table 2.1 depicts a number of socioeconomic indicators by broad developing region of the world over the period 1960–1999: East Asia and the Pacific basin, South Asia, the Middle East and North Africa, sub-Saharan Africa, and Latin America.[3] The 11 European Union countries that first adopted the euro (i.e., the EMU-11) are also used as a benchmark. As shown in this table, European GDP growth, in constant US dollars, more than doubled between 1960 and 1999. The growth performance of South Asia during the same period (at 139%) surpassed the EMU-11 level, whereas that of East Asia literally exploded (a sixfold increase). By contrast, growth in Latin America lacked vigor, whereas the Middle East and Africa grew only marginally (17.5% increase overall in sub-Saharan Africa).

Data on other macroeconomic variables corroborate these dissimilar growth trends. These data show that the dynamism of investment (defined here as the

[3] See Appendix 2.1 for a list of countries encompassed in each group.

ratio of gross fixed capital formation over GDP) in both East Asia and the Pacific contrasts with a sluggish ratio in sub-Saharan Africa. Compared with sub-Saharan Africa, investment rates are higher in Latin America, but they are still below those of the EMU-11 area, an economic area characterized at the turn of the millennium by a lack of business confidence and moderate growth. Sustained investment levels have nurtured high growth rates in East Asia and the Pacific. Also, much of this investment and growth boom in Asia has allowed a great deal of structural change in these economies.[4] Column 4 of the table depicts the way the East Asian and Pacific basin economies have changed structurally over time. In 1999, one third of the value added in the countries of these regions was generated by manufacturing activities, against a low 14–16% in other developing regions, with the exception of Latin America. Note that the low share for the EU is, in contrast to other less developed regions, explained by the importance of services to the economy.

When examining the selected economic and social indicators together, an incontestable broad picture emerges. First of all, East Asian and Pacific countries have caught up rapidly with western levels, although there is still room for improvement in terms of social indicators. Second, economic quasi stagnation in Africa seems to have seriously slowed down the process of social convergence of this region in comparative terms. Third, the rapid catching up in Asia (particularly in both East Asia and the Pacific basin region) combined with slow and insufficient improvements elsewhere (notably in Africa, but also in the Middle East) together led to a widening gap between Asian and African countries over the period under analysis. Latin American countries lie in an intermediate position. Again, these broad trends by major region of the world do not imply convergence within broad regions, but this issue is outside the remit of the present work. Clearly, Asia on the one hand – in particular East Asia and the Pacific basin region – and Africa on the other seem to have followed a diverging path in terms of socioeconomic growth in the past few decades.[5]

2.3 Economic Growth, Development, and Poverty

Sustained economic growth and structural change are not however synonymous with development, as François Perroux already warned in the 1980s (Perroux 1983). According to this author, growth can indeed take place without development. In his own words:

> This danger [of growth without development] obviously exists in developing countries when economic activity is concentrated around branches of foreign firms [...]. Even in

[4] Structural change typically manifests itself by the movement from the mineral and agricultural sectors to the manufacturing and services sectors.

[5] The explanations for the dismal socioeconomic performance in Africa (and particularly for slow growth) can be grouped into four different categories: country-specific characteristics, degree of openness (defined by the exports + imports to GDP ratio), lack of capital, and others causes.

> developed countries we see that, as growth progresses, the benefits of development are being unevenly distributed in geographical terms, because relatively "empty" regions still exist, and in social terms, because "pockets of poverty" have not disappeared (Perroux 1983: 36).

Economic growth can take place without much (socioeconomic) development. It all depends on the intensity and quality of the redistribution policy and on policy choice. With regard to developing countries, Kuznets' law (Kuznets 1955), according to which the take-off stage of economic development in a given country is characterized by increasing income inequalities, is a phenomenon that has been observed and studied at length.

In the case of developed countries, higher educational attainments and more sophisticated information networks tend to nurture the opposition to greater inequality (through social movements) particularly in times of economic downturn or crises. Wilkinson and Pickett (2009) argue that in the case of industrialized countries, more equal societies almost always do better on several accounts: health, security, and social cohesion. By contrast, large income inequality within countries, combined with poverty, jeopardizes social cohesion. Unequal and poverty-ridden societies are also likely to be societies wherein trust and social capital are low.[6] Although economic growth does not prevent the rise of income inequality, of poverty, and of social unrest – as indicated by Perroux – periods of economic downturns (crises) are however more likely to witness a sharp decline in "the quality of institutions, political stability, voice and accountability, regulatory framework, rule of law, and government effectiveness" (IBRD and World Bank 2010: 3). According to this latter source, "vicious circles during crises are stronger than virtuous ones during prosperous times" (Ibid). These elements imply therefore that the issue of social cohesion takes a particular resonance in times of economic crises: when economic growth is low, inequality, poverty, social unrest, and political instability become paramount issues to monitor and address. Given the emphasis of this chapter on economic issues, the ensuing sub-section will throw some light on poverty and inequality trends before and since the current economic crisis.

2.3.1 Broad Trends in Terms of Poverty and Inequality

By setting the poverty line at $1.25 a day (instead of $1 a day in previous estimates), the World Bank (2008) found that, in 2008, 1.4 billion people in the world lived at or below this poverty threshold, before the effects of the 2007–2008 food and global

[6] As is shown in the sociology and political science literature on the issue, there is a strong link between inequality on the one hand and violence on the other. According to this literature, poverty, rather than inequality *per se*, seems to impact more on social cohesion. On the issue of social capital and inequality, the interested reader can refer to Putnam (2000).

Table 2.2 Regional poverty estimates

Region	1981	1990	1999	2005
People living on less than 2005 PPP $1.25 a day (millions)				
East Asia and Pacific	1,071	873	635	316
Of which: China	835	683	447	208
Europe and Central Asia	7	9	24	17
Latin America and Caribbean	47	50	55	45
Middle East and North Africa	14	10	12	11
South Asia	548	579	589	596
Sub-Saharan Africa	212	298	383	388
Total	1,900	1,818	1,698	1,374
Share of people living on less than 2005 PPP $1.25 a day (%)				
East Asia and Pacific	77.7	54.7	35.5	16.8
Of which: China	84.0	60.2	35.6	15.9
Europe and Central Asia	1.7	2.0	4.6	3.7
Latin America and Caribbean	12.9	11.3	10.9	8.2
Middle East and North Africa	7.9	4.3	4.2	3.6
South Asia	59.4	51.7	44.1	40.3
Sub-Saharan Africa	53.4	57.6	58.4	50.9
Total	51.9	41.7	33.7	25.2

Source: PovcalNet, World Bank (2008)

crises as well as rising costs of energy were taken into account.[7] Worldwide, poverty has declined by 30% since 1990 and by 1 percentage point per year over the 1981–2005 period. This favorable trend was made possible by high growth and appropriate policies in many regions and countries, notably in East Asia and China where the incidence of poverty declined from roughly 55 and 60 to 17 and 16%, respectively, between 1990 and 2005 (IBRD and World Bank 2010; and Table 2.2). However, by excluding China, world poverty rates would have fallen much less since China alone accounts for a large share of the world's reduction in poverty over the period (World Bank 2008). Table 2.2 also shows that the number of poor people has increased in both Europe and Central Asia as well as in South Asia during the period 1981–2005.

These preliminary statistics ought to be complemented, compared, and analyzed with additional figures from different sources. In the case of the European Union, EU-based statistics define an individual as being "poor" or "at risk of poverty" as someone with less than 60% of the median national income.[8] Before the current crisis, this definition applied to 16% of the total EU population (or 79 million people), a figure which is rather different from that inferred by the data shown in Table 2.2.

[7] The World Bank acknowledges the fact that previous data had underestimated the cost of living in most developing countries. Poverty lines used by the World Bank also refer to $10 a day in the case of poverty in a wealthy country, such as the United States.

[8] This definition holds for the household as the reference unit of analysis, by taking into account its composition; therefore, the data are "equivalized."

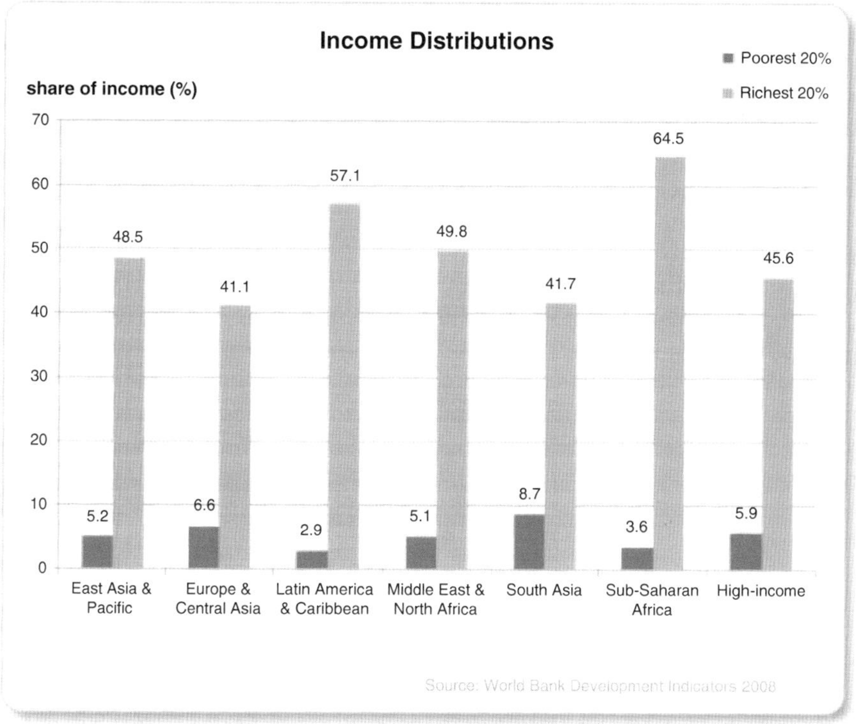

Fig. 2.1 Income distribution by broad region of the world (*upper* and *lower* quintiles) (Source: World Bank Development Indicators 2008)

Of particular note is the increasing phenomenon of the "working poor" in Europe, representing some 8 % of the total EU labor force.[9]

In spite of a reduction in overall poverty rates worldwide, inequality, defined on the basis of income distribution, is persistently high in many regions around the world. As can be seen in Fig. 2.1, when compared with sub-Saharan Africa, Europe and Central Asia, and East Asia and Pacific are among the least unequal regions in the world.[10] However, the relative importance of the lowest quintile (poorest 20%) is greater in Europe and Central Asia (6.6%) than in the East Asia and Pacific region (5.2%).

Also, between-country inequality, measured with the help of the Gini coefficient, has risen in Africa since the 1960s, whereas it has decreased in Asia from the 1980s (Wodon and Yitzhaki 2003).[11]

---

[9] These figures are from the EU Statistics on Income and Living Conditions (EU-SILC) for 2007.

[10] Note that the USA has the largest gap between rich and poor compared to all other industrialized nations, with this gap being the widest in 70 years.

[11] The Gini coefficient is the most well-known measure of (income) dispersion. Based on the Lorenz Curve which relates the percentage of total income earned to the percentage of a given

2.3.2 Impact of the Recent and Current Economic Shocks

Some of the progress in terms of fighting poverty over the past decades has been somewhat lessened by a number of recent economic shocks. First, the 2008 food and energy crisis, caused by historically high prices, explains the sudden deterioration in human development indicators. Some countries saw their food prices almost double, with no corresponding adjustment in earnings (de Walque et al. 2011). The IBRD and World Bank (2010) estimate that by the end of 2010, the current global crisis would have negatively affected more than 110 million people worldwide: some 53 million more people will remain in extreme poverty by 2015 than would have been the case otherwise, and an additional 64 million people worldwide will fall into the extreme poverty trap as a result of the current crisis.

There are two main channels through which the crisis leads to increased poverty: one is through depressed disposable incomes due to reduced economic activity and the other is through increased pressures on social spending due to contracting budgetary receipts, the latter being particularly prominent in western (European) economies. The IBRD and World Bank report stated that declines in disposable incomes had been felt by about a third of emerging and developing countries in 2008–2010, particularly in Central and Eastern Europe, which was the hardest hit region in the group of "emerging countries." Countries such as Greece, Latvia, Lithuania, Romania, Poland but also Ireland and Spain resorted to large cuts in both several areas of public spending as well as wage earnings. According to Caritas (2010), more than 23% of the EU-27 population were estimated to be at risk of poverty or social exclusion in 2010; the proportion of the Spanish population classified as being either moderately or severely poor reached the figure of 22.7% of the population in the second half of 2009, an increase of 3.4 percentage points compared with the 2007 figure. The economic crisis has also led to an increase in the number of working poor people in EU countries such as Portugal, Spain, and Ireland.

It is therefore clear that the economic crisis is also a social crisis with asymmetric effects, a crisis that jeopardizes the cohesion of the EU social fabric. It hits particularly vulnerable groups of individuals such as women and children, and it tends to threaten the standard of living of already poor households. Increasing poverty may have a bearing on economic convergence and on equality, two issues explored in the next section.

2.4 Convergence and Equality in the EU

In the economics literature on convergence in the case of EU countries, the emphasis has been placed on GDP per capita performance between countries and between regions at the sub-national level. This section briefly discusses this level of analysis

---

population, cumulated from the poorest to the richest, it is calculated as the area lying between the line of perfect equality (diagonal) and the Lorenz curve: the higher the coefficient, the higher the level of inequality.

before turning to the issue of convergence of incomes and equality within EU countries.

2.4.1 Between-Country Economic Convergence

Convergence of economic performance (i.e., of living standards) at the highest possible level of welfare was the final objective of economic integration as stated in the *Principles* of the 1957 Treaty of Rome. In the eyes of the Commission, the concept of convergence contained at the time an efficiency objective and a distributive objective, which implied closing the gap between the rich and the poor areas of the then Common Market. This vision implied that the market equilibrium paradigm, which served as a theoretical basis for the creation of the European Market in 1957, was not at the outset seen as sufficient for attaining the convergence objective. Indeed, government intervention through the implementation of common policies (Common Agricultural Policy, Regional Policy, Social Policy, all policies later encompassed in the Structural Funds) was a clear proof that the EU needed more than trade liberalization for the promotion of such convergence. The work on convergence in the case of the EU, and measured by GDP per capita, shows that convergence reversed in the beginning of the 1980s (de la Fuente and Vives 1995; Neven and Gouyette 1995; Fagerberg and Verspagen 1996; Cappelen et al. 2003). After a period of rapid catching up by either the poorest countries (Fagerberg and Verspagen 1996) or poorest regions (la Fuente and Vives 1995) between 1945 and the late 1970s, the convergence phenomenon came to a halt in the EU. These findings are in line with other studies done at world level, which highlight two distinct chronological periods in terms of income convergence (and distributional convergence); after the "golden age" period stretching from the 1950s to the first oil shock, divergence has tended to occur (Epstein et al. 2007).

2.4.2 Convergence Across Socioeconomic Groups in the EU

Another level of analysis consists in looking at income convergence within different EU countries across various income groups. EU studies along these lines are of a more recent vintage since the emphasis of economic integration was placed at the outset on *between-country* convergence rather than on *within-country* convergence. With the official endorsement of the concepts of "Social Cohesion" in the 1980s, and with the development of statistical indicators depicting social exclusion and poverty endorsed at the Laeken European Council in December 2001 (see Appendix 2.2), poverty trends are now being monitored at the EU level.

Income inequality trends invariably show that countries such as the Netherlands, Sweden, but also the Czech Republic display the lowest percentage of households below the 60% median income threshold, and that other "old" EU countries such as

Table 2.3 Top quintile to bottom quintile equivalized income (selected EU countries and years)

	1998	1999	2000	2001	2002	2003	2004	2005	2006	2007	2008
EU-25	4.6	4.6	4.5	4.5	–	4.6	4.8	4.9	4.8	4.8	4.8
EU-15	4.6	4.6	4.5	4.5	–	4.6	4.8	4.8	4.7	4.9	4.9
Ireland	5.2	4.9	4.7	4.5	–	5.0	4.9	5.0	4.9	4.8	4.5
Greece	6.5	6.2	5.8	5.7	–	6.4	5.9	5.8	6.1	6.0	5.9
Portugal	6.8	6.4	6.4	6.5	7.3	7.4	7.0	7.0	6.7	6.5	6.1
Sweden		3.1		3.4	3.3		3.3	3.3	3.6	3.3	3.5

Source: Eurostat: EU-SILC, Luxembourg

Greece have the highest percentage in the sample. In the former group of countries, the incidence of poverty – defined on the basis of the median equivalized income – affected 10% of the population before the current crisis, whereas in countries such as Estonia, Greece, Italy, and Spain, this ratio stood at or above 20% (18% in the case of Ireland) (INSEE 2010). These trends in income inequality can be related to trends in low pay category earners. International comparisons show that Nordic countries (Sweden in particular) have the smallest proportion of workers classified as low-paid workers. A dynamic analysis shows increasing earnings dispersion in countries such as the United Kingdom (UK) and Portugal (and also the United States [USA]) in the 1980s and in the 1990s. In the UK, the Gini coefficient rose from 0.32 to 0.34 between 1995 and 2008, whereas in Portugal, the coefficient rose from 0.37 in 1995 to 0.41 in 2005 with a slight decrease until the beginning of the 2008 crisis.[12] In spite of unprecedented high growth rates in Ireland during its so-called Celtic tiger era, the Gini coefficient was quite stable up until the beginning of the current crisis and was still above the EU-15 average in 2005 (Callan et al. 2010).

The example of Ireland mirrors both the inability of its various governments to address satisfactorily the issue of poverty and the gap existing between economic growth and (human) development. In France, diverging trends preceded the crisis. INSEE figures show that, over the period 2005–2007, inequality increased due to higher than average rising incomes for the top 1% of the population; nearly 50% of the income acquired by this top percentile was made up of "exceptional income" such as stock options (INSEE 2010) (Table 2.3).

Figure 2.2 corroborates these findings. It shows the proportion of individuals living in households with an equivalized disposable income below 60% of the median equivalized income of the country in which they lived during 2009. This proportion is defined as being "at risk of poverty." More than 16% of the EU population was at risk of poverty in 2009, with a small proportion registered in the Czech Republic and in the Netherlands, contrasting with high proportions in Latvia and Greece (more than 20%), the very same countries where budgetary cuts and depleted wages and

[12] These figures are from the Eurostat New Cronos database; Eurostat, online database and Eurostat/EU-SILC. July 2010.

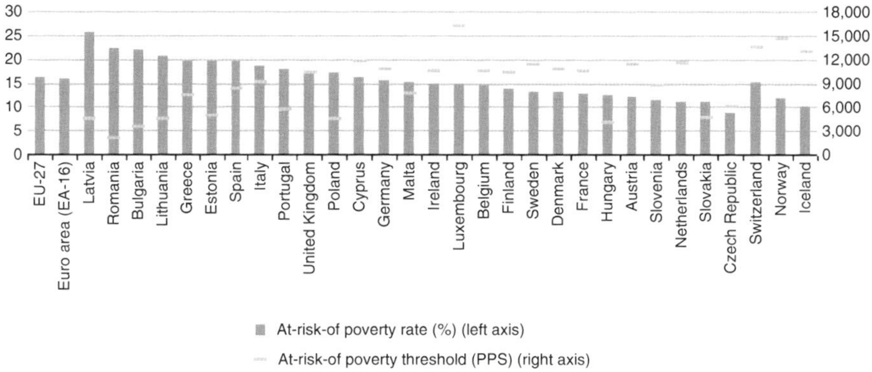

Fig. 2.2 At-risk poverty rate, total population, 2009

other earnings have been the most severe since the 2008 crisis.[13] This indicator can further be complemented with a ratio comparing the total equivalized income received by the top income quintile (20% of the population with the highest equivalized income) to that received by the bottom income quintile. In 2008, the EU-25 average is 4.8, an increase from 4.6 ten years earlier. Large variations between the different countries imply a low ratio for Sweden (3.5 in 2008), compared with a ratio above 6 in Portugal. Inequality between rich and poor has tended to decline slightly between 2005 and 2008 in Ireland, Greece, and Portugal. Again, the few years preceding the current crisis seemed to have witnessed more favorable socioeconomic performance, a commendable result that was soon to be put into question.

Standard explanations for this poor ability to tackle the problem of income disparities since the 1980s are globalization and greater competition from developing countries leading to wage squeezes particularly in the case of low-skilled jobs. However, unsuccessful taxation, budgetary, and social policies in various EU countries and at EU level should not be dismissed as major causes of persistent poverty.

2.5 The Case of Asia

2.5.1 Convergence Across Asian Countries

Using per capita income data, Karras (2009) shows that there has been more convergence over time in Asia than in the rest of the world, and that the speed of convergence

[13] Note that some countries, such as Ireland, appear quite favorably under this criterion. This is due to the downward revision (more than 15 %) of the "at risk of poverty" threshold in purchasing power parity terms in these countries since 2008. Some of this downward revision can be explained by low inflation rates and by deflationary tendencies since the beginning of the crisis (−1.6 % in 2010 in Ireland).

has been far from being constant over time, with maximum values in the 1980s. With the help of a Theil entropy index, Park (2003) finds no evidence of convergence for Asia-Pacific countries (including, e.g., Australia and Papua New Guinea) over the entire period 1960–2000, although convergence seems to appear during the latter part of the period.[14] Hsiao and Hsiao (2004) find evidence of real GDP per capita convergence of South Korea and Taiwan toward the GDP per capital levels of Japan and of the USA. These analyses rest however on traditional (i.e., income-based) measures of convergence, and on convergence seen as a uni-model process, i.e., as characterizing a situation where the growth to the steady state equilibrium is the same for all countries.

Owing to the fact that Asian countries have embarked upon a process of fast economic growth since the 1950s, the remaining analysis will rest on socioeconomic indicators of convergence. In the case of Asia, a longitudinal cross-country analysis of economic and social performance suffers from a number of caveats: lack of harmonization of socioeconomic indicators, discontinuity in the time series, manipulations by national statistical offices leading to over or under reporting, etc. Bearing all these limitations in mind, a tentative statistical appraisal of socioeconomic convergence in Asia compared to other "Bandung countries" can be attempted, using a combination of statistics released by the World Bank and by Maddison (2001).

Since the aim here is to measure *socioeconomic* convergence, our first task is to construct for each country a composite indicator (an index) capturing its economic as well as social characteristics. This "human development" index (HDI) thus combines GDP per capita, literacy, life expectancy, and children's rights, and it will be referred to as "HDI-4."[15] The higher the value of the composite indicator (such as in the case of Japan), the more developed economically and socially the country is. Such an indicator can be computed for each country at discrete time intervals (i.e., starting in 1960). The Human Development Index devised by Anand and Sen (1999) can be used for measuring convergence in welfare terms. The calculation of the HDI is as follows:

$$HDI_{jt} = \frac{1}{n}\sum_{1}^{n}\left(\log A_{ijt} - \log A_{iMin}\right)/\left(\log A_{iMax} - \log A_{iMin}\right) \tag{2.1}$$

where HDI_{jt} is the human development index of country *j* in year *t*. This is composed of *n* variables *Ai* (such as life expectancy). A_{ijt} is therefore the value of variable *Ai* for country *j* in year *t*, and A_{iMin} and A_{iMax} are the minimal and maximal values for a given variable observed in the entire sample of countries for the various years,

[14] The Theil entropy index borrows from information theory and measures nonrandomness or inequality. Its main advantage is that it can be decomposed into several groups of individuals, and that it allows therefore to measure *within-groups* as well *between-groups* inequality.

[15] As a proxy for children's rights, we use 1 minus the proportion of children aged 10–14 in the labor force.

respectively. The only difference between the measure of the HDI presented above and that of the UNDP is that the present one takes into account variations across countries but also within a given period of time (1960–1998 in our study). As stated above, our human development indicator combines per capita GDP with life expectancy, literacy, and children's rights; this is a different indicator from the one used by the UNDP.

The second task is to define the most appropriate methodology. The analysis of convergence between countries and groups of countries has relied mostly on *static* models using beta and, more rarely, sigma convergence. A standard convergence equation is used which relates the growth of income rates with income levels; less simple models include other (mostly economic) variables on the right-hand side of the equation, such as human capital variables, stressing thereby the importance of knowledge to economic growth. Later convergence studies have used *dynamic* models (see Quah 1996; Epstein et al. 2003), highlighting the existence of two or more convergence clubs in the process. The most popular models, the beta-convergence models, have however been criticized for their lack of consistency: different authors control for different combinations of variables, and there is therefore a crucial problem of how sensitive the various convergence results are to the inclusion or omission of specific variables. In contrast with the beta-convergence method, the sigma-convergence tool does not provide any information on the rate of convergence.[16] This is why our analysis rests primarily on a different methodology: the Euclidian distance.

The *Euclidean distance* is a metric that meets four properties: (1) minimum distance is 0; (2) the distance should be a positive real number; (3) symmetry; and (4) triangular inequality. It is computed applying Pythagoras' formula to country-points positioned in an *N*-dimensional space (Euclidean space), and it can be calculated for each time period. The idea is to see whether the distance (or socioeconomic gap) has shrunk over time, for the same group of countries. The Euclidian distance has rarely been used in convergence studies, in spite of a clear advantage of this indicator, which is that it can be calculated for different groups and subgroups of countries. For our purpose, the Euclidian distance between two reference years t and $t+k$ and n countries is calculated as follows[17]:

$$d(x,z)_t = \|x - z\| = \sqrt{\left[\sum_{i=1}^{28} (x_i - z_i)^2\right]} \tag{2.2}$$

[16] Sigma convergence simply refers to the coefficient of variation (CV), which is simply equal to σ/μ. In its most standard form, it is measured as the unweighted coefficient of variation of per capita income. Beta convergence is obtained by regressing the growth rate of per capita incomes against its initial levels (see, e.g., Barro and Sala-i-Martin 1992; Ben-David 1994). A negative relationship between initial GDP per capita and growth rates denotes convergence.

[17] Note that because of the lack of data, Ethiopia and Libya are not included in the calculations.

Table 2.4 Using the Euclidian distance for the measurement of convergence in the Asian and other "Bandung countries"

	Economic indicator (GDP/cap index)	Socioeconomic indicator (HDI-4 index)
$d(x, z)_{1960-1980}$	0.8208	0.7017
$d(x, z)_{1980-1999}$	0.8397	0.7076

Note: Jordan is excluded from the calculation of socioeconomic convergence

Table 2.5 Inequality in Asia and in other Bandung countries (various years)

Country	UN R/P 10 %	Gini coefficient (×100)	Year
Cambodia	12.2	41.7	2004
China (PRC)	21.6	46.9	2004
India	8.6	36.8	2004
Indonesia	7.8	34.3	2002
Japan	4.5	24.9	1993
Laos	8.3	34.6	2002
Nepal	15.8	47.2	2004
Pakistan	6.5	30.6	2002
Philippines	15.5	44.5	2003
Sri Lanka	11.1	40.2	FY 2003/2004
Thailand	12.6	42	2002
Vietnam	6.9	34.4	2004
Other Bandung (non-Asian)			
Egypt	8	34.4	2000
Ethiopia	6.6	30	2000
Ghana	14.1	40.8	1999
Iran	17.2	43	1998
Jordan	11.3	38.8	2003
Turkey	16.8	43.6	2003

Source: UN Development Program

For any country, i, x_i, and z_i correspond to the HDI-4 index as developed above at two different time intervals. This distance can therefore be calculated at several time intervals. In particular, the Euclidian distance for the two selected time periods is denoted by $d(x, z)_{1960-1980}$ and $d(x, z)_{1980-1999}$. If $d(x, z)_{1960-1980} > d(x, z)_{1980-1999}$, this implies convergence over the long period of time under review. Again, these calculations can be compared with calculations pertaining to GDP per capita only (i.e., we compare socioeconomic convergence with "pure" economic convergence). The results of these calculations are shown in Table 2.4.

As can be seen, neither indicator provides an indication of convergence between the two time periods. According to this indicator, there seems to have been a slight economic divergence as well as socioeconomic stability over the long period under review. Note however that these results mirror one of the drawbacks of this indicator, which is its sensitiveness to the inclusion of some countries, such as China, in the analysis.

2.5.2 Convergence Across Socioeconomic Groups in Asia

Finally, and in line with the analysis conducted above, a glance at Gini coefficients in the case of Asian and Bandung countries (column 3 of Table 2.5) shows a wide disparity between relatively equal countries (Japan) and fairly unequal countries (Nepal, China, and the Philippines). Column 2 of the table depicts the ratio between the average income of the richest 10% (top decile) and the average income of the poorest 10%. It is interesting to note that China, the country that is responsible for most of the reduction in the world poverty rate, is actually the most unequal Asian country when assessed on the basis of the gap between the top wealthy and bottom deciles. Here again, Japan, a country that has managed to grow and to develop while putting in place the appropriate policies aimed at social cohesion, is the least unequal of all countries in this group.

2.6 Conclusions

In the economics literature, convergence has mostly been appraised in reference to economic convergence (using GDP per capita figures) between countries. Results at the global level broadly show that economic convergence in Asia has been above the world average since WWII and that between-country convergence came to a standstill in the EU at the end of the "golden age." The former phenomenon is partly explained by vigorous economic growth in Asia over the 1960–1998 period, notably in East Asia and in some of the South East Asian countries. However, an important issue raised by François Perroux, Amartya Sen, and others is that economic growth can unfold without much economic and social development. This is why this chapter has placed an emphasis on socioeconomic indicators and on within-country convergence. The analysis of socioeconomic performance and convergence since the early 1960s in the EU and Asia (the latter being compared with the "Bandung countries") offers a few unambiguous conclusions. It shows that within-country convergence, appraised with the help of the Gini coefficient, has not materialized in the EU since the oil shocks of the 1970s. Poverty levels have slightly diminished between 2003 and 2008 in countries such as Greece, Portugal, and Ireland, where approximately 20% of the respective national populations were at risk of poverty in 2003 (compared with less than 10 % in Luxembourg). Given that the economic crisis has hit these three countries harder than the EU core (i.e., Germany or Belgium), prospects in terms of income and socioeconomic convergence since 2008 are rather compromised.

In the convergence literature relating to Asian countries, the use of socioeconomic indicators is rare. This chapter has therefore provided a quantitative analysis of socioeconomic convergence in Asia, with reference to the Bandung group of countries, by constructing a composite indicator and by using the Euclidian distance. The indicator combines economic performance measures with social performance measures, such as life expectancy. The results do not show evidence of socioeconomic convergence within the group of the "Bandung countries" over the period 1960–1998. Finally, inequality (or within-country divergence) is much higher in Asia than in the EU. This issue seems to be an increasing problem for China, a country where the Gini coefficient is twice that of Japan. This is in spite of the fact that high sustained growth in China explains much of the poverty reduction at world level.

It might be inferred from the above that both the EU (notably since the current crisis) and China (since the implementation of its economic reforms) are sliding on the dangerous path of socioeconomic divergence, undermining social cohesion and ultimately political stability. In the case of EU countries, relatively high educational attainments and sophisticated information networks tend to nurture the opposition to greater inequality (through social movements), particularly during times of hardship (post-2008 crisis Ireland is a case in point). Whenever essential consumer commodities are threatened by high price rises (such as in the case of foodstuff in 2008 and at the time of writing) leading to increased inequality and poverty, food riots or consumer protests tend to flourish not only in developing countries but also in Europe (see Chaps. 6 and 9 in this volume). In March 2011, the repeated reaction and vigilance of the Chinese authorities to prevent gatherings in several cities of China – leading to a potential "Jasmine Revolution" – attest to the Chinese government's awareness that perceived inequality can ultimately jeopardize social cohesion and political stability in the country (see Chaps. 4 and 14 in this volume).

2.7 Appendices

Appendix 2.1 List of Countries Included in the Major World Regions (See Table 2.1)

East Asia and Pacific	South Asia	Middle East and North Africa	EMU-11
Am. Samoa	Afghanistan	Algeria	Austria
Cambodia	Bangladesh	Bahrain	Belgium
China	Bhutan	Djibouti	Finland
Indonesia	India	Egypt	France
Kiribati	Maldives	Iran	Germany
Lao	Nepal	Iraq	Ireland
Malaysia	Pakistan	Jordan	Italy

(continued)

Appendix 2.1 (continued)

East Asia and Pacific	South Asia	Middle East and North Africa	EMU-11
Marshall Islands	Sri Lanka	Lebanon	Luxembourg
Micronesia		Libya	Netherlands
Mongolia		Malta	Portugal
Myanmar		Morocco	Spain
North Korea		Oman	
Palau		Saudi Arabia	
Papua New Guinea		Syria	
Philippines		Tunisia	
Samoa		West Bank of Gaza	
Solomon Islands		Yemen	
Thailand			
Tonga			
South Korea			
Vanuatu			
Vietnam			

Source: World Development Indicators, CD Rom

NB: Sub-Saharan Africa comprises all the countries of the continent, except those of North Africa, and includes Mauritius, Madagascar, and other islands. Latin America encompasses all of the countries of that continent, including those from Central America, and islands such as Trinidad, etc

Appendix 2.2 Indicators Developed (or Being Developed) by the Commission so as to Measure Social Cohesion (Sample)

Material deprivation rate		Eurostat/EU-SILC
Housing	To be developed	Eurostat/EU-SILC
Self-reported unmet need for medical care by income quintile	Under preparation	Eurostat/EU-SILC
Utilization of medical care services	Under preparation	National data
Child well-being	To be developed	Eurostat/EU-SILC
Persons with low educational attainment		Eurostat/LFS
Low reading literacy performance of pupils	Under preparation	OECD/PISA
Depth of material deprivation		

Note: The European Community Household Panel (ECHP) is the primary source of data used for the calculation of these indicators in the field of income, poverty, and social exclusion

References

Anand, S., & Sen, A. (1999). *The income component of the HDI: Alternative formulations* (UNDP Occasional Papers). New York: United Nations Development Bank.

Barro, R., & Sala-i-Martin, X. (1992). Convergence. *Journal of Political Economy, 100*(2), 223–251.

Ben-David, D. (1994). Income disparity among countries and the effects of freer trade. In L. Pasinetti & R. Solow (Eds.), *Economic growth and the structure of long-term development*. Basingstoke: Macmillan.

Callan, T., Nolan, B., Keane, C., & Walsh, J. (2010). Inequality and the crisis: The distributional impact of tax increases and welfare and public sector pay cuts. *The Economic and Social Review, 41*(4), 461–471.

Cappelen, A., Castellacci, F., Fagerberg, J., & Verspagen, B. (2003). The impact of EU regional support on growth and convergence in the European Union. *Journal of Common Market Studies, 41*(4), 621–644.

Caritas. (2010). *2010 survey*. Madrid: FOESSA Social Studies Foundation.

De Walque, D., Kazianga, H., Over, M., & Vaillant, J. (2011, January). *Food crisis, household welfare and HIV/AIDS treatment: Evidence from Mozambique* (Policy Research Working Paper No. 5522). The World Bank Development Economics Development Research Group Workshop. http://www-wds.worldbank.org/external/default/WDSContentServer/IW3P/IB/2011/01/05/000158349_20110105143534/Rendered/PDF/WPS5522.pdf. Last accessed on 10 June 2011.

Epstein, P., Howlett, P., & Schulze, M.-S. (2003). Distribution dynamics: Stratification, polarization and convergence among OECD economies, 1870–1992. *Explorations in Economic History, 40*(1), 78–93.

Epstein, P., Howlett, P., & Schulze, M.-S. (2007). Trade, convergence, and globalisation: The dynamics of the international income distribution, 1950–1998. *Explorations in Economic History, 44*(1), 100–113.

Fagerberg, J., & Verspagen, B. (1996). Heading for divergence? Regional growth in Europe reconsidered. *Journal of Common Market Studies, 34*(3), 431–448.

Hsiao, F. S. T., & Hsiao, M.-C. (2004). Catching-up and convergence: Long-run growth in East Asia. *Review of Development Economics, 8*(2), 223–236.

IBRD and World Bank. (2010). *Global monitoring report 2010: The MDGs after the crisis*. Washington, DC: World Bank.

INSEE. (2010). *Les revenus et le patrimoine des ménages*, Édition 2010. Paris: Institut National de la Statistique et des Études Économiques.

Karras, G. (2009). Economic growth convergence in Asia, 1970–2003: Empirical evidence from the Solow model. *The IUP Journal of Monetary Economics, VII*(3–4), 73–84.

Kuznets, S. (1955). Economic growth and income inequality. *American Economic Review, 45*(1), 1–28.

la Fuente, D., & Vives, X. (1995). Infrastructure and education as instruments of regional policy: Evidence from Spain. *Economic Policy, 10*(20), 11–54.

Maddison, A. (2001). *The world economy: A millennial perspective*. Paris: OECD Development Centre Studies.

Neven, D., & Gouyette, C. (1995). Regional convergence in the European community. *Journal of Common Market Studies, 33*(1), 47–65.

Osberg, L., & Sharp, A. (2002). An index of economic well-being for selected OECD countries. *Review of Income and Wealth, 48*(3), 291–316.

Park, D. (2003). An empirical examination of income convergence in the Asia-Pacific region. *Journal of Asian Economics, 14*(3), 497–502.

Perroux, F. (1983). *A new concept of development*. London: Croom Helm.

Putnam, R. (2000). *Bowling alone: The collapse and revival of American community*. New York: Simon & Schuster.

Quah, D. (1996). Twin peaks: Growth and convergence in models of distribution dynamics. *The Economic Journal, 106*(437), 1045–1055.

ul Haq, M. (1995). *Reflections on human development*. Oxford: Oxford University Press.

Wilkinson, R., & Pickett, K. (2009). *The spirit level: Why more equal societies almost always do better*. London: Penguin.

Wodon, Q., & Yitzhaki, S. (2003). Growth and convergence: A social welfare framework. *Review of Income and Wealth, 51*(3), 443–454.

World Bank. (2008). *World development indicators, poverty data, a supplement to the WDI 2008*. Washington, DC: The World Bank.

Chapter 3
European Integration, Social Cohesion, and Political Contentiousness

Christian Lahusen

3.1 Introduction

Social cohesion has become a prominent issue of political debates addressing processes and consequences of European integration. For over two decades, the institutions of the European Union (EU) and the Council of Europe (CoE) have encouraged these debates because they were worried about rising economic disparities, social inequalities, and cultural divergences within the enlarging European Union (CEC 2009; Council of Europe 2008). Both, the EU and the CoE, have proposed remedial actions that focus on two levels.

On the one hand, attention was paid to territorial cohesion (CEC 2008). Here, we can refer to the EU's own regional policy that aims to combat the persisting disparities in the economic development of European member states and their regions – disparities that have tended to increase throughout the various enlargements of the European Community (EC). Throughout its history, the EC/EU has developed several funding schemes and invests today more than 30 billion of its 140 billion euro budget in regional development and convergence policies, with the aim of improving regional infrastructures (e.g., transport, telecommunication), restructuring and developing regional economies, and thus promoting economic convergence and integration across the European social space.

On the other hand, the EU is also concerned about social cohesion. The focus is not on territorial disparities between regions but on social inequalities, cleavages, and segregations within nations or regions according to population groups. The objective is to combat social exclusion of individuals, in particular among vulnerable groups of the society (e.g., the elderly, youth, migrants, single parents). The main strategy consists in furthering social inclusion, that is, the participation of

C. Lahusen (✉)
Department of Social Science, University of Siegen, Siegen, Germany
e-mail: lahusen@soziologie.uni-siegen.de

B. Andreosso-O'Callaghan and F. Royall (eds.), *Economic and Political Change in Asia and Europe: Social Movement Analyses*, DOI 10.1007/978-94-007-4653-4_3,

individuals within societal life by granting basic civic, political, and social rights to the European citizenry, for example, through the Council of Europe's two fundamental rights instruments (the *European Convention on Human Rights* and the *European Social Charter*), and by investing more than ten billion euros into labor market inclusion through the European Social Fund. Moreover, emphasis is put on the coordination and harmonization of national regulations in the realm of labor markets, employment, education, antidiscrimination, and social security systems (for instance, within the so-called Lisbon Strategy since 2000). Finally, European institutions encourage the incorporation of civil societies and nongovernmental organizations (NGO) into policy-making and service delivery, for example, by means of the European civil dialogue (Prodi and Kinnock 2001).

There is a growing awareness, however, that these approaches have a limited impact. Indeed, the EU and the CoE are concerned by the fact that the current situation is far from reaching the stipulated objectives. In 2008, the Council of Europe's own Task Force on Social Cohesion describes the challenge as follows:

> Democracy has spread across the continent, levels of well-being are higher than they have been in the past, social stability is widespread and Europeans generally express satisfaction with their lives. However, there are grounds to question whether the conditions still prevail for a strong social commitment. The socio-economic transformation attendant on globalisation and the rewriting of the European political map bring new pressures to bear on and raise questions about the [Council of Europe's, C.L.] social cohesion approach. (…) Things have obviously changed. There is no doubt either, however, that a healthy and vibrant society is the cornerstone to continued progress. Given this, Europe has to find ways of adapting its social (policy) achievements to changing needs and circumstances without losing their essential character. (Council of Europe 2008: 5)

The report stresses that there are various challenges to social cohesion: economic globalization, the demographic transition (e.g., its effects on family models, gender roles, transition from education to work, care responsibilities, and social security), increasing migration and cultural diversity, shifting political realities (e.g., changing political behavior, multilevel systems of decision-making, privatization), and socio-economic changes (e.g., new risks of poverty, social inequality, and health) (Council of Europe 2008: 19–28).The worries of the European institutions are well founded, particularly since the EU is affected by a serious financial and economic crisis from 2008 onwards. The EU is not only facing societal transformations and economic problems, but it must also face stagnating rates of public acceptance, political support, feelings of belonging, and European identification. The latter have effects on the "European project" because further steps toward European integration and enlargement can no longer depend on the "permissive consensus" of European citizens. This was amply demonstrated in the cases of the mobilizations in the Netherlands and in France against the European Constitution in 2005 and those in Ireland against the Lisbon Treaty in 2008.

These protests illustrate that the EU and European integration are more contentious than ever. Political parties that criticize or reject the European Union are elected recurrently in national elections to the European Parliament and are thus represented in this political body (Hix and Marsh 2007). At the same time, more and more groups, organizations, and social movements oppose specific European initiatives or regulations by means of public protest activities and campaigns as, for instance, when unions criticized the EU's Service Directive in 2005, environmentalists opposed the EU regulations on chemical substances in 2007, or when farmers protested against the inactivity of the EU in fighting tumbling milk prices in 2009 (Balme and Chabanet 2008).

Studies have provided persuasive evidence for this rising contentiousness within the EU, which is mirrored by EU-related political mobilizations and protests at the local, national, and supranational levels (Imig and Tarrow 2001). Most often, researchers attribute these developments to the institutional framework of the EC/EU, which established a proper "political opportunity structure," new targets and incentives for political protest (Marks and McAdam 1999; Balme et al. 2002; Rucht 2001; Lahusen 2004). The consequences are more EU-related political mobilizations and protest actions. However, these developments do not speak for an unconditional "Europeanization" of political contentions, in the sense that political mobilizations are transferred to a supranational (European) level. I wish to make two qualifying remarks here. On the one hand, scholars argue that a wealth of different issue-specific groups and/or coalitions with strong domestic roots and activities initiate EU-related mobilizations and protests. Hence, while there are supranational associations and networks operating in Brussels, European mobilizations and protests are dominated by a strong domestic or local component (Imig and Tarrow 1999; Rucht 2002; della Porta and Caiani 2011). This has to do, on the other hand, with the rather strong selectivity of EU-related policy-making. The much acclaimed involvement of civil society organizations is more rhetorical than real. Additionally, the EU privileges an "elitist" civil dialogue and conventional forms of lobbying, which are quite distant from grassroots movements and mobilizations (Kohler-Koch 2010; Kohler-Koch and Quittkat 2011). Moreover, European-wide protests of weak interests do happen, as the example of the Euro-Marches against unemployment, job insecurity and social exclusions show since 1997 (Chabanet 2008). They are, however, the exception rather than the rule (Balme and Chabanet 2008).

This chapter aims to analyze the societal context of the political contentiousness of the EU in its specific features. It asks whether European integration and enlargement has an effect on mobilization potentials in general and on the likelihood of "Europeanized," transnational mobilizations in particular. This research question is devoted to a sociological perspective on political contentions, which was prominent in earlier studies (Touraine 1971; Melucci 1989; Buechler 1999), because it puts an emphasis on the analysis of societal structures and developments. These societal factors do not translate directly into political protest action, as demonstrated persuasively by social movement analysis (McCarthy and Zald 1977; McAdam et al. 2001). Nevertheless, they structure the context within which political mobilizations emerge and evolve, and they do so at least on two dimensions, which will be at the center of attention in this chapter: grievance structures on the one side and mobilizing resources (social capital and collective identities in particular) on the other. Therefore, two questions will guide the following analysis: Are European integration and enlargement altering (possibly Europeanizing) the structure of societal grievances and, second, are European integration and enlargement changing (possibly Europeanizing) the structure of (transnational) social capital and collective identities? The empirical and analytical answers to these questions will help to understand the strong domestic roots and the marked selectivity of political contentions and mobilizations within the EU, as mentioned above.

The argument of this chapter will be developed in three steps. First, I will demonstrate that the process of European integration is indeed impinging on the structure of societal cleavages and grievances, leading to a territorial differentiation of social problems and a multiplication of grievances. In particular, I will note a reemergence of "old" grievances. These observations will help to explain the burgeoning and domestication of political protest outlined above. Second, I will illustrate that European integration is also altering the structure of social capital and collective identities. I will illustrate that the distribution of these social resources throughout the European continent improves the mobilization potentials among groups of the population with higher degrees of transnational social capital and identity. This helps to understand better the marked selectivity of Europeanized mobilizations mentioned above. Finally, I will come back to the institutional approach in order to show that the EU is establishing a normative discourse about shared grievances and common norms and objectives, and that it is institutionalizing common procedures of monitoring, policy evaluation, and learning. I will discuss whether this is having an effect on the emergence of a less selective, more inclusive, and better-integrated arena of EU-related mobilizations and transnational protests and claims.

3.2 The European Structure of Grievances: The Renaissance of "Old" Issues

It has become quite common in scientific and public debates in Europe in the 1980s and 1990s to refer to "new" risks and conflicts in modern societies (Beck 1992; Giddens 1999). Some scholars argue that these "new" risks and conflicts have given rise to claims and protest actions by new social movements (Touraine 1971; Melucci 1989; Buechler 1999). Indeed, "new" grievances and contentions have emerged on various issues such as environmental degradation, peace, gender equality, sex and civil liberties, technological hazards, ethical implications of scientific progress such as genetic engineering, and animal rights, among many others. In many of these areas, the EU has acquired policy-making competencies because member states saw the need for a concerted approach to problem-solving. This has provided opportunities and incentives for a Europeanization of "new" public interest groups and related mobilizations. However, I argue that European integration and enlargement processes are once again putting "old" grievances on the public agenda by generating awareness, for example, about economic disparities, social inequalities, risks of poverty and marginalization, interethnic conflicts, and xenophobic tendencies.

Empirical evidence persuasively corroborates this assumption. Today, the European Union is comprised of 27 member states with quite different levels of economic development, social inequalities, and standards of life. The consecutive rounds of EU enlargement[1] have increased the disparities within the EC considerably by integrating some of the least and most developed European economies (see Table 3.1). In fact, data on gross domestic product (GDP) per capita show that there is a pronounced east/west and north/south divide: northern and western countries are economically much more powerful than the EU average, the accession countries lag far behind (i.e., between two-thirds and half of western GDP rates), while most southern countries are closer to the average scores of GDP per capita. During pre-accession negotiations, the EU and national governments were optimistic that the new member states would gradually catch up economically, using the possibilities provided by the integrated market and the monetary union. This optimism was nurtured by the strong economic development since the beginning of the millennium and which was of particular benefit to some of the poorer, older member states (Spain, Greece, and Ireland) and to most accession countries, whose GDP growth rates exceeded 8% per annum (the Baltic countries) or 5% (most other eastern European countries). However, since 2008, the economic situation has deteriorated and many of the new member states with growing economies were struck particularly hard by the recession. In fact, the global financial and economic crisis affected in particular the weaker southern and eastern European economies, such as the Baltic countries, whose GDP decreased more sharply than the European average (see Table 3.1). Former role models of European integration such as Ireland but also other countries like Portugal and Greece now require the assistance of the EU to prevent financial bankruptcy. This development places fiscal austerity high on the agenda of most European governments and increases the pressure to adopt welfare state retrenchment policies.

Economic development has had an effect on the situation of European citizens by reducing employment rates and increasing the number of jobless people for instance. Social exclusion affected the European countries differently, depending on the structure of national labor markets and employment regimes (Muffels and Fouarge 2001). In this respect, cleavages exist along north/south and east/west axes. Available data distinguishes a group of countries that have high levels of employment rates and low numbers of unemployed people, thus providing citizens of these countries with an easier access to the labor market (see Table 3.1). This group consists of the Scandinavian countries, Austria, Germany, the Netherlands, and the United Kingdom (UK) but also of Slovenia. By comparison, there are countries with lower employment rates and higher shares of joblessness, thus exhibiting more exclusive labor markets (the Baltic countries, Hungary, Slovakia, Greece, Spain, but also France and Ireland). Other countries, among them the remaining Mediterranean and east European countries, are placed at an intermediate position. These differences are particularly relevant because joblessness is one of the main determinants of social inequalities.

[1] The EU has had six enlargement rounds: in 1973 in a northwestern direction (Denmark, Ireland, and the United Kingdom (UK)); in 1981 and 1986 toward the south (Greece, Spain, and Portugal); in 1995 toward the north (Finland and Sweden, and also Austria); in 2004 toward the east (Estonia, Latvia, Lithuania, Poland, the Czech Republic, Hungary, Slovakia, Slovenia, Malta, and Cyprus); and in 2007 toward the southeast (Bulgaria and Romania).

Table 3.1 The socioeconomic structure of EU member states

GEO	GDP/capita (€, 2010)	GDP/capita (PPS, 2010)	GDP growth rate (%, Ø 2003–2007)	GDP growth rate (%, Ø 2008–2010)	Employment rate (%, 2010)	Unemployment rate (%, 2010)	Risk at poverty rate (%, 2010)	Income inequality: income quintile share ration (2010)	Material deprivation rate – 4 goods (2010)
EU 27	24,400	100	1.94	–0.7	64.1	9.7	16.4	5.0	8.1
EU 25	25,600	103	1.86	–0.7	64.5	9.8	–	–	–
EU 15	28,400	110	1.62	–0.8	65.4	9.6	16.3	5.0	5.2
Austria	34,100	126	2.10	0.0	71.7	4.4	12.1	3.7	4.3
Belgium	32,600	119	1.72	0.2	62.0	8.3	14.6	3.9	5.9
Bulgaria	4,800	44	6.94	0.3	59.7	10.2	20.7	5.9	35.0
Cyprus	21,600	99	1.82	0.9	69.7	6.2	16.2[a]	4.2[a]	7.9[a]
Czech Rep.	14,200	80	5.22	0.4	65.0	7.3	9.0	3.5	6.2
Denmark	42,500	127	1.72	–1.8	73.4	7.4	13.3	4.4	2.7
Estonia	10,700	64	8.64	–5.2	61.0	16.9	15.8	5.0	9.0
Finland	33,500	115	3.42	–1.5	68.1	8.4	13.1	3.6	2.8
France	29,800	108	1.30	–0.4	63.8	9.8	13.5	4.5	5.8
Germany	30,300	118	1.60	–0.1	71.1	7.1	15.6	4.5	4.5
Greece	20,100	90	4.02	–2.3	59.6	12.6	20.1	5.6	11.6
Hungary	9,700	65	3.44	–1.5	55.4	11.2	12.3	3.4	21.6
Ireland	34,900	127	2.98	–3.5	60.0	13.7	15.0[a]	4.2[a]	6.1[a]
Italy	25,700	101	0.36	–1.6	56.9	8.4	18.2	5.2	6.9
Latvia	8,000	51	10.34	–7.1	59.3	18.7	21.3	6.9	27.4
Lithuania	8,400	57	9.20	–3.5	57.8	17.8	20.2	7.3	19.5
Luxembourg	79,500	271	3.08	–0.6	65.2	4.6	14.5	4.1	0.5
Malta	14,800	83	1.74	1.5	56.1	6.9	15.5	4.3	5.7
Netherlands	35,400	133	2.10	0.0	74.7	4.5	10.3	3.7	2.2
Poland	9,300	63	5.24	3.5	59.3	9.6	17.6	5.0	14.2

Portugal	16,200	80	0.60	−0.5	65.6	12	17.9	5.6	9.0
Romania	5,800	47	6.66	−0.3	58.8	7.3	21.1	6.0	31.0
Slovakia	12,100	73	7.04	1.7	58.8	14.4	12.0	3.8	11.4
Slovenia	17,300	85	4.62	−1.0	66.2	7.3	12.7	3.4	5.9
Spain	22,800	100	1.80	−1.0	58.6	20.1	20.7	6.9	4.0
Sweden	37,000	123	2.96	−0.1	72.7	8.4	12.9	3.5	1.3
UK	27,400	112	2.12	−1.1	69.5	7.8	17.1	5.4	4.8

Source: European Union (1995–2011), Eurostat online statistics at http://epp.eurostat.ec.europa.eu/

[a]This data refers to the year 2009

In fact, these differences mirror variations in national levels of poverty – when identifying income poverty by means of households with less than 60% of the mean national household income. According to this criterion, Austria, Denmark, France, Finland, the Netherlands, and Sweden but also the Czech Republic, Hungary, Slovakia, and Slovenia perform better when compared with the average rates within the EU 27, with only 8–14% of the population suffering income poverty (see Table 3.1). The risk of poverty is much more pronounced in the European south and east, for instance in Greece, Portugal, Italy, and Spain, in Bulgaria, Romania, Lithuania, and Latvia – with 18–21% of the population living in precarious financial circumstances (see also Böhnke 2006: 117). These differences are not only determined by the level of economic development, structure of labor markets, working conditions, and wages but also by social security systems and policies which differ quite strongly between the European countries, depending on the welfare regimes in place (Esping-Andersen 1990). In fact, social transfers reduce the risks of poverty by at least 50% in the Scandinavian countries, the Czech Republic, and the Netherlands, and between 40 and 50% in the other western welfare states, such as the Austria, Belgium, France, Germany, Luxembourg, and the UK, and in some east European countries (Slovenia, Slovakia, Hungary, and Poland). This effect is rather restricted in the southern and the other east European countries (Caminada and Goudswsaard 2009).

European integration seems to affect the income situation of European households over time. Beckfield (2006), for instance, argues that European integration has increased income inequalities within western European nations between the early 1970s and the late 1990s, due to economic and political integration, external and internal pressures on labor and labor organizations, and demands for the relaxation of social security. Other studies paint a more differentiated picture. Härpfer and Schwarze (2006) demonstrated that income inequalities have declined slightly on average throughout Western Europe between 1997 and 2001. But this is the case only because southern countries (e.g., Spain, Greece, or Italy) were able to benefit from the European market, economic growth, labor-market flexibility, and higher rates of employment. At the same time, however, income inequalities increased in other countries and most markedly in the developed welfare states such as in Sweden, Finland, and Denmark (Härpfer and Schwarze 2006). Scholars point to two possible reasons for this state of affairs. While welfare states have demonstrated a quite considerable resistance to convergence (Castels 2004: 73–92), it is argued that European integration is putting more pressure on welfare state retrenchment. At the same time, labor market policies are under review since the European Lisbon Strategy of 2000, favoring the flexibility and liberalization of labor markets in an attempt to increase employment (Countouris 2007: 87–105). This development has had an impact on the labor force. Scientific estimates suggest that flexible employment has increased by approximately 15% in the EU between 1985 and 1995 (de Grip and Hoevenberg 1997; Muffels and Fouarge 2001). By the late 1990s, one job in four in the EU was considered to be precarious or of a low quality (ESOPE 2004: 10). This development seems to have alleviated the problem of income inequalities by bringing more people into work in some of the Mediterranean countries but just to increase the risk at poverty due to precarious employment. Income inequalities thus remain high in many eastern and southern European countries and are gradually increasing in more egalitarian member states.

These socioeconomic indicators only give an incomplete picture of the prevailing living conditions and standards of life in the various member states, because they do not take sufficiently into consideration the local accessibility of goods. For this reason, scholars have been using the *European Quality of Life Survey* to look at material deprivations, defined as the lack of at least four out of nine different types of goods (e.g., heated housing, regular meals with fish and meat, short holidays, a washing machine, a television, a car, and a computer). According to this definition, deprivation is a reality for less than 5% of the population in Austria, Denmark, Finland, Germany, Luxembourg, the Netherlands, Spain, Sweden, and the UK, while it affects large proportions of the population in Portugal (9%), Greece (11.6%), Slovakia (11.4%), Poland (14.2%), Lithuania (19.5%), Hungary (21.6%), Latvia (27.4), Romania (31%), and Bulgaria (35%) (see also Böhnke 2006: 117). Moreover, standards of living are very different even for the more privileged strata of the population. For instance, the richest income group in Romania, Bulgaria, Poland, and the Baltic countries reports a level of access to material goods and housing that is comparable to the lowest income group in Luxembourg, the Netherlands, Austria, and the Scandinavian countries (Alber and Lenarz 2008). This does not necessarily reflect identical, objective living conditions but comparable accessibility to goods. Finally, European countries also exhibit a varying degree of internal differences between the standards of life of the lowest and highest income groups of the population. In the Northern countries such as Scandinavia and the Netherlands, standards of life are comparable, while they are particularly unequal in the European south and east and in the UK and Ireland (Alber and Lenarz 2008), subjecting underprivileged groups of the population, therefore, to considerable material deprivations.

In sum, nations do make a considerable difference with respect to the living conditions of the European citizenry. This observation is plausible, but it disregards regional disparities in economic wealth, for example, when measured in GDP per capita. In fact, nation-states are not homogenous social spaces, but all have considerable internal variances. Overall, scholars agree that regional disparities are the major challenge to European integration. The good news is that socioeconomic disparities between nations tend to diminish or stagnate over time. At the same time, however, there is a substantial increase in regional disparities that reproduce and/or aggravate existing core-periphery relations (Heidenreich and Wunder 2008). This situation was true for the pre-accession EU of 15 member states and it still prevails in these countries. In fact, the poorest regions today are located in the southern periphery, that is, in the southern parts of Spain, Italy, and Greece. There are also deprived regions in the developed countries of central Europe such as the new "Länder" in Germany or the old industrial areas of Belgium.

The eastward enlargement process increased disparities considerably. According to Brasche (2008: 208–210), only 8% of the population of the old 15 member states lived in poor regions in 1995, that is, the areas generating a GDP per capita that is below 75% of the EU average. This picture changes drastically when the situation in the 12 accession countries is taken into consideration because here 97 % of the people in these countries lived in poor regions in 1995, and 88 % continued to do so in 2004. In these countries, the core-periphery structure is much more pronounced because the socioeconomic development is strongly concentrated in the big cities and principally in metropolitan areas. These urban development areas shelter the biggest share of the population, attract most of foreign investments, and promote the service sector, information and telecommunication technologies, knowledge-based goods and labor markets, thus generating high growth rates. Cities such as Prague, Bratislava, Budapest, and Warsaw are therefore far above the GDP EU average per capita (Brasche 2008: 212–218).

The reasons for these regional disparities are manifold and have to do with migration movements and different demographic dynamics, diverging socioeconomic structures (e.g., the importance of agrarian, industrial, or service and knowledge-based sectors), their competitiveness within the liberalizing European markets, private and public transfers, and regional policies, among many others. For my purposes, it is important to stress that regional disparities seem to increase in most countries, thus contradicting the hopes of the EU that the more prosperous core regions might spur the economic transformation and take-off of peripheral regions, thus leading to a gradual convergence. In fact, Heidenreich and Wunder (2008) have shown that regional disparities in GDP per capita have grown between 1995 and 2003 in most EU member states. A decrease of disparities was only noted in Italy and Denmark. At the same time, disparities more than doubled in Poland, Latvia, and Portugal and increased strongly in the other central and east European countries and in Ireland, Sweden, and Finland. These countries are moving closer to the more heterogeneous structure of the older member states, such as the UK, France, Germany, Austria, and Belgium, where the richest regions are from two to five times more prosperous economically than the poorest regions.

Hence, throughout the European continent, the picture of core-periphery structures and regional disparities is being reproduced and magnified, thus generating quite different life chances and forms for its citizens. It is to be assumed that prosperous metropolitan regions such as Madrid, London, Stockholm, Prague, or Bratislava have many more societal features in common than with their neighboring areas and rural peripheries. This core-periphery structure implies contrasting grievances and problems. Peripheral regions have to struggle with depopulation and pronounced aging, badly developed transport and communication infrastructures, limited access to social, cultural, or health services, to higher education and knowledge-based labor markets, while more developed metropolitan regions are confronted with urbanization, migration and spatial segregation, insufficient (affordable) housing and public services, traffic congestions, and environmental degradation, among many others (ESPON 2007).

All these findings lead to the conclusion that European integration has had strong effects on the socioeconomic structures within Europe by establishing liberalized markets (capital, goods, labor, and services), pushing nations and regions into economic competition and subsequent economic transformations. However, this does not eliminate national and regional differences in economic development, welfare regimes, labor markets, income patterns, and living standards, as demonstrated above. Hence, what happens in Europe is a process of constant societal change without convergence. What I mean by this is that on the one hand, it becomes apparent that European societies are changing very quickly. This is not determined by European integration alone but by underlying societal transformations, such as the demographic transition, urbanization, the shift toward the service sector, educational and technological revolutions, etc. The EU is actively engaged in furthering these "modernization processes," particularly with respect to accession countries that have to adapt to the Copenhagen Criteria and to the European "acquis communautaire," which stipulate liberal market economies, the rule of law and democratic governance, civil societies, and a civic and secular culture as the role model for all member states. More specifically, the EU is committed to improving transport and communication infrastructures to increase individuals' access to the liberalized, Pan-European markets of goods, services, capital, and labor it is constructing. The EU is committed to harmonize educational systems in order to promote educational and career mobility. It is engaged in increasing employment rates by means of labor market flexibility and activation. The EU is committed to antidiscrimination measures to improve the access of women, handicapped, or migrants to economic and social life. Finally, the EU supports research and innovation in order to promote an information and knowledge-based European society. Therefore, Europe faces rapid societal change that affects all aspects of people's lives. This comment does not only apply to the east European accession countries, as mentioned above, which had to commit to fundamental changes to their economic, political, and legal institutions when they applied for EU membership. A similar observation is true for the older accession countries such as Italy, Spain, and Greece. This implies an accelerated shift of societal problems and conflicts. For instance, Italy, Spain, and Greece quickly left the high emigration rates from the 1960s and 1970s behind them and have been confronted these past 10 years with high rates of legal and illegal immigration flows across the southern EU borders.

This generalized and constant societal change, however, does not generate more convergence between European societies, due to the different developmental stages and structural positions of the various countries in the European space and given the different institutional path dependencies and cultures in place. Moreover, I have indicated that the fault lines between center and periphery are also deepening within nation-states. Finally, Europe is witnessing the reemergence of "old" cleavages and grievances, and thus a multiplication of "old" and "new" conflict lines, because environmental degradation, technological hazards, gender discrimination, and many other "new" issues are still important public concerns but are now confronted more clearly by "old" issues such as poverty, precarious working conditions, migration inflows, or xenophobia, which tend to rank high public and policy agendas.

The multiplication and fragmentation of cleavages and grievances provide a valuable societal background story to understand better the domestication or localization of EU-related mobilizations and protests. Indeed, available data seems to point to a marked localization of societal problems: people living in the region of Extremadura, Severozápad, or Calabria, for instance, will have other societal grievances and problems to cope with compared to their fellow citizens in Madrid, Prague, or Milan. This does not make EU-related mobilizations and protests unlikely but rather it requires that they resonate with the specific grievances, conflicts, and agendas of local constituencies. This development has two implications. On the one hand, this grievance structure will increase the probability of more issue-specific and constituency-specific collective action with diverse and/or competing claims. On the other hand, "Europeanized" collective action will require a specific form, namely, broader and changing protest coalitions adapted to the fragmented structure of local cleavages and grievances.

3.3 Social Cohesion in Europe: Spatial and Social Cleavages

The EU institutions are aware of the difficulties associated to European integration and highlight a number of problems: rising spatial and social disparities, weak social bonds, and limited feelings of belonging and shared identities among EU citizens of different social backgrounds and cultures (Council of Europe 2008: 8). Ultimately, EU institutions are worried about decreasing rates of public acceptance of the "European project" and of its institutions. A less cohesive EU would also increase the risk of more EU-related conflicts about the definition of the guiding values, ideas, and goals of the "European project" and about the distribution of resources between member states, regions, and groups. Are these worries ill-founded? Available data tends to confirm that levels of social cohesion are not well developed in Europe. This is true when looking at the level of social capital (i.e., social relations and ties, mutual feelings of trust) across the European continent and to the development of shared values and identifications (Jeannotte 2000; Chan et al. 2006; Osberg 2003). These deficiencies have an impact on political mobilization potentials because social capital and collective identities are important mobilizing resources. A low degree of European social cohesion will have detrimental effects on the prospects of transnational mobilizations. While this worry is justified, two exceptions need to be highlighted. On a spatial dimension, a "core Europe" of older member states with higher levels of social cohesion, against the "peripheral," newer and "not yet" European member states can be identified (Eder 2005). On a social dimension, social cohesion is marked by a class bias because the upper social classes benefit more strongly from "Europeanized" social capitals and shared identifications (Fligstein 2008).

3.3.1 Social Cohesion: The Core and the Peripheries

Studies using the indicators outlined above have shown that social cohesion is unevenly developed across member states within the EU. This is true, in first instance, with respect to social capital, which is measured by focusing on informal contacts (e.g., to friends and family members), participation in civic organizations and/or protest events, and relations of trust to fellow citizens and/or institutions. National differences within the EU are quite strong and follow cleavages along the north/south and west/east divide (Fuchs and Klingemann 2002). For instance, when Sweden is compared with Portugal or Poland, there is divergence in the average number of organizational memberships, that is, 1.43 compared to 0.20 and 0.19. The proportion of people participating in mass protests is 89% compared to 27 and 26%; the proportion that refer to the importance of friends is 75% compared to 42 and 33%, and the proportion that expresses interpersonal trust is 64% compared to 10 and 18% (Voicu 2005). The available data thus classifies European countries into four groups: a northern group with highest scores on all dimensions (Sweden, the Netherlands, Finland, Denmark, and Iceland); a western group with the second highest scores, particularly in regard to institutional trust and protest participation (Ireland, the UK, Germany, France, Italy, and Switzerland); a southern ex-totalitarian group with low scores on all indicators, except for friendships (Greece, Spain, Portugal, and ex-Yugoslavia); and an eastern ex-totalitarian group with the lowest rates on all dimensions (Voicu 2005). However, this does not mean that southern and eastern European countries lack any kind of social bonds, trust, and feelings of belonging. They are rather marked by a much stronger dominance of private forms of social relation that are more strongly restricted to family and kinship. Generalized trust and organized civil societies are weaker in these countries (Howard 2003). These findings corroborate the continuing importance of the nation-state: social capital seems to be determined by the "supply side," either by different welfare regimes (Salamon and Anheier 1998) or existing civil societies that provide opportunities for the development of civic engagement and generalized trust (Baldassarri and Diani 2007). Hence, it is the "core Europe" of older member states that has higher levels of generalized social cohesion.

These observations are well documented, yet say little about transnational social cohesion – about social ties, relations of trust and cultural values shared by people from different EU countries. In this regard, scholars tend to confirm the spatial segregation of Europe because they differentiate, in first instance, between a "core" group of countries with high levels of mutual trust and a "periphery" of less trusted and less trusting societies. This has been demonstrated by Delhey (2007) on the basis of *Eurobarometer* data from 1976 to 1997. He shows that people from the six founding EC members trust each other quite strongly. Northwestern enlargement countries (Ireland, the UK, and Denmark) and the northern enlargement countries (Sweden, Finland, but also Austria) stabilized and increased mutual trust levels, not only because these countries were considered trustworthy by the citizens of the old member states but also because these newer member states exhibited higher trust rates themselves. However, the southern enlargement countries reduced these rates considerably, and this is particularly true with respect to the eastern European accession countries. People from these countries are much less trusted but tend also to trust less – even each other. Lack of trust concerns Romania, Bulgaria, and Turkey – an EU candidate country.

A similar picture of a segregated social cohesion within Europe emerges when considering the EU's cultural diversity in terms of cultural values, attitudes, and political agendas. Research has shown that citizens, national governments, and EU institutions tend to have different policy priorities (Hooghe 2003). But these differences are also marked when comparing member states. Gerhards (2007), for instance, has demonstrated on the basis of survey data that cultural values within the old member states (here, in particularly within the EU-6 and EU-9 countries) are more in tune with the liberal and secular "script" of the EU's own modernization project in many policy areas (e.g., economic, employment, social, gender, family policies). The "compatibility" is less marked among the new, eastern European and candidate member states because their citizens favor traditional and materialistic value systems, as corroborated by Ingelhart (1997).

European enlargement and further integration thus increase the probability of societal conflicts on the guiding values and the objectives of European unification. These conflicts are the more probable because the EU is marked by rather low levels of European identifications among their citizens, as has been illustrated recurrently. In fact, identifications with the EU are more rational than emotional and more civic than cultural (Bruter 2004). Moreover, European references always rank second compared to national and/or regional identifications (Westle 2003; Karolewski and Kaina 2006). Citizens feel attached to the EU because of the advantages of the economic and legal "community" (e.g., the free movement, a shared currency, and common rights) and because of a common civilization and society. Cultural traits, such as a common history, ancestry, and symbols, are mentioned far less often (Pichler 2005). While most citizens claim that membership of the EU is a good thing (around 50 %), only a small minority of citizens identify exclusively with Europe (less than 7 %). Europe is not irrelevant, though, because more than 50 % identify with the nation-state and Europe at the same time (Westle 2003; Fuss and Grosser 2006). Thus, a "European identity" is only a secondary reference point, which implies that feelings of belongingness to the EU lose in comparison with "older" political identities, as soon as exclusive identifications become a matter of interest. These issues point to a structural weakness of European identifications: in case of conflicts of interest or value, people will tend to feel attached to "primary" collectivities, such as the nation or the region and not to the EU.

Overall, available evidence confirms the above stated argument about the segregation of Europe with respect to social cohesion along a core-periphery structure. On the one hand, there is a core group of northern and western European member states with higher levels of internal social capital, with stronger mutual relations of intercultural trust, and with a more pronounced degree of "fit" between their cultural values and the political mission of the EU. On the other hand, southern and eastern European countries are placed at the periphery because they bring in less generalized social capital, are more excluded from transnational relations of trust, and share less "European" (i.e., EU-related) values and policy ideas, thus belonging to a group of "not really" or "not yet European" countries (Eder 2005). This core-periphery structure is complemented by a similar internal cleavage because regional disparities in social cohesion exist within each country as well. Indeed, while levels of social capital are quite high in Europe when compared worldwide (van Oorschot et al. 2006), Europe has higher levels of generalized trust and civic participation in more urbanized and developed core regions, while they are less developed in peripheral areas such as in southern Italy and southern France, western and southern Spain, northern England, and Scotland (Beugelsdijk and van Schaik 2005).

3.3.2 Social Cohesion and Class

Empirical evidence also corroborates my second hypothesis, namely, that the state of social cohesion in Europe is determined by social class as well. The amount of social bonds, organizational memberships, and interpersonal and institutional trust is strongly determined by income, employment, social status, and education, regardless of the country or region (van Oorschot et al. 2006). Scholars thus speak about cumulative deprivations: people subjected to income poverty and material deprivation also suffer social poverty in the sense of having fewer social contacts and relations of support. However, this cumulative effect is stronger in the more developed Northern countries of the EU and less evident in the southern and eastern European countries, where family and private forms of social relation and support are more stable and important (Böhnke 2006).

At the same time, more privileged social classes tend to have more social capital in general but also more transnational social capital in particular. In fact, Mau (2007) has demonstrated for Germany that almost one in two Germans has close friends or relatives abroad with which he or she is in regular contact. One in six is married to a foreigner, and one in eight has spent a long period of time abroad. This transnationalization is particularly pronounced among the more privileged social classes because people with the highest educational attainment have twice as many transnational contacts than their fellow citizens with a low level of education (Mau 2007: 106). These findings fit to the general picture portrayed by scholars: the upper social strata have "Europeanized" the most with respect to social capital and collective identities. Indeed, it is the well educated with better jobs and higher social status that know more about the EU, are more happy with an EU membership of their country, and feel more European (Petithomme 2008). At the same time, they have assembled key transnational resources. This applies, above all to linguistic competence, a significant resource in the EU. Data shows that more than 50% of all EU citizens do not speak a foreign language, 25% speak one foreign language, and another 25% speak two or more foreign languages. While unskilled workers are the least well equipped, the higher professionals, executives, and self-employed are the best qualified (Gerhards 2008b). Hence, it is this social stratum that can best benefit from the opportunities provided by the process of European integration. Although we are not witnessing the advent of an integrated European elite (Hartmann 2007), available evidence seems to indicate that they at least develop a more "transnational" lifestyle, with more mobility, more transnational contacts, and related experiences (Favell 2008; Fuss and Grosser 2006; Gerhards 2008a).

These observations lead me to the same conclusions presented by Fligstein (2008). The process of European integration has generated a more cohesive "European society" for the more privileged strata of the European citizenry, because the latter are better equipped to benefit from the opportunities generated by the EU and are thus able to develop a more transnational economic, social, and human capital. In Fligstein's perspective, this will intensify the contentiousness within the EU by confronting three different constituencies with different social interests and political orientations: a group of well-educated, young professionals, managers, and white-collar workers who will use and defend proactively European integration; a stratum of older and less-educated working poor, jobless, and blue-collar workers who will defend the national welfare state against an intrusive EU; and a middle-class constituency who shares a more positive view on the EU but is not unconditionally in favor of furthering integration, thus being a potential ally of both fractions. Moreover, this class-biased structure of social cohesion provides better societal opportunities for middle- and upper-class mobilizations and protests because these groups have more (transnational) social relations and organizational memberships, feel more European, are better informed about the EU, and are more in tune with the EU's own ideas and missions.

3.4 Discussion and Conclusions: Social Cohesion and the Political Sociology of Europe

In this chapter, I have argued that the process of European enlargement and integration is having a series of effects on the social structure of the EU. The main conclusion to these observations is that Europe is not governed by one big and core fault line but rather that societal developments lead to a multiplication and fragmentation of societal grievances along national and regional divisions and along social class structures. In fact, there seems to be the renaissance of "old" grievances, namely, those related to social inequalities, poverty and exclusion, and nationalism and xenophobia, which complement "new" issues, such as environmental degradation, technological hazards, gender equality, sex and civil liberties, and others.

Grievances do not translate automatically into unrest. The multiplication and fragmentation I described so far can therefore bring about quite different dynamics. On the one hand, we might expect a stronger segregation of contentions along spatial disparities and social divisions: "old" grievances and issues being more present in the European periphery and among underprivileged population groups, while "newer" grievances prevail in more developed, urban environments and in the more affluent strata of the population. On the other hand, it is possible that the European integration process provides arenas and incentives for a stronger interrelation and conjunction of various issue areas and political contentions. This is true in the case of the movement activists who promote more comprehensive debates about environmental justice, gender mainstreaming, and antidiscrimination policies, and who aim to link "old" and "new" conflict lines and claims. Many Pan-European advocacy networks have embarked in this venture. This is the case of the European feminism and women's movements that have to reconcile the different interests, political traditions and claims of their constituencies from western and eastern European member states (Roth 2008).

Against this backdrop, there is a real chance that the European Union will make a difference in blending the various cleavages and claims into more integrated protest and policy agendas. Here, I come back to an argument presented earlier in this chapter: the EU is an institutional arena with its own policy debates and priorities, proper political opportunities structures and incentives. The EU is thus able to drive public interests onto the European scene and to accommodate them within the consultative practices of the Brussel's policy communities (Marks and McAdam 1999; Rucht 2001; Balme and Chabanet 2008). This integrative pressure might have catalytic effects on political contentions far beyond the supranational level of the EU institutions. While living conditions remain very different within Europe, depending on where citizens live, it is true at the same time that the EU is redefining and reframing national problems and local grievances within a Pan-European frame of reference. In fact, the EU is defining economic and social indicators for all of its member states and is gathering comparable data and encouraging a continuous process of monitoring in many areas of activity such as economic integration, employment, poverty, and social exclusion. The EU is thus promoting the idea of a common European social space with a shared social structure, within which citizens, regions, and nations can and must be compared. Finally, the EU engages into a normative discussion about social cohesion, as we have illustrated above, and this debate provides a target and a frame for political contentions because it erects procedures, guidelines, and norms for evaluating and criticizing the performance of EU institutions, nations, and regions in their ability to reach the common objectives.

Consequently, even if the process of European integration is leading to a more fragmented field of societal grievances and political contentions, it is possible that the EU as an institutional arena effectively alters the definition and perception of societal grievances, conflicts, and issues by erecting a Pan-European frame of reference and a vision of a common European space. This seems to be the case to a certain extent. On the one hand, the academic community has been advocating the idea of an emerging common "European society" (Outhwaite 2008; Beck and Grande 2007; Delanty and Rumford 2005), and attempts are made to reconstruct its culture, identity, and collective memory (Giesen 2003; Eder 2005). On the other hand, there is evidence for the fact that citizens start to assess their situation in Pan-European categories, for example, by comparing their position with those of other European citizens. Delhey and Kohler (2006), for instance, have demonstrated through a survey in three European countries (Germany, Hungary, and Turkey) that the great majority of respondents (75–90%) do compare themselves not only with closer reference groups (neighbors, family, fellow citizens) but also with the situation in other countries. Moreover, people tend to compare themselves more readily with more affluent countries. This comparison affects their subjective well-being, thus generating feelings of relative deprivation.

These findings suggest that transnational mobilizations and EU-related protests might well rise in the future, as soon as local constituencies become aware that they are worse off than fellow citizens when compared with common standards, as soon as they start to defend their higher standards of living against those EU citizens living in more precarious situations, and/or as soon as they perceive to share grievances with many other people throughout Europe. This scenario is probable and confirmed by transnational and EU-related mobilizations (Chabanet 2008; Balme and Chabanet 2008). However, this observation needs to be qualified with respect to the more general picture portrayed here. My previous analysis has demonstrated that social cohesion within the EU is strongly patterned by core-periphery relations and class structures. This decreases the scope of issues and constituencies that can be mobilized effectively and over time.

On the one hand, constituencies of the socially underprivileged, excluded, or marginalized have less information about the EU and the "system of European grievances" it monitors and addresses. Their cultural and social capital is more restricted and less transnationalized and is thus badly equipped for mobilizing a spatially dispersed and complex European constituency with different agendas, belief systems, and social relations. Moreover, these constituencies are much more dependent on the nation-state and on its welfare institutions, thus being more inclined to mobilize on their behalf and against EU-specific policies, particularly if they are viewed as a threat to the national welfare state (Fligstein 2008). Finally, the process of European integration follows a liberal modernization project with strong path dependencies. Protests that aim to redirect the path of European integration toward new goals (e.g., social welfare) meet more resistance and challenges (Hooghe 2003) than those aiming at continuing, improving, or correcting the direction of European unification. Their protests become more oppositional and "anti-systemic" and ask for more perseverance, organizational continuity, and commitment, thus requiring additional material and symbolic resources (e.g., funds, social relations, information, shared identities) to which the underprivileged have a more restricted access. To this, we have to add the observation made by the "political opportunity structure" approach stated before. The EU establishes a system of political consultation and decision-making with clear rules that push public interest groups toward an institutionalization and professionalization of claims-making (Rucht 2001; Marks and McAdam 1999; Lahusen 2004; Kohler-Koch 2010).

On the other hand, it is to be expected that mobilization processes will be structured also along the spatial patterns identified before. In regard to grievances, we need to count with a continuing domestication of contentions, as some scholars have proposed (Imig and Tarrow 2001), accounting for the fact that political protests within the EU are still primarily local phenomena with specific constituencies, issues, and claims. This has to do with the fact that living conditions, forms, and aspirations diverge between countries and their regions. Moreover, the nation-state is still the main addressee of political claims-making because the latter is democratically legitimized and legally accountable to act in all policy fields, even in those "Europeanized" issue areas where it is responsible for legally adopting and implementing European objectives and directives. Pan-European mobilizations and protest thus depend on the ability of activists to build coalitions and to identify claims that mirror the different grievances of local constituencies throughout Europe. In this sense, there are chances to successfully transnationalize protest.

However, transnational protest mobilization also seems to be constrained by the structure of social cohesion within the EU. As we have seen, social cohesion within the EU is marked by a core-periphery structure which tends to translate into mobilization cleavages. Transnational protest across the "core" of Europe is probable, given the fact that people in these countries share higher levels of social capital, transnational contacts and trust, and comparable values and beliefs; while protest is much less probable across the European periphery because people tend to expose lower levels of civic engagement, transnational contacts and trust, and shared values and identifications. It is to be expected that these cleavages increase due to the financial and economic crisis within the EU and the austerity measures governments in Greece, Spain, Portugal, and Italy are implementing. Protest mobilization is particularly strong in Greece where citizens oppose the austerity packages demanded by bailout creditor countries, in particular France and Germany. However, protests in the European periphery tend to be locally contained. Moreover, they can count with less solidarity and support from core European countries. Under these circumstances, it is to be hoped that weak interests and constituencies from the European periphery will be able to voice their grievances and claims perceivably in order to have a say in the ongoing construction of the European Union.

References

Alber, J., & Lenarz, P. (2008). Wachsende soziale Ungleichheit in Europa. *Informationsdienst Soziale Indikatoren, 39*, 1–5.

Baldassarri, D., & Diani, M. (2007). The integrative power of civic networks. *American Journal of Sociology, 113*(3), 735–780.

Balme, R., & Chabanet, D. (2008). *Collective action and European democracy*. New York: Rowman & Littlefield.

Balme, R., Chabanet, D., & Wright, V. (Eds.). (2002). *L'Action collective en Europe*. Paris: Presses de Sciences Po.

Beck, U. (1992). *Risk society: Towards a new modernity*. New Delhi: Sage.

Beck, U., & Grande, E. (2007). *Cosmopolitan Europe*. Cambridge: Polity Press.

Beckfield, J. (2006). European integration and income inequality. *American Sociological Review, 71*, 964–985.

Beugelsdijk, S., & van Schaik, T. (2005). Differences in social capital between 54 Western European regions. *Regional Studies, 39*(8), 1053–1064.

Böhnke, P. (2006). Einkommensarm, aber beziehungsreich? Zum Zusammenhang von Armut und sozialen Beziehungen in der erweiterten EU. In J. Alber & W. Merkel (Eds.), *Europas Osterweiterung: Das Ende der Vertiefung?* Berlin: Sigma.

Brasche, U. (2008). *Europäische Integration. Wirtschaft, Erweiterung, Regionale Effekte* (2nd ed.). Munich: Oldenburg.

Bruter, M. (2004). On what citizens mean by feeling 'European': Perceptions of news, symbols and borderlessness. *Journal of Ethnic and Migration Studies, 30*(1), 21–39.

Buechler, S. (1999). *Social movements in advanced capitalism*. Oxford: Oxford University Press.

Caminada, K., & Goudswsaard, K. (2009). Effectiveness of poverty reduction in the EU: A descriptive analysis. *Poverty and Public Policy, 1*(2), 1–49.

Castels, F. (2004). *The future of the welfare state: Crisis myths and crisis realities*. Oxford: Oxford University Press.

Chabanet, D. (2008). When the unemployed challenge the European Union: The European marches as a mode of externalization of protest. *Mobilization, 13*(3), 311–322.

Chan, J., To, H.-P., & Chan, E. (2006). Reconsidering social cohesion: Developing a definition and analytical framework for empirical research. *Social Indicators Research, 75*, 273–302.

Commission of the European Communities (CEC). (2008). *Green paper on territorial cohesion: Turning territorial diversity into strength*. Brussels: Communication from the Commission to the Council, the European Parliament, the Committee of the Regions and the European Economic and Social Committee (COM 2008 616 final).

Commission of the European Communities (CEC). (2009). *Sixth progress report on economic and social cohesion*. Brussels: Report from the European Parliament and Council, COM 2009 295 final.

Council of Europe. (2008). *Report of high-level task force on social cohesion: Towards an active, fair and socially cohesive Europe*. Strasbourg: Council of Europe.

Countouris, N. (2007). *The changing law of the employment relationship: Comparative analysis in the European context*. Aldershot: Ashgate.

de Grip, A., & Hoevenberg, J. (1997). Atypical employment in the European Union. *International Labor Review, 136*(1), 49–72.

Delanty, G., & Rumford, C. (2005). *Rethinking Europe: Social theory and the implications of Europeanization*. London: Routledge.

Delhey, J. (2007). Do enlargements make the European Union less cohesive? An analysis of trust between EU nationalities. *Journal of Common Market Studies, 45*(2), 253–279.

Delhey, J., & Kohler, U. (2006). From nationally bounded to Pan-European inequalities? On the importance of foreign countries as reference groups. *European Sociological Review, 22*(2), 125–140.

della Porta, D., & Caiani, M. (2011). *Social movements and Europeanization*. Oxford: Oxford University Press.

Eder, K. (2005). National identities and collective memory in an enlarged Europe. In W. Spohn & K. Eder (Eds.), *Collective memory and European identity: The effects of integration and enlargement*. Aldershot: Ashgate.

ESOPE. (2004). *Precarious employment in Europe: A comparative study of labor market related risks in flexible economies*. Brussels: European Commission, Directorate General for Research (Final Report of the Project HPSE-CT2001-00075).

Esping-Andersen, G. (1990). *The three worlds of welfare capitalism*. Cambridge: Polity Press.

ESPON. (2007). *Scenarios on the territorial future of Europe*. Brussels: ESPON.

Favell, A. (2008). *Eurostars and Eurocities: Free movement and mobility in an integrating Europe*. Oxford: Blackwell.

Fligstein, N. (2008). *Euroclash: The EU, European identity, and the future of Europe*. Oxford: Oxford University Press.

Fuchs, D., & Klingemann, H.-D. (2002). Eastward enlargement of the European Union and the identity of Europe. *West European Politics, 25*(2), 19–54.

Fuss, D., & Grosser, M. (2006). What makes young Europeans feel European? Results from a cross-cultural research project. In P. I. Karolewski & V. Kaina (Eds.), *European identity: Theoretical perspectives and empirical insights*. Münster: Lit-Verlag.

Gerhards, J. (2007). *Cultural overstretch? Differences between old and new member states of the EU and Turkey*. London: Routledge.

Gerhards, J. (2008a). Die kulturelle Elite Europas. Eine vergleichende Analyse der 27 Mitgliedsländer der EU auf der Grundlage einer Auswertung des Eurobarometers. *Berliner Studien zur Soziologie Europas, 13*, 1–32.

Gerhards, J. (2008b). Transnationales linguistisches Kapital der Bürger und der Prozess der europäischen Integration. *Berliner Studien zur Soziologie Europas, 17*, 1–28.

Giddens, A. (1999). *Runaway world: How globalization is reshaping our lives*. London: Profile.

Giesen, B. (2003). The collective identity of Europe: Constitutional practice or community of memory? In W. Spohn & A. Triandafyllidou (Eds.), *Europeanisation, national identities and migration: Changes in boundary constructions between western and eastern Europe*. London: Routledge.
Härpfer, M., & Schwarze, J. (2006). Wie gleich ist Europa? Empirische Befunde zur Entwicklung der Einkommensungleichheiten in den bisherigen EU-Mitgliedsstaaten. In M. Heidenreich (Ed.), *Die Europäisierung sozialer Ungleichheit: Zur transnationalen Klassen- und Sozialstrukturanalyse*. Frankfurt: Campus.
Hartmann, M. (2007). *Eliten und Macht in Europa: Ein internationaler Vergleich*. New York: Campus.
Heidenreich, M., & Wunder, C. (2008). Patterns of regional inequality in the enlarged Europe. *European Sociological Review, 24*(1), 19–36.
Hix, S., & Marsh, M. (2007). Punishment or protest? Understanding European parliament elections. *Journal of Politics, 69*(2), 495–510.
Hooghe, L. (2003). Europe divided? Elites vs. public opinion on European integration. *European Union Politics, 4*(3), 281–304.
Howard, M. M. (2003). *The weakness of civil society in post-communist Europe*. Cambridge: Cambridge University Press.
Imig, D., & Tarrow, S. (1999). The Europeanization of movements? Contentious politics and the European Union: October 1983–March 1995. In D. della Porta, H. Kriesi, & D. Rucht (Eds.), *Social movements in a globalizing world*. New York: Macmillan.
Imig, D., & Tarrow, S. (2001). Mapping the Europeanisation of contention: Evidence from a quantitative data analysis. In D. Imig & S. Tarrow (Eds.), *Contentious Europeans: Protest and politics in an emerging polity*. Lanham: Rowman and Littlefield.
Ingelhart, R. (1997). *Modernization and postmodernization*. Princeton: Princeton University Press.
Jeannotte, S. (2000). *Social cohesion around the world: An international comparison of definitions and issues*. Gatineau: Strategic Research and Analysis, Canadian Heritage (SRA-309, December).
Karolewski, I. P., & Kaina, V. (Eds.). (2006). *European identity: Theoretical perspectives and empirical insights*. Münster: Lit-Verlag.
Kohler-Koch, B. (2010). Civil society and EU democracy: 'Astroturf' representation? *Journal of European Public Policy, 17*(1), 100–116.
Kohler-Koch, B., & Quittkat, C. (2011). *Die Entzauberung partizipativer Demokratie: Zur Rolle der Zivilgesellschaft bei der Demokratisierung von EU-Governance*. Frankfurt: Campus.
Lahusen, C. (2004). Joining the cocktail-circuit: Social movement organizations at the European Union. *Mobilization, 9*(1), 55–71.
Marks, G., & McAdam, D. (1999). On the relationship of political opportunities to the form of collective action: The case of the European Union. In D. della Porta, H. Kriesi, & D. Rucht (Eds.), *Social movements in a globalizing world*. London: Macmillan.
Mau, S. (2007). *Transnationale Vergesellschaftung: Die Entgrenzung sozialer Lebenswelten*. Frankfurt: Campus.
McAdam, D., Tarrow, S., & Tilly, C. (2001). *Dynamics of contention*. Cambridge: Cambridge University Press.
McCarthy, J., & Zald, M. (1977). Resource mobilization and social movements: A partial theory. *American Journal of Sociology, 82*(6), 1212–1241.
Melucci, A. (1989). *Nomads of the present: Social movements and individual needs in contemporary society*. Philadelphia: Temple University Press.
Muffels, R., & Fouarge, D. (2001). *Working profiles and employment regimes in European panel perspective* (MPRA Paper No. 1329). Munich. http://mpra.ub.uni-muenchen.de/13295/. Last Accessed 12 June 2011.
Osberg, L. (2003). *The economic implications of social cohesion*. Toronto: University of Toronto Press.
Outhwaite, W. (2008). *European society*. Cambridge: Polity Press.

Petithomme, M. (2008). Is there a European identity? National attitudes and social identification toward the European Union. *Journal of Identity and Migration Studies, 2*(1), 15–36.
Pichler, F. (2005). *Affection to and exploitation of Europe*. Vienna: Institut für Höhere Studien.
Prodi, R., & Kinnock, N. (2001). *The Commission and non-governmental organisations: Building a stronger partnership*. Brussels: The Commission of the European Union, Discussion Paper.
Roth, S. (Ed.). (2008). *Gender politics in the expanding European Union: Mobilization, inclusion, exclusion*. New York: Berghahn Books.
Rucht, D. (2001). Lobbying or protest: Strategies to influence EU environmental policies. In D. Imig & S. Tarrow (Eds.), *Contentious Europeans: Protest and politics in an integrating Europe*. Boulder: Rowman & Littlefield.
Rucht, D. (2002). The EU as a target of political mobilization: Is there a Europeanisation of conflict? In R. Balme, D. Chabanet, & V. Wright (Eds.), *L'action collective en Europe*. Paris: Presses de Sciences Po.
Salamon, L., & Anheier, H. (1998). Social origins of civil society: Explaining the nonprofit sector cross-nationally. *Voluntas, 9*(3), 213–248.
Touraine, A. (1971). *Post-industrial society; Tomorrow's social history: Classes, conflicts and culture in the programmed society*. New York: Random House.
Van Oorschot, W., Arts, W., & Gelissen, J. (2006). Social capital in Europe: Measurement and social and regional distribution of a multifaceted phenomenon. *Acta Sociologica, 49*(2), 149–167.
Voicu, B. (2005). Social capital: Bonding or bridging Europe? In H. Rusu & B. Voicu (Eds.), *European integration process from East to East: Civil society and ethnic minorities in a changing world*. Sibiu: Psihomedia.
Westle, B. (2003). Europäische Identifikation im Spannungsfeld regionaler und nationaler Identitäten. Theoretische Überlegungen und empirische Befunde. *Politische Vierteljahresschrift, 44*(4), 453–482.

Chapter 4
Images and Frameworks of Collective Action in China

Carsten Storm

4.1 Assumptions from a Western Concept

The Western discourse on collective action has established a concept that epistemologically combines terms like marginalization (inequality, oppression, etc.), shared intentions, resistance, civil society, and democratization and that forms a fixed narrative, thus indicating legitimate reasons and starting points of collective action; further, aspects of developing informed opinions, decision making, and self-organization; forms of actions and implementations; as well as aims and outcomes. Luis Medina, for instance, argues that "collective action is a potent mechanism of social change" and that "the members of society can destroy all its existing institutions, no matter how old and revered, through collective action" (Medina 2007: xiii and xv). Although he admits that such impacts are exceptional, there is clearly a hope for resistance and change detectable in sentences like these. With regard to non-Western societies, the Western notion of this concept therefore has often ideological and to a certain extent "missionary" impacts aiming at developing especially non-Western societies into modern "Westernized" states that guarantee high levels of freedom (both individual and collective), competition (most notably economic, political, and cultural), democracy, free access to markets, and peaceful integration into a (Western-type) globalization. In the (not exclusive) case of China, it is primarily this logic which is exported and which shall be inscribed into societal practices. As a result, a Western logic meets an indigenous tradition of collective action as well as convictions concerning the reasons which legitimize collective actions, the organizational patterns and outcomes they have, and the question of how to value them.

A random review of Chinese research literature on collective action (*jiti xingdong* 集体行动) of the last decade reveals a range of parallel approaches that partly take

C. Storm (✉)
Chinese Studies, Friedrich-Alexander University Erlangen-Nürnberg, Erlangen, Germany
e-mail: carsten.storm@tu-dresden.de

B. Andreosso-O'Callaghan and F. Royall (eds.), *Economic and Political Change in Asia and Europe: Social Movement Analyses*, DOI 10.1007/978-94-007-4653-4_4,

the Western debate into account. A first refers to an understanding of upheaval and rebellion, in the tradition of the White Lotus, Taiping, etc., nowadays: rural or ethnic protests or wage upheavals; a second puts emphasis on a Chinese cultural proximity toward a sense of collectivity resulting from tradition and cultural heritage; a third deals with the influence of Western ideas of participation, democracy, and/or capitalism constructed as action confronting the authoritarian Chinese Communist Party's (CCP) state power. Depending on the political disposition of the authors, alternatively a mode of rejection or consent is employed. A final approach refers to an interest in the practical forms of collective action in China (by both indigenous and foreign actors), like their functioning, styles of working, their cooperation with or hindrances by state organs or bureaucracy, or their impact. All these approaches, Western as well as Chinese, differ to various degrees concerning their definitions and understandings of what collective action means.

Collective action does not merely address any kind of action undertaken by at least two persons. All actions that might be labeled natural actions in the sense of Miller (2001) are not part of it because they are lacking a socially defined aim. Academic writing on collective action in China – especially of Chinese or sinological provenance – often constructs an image of a Chinese commitment to collective action which differs from a Western type. It is claimed to be determined by a specific cultural heritage and an almost essential orientation of the Chinese human being toward a nonindividualistic self-awareness (Hao 2009; Lai 1995; Shen 2007; Song et al. 2004; Sun and Feng 2008; Tsui and Farh 1997; Yang 2009). I will argue that the elements of the Chinese tradition employed in order to strengthen this argument are hinting toward interpersonal "one-to-one" links rather than to collectivity in the sense of collective action.

An assumption very typical within today's cultural discourses is that transcultural flows are causing modifications of both the ideas and the concluding practices. Does the contact with Western ideas of collective action in contemporary China result in what might be called a form of "sinizising" the concept, or in establishing a notion of "collective action with Chinese characteristics"? I attempt to show, that at least some of the differences in theories and practices of collective action are rather to be explained as different traditions in ideas of statehood and state legitimacy than as essentialized visions of a primordial Chinese self.

4.2 Reconstruction of a Chinese Traditional Heritage

4.2.1 Interpersonal Relations, Intention, Ritual, and Mankind

Confucian notions, especially concepts like *ren* 仁 and *wulun* 五倫 (five bonds), are often indicated as being characteristics of a particular Chinese self-awareness, identity, and outlook. "Ren," one of the fundamental concepts of Confucianism, can roughly be translated as benevolence, humanness, or human-heartedness. The crucial point used in many current arguments is the term's etymology: it consists of the characters "man" (*ren* 人) and "two" (*er* 二), thus denoting a fundamental connection of the human being toward a counterpart, an existence in correlation and relation to others (Yang 2009: 53; Gold et al. 2002: 10; Sun and Feng 2008; Zhou 2004; Shen 2007).

In a similar way, the notion of the five bonds is employed as evidence of a cultural affinity toward collectivity. The five bonds, namely, ruler–subject, father–son, elder–younger brother, husband–wife, and friend–friend, describe a general relatedness of human beings to each other and are thus interpreted as a fundamental collective disposition. However, the five bonds are framing social relationships in a hierarchical order. The Confucian ideal of an orderly world relies on a ritually structured society in which the relative position of self and other determines appropriate moral behavior. Accordingly, even the fifth bond (friend to friend), which nowadays is often, yet erroneously, understood as a relationship between equal partners, does in fact hint at different social positions that, according to Confucian thinking, two friends necessarily do have. Most importantly, the five bonds constitute a mandatory behavior. They cannot be freely chosen neither in the sense of an option of obedience or denial nor in the sense of choosing or determining their specific form.

It is thus highly problematic to rely on the concepts of *ren* as well as the five bonds in order to legitimize the argument of a general Chinese affinity to collectivity. Both concepts deal with situational one-to-one relationships and thus belong to a category that Miller calls interpersonal and which is "directed to a single person" (Miller 2001: 3) but not to any collective. Hence, the transition from these bipolar interpersonal relations toward larger groups, from the hierarchical orientation drawn from personal relationship toward a (not necessarily nonhierarchical) group constituted by a specific social instrumental aim is not discussed in Chinese academic writing. In fact, the reevaluation of primarily Confucian virtues construes a primordial disposition of the Chinese mind so fundamental that the problem of the "I → us" transition becomes irrelevant within this framework.

With their focus on bipolar and/or highly ritualized relationships, these concepts provide only slight evidence for a traditional indigenous Chinese way of forming groups constituted by shared social interests. Instead, these forms of orientation toward other humans focus on interpersonal relationships and, apart from a general moral standard, they do not follow any specific social aim that shall be achieved. They do, however, provide possible explanations of how these groups organize themselves, how they operate (both internally and externally), and which forms of engagement and action they choose. As a kind of self-fulfilling prophecy, an awareness of a reconstructed tradition might play a decisive role in the functional and operational modes and the ways these are received and/or communicated.

A completely different approach, that is not limited to bipolar relations, refers to the first systematic Confucian philosopher, Xunzi. Fan Hao employs a quotation from the *Xunzi* to illustrate the fundamental understanding of cooperation and collective action within Chinese philosophical thinking. The *Xunzi* chapter "On the Regulations of a King" (*Wang zhi* 王制) formulates a fundamental ability of mankind to organize oneself in groups which separates the human from other beings. Concerning the special ability of mankind, it remarks:

> In physical power they are not so good as an ox, in swiftness they do not equal the horse; yet the ox and the horse can be put to their use. Why is that? I say it is because humans alone can form societies and animals cannot. Why can man form a society? I say it is due to the division of society into classes. How can social divisions be translated into behavior? I say it is because of humans' sense of morality and justice. (Knoblock 1990: 104)

> 力不若牛,走不若馬,而牛馬為用,何也?曰: 人能群,彼不能群也。人何以能群?曰: 分。分何以能行?曰: 義。(Xun 2001: 77)

Thus, the Western difficulties to transgress the boundaries of individuality and explain the act of saying "we" becomes obsolete. To organize as "we" or to engage in collective action is mankind's innermost and fundamental capability which all men inherit by birth (古人生不能無群, Xun 2001: 77). It is therefore essential and "a priori." This capability, however, is not specifically Chinese but generally human and part of a discourse which was intended to be universal rather than culturally specific at its time and which aimed at explaining and legitimizing mankind's unique position in the cosmic triad of heaven, earth, and mankind. On the contrary, the mainstream Western approach would emphasize mankind's ability to develop self-awareness and thus to say "I." Both positions have come under scrutiny by recent biological, anthropological, and psychological research such as Martin Nowak's notion of "natural cooperation" (Nowak 2006) or Samuel Bowles' use of the term "parochial altruism" (Choi and Bowles 2007). More importantly, for Xunzi, collective action is not an end in itself: it needs a moral basis expressed by the concept of righteousness (*yi* 義). For Xunzi, righteousness was a ritualized understanding of ethically appropriate and canonically mandatory ways of behavior. Therefore, it is terminologically difficult to employ Xunzi, since the text does not hint toward an engagement in collective action out of free will or following particularistic intentions.

Nonetheless, intersubjective, societal morality is seen as a decisive factor that eclipses individuality and thus constitutes an affinity toward the collective. Fan Hao employs a moral framework (*lunli tiaojian* 伦理条件) plus an objective basis (*keguan jichu* 客观基础) as agents, which he believes are capable of harmonizing divergent outlooks of the individual and the collective (Fan 2006: 18). He thus contradicts the Western focus on the fundamental difficulties concerning the boundary between the individual and the collective (Fan 2006). Fan's statement has to be understood in the context of a Chinese history of statehood as well as of the notion of a harmonious society currently advocated by the Chinese government (see below).

Other concepts that play a crucial role in academic writing and economic guidebooks on Chinese forms of collectivity are those of *guanxi* 关系, roughly translated as connection, relation, or relationship, as well as face (*mianzi* 面子). In 2002, Gold et al. (2002: 3) stated that *guanxi* was "the latest Chinese word to gain entry into English parlance," thus denoting an awareness of a real or imagined ultimate importance of a specific Chinese way to connect that was arising among Western business people engaged in China.

Guanxi is described as a connection characterized by factors like reciprocity, obligation, indebtedness, trust, and sentiment. It can be established toward different persons and/or groups simultaneously. Concomitantly, each single person as a holder of different *guanxi* connections is perceived as being located in a respective center of *guanxi* networks, which form a web of different, alternative, or parallel connections (Fei 1992: 65). The centric position provides the possibility to ascribe individualistic notions due to a person's ability to establish, maintain, or break ties (Yang 2009: 54). However, due to its kinship origins, *guanxi* remains a relationship that bears a strong influence of rituality and fixed role patterns which organize relations. At the same time, reciprocity and obedience to obligation are major elements in ascribing "face." "Face" has often been related to a shame culture, thus defining (non)obedience as a decisive factor in personal and collective forms of judging a person and defining his/her social position.

Problematic in terms of collective action is the formation of particularistic ties within *guanxi*.

> These ties are based on ascribed or primordial traits such as kinship, native place, and ethnicity, and also on achieved characteristics such as attending the same school (even if not at the same time), serving together in the same military unit, having shared experiences, such as the Long March, and doing business together. (Gold et al. 2002: 6)

Thus, the typical *guanxi* group is constituted by factors of shared fate (kinship, lineage, place, ethnicity) or shared histories (school, army, experiences) but not initially by shared intentions. The factor of business seems to fit badly into this finding. However, reliable *guanxi* exist only after completing a business transaction. Logically, aspects of reciprocity need the accomplishment of at least one act before obligation turns into an effective agent. Acts are thus turned into shared history.

While the typical Western notion of collective action (especially as a citizen movement, a non-governmental organization (NGO), or something else) quite generally implies that its establishment starts with shared intentions, continues with interest-driven particularistic ties, and then results in organizational forms, the Chinese notion is different. Intention is brought into or arises out of group ties which are at least partly preexistent. All these cultural features describe relationships which are ritualized and which depend on role patterns. Furthermore, their agenda is the integration of the individual into a social framework as well as the self-positioning of the individual in order to provide him/her with reliable and useful networks. Thus, a person is constituted as a network member *and* an individual as well as by value-oriented *and* utilitarian dispositions. However, *guanxi* in this connotation does not target a specific social agenda (like health care, charity, environment, or something else). Instead, it is multi-instrumental and thus defined by its ability to serve many intentions and agendas. As such, it reflects a general idea of a way of life or, more essentially, a way of existence which, however, may (or may not) transcend into specific social concerns and actions. Yet, theoretically speaking, the shift from rituality and role patterns toward specific instrumental ends remains problematic. However, it might precisely be the aspect of rituality and mutual obligation which enables effective channeling of preexistent, multi-instrumental *guanxi* relations into intentional collective action.

Relying on the Chinese philosophical canon and anthropological images in order to constitute a socially effective tradition and identity within the Chinese populace is difficult for at least three reasons. A first reason is that a direct, or at least in important parts, continuous, and consistent trajectory is drawn from pre-imperial China to present times neglecting major changes and developments throughout Chinese history. History here is employed to legitimize an essentialization of the Chinese mind in order to construct an alternative to Western modernity. A second reason is that the influence of ethno-national borders between cultures (i.e., Chinese and European) might be overemphasized, thus advocating non-temporal differences between cultures while temporal borders are almost ignored. A (post) modern, industrialized, and globalized Chinese culture might in many aspects be closer to a contemporary Western than to a premodern, preoptional, agrarian, and imperial Chinese one. A third reason is that the vision of a cultural heritage that generally separates Chinese collective action from a Western-type one is the result of both, a Western construction of China as the "other"[1] and a Chinese self-orientalization. The latter is in itself an ambivalent phenomenon combining two contrary yet interdependent aspects: (1) an adaptation of Western ideas and theories resulting from the academic dominance of the West and (2) a Chinese reevaluation of Confucianism that is connected to the so-called modern Neo-Confucianism (*dangdai xin rujia* 當代新儒家) arising since about the 1950s and connected to philosophers like Liang Shuming 梁漱溟 (1893–1988), Carsun Chang 張君勱 (Zhang Junmai, 1887–1969), Qian Mu 錢穆 (1895–1990), and later on Tu Weiming 杜維明 (b. 1940) and Yu Ying-shih 余英時 (b. 1930). However, the agenda of the modern Neo-Confucians has risen outside of the People's Republic of China (PRC) and has strongly opposed the CCP's regime. In relation to the Chinese mainland, the emphasis on the Confucian tradition and heritage is a relatively new phenomenon. It arises after a history of roughly 100 years in which Confucian values were vehemently rejected and blamed for China's national decline. It also must be highlighted that public promotion and valuing of ethical standards, no matter whether in the past or at present, do not imply that these standards are realized in everyday life. Rather, a deficient situation is obviously perceived so that ideal behavior has to be propagated permanently.

However, all these concepts refer to a current understanding of the Chinese self, in which concepts of "Chineseness" and Confucianism do play an important part. Such concepts often reveal either alternative "layism" or severe adaptations of modernity (Cheung et al. 2006; Tu 2001b). Nonetheless, they are impacting on current ways of thinking and of constructing a Chinese reading of society and collective action.

---

[1] There are of course also more balanced studies that successfully avoid the construction of China as the other. Edwards Shils' (1996) study on civil society and civility in China may serve as an example.

4.2.2 Traces of Collectivity in Chinese History

The (often cliché-like) concern for traditional Chinese values results in a focus on anthropological and philosophical concepts. Thus, an own historical tradition of collective action which aimed at sociopolitical change or improvement is often neglected within current academic writing on the topic. Chinese history provides ample evidence of collective actions which were not (or only in the beginning) organized along ritualized *guanxi* connections. Instead, they were established along shared intentions and interests. Among these are, for instance, upheavals and rebellions motivated by corruption, decadence, tax exploitation, or poverty, and, at the end of the Qing Dynasty, also ethnic oppression.[2] Injustices by the government and its representatives provided a legitimate motive for rebellion throughout Chinese history starting from the Mencian dictum on a right to assassinate an immoral emperor and hence a tyrant (Mengzi 1B 6 and 8).[3] New dynasties quite generally came to power after taking leadership in such rebellions. Two of the most well-known and influential traditional novels, *The Three Kingdoms* (*Sanguo zhi yanyi* 三國志演義) and *Outlaws of the Marsh* (*Shuihu zhuan* 水滸傳), describe resistance against immoral emperors and/or governments as a heroic endeavor.

Guilds of artisans and merchants, not forgetting state-organized forms of collective action (primarily under the responsibility of the boards of revenue and works: *hubu* 戶部 and *gongbu* 工部), which increasingly became important since the end of the Ming Dynasty, may also serve as yet another example of collective action that was not restricted to ritualized forms of *guanxi*. However, only the former was, at least partly, based on initially shared intentions and interests, while the latter was state enforced collective action.

Buddhism and Daoism have also been driving forces in protest movements at the end of Imperial China, when a syncretistic approach of Buddhist and Daoist beliefs in martial art and magic power was employed to counter the Manchurian authority during the Qing Dynasty as well as an increasing Western dominance. Upheavals of the White Lotus Sect 白蓮教 or the Boxer Rebellion 義和團運動 for instance both reconstructed religious beliefs as a stronghold of Han Chinese ethnicity vis-à-vis foreign powers. However, more important here is the channeling of religious concerns

[2] Neglecting this tradition might be caused by the traditionally negative connotation of rebellion, turmoil, and chaos which contradict the usually affirmative and harmonious notion in the construction of the Chinese self. The most prominent exception is possibly the CCP historiography which focused on peasant rebellions as manifestations of prerevolutionary consciousness. However, the CCP's notion of historiography is highly informed by a Marxist understanding of development.

[3] It needs to be emphasized that this was by no means a general right which could be understood as being predemocratic. Evaluating the ruler as being a tyrant as well as the actual act of assassination had been the sole task of the political elite, most notably members of the ruler's family. For the respective text, see Legge (1983: 164–165 and 167). The reference refers to a universal reference system for the book of Mengzi and applies to all editions irrespective of page numbers: Book 1, Part B, Chaps. 6 and 8.

and spirituality into forms of collective charity engagements which became an increasingly influential factor during the nineteenth century. Predominantly organized within religious (Daoist and Buddhist) frameworks, they translated religious beliefs of social order and commitment into non-kinship-organized action. As such, they also play a crucial role in modern religious movements. The so-called *daotan* 道壇 (Daoist altar) organizations which addressed the crisis of the late Qing Dynasty may serve as an example.

> Around the turn of the century, local elites were caught up in an eschatological sentiment and the hope of salvation from "the great catastrophe" in response to the social disorder by frequent disasters, epidemics, and wars. Responding to these conditions, the *daotan* movement began to lean more toward charitable activities and spread further into the lower classes. Traditionally, *xianguan* [仙館, literally the immortal's office, C.S.] had been hermitages for the upper classes, but now many began to shift their concern from esoteric Daoist knowledge and individual cultivation to moral reformation and practice of goodness. (Shiga 2002: 200)

In this case, eschatological beliefs did serve as a motive for collective action. A link is constructed between public or even mass behavior, disasters, and epidemics which appear as a punishment for sins. Charity plus a restrengthened sense of public morality were seen as tools countering the effects of a sinful and decadent world. One of the morality books (*shanshu* 善書) of the time, the *Shan yu rentong lu* 善與人同錄 (*Record of Being Good to the Human Community*), "advises its followers to confess sins, be without fault, act with charity, and appeal to the Emperor of Heaven" (Shiga 2002: 201). Here, charity is not an individual but an ultimately collective endeavor. "They believed that while the goodness practiced by one person might be small, the collective practice of goodness would be significant. [...] establishing charitable societies is a very effective way to escape the great catastrophes" (Ibid.: 201). Its aim is not the eternal salvation of the individual who engages in charity actions – as it tends to be in monotheistic religions – but the salvation of an "us," which therefore has to be undertaken by a collective "us." Self and society are interdependent parts within a holistic world view. The human realm is but one part within a cosmic order, yet different from earlier, especially philosophical Daoist notions, it becomes a realm of higher importance.

To some extent similar in outlook are contemporary Buddhist forms of charity as they are performed, for instance, within the Taiwan-based "Engaged Buddhism" (*renjian fojiao* 人間佛教). Other common Chinese expressions adopted as alternatives of *renjian fojiao* but indicating the same phenomenon are *canyu de fojiao* 參與的佛教 (Buddhism that participates), *shehui canyu de fojiao* 社會參與 的佛教 (socially participating Buddhism), and *rushi fojiao* 入世佛教 (Buddhism entering the world) (Travagnin 2007: 79). The terms elucidate a fundamental worldly and social involvement of its supporters. Like many Buddhist organizations, the Engaged Buddhism is monastic in spite of its large laity. It is engaged in traditional forms of charity (poverty and health programs) but also does have strong concerns for the environment or animal rights, which are typical NGO agendas in the West. However, it resembles the *daotan* form in its orientation on religious salvation. A conviction prevails that caring for the salvation of the self and the world by trying to avoid bad *karma* and hoping to escape the fate of reincarnation has to be accompanied and in fact can be fostered by a social commitment that addresses society and welfare.

4.3 The Affirmative Societal Role of Collective Action

4.3.1 Statehood, Citizens, and Welfare

From a Western perspective, the general notion of collective action as a potential toward change and democratization, justified or not, determines the discursive boundaries of collective action in Asia – and to some extent the non-West. It defines what legitimately counts as collective action and therefore is worthy of recognition and academic research. Due to this general setting, we tend to neglect forms of collective action in Asia which are nonoppositional in the broadest sense, that is, collective action which is affirmative toward its own society and state. However, collective action might be understood as both a result of the authoritarian state order in China (but not only in China) and a legacy of China's imperial past which tends to perceive even random forms of opposition as manifestations of rebellion which call for massive state reactions.

It might be useful to elaborate briefly on a distinctive feature in the Chinese history of state theory that still influences the relationship between the state and the citizens. The task to provide welfare for its populace is among the most central categories of successful statehood and thus a major legitimizing factor of power. Starting from the positions of the early Confucians (especially Mengzi and Xunzi and the praise of the examples of good governance of the holy kings of the early Zhou Dynasty or, respectively, the condemnation of the tyrants of the past) and, to some extent, also from philosophical Daoism, the welfare of the people was among the noblest aims to be achieved by the king and later on the emperor. "Welfare" addresses a peaceful, well-ordered, and protected society, plus moral communal life free of poverty, oppression, and exploitation. Upheavals motivated by exploitative taxes, poverty, or corruption were seen as indicators that the emperor had lost the mandate of heaven and thus was no longer to be regarded a legitimate ruler.

There is ample evidence throughout Chinese history that verifies the consistent validity of the welfare principle. Most importantly here, the idea of welfare remained a central issue in the time of transition from late Imperial China to modernity. The premodern history of the idea ends with philosophers like Tang Zhen 唐甄 (1630–1704) who explicitly "advised the rulers to lend their ears to public opinion [that] the vocation of the officials and bureaucrats was to 'nourish the people', and that it was with reference to their achievement in this respect that their merits and defects should be judged" (He et al. 1991: 381). Gu Yanwu 顧炎武 (1613–1682) likewise insisted that "priority should be given to the wealth of the people rather than to the wealth in the imperial treasury [stressing] the necessity of alleviating the over-exploitation of the people" (Ibid.: 383). The turn to modernity in China did not change the importance of welfare, as expressed in the works of Kang Youwei 康有為 (1859–1927) and his utopian outline of an all-embracing world statehood or Sun Yat-sen's 孫中山 (1866–1925) Three Peoples' Principles (*sanmin zhuyi* 三民主義), consisting of nationalism, democracy, and peoples' livelihood. Carsun Chang advocated a synthesis of Western notions of law and Confucian notions of morality, hence the integration of morality and law (*de fa heyi* 德法合一). The ultimate aim was, however, to create a Chinese nation in which a moral status of "sage inside and king outside" (*nei sheng wai wang* 内圣外王) could be established (Wang 2009). Likewise, the specific Maoist notion of Chinese Marxism did not abolish these ideas but rather translated notions of welfare into a party task. The degree of penetration into all levels of society by state organs increased due to modern communication structures and administration strategies. Thus, options of control grew, yet also expectations in a moral legitimacy of rule and, hence, options for the state to fail as well.

4.3.2 Authoritarianism, Democratization, and Collective Action

Since the founding of the People's Republic of China in 1949, the CCP's discourse gained dominance. Collective action was primarily framed as mass action under the leadership of the CCP. In this sense, the meaning of the collective in China was transformed into an ambivalent concept addressing two entities: the masses as the "body" of the collective and the party as the "brain" of the collective. In the West, communist mass action and mass mobilization were often constructed as a form of indoctrination. In Western marginalization discourses, "truly" shared intentions are primarily regarded as the result of an individual plus self-conscious awareness toward a specific situation of inequality. This includes personal experience and individual decision, hence a notion of authenticity legitimating personal engagement and moral strictness. While this might be regarded as a process from self to collectivity, mass mobilization is constructed as invoked by external agents (party, state, cadres) and more often than not as violating people's "true" intentions.

Yet, research into the early phase of the CCP rule suggests a more ambivalent reading of mass mobilization and mass action. The rule of the CCP and the abolishment of the old system came along with an empowerment of many formerly exploited citizens. This might not only explain the extent of admiration and trust many Chinese had in the CCP, especially in the 1950s and early 1960s. It also provides evidence for two further dimensions: (1) for the willingness to engage in collective action such as the cleaning campaigns (*dasaochu* 大扫除), programs against illiteracy (*saomang ban* 扫盲班), or the steel melting campaign (*da liangang* 大炼钢); and (2) for the willingness to follow local cadres and to participate in the organized actions. The fact that many collectively organized actions improved the living conditions of those involved additionally legitimated the CCP as the leader of collective action. However, and somehow resembling traditional notions, the ethical disposition of local cadres was among the most important factors. Ho

Wing Chung's study on a Shanghai Socialist "Model Community" shows that recruitment for collective action was easy as long as the participants trusted in the incorruptibility and selflessness of the cadres (Ho 2006). Here, the understanding of collective actions hints at very concrete situations that can be changed by temporary mass action but not at problems which are defined as long lasting and possibly structural. Neighborhood and thus locality were important recruitment factors of this kind of collective action. But these factors again bear dimensions of fate. From a democratic point of view, one might add that recruitment by CCP cadres also includes enforcement. Yet, the numbers Ho provides for the specific community tell a different story. With one exception, no more than 150–200 residents out of 1,800–1,900 households participated in the actions mentioned above. Free will and personal intention are thus likely to be important factors despite CCP leadership.

Within the welfare framework, collective action targeting social dimensions such as health care, poverty, or injustices instantly addresses deficiencies of the state in meeting its primary task. Marking a lack in providing the citizens' livelihood and formulating a necessity to act via non-state-controlled collective action somewhat automatically challenges the state's legitimacy. It is thus easily perceived as action confronting state power (by the CCP and Western observers alike, even though they are following quite different patterns of valuing resistance). Consequently, pure governmental oppression of collective actions addressing deficiencies easily results in an increasing loss of legitimacy, as the reactions on breaking down the June 4th movement on Tiananmen Square in 1989 have shown. The latent disillusionment of parts of the rural populace (often constructed as a stronghold of CCP power) induced through violent suppression of wage strikes may serve as another example. Ideally, the state's task is to address the problems by implementing ethically adequate frameworks and enforcing them against corrupt or otherwise immoral local officials. Legitimate public protest needs to be eased by ethically based governmental action (Ying 2007). Instead of an oppressive ideological reaction motivated by materialistic rationality, relying on aspects like sentiment, ritual, and religious beliefs might strengthen the government's legitimacy (Qiao 2009).[4] There is obviously a gap between ideal and "praxis." In fact, triggering individual critique through encouragement to "speak out" and the convergence of critique into state-induced collective or mass action can be regarded – to a certain extent sarcastically – as a method regularly used by the CCP to address (real or ideological) injustices within the society (Zhou 1993).

It is, however, not only authoritarian state power that reacts with enmity toward collective action and tries to limit its range and impacts which often are perceived as competing forms of power. But it is also a large part of society which often reacts with distrust and lack of understanding toward organizational forms of collective

[4] This might also partly explain why the Chinese government reacts toward the millions of illegal NGOs with a policy of Three Nos, that is, no recognition, no banning, and no intervention, as long as a particular NGO's activities are not seen as a challenge toward state power. On this issue, see also the contribution by Birgit Haese in this volume.

action, since the collective is still predominantly envisioned as the populace as a whole. Interests of a particular group are thus in danger to be perceived as individual and particularistic interests that do not meet the interests of the whole society.

Since the mid-1990s, the notion of the harmonious society (*hexie shehui* 和谐社会) has become one of the major goals of societal development and is fervently promoted by the government as a specific Chinese future vision of the nation state aiming at minimizing turbulences between government and citizens. A notion of Confucian harmony is also advocated by many intellectuals who interpret the specific combination of traditional Chinese values and governance as a Chinese contribution to a global world (Tu 2001a, b). The intended institutional setup of the harmonious society includes resident participation at least at communal levels. The currently low level of resident participation and an unawareness of resident self administration or autonomy (*jumin zizhi zuzhi* 居民自治组织) are seen as a major obstacle in the process of implementing the new order. However, collective action in this sense is affirmative and part of a cooperative formation of three bodies: party, government, and residents on a community level (Jiang and Wang 2009). Its aim is not to confront state power as such or to overthrow the authoritarian communist regime but to alleviate local or otherwise particular deficiencies.

Hence, even the aims to establish grassroots democracy via direct election can become highly ambivalent, as the example of residents' committees in Shanghai in 2003 illustrates. Gui et al. (2006) describe the difficulties of local cadres to convince people to take part in elections. Besides administrative changes in the committees' tasks and competences, the authors argue that a modern urban loss in local cohesion of neighborhoods is one important factor for low-level interest in participation. While one would expect urban residents to be, on average, better educated and thus more interested in political participation, the state-induced democratization process seemed to be an improper tool. In this regard, urban residents differ from rural populace which has turned the democratization process at lower levels into a success story.[5] Instead, urban residents prefer to organize themselves in nonlocal interest groups as, for instance, ownership councils which they believe to be more effective tools to represent their interests. Fractured locality is of course one result of globalization. Neighborhood turns into a fate of geographical setting which limits personal perspectives and options rather than offering a meaningful framework to establish new connections and to engage in self-imposed action and alliances of responsibility (*Verantwortungsgemeinschaft*).

The history of collective action in China results in a lasting, in some aspects even increasing, importance of the morally legitimate state as an actor in the social field, which is only gradually weakened by the change in recruitment strategies.

---

[5] Despite many difficulties in the election processes and accomplishing competences vis-à-vis party bureaucracy and higher administrative levels, village and township elections have brought forth local forms of governance by implementing local policies initiated by elected citizens (Jacobson 2004). Differences in social cohesion between urban and rural communities might be a major reason for the varying attitudes toward local elections.

The prevailing status of the state and the importance of ethics (societal, national, cultural, etc.) are challenging Western mainstream narratives of collective action. The fundamental link between political aspects (democratization, liberalism, empowerment, individuality) and sociological ones (motives, functions, impacts) of collective action becomes visible as a Western hope, at best, if not as an ideological mission. Engagement in collective action and a state-induced capitalism do not automatically transcend into a civil society fostering or even causing a Western-type democracy for two important reasons. In the first instance, the elites engaged in state action and the elites benefiting from the economic change are mainly identical (Wang 2003: 177). These elites rather advocate a conversion of diverse interests that might be labeled as public, private, societal, governmental, intentional, or something else.[6] Second, nonelites are often more interested in alleviating particularistic injustices or deficiencies instead of engaging in collective actions that are aiming at structural and/or national levels.

State and citizens are not necessarily to be seen in opposition to each other. Instead, the welfare legacy might be an important reason why collective action in a Chinese environment often tends to be affirmative and cooperative in character instead of purely oppositional. However, the shift from NGO to an embedded NGO and on to GONGO (government organized NGO) is problematic, although it might primarily be so from a Western point of view. It has to be stated though that within the modern Western tradition of a liberal state which defines itself explicitly as non-all-embracing, collective action gains a different importance. In the West, independence of NGOs and other organized citizen groups and distance from state organs are not only a question of being not corrupted in one's intentions and agendas. It is also part of the state's self-awareness to merely provide a framework in which citizens are expected to act collectively.

4.4 Collective Action with Chinese Characteristics

Within the debate of collective action in China, two theses have gained momentum. First, the cultural heritage thesis formulates a vision of a Chinese cultural tradition which enables or rather causes a primordial sense for collectivity. Second, the democratization thesis advocates a (Western) conviction that implementing collective action somehow automatically results in a strengthening of individuality, liberalism, and democracy in China and thus weakens the authoritarian communist state. The first thesis flourishes rather (although not exclusively) within economic debates on management, contract, and networking practices and social-economic debates on collective actions which do not have primarily political agendas. The assumed

[6] Critical elites, like the supporters of the *Charter 08* (*Lingba xianzhang* 零八宪章), are still a minority compared to affirmative elites despite the attention the former ones receive from Western observers.

primordial networking capability of the Chinese is seen as potentially superior to the West and thus as a factor that challenges Western dominance or at least its economic strength. Strange enough, seen from a cultural studies' point of view, essentialized primordial settings are shifted from marginalizing tools to valuable assets. The second thesis is rather advocated within the political, sociological, and sometimes ideological sphere. Here, the Western system of liberalism, individuality, capitalism, and law-enforced civil society is seen as clearly superior to the non-West, and, accordingly, the specific Chinese way into an authoritarian modern state is valued as inferior to Western practices. Obviously, the images produced within these theses are quite contradictory, which clearly marks them as highly constructed. These images are advocated by both Chinese and Western actors although caused by different motives.

As argued above, both theses have their obstacles. Terms of the premodern philosophical and cultural Chinese past are ill-fitting into a matrix of modern epistemology employed within the debate on shared intentions and collective action. Likewise, the notion of a reliable link between collective action and a development toward democracy and civil society inspired by the Western example is not convincing in itself either. Rather, both concepts are adapted to a modern-cum-Chinese framework in current academic, economical, political, cultural, etc., practices.

This being the case, the question remains whether the Western concept of collective action is a meaningful analytic tool for a Chinese environment. Yet, the discourse on collective action is well received in China and is frequently adopted and altered by Chinese practitioners and authors. It has to be emphasized here that stating an improper reference to tradition in constructing a primordial Chinese affinity toward collectivity does not legitimize a category like "conformity to Western concepts of collective action" as a valid tool for evaluation. Like the Chinese tradition which is selectively used (and thereby altered) to construct a Chinese modernity and a Chinese understanding of collective action, the Western concept is used and altered accordingly. The use (and misuse) of deliberate selections from tradition or transcultural flows in order to construct a primordial cultural heritage is by no means a particularly Chinese phenomenon. Rather, it is a phenomenon of nationalism and, maybe, of modern identity formations in general.

The major question therefore is: Does the constant promotion and/or propagandizing of the morality of the collective – as being specifically Chinese/Confucian – transcend into a sustainable mental entity of its own? Instead of targeting a somewhat improper and hollow use of the Chinese tradition and Western concepts, an alternative possibility has to be considered. As a self-fulfilling prophecy, the constructed image of a sense of collectivity provided by Chinese concepts of heritage and identity might in fact cause a different affinity toward and maybe even different manifestations of engagement and practices in collective action in the future.

Meanwhile, the practices of collective action are changing. The decreasing importance of traditional recruitment strategies in forming groups, like fate and history, leaves place for initial interest and intention. They are thus translated from past to present. This matches new ways of networking that are coming along with digital and virtual communication. The abolishment of locality as a formative factor in constituting groups, or in other words, the anonymization process especially of urban lifestyles paves the way for an emphasis of personal concerns and intentions. It has to be noted, however, that this tendency does not necessarily include or result in a strengthening of Western-type individuality. First of all, it represents an adopted way of networking which may, but does not automatically, change the operational or functional structures of these groups, although increasing numbers of practitioners in (illegal) NGOs who demand to work free from state control have to be listed as well.

Obviously, the moral dimension still has its impacts. There is an ongoing belief in the link between welfare, morality, and legitimacy which is effective among government officials and many citizens alike, no matter whether this link is imagined, constructed, or real. Until now, the increasing gap between moral claim and moral reality is not necessarily perceived as a structural problem or a general failure of the political system. Often enough, it is perceived as a problem of globalization and as a Western ethical setup that is regarded as improper for China. It is also not turned into general doubts about the CCP's ethical mandate to claim power. In some aspects, one might be reminded of the verdict in the Ming Dynasty novel *Outlaws of the Marsh*: the dynasty's rule as such is good and ethically superior; it is the decadence and corruptness of particular ministers and other officials or (now) the greed of managers that causes injustices, triggers discontent, and brings about a necessity to act collectively. Collective action therefore tends to be affirmative by alleviating inequalities, and it aims at restoring moral and/or legal rule by eliminating those obstructing the moral rules.

References

Cheung, T. S., Chan, H. M., Chan, K. M., King, A. Y. C., Chiu, C. Y., & Yang, C. F. (2006). How Confucian are contemporary Chinese? Construction of an ideal type and its application to three Chinese communities. *European Journal of East Asian Studies, 5*(2), 157–180.

Choi, J.-K., & Bowles, S. (2007). The coevolution of parochial altruism and war. *Science, 318*, 636–640.

Fan, Hao 樊浩. (2006). Daode zhexue tixi zhong de geti, jiti yu shiti 道德哲学体系中的个体、集体与实体 [The individual, the collective and substance within the ethical philosophical system]. *Daode yu wenming* 道德与文明, *3*, 16–20.

Fei, X. (1992). *From the soil: The foundation of Chinese society*. Berkeley: University of California Press.

Gold, T., Guthrie, D., & Wank, D. (2002). An introduction to the study of *Guanxi*. In T. Gold, D. Guthrie, & D. Wank (Eds.), *Social connections in China: Institutions, culture, and the changing nature of 'Guanxi'*. Cambridge: Cambridge University Press.

Gui, Y., Cheng, J., & Ma, W. (2006). Cultivation of grass-roots democracy: A study of direct elections of residents committees in Shanghai. *China Information, 20*(1), 7–31.

Hao, Xiaobing 郝晓兵. (2009). Kongzi renai sixiang dui peiyang dangdai Zhongguo gongmin daode yizhi de jiji zuoyong 孔子仁爱思想对培养当代中国公民道德意识的积极作用 [The positive role of using Confucian humanistic thought for fostering contemporary moral consciousness of the Chinese citizens]. *Xue lilun* 学理论, *30*, 75–76.

He, Z., Bu, J., Tang, Y., & Sun, K. (1991). *An intellectual history of China* (Z. He, Revised and Trans.). Beijing: Foreign Languages Press.

Ho, W. C. (2006). From resistance to collective action in a Shanghai socialist 'model community': From the late 1940s to early 1970s. *Journal of Social History, 40*(1), 85–117.

Jacobson, L. (2004). Local governance: Village and township direct elections. In J. Howell (Ed.), *Governance in China*. Lanham: Rowman & Littlefield.

Jiang, Jihong 姜继红, & Wang, Qingyao 汪庆尧. (2009). Shehui zhuanxing shiqi de hexie shequ jianshe – lai zi Yangzhou shi de shizheng yanjiu 社会转型时期的和谐社区建设 – 来自扬州市的实证研究 [The construction of a harmonious community in the transforming era – An empirical study on Yangzhou]. *Yangzhou daxue xuebao (renwen shehui kexue ban)* 扬州大学学报（人文社会科学版）, *13*(3), 34–41.

Knoblock, J. (1990). *Xunzi: A translation and study of the complete works. Vol. II. Books 7–16*. Stanford: Stanford University Press.

Lai, K. (1995). Confucian moral thinking. *Philosophy East & West, 45*(2), 249–272.

Legge, J. (1983). *The Chinese classics with a translation, critical and exegetical notes, prolegomena, and copious indexes: Vol. 1. Confucian analects, The great learning, and The doctrine of the mean. Vol. 2. The works of Mencius*. Taipei: Huangjia tushu.

Medina, L. F. (2007). *A unified theory of collective action and social change*. Ann Arbor: The University of Michigan Press.

Miller, S. (2001). *Social action: A teleological account*. Cambridge: Cambridge University Press.

Nowak, M. (2006). Five rules for the evolution of cooperation. *Science, 314*, 1560–1563.

Qiao, Shidong 乔世东. (2009). Shehui ziyuan dongyuan yanjiu 社会资源动员研究 [A study of social resource mobilization]. *Shanghai jiaotong daxue xuebao (zhexue shehui kexue ban)* 上海交通大学学报（哲学社会科学版）, *17*(5), 18–24.

Shen, Yi 沈毅. (2007). 'Ren', 'yi', 'li' de richang shijian: 'guanxi', 'renqing' yu 'mianzi' – cong 'chaxu geju' kan Rujia 'da chuantong' zai richang 'xiao chuantong' zhong de xianshi dingwei "仁"、"义"、"礼"的日常实践:"关系"、"人 情"与"面子" – 从"差 序格局"看儒家"大传统"在日常"小传统"中的现 实 定位 [The daily practice of 'benevolence', 'righteousness', and 'ritual': 'Guanxi', 'sentiment', and 'face' – The real position of the Confucian 'high tradition' within the daily 'lower tradition' seen from an 'alternative mode']. *Kaifang shidai* 开放时代, *4*, 88–104.

Shiga, I. (2002). Manifestations of Lüzu in modern Guangdong and Hong Kong: The rise and growth of spirit-writing cults. In L. Kohn & H. Roth (Eds.), *Daoist identity: History, lineage, and ritual*. Honolulu: University of Hawaii Press.

Shils, E. (1996). Reflections on civil society and civility in the Chinese intellectual tradition. In Tu Weiming (Ed.), *Confucian traditions in East Asian modernity: Moral education and economic culture in Japan and the four mini-dragons*. Cambridge, MA: Harvard University Press.

Song, Ruizhi 宋瑞芝, Tang Yunbo 唐云波, & Li Haibo 黎海波. (2004). Shangxia xietiao, liangxing hudong. 'Wulun' ji qi xiandai yiyi shuping 上下协调良 性互动"五伦"及其现代意义述评 [Harmonizing high and low, making goodness mutual. The five bonds and a commentary on their contemporary meaning]. *Hanshan shifan xueyuan xuebao* 韩山师范 学院学报, *25*(1), 36–40.

Sun, Liangwei 孙良微, & Feng Hao 冯浩. (2008). Cong Kongzi 'ren' de xueshuo kan xiandai renji guanxi 从孔子"仁"的学说看现代人际关系 [Human relations seen from the Confucian concept of 'ren']. *Shidai wenxue* 时代文学, *4*, 89.

Travagnin, S. (2007). Master Yinshun and Buddhist nuns in/for the human realm: Shift and continuity from theory to practice of *renjian fojiao* in contemporary Taiwan. In C. Storm & M. Harrison (Eds.), *The margins of becoming: Identity and culture in Taiwan*. Wiesbaden: Harrassowitz.

Tsui, A., & Farh, Jiing-lih Larry. (1997). Where *Guanxi* matters: Relational demography and *Guanxi* in the Chinese context. *Work and Occupations, 24*(1), 56–79.

Tu, W. (2001a). *Confucian humanism as a spiritual resource for global ethics* (Tasan Lecture no. 4, Korea). http://tuweiming.com/lecture.8.html. Accessed 8 Aug 2010.

Tu, W. (2001b). The ecological turn in new Confucian humanism: Implications for China and the global world. *Daedalus (Journal of the American Academy of Arts and Science), 130*(4), 243–264.

Wang, H. (2003). *China's new order: Society, politics, and economy in transition*. Cambridge, MA: Harvard University Press.

Wang, Xiaoli 王晓黎. (2009). Cong 'de fa heyi' dao 'nei sheng wai wang': Zhang Junmai 'de fa heyi' de lunshuping 从"德法合一"到"内圣外王" – 张君劢"德 法合一"的论述评 [From 'synthesizing ethics and law' to 'sage within, king outside': A study on Zhang Junmai's 'synthesizing ethics and law']. *Xuzhou shifan daxue xuebao (zhexue shehui kexue ban)* 徐州师范大学学报(哲学社会 科学版), *35*(2), 113–116.

Xun, Kuang 荀况. (2001). *Xunzi* 荀子 [Xunzi] (Xie Dan 谢丹 & Shu Tian 书田, Trans.). Taiyuan: Shuhai chubanshe.

Yang, Y. (2009). Guanxilization or categorization: Psychological mechanisms contributing to the formation of the Chinese concept of 'us'. *Social Sciences in China, 30*(2), 49–67.

Ying, Xing 应星. (2007). 'Qi' yu Zhongguo xiangcun jiti xingdong de zaishengchan "气"与中国乡村集体行动的再生产 ['Vital force' and the reproduction of collective action in Chinese rural villages]. *Kaifang shidai* 开放时代, *6*, 106–120.

Zhou, X. (1993). Unorganized interests and collective action in communist China. *American Sociological Review, 58*(1), 54–73.

Zhou, Shanfu 周善甫. (2004). 'Ren' yu 'ge' "仁"与"个" [Benevolence and the individual]. *Shidai jinrong* 时代金融, *5* [no pagination].

Chapter 5
European Governance and Democracy

Didier Chabanet

5.1 Introduction

Who benefits from Europe? A pluralist interpretation of the building of Europe would stress the openness of European Union (EU) institutions to different interest groups and even their capacity to provide alternative forms of access to actors underrepresented in national institutions, while a more elitist interpretation, sensitive to political domination, would put the emphasis on the filters at work in the process. The question arises, in particular, with regard to a set of rights politically structured well after the formation of cleavages stabilized within the framework of the nation-states. In this chapter, we shall examine two areas of public policy and mobilization corresponding to (1) the defense of the rights of migrants and (2) unemployed people, the latter being one of the pioneer expression of the so-called (3) alter-globalization movement.

5.2 Immigration and Citizenship: Building the Fortress

One of the distinctive features of European migration policy is that it hinges much more on intergovernmental collaboration than on overall coordination between EU institutions, even if EU provisions in this field have developed somewhat in recent times. These provisions focus on population groups that are highly diverse in ethnic terms and sociologically very mixed. Our main concern here is non-EU migrants aspiring long-term residence on EU territory, especially when their presence is illegal or they are seeking asylum.[1] In 1975, the founding of the Trevi Group, comprising the

[1] Every year, some 2.45 million persons from non-member states migrate to the EU, to which figure must be added, according to the most trustworthy estimates, 120,000–500,000 illegal immigrants.

D. Chabanet (✉)
Badia Fiesolana (SPS Department), European University Institute,
Via dei Roccettini, 9. 50014 San Domenico di Fiesole, Italy
e-mail: didierchabanet@hotmail.com

B. Andreosso-O'Callaghan and F. Royall (eds.), *Economic and Political Change in Asia and Europe: Social Movement Analyses*, DOI 10.1007/978-94-007-4653-4_5,

ministers for the interior and for justice of the EU member states, marked a significant first step toward enhanced cooperation between police forces and intelligence agencies. Its field of action expanded rapidly, and by the early 1980s covered the preconditions for harmonization of the granting of visas and asylum status in Europe. Shortly afterward, the Schengen Agreements, signed by France, Germany, and the Benelux countries in June 1985 and taking effect 10 years later, implemented a set of provisions allowing for reduced internal customs checks while stepping up surveillance on external frontiers. At the time the agreements constituted an intergovernmental charter which, as such, involved no transfer of powers to the EU.

The Dublin Asylum Convention, signed in 1990, increased this focus on coordination by setting up convergence criteria for the examination of requests for asylum and specified that applications could henceforth be made in only one country. In 1992, the Treaty of Maastricht defined a set of migration issues—the right to asylum, border controls, and policies regarding migrants residing inside and outside the EU—that basically continued to depend on individual state sovereignty, even though they fell within a field of interest common to the Commission and the Council. Significantly, the European citizenship sketched out in the treaty was not immune to this sovereignty, being subject to the possession of civil rights in one or other of the member states. The Amsterdam Treaty, signed in 1997 and put into effect in 1999, brought significant modifications, providing for the transfer of migration matters, which after a 5-year transition period would be placed under the responsibility of European institutions. At this point, the Schengen Agreements became part of EU law, and after consulting the European Parliament, the Council could henceforth unanimously decide to apply the co-decision rule and qualified majority voting.

This Europeanization remained limited, however, since the procedure was not automatic and remained at the discretion of the states—which, moreover, retained the possibility of having their own policies as long as these were compatible with the Treaty. In addition, England and Ireland were exempted from these provisions by a special waiver. At Tampere, in 1999, the Council laid down the rules for a common system for refugees and asylum seekers that would both limit and better distribute the entry of migrants into Europe. In Seville in June 2002, the EU's heads of state and government decided to speed up application of this program. As a result, the Dublin Convention, remodeled and extended in February 2003, became an EU regulatory regime backed up by the Eurodac databank, a system allowing for comparison of the fingerprints of asylum seekers and illegal immigrants and thus the identification of persons attempting fraudulent entry.

At the November 2004 summit in The Hague, a program of action for 2005–2010 was adopted that notably aimed at developing the "capacity for migration management" of non-EU countries: the intention, in other words, was to contain illegal immigration by tighter controls upstream, away from EU borders. Current conditions of entry and residence for legal immigrants are still marked by clear differences between member states in terms of demographic developments, manpower requirements, and traditions of integration, and remain relatively unharmonized; on the other hand, anti-illegal immigration policies have become steadily tougher over the last 30 years.

Here too, however, major national differences remain: in the early 1990s, Italy and Spain conferred resident status on hundreds of thousands of illegal entrants, while in France the figures were very much lower. Requests for asylum, once one of the main avenues for foreigners seeking residence in Europe, have been subject to much more selective treatment since the mid-1970s and likewise continue to show marked national disparities: in 2004 Austria granted refugee status to over 50% of applicants, while in Greece the figure was 0.3%. These variations should not, however, be allowed to obscure a pronounced and convergent tendency toward increased no acceptance. Austria aside, throughout Europe between 85 and 99.9% of applicants are now turned down: in some countries, like Italy, Switzerland, and to a lesser extent the United Kingdom (UK) and Germany, the refusal ceiling was already reached in the late 1980s, while in others, like France, Belgium, Spain, and Greece, it came later (Valluy 2005). "Fortress Europe"—on the whole extremely rich—thus threw up a rampart against more or less neighboring countries stricken by poverty, underdevelopment, and/or war.

Some members of the European Parliament (EP) have taken an interest in these matters, notably denouncing the racism and discrimination to which migrants can be subject, but often in a polemical vein more aimed at boosting their personal political credibility than at getting the issue onto the European agenda. Episodically, the EP gives advocates of migrant rights the chance to make themselves heard and is doubtless one of the access points most receptive to their cause. In a report published early in 2006, the EP even went as far as addressing a strongly worded warning to the heads of Europe's states and governments, summoning them to put a stop as soon as possible to certain modes of detention of illegal entrants, seen as detrimental to human dignity.

If the opportunities are so reduced at the European level, it is not solely because of the incompleteness of migration policy integration but also because the organizational difficulties encountered by migrant defense bodies have prevented them from seizing certain chances for action. The trajectory of the European Migrants' Forum is an eloquent illustration of the migrant movement working to provide itself with a lasting, effective structure in relation to EU institutions. Created at the instigation of the Commission in 1991, this consultative organization for migrant populations in Europe functioned for a decade or so as an immigrant rights lobby, notably within the framework of the European citizenship project. However, its influence rapidly declined to the point where it was justifiably dissolved: first of all because its level of expertise proved insufficient to meet the requirements of the Commission and second because its internal divisions prevented it from developing a rationale acceptable to its various national components.[2]

In this case, as in others, migrant mobilization, rooted in national political and legal contexts very different from each other, failed to find effective unity in European terms.

[2] In this context, it is probable that the scope of European programs against discrimination based on "race, ethnic origin, religion or beliefs, age, or sexual orientation" has, for the migrants themselves, been considerably reduced.

Their multifarious claims and the equally varied responses supplied by each member state caused dissension at the very heart of the European networks that were supposed to represent their interests, the result being that the few organizations now capable of giving migrants access to EU institutions generally settle for pacific, low-profile modes of action. Many of them are solidly embedded in northern European countries and are not the organizations most directly confronted with the issues raised by migrant flows to EU borders. Other bodies, such as the European Citizenship Action Service, are more like service providers, giving assistance with administrative procedures for migrants—often with legal status—who are already on the road to integration. Their concerns are with promotion of civil rights and policies of equality but are not really attuned to the situation of migrants whose status and presence in Europe are problematic. Lastly, among the non-governmental organizations (NGOs) defending migrant rights, only Amnesty International and the European Council on Refugees and Exiles (ECRE) enjoy regular, official contact with the Commission; even so, the former does not specialize in asylum and immigration matters, while the latter has only limited scope for putting its case forward.

All in all, then, migrant movement action is characterized by marked fragmentation, the actors involved in European networks having only tenuous links with those active in member states (Guiraudon 2001). It may be that the national organizations are reinforcing their connections with European NGOs, and ECRE in particular, in response to the ongoing integration of EU migration policy. This process nonetheless remains emergent, Europeanization taking place more "from below," from outside, or on the margin of European institutions and in opposition to them. With its virulent denunciations of EU migration policy, the Migreurop association, formed at the European Social Forum (ESF) in Florence in November 2002, is a perfect example of this phenomenon. All members, within the framework of their respective national associations, are charged with monitoring European asylum and immigration policies (this testifies to clear specialization), and within their network, they pursue information exchange and the formalization of a common discourse designed to increase public awareness. Their stances are based on a very real expertise generally allied to a strategy of outrage. Recourse to provocative rhetoric (e.g., the comparison of the migrant detention policy at EU frontiers to the "Europe of the camps," in a deliberate analogy to the Nazi experience) is intended as a way of compensating for their institutional isolation and the recurring handicap of their meager logistic and financial resources. Even if the influence of this kind of European network remains extremely limited, the pooling of analyses enhances the capacity for action of national militants, especially in their negotiations with governmental executives.

The discrimination to which migrants can be subject to seems explicable, if not justifiable, to a part of European public opinion, very likely disturbed by the more or less insidious connections and confusions between immigration, crime, and terrorism. It is this combination of institutional and cognitive factors that explains why the fate of migrants causes so little mobilization in Europe. The subject being especially sensitive for politicians and investigation being particularly difficult for journalists, the general public is under-informed. For population groups as vulnerable and little organized as migrants, the media barrier can be insurmountable and represents, beyond any doubt, one of the major drags on the defense of their rights. Here, the absence of an independent, broad-audience European medium is cruelly felt and makes it difficult to imagine strategies for getting the right questions asked. Recent events have demonstrated that when the fate of illegal immigrants—turned back at the gates of the European Eldorado and dying by dozens—claimed the attention of the media, Europe's politicians as a whole were challenged and forced to attempt a justification of current migration policy. Nor did the heads of state and government fail to get the message about the strategic impact of this media coverage: they decided to create detention areas on non-EU territories that will henceforth have to accept responsibility for them and are less in the media spotlight. At the same time, the capacity for expression of migrants and those who represent them is generally low, in the majority of cases not exceeding 10% of the stances taken on the subject.[3] In addition, migrants are isolated from other civil society actors, in particular trade unions, as illustrated by the UK, which is, nonetheless, one of the countries most favorable to their mobilization.

Regarding immigration, and ethnic relations in particular, citizenship systems as the expression of the national state channel public debate and significantly influence the choices of collective actors (Monforte and Dufour 2011). In each country, greater or lesser recognition of the political rights and cultural particularities of migration-based groups points up different models.[4] On the one hand, when migrants do not acquire the nationality of the host country and remain largely excluded from the national community, the great majority of their political utterances bear on the country of origin; conversely, when acquisition of civil rights is facilitated, their demands are very largely aimed at the host society and its institutions. Meanwhile, greater (or lesser) public and political acceptance of their ethnic, religious, or cultural particularisms encourages (or discourages) their participation. According to these criteria, Switzerland and Germany are fairly segregationist, France is universalist, and the UK and the Netherlands are multiculturalist (Fig. 5.1).

In line with this dual logic, mobilization of migrants is lowest in Switzerland (5% of all stances taken on immigration and ethnic relations), followed by Germany (7%), the Netherlands (9%), France (10%), and the UK (18%) (Koopmans et al. 2005).

In countries in which immigrants remain mainly foreigners and do not have the right to vote, their opportunities for action are limited. The mechanisms for public action on their behalf are few and cannot provide reasons, or targets, for protests. By contrast, in the Netherlands and the UK, measures in favor of equal opportunity and against discrimination are highly developed and represent real incentives to participation and the making of claims. Given this, mobilization of migrants in the Netherlands can appear surprisingly low, suggesting that when cultural differences are very marked and, above all, socially accepted, ethnic communities tend to organize

[3] See the Mobilisation over Ethnic Relations, Citizenship and Immigration (MERCI) project website for studies of France, Germany, the Netherlands, the UK, and Switzerland over the period 1992–1998, ics.leeds.ac.uk/eurpolcom/research_projects_merci.cfm. Accessed 24 Mar 2011.

[4] We use here the main conclusions of the MERCI research.

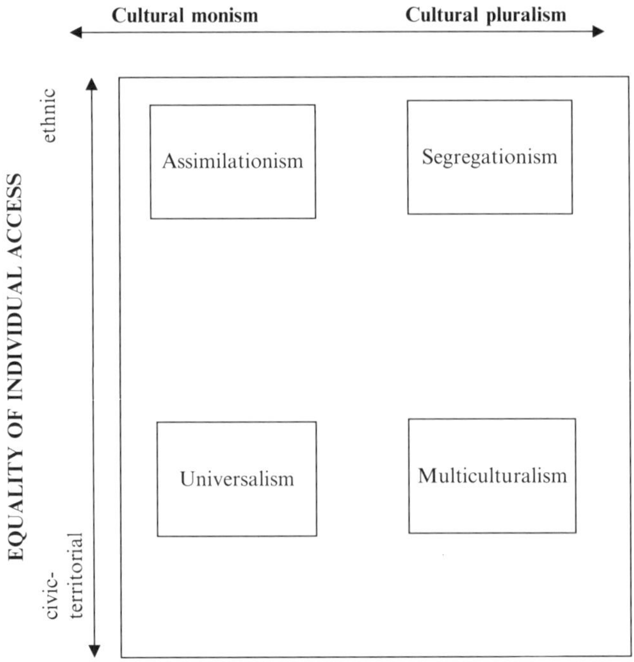

Fig. 5.1 A two-dimensional space for situating conceptions of citizenship (Source: Koopmans et al. 2005: 10)

on self-sufficient lines and involve themselves less in public debate. The in-between situation in France is revelatory of the ambivalence of its integration model: it readily accords political rights to migrants but not the right to express communitarian claims in organized political form.

The types of claims made are also very different from one country to another. In Germany and Switzerland, religious and cultural demands are almost nonexistent, whereas they loom conspicuously larger in the three other countries, including France. The acceptability of demands in terms of the group of origin obviously plays a part here, but so too does their impact within the host society. In France, where particularistic claims are less tolerated, these issues are the subject of debate and have a polarizing effect. Lastly, the forms of action are most moderate in the UK, closely followed by the Netherlands, then France, Germany, and Switzerland. In other words, in the countries in which the opportunities for political expression are most restricted, the action taken is more reactive and violent.

In contrast with the two preceding examples, the EU does not favor defense of migrant interests and does not represent an alternative space allowing for greater assertion of rights than nationally. To a large extent, free movement of persons and goods within the Union is being matched by a toughening of access conditions to European territory for non-EU population groups. In this field, member states are clinging to their sovereignty and retaining most of their basic prerogatives.

Thus while the EU is equipping itself with common rules for border checks, integration modalities remain within the sphere of national governments. This configuration leaves little maneuvering room for migrant rights defenders, who find themselves faced with sets of regulations basically hostile to their cause. These institutional obstacles are aggravated by the fact that the population groups concerned have few resources and, lacking adequate support, are unable to take advantage of the windows of opportunity and mobilize effectively. In this context their forms of participation and representation remain profoundly linked to the historical and political specificities of each host country, without there being currently any sign of convergence.

5.3 Organizing the Unemployed Within the Member States

Despite the exacerbation of situations of precariousness, mobilization by the unemployed was long considered highly improbable. The obstacles to overcome have been outlined in the literature and related to powerful forces for social and political atomization. However, in the light of the recent rise of collective action by the unemployed, such analyses require substantial qualification. This section is devoted to a quick survey of action taken in different European countries—Belgium, Ireland, Italy, Finland, Germany, and France—and then to the lessons to be drawn more systematically from the way they operate.[5]

A first country category, comprising Belgium and Ireland, is characterized by a *limited, residual* capacity for mobilization. In Belgium, almost 85% of the unemployed are trade union members. This atypical situation is the result of historical compromises leading to the payment of unemployment benefits via the unions, which have always defended the rights of the unemployed in respect of benefit, if for no other reason than to resist pressure for lower wages. Despite the considerable rise in unemployment that began in the mid-1970s, the level of protection for jobseekers has been kept at a level well above the average in other countries. Belgium, for example, is the only EU country in which there is, in theory, no time limit on benefit payments. Over recent years, however, restrictions and, especially, controls have been instituted regarding beneficiaries living in the same household as someone receiving earned income.[6] The unemployed have vigorously condemned these measures, which involve surprise home visits generally perceived as violations of privacy, and the government has responded by reducing their severity. Thus, Belgium is an example of a welfare state providing a high level of protection even in times of serious labor market recession.

[5] In this section, we summarize the content of a collective project devoted to mobilization by the unemployed in Europe. The contributions were presented at an encounter at the University of Oxford on June 10–11, 2005. For each country, invaluable assistance was provided by, respectively, Jean Faniel, Frédéric Royall, Simone Baglioni, Eeva Luhtakallio and Martti Siisiäinen, Christian Lahusen, and Britta Baumgarten.

[6] See Chap. 10 by Jean Faniel in this volume.

Paradoxically, however, mobilization by the unemployed is unquestionably hampered by the level of protection from which they benefit in these countries, as it decreases their feeling of being ignored and excluded. Even when measures aimed at cutting back benefits are introduced, the social and political representation they enjoy drastically limit the tendency toward protest. Infrequent, small-scale mobilization generally has major political consequences, as it often generates a positive institutional response.

In Ireland, too, each wave of unemployment has seen the emergence of unemployed organizations. This was the case in 1983, with the creation of the Dublin Unemployed Alliance, which quickly obtained a major negotiating status with the authorities and 4 years later became the Irish National Organisation of the Unemployed (INOU). Expanding rapidly, it is now considered the representative body for the unemployed: it had 100 affiliate groups in 1994 and some 180 in 2003. Devoting its energies mainly to community aid for the unemployed and assessment of employment policies, the INOU has continued to shun forms of action involving conflict. In a context of pronounced administrative centralization and a political system marked by a strong respect for authority, the expected challenges were snuffed out. The INOU has been entrusted with steadily growing responsibilities in terms of providing services to the unemployed and can be considered a force for social pacification. A further result was that its member organizations gradually toned down their demands, especially when the drastic fall in unemployment that began in 1996 ushered in an unprecedented period of prosperity. The Irish example thus highlights the fact that unemployed associations do not necessarily work in favor of active protest, especially when they have been coopted by the state apparatus.

A second category groups countries like Italy and Finland, in which mobilization is *moderate and limited*. In Italy, the phenomenon is concentrated in certain urban parts of the South, mainly Naples and its region, where unemployment of over 30% has been endemic for some decades. Its roots go back to June 1975, when almost 2,000 jobless people, wearied by more than a year of protest in Naples, marched to Rome and were received by the government. At this meeting, a promise was made to create 10,500 new jobs for the mobilized unemployed; and the same day, the City of Naples offered 700 mobilized unemployed persons a 1-year work contract financed by a state assistance fund. This success led Naples to the creation of numerous committees of the unemployed, which then negotiated hiring terms for members with the local and national authorities.

These groups have since become part of the political landscape and are now officially considered legitimate negotiating partners; they play a central role in the labor market, functioning as a kind of employment agency and compensating to some extent for the shortcomings of a welfare state whose benefit payments are among the lowest in Europe. Italy represents a specific case, with action by the unemployed having a strongly regional character. There is certainly no other example in Europe of an autonomous unemployed movement's having achieved such political recognition and influence, but these factors only operate locally and in contrast with the lack of mobilization in the rest of the country.

In Finland, unemployment rose abruptly from 3.2% in 1990 to 16.6% in 1994, then stabilized at just over 10% until 2000. This jump led to the creation of a host of unemployed organizations—220 between 1990 and 1997—which came together as the National Cooperation Association of the Unemployed, founded in 1991. Largely under the control of wealthy and powerful trade union organizations with real influence on the functioning of public sector action, these bodies played a decisive part in the antigovernment front, denouncing the restrictive measures of a welfare state until then reputed throughout the world for its generosity. The movement's high point came on "Revolution Thursday"—November 4, 1993—when a call from the unemployed brought 20,000 people onto the street in Helsinki. The largest demonstration the country had seen since the end of World War II, this compares more than favorably with the 6,000-strong nuclear weapons protest in 2002 and, subsequently, the turnout of 10,000 against the war in Iraq in 2003. Its impact, however, was short-lived, the arrival of a progressive coalition government in 1995 leaving the unemployed organizations isolated and deprived of the support of the unions and other militant groups. Thus, the situation in Finland testifies to the capacity for mobilization of the unemployed but also to their vulnerability, given that their impact depends on exceptional political circumstances over which they have almost no control. The case of Finland is also paradoxical: relatively well organized, the unemployed are capable of taking part—and sometimes even provoking—mass action, yet without mastering the dynamics of protest, whose driving forces are mainly external.

A third category, the one Germany and, even more so, France belong to, is that of *long-term, large-scale* mobilization. France is unquestionably the EU country in which the unemployed have achieved greatest visibility. Over the last 20 years, they have mobilized massively on several occasions and shown a certain capacity for ongoing action. Their organizations have built up a network that, while more active in some regions than in others, enjoys both a national presence and alliances with trade unions and far-Left bodies that help reduce their political isolation. Despite its limited resources, the French unemployed movement has succeeded in maintaining a certain autonomy of action. The first-ever Syndicat National des Chômeurs (SNC) was formed in 1982 at the instigation of a handful of leftist Catholic militants. On May 30, 1985, it was the driving force behind a protest march in Paris—some 5,000 unemployed—that remains the SNC's largest demonstration to date. Weakened by internal divisions, the SNC split in 1985, giving rise to the Mouvement National des Chômeurs et Précaires. The year 1987 saw the formation, by communist party leaders from the Paris suburbs, of the Association pour l'Emploi, l'Information et la Solidarité des chômeurs et travailleurs précaires. In 1993, "Agir ensemble contre le chômage!" was jointly launched by unionists, unemployed association leaders, and intellectuals. Also deserving of mention is the CGT trade union's unemployed defense section, founded in 1983, which plays a vital role in the south of the country. All these organizations were formed in the course of the decade beginning in 1982, a period marked by mass unemployment, the emergence of the new poverty, the failure of the Left in respect of employment, and acceleration of the process of European integration which, since the ratification of the Treaty of Maastricht, prohibits any reflationary policies.

The same period brought a substantial drop in unionization and a growing mistrust of political parties, both of which favor the autonomy of social movements. It was against this background, then, that the unemployed expressed their discontent and their determination to speak up on their own behalf. Unable to count on the support of any party—with the exception, sometimes, of the Trotskyist Ligue Communiste Révolutionnaire (LCR) and the Parti Communiste Français (PCF)—and in constant conflict with most union organizations apart from the CGT, they did, however, benefit from public opinion support. In November and December 1995, they found a favorable context in taking part in what was the largest movement of social protest the country had known since May 1968. In the winter of 1997 and again in 1998, they demanded and ultimately obtained—once again in a climate of considerable unrest—a "Christmas bonus" equivalent to 1,500 francs (approx. $250). Since then, unemployed mobilization increasingly is aimed at using the courts to challenge restrictions on benefit payments but invariably runs up against official refusal to recognize the representativeness of their organizations, this being a status legally confined to trade unions.

In Germany too, unemployed mobilization significantly developed, driven by the combination of rising unemployment and a series of reforms. It mounted considerably in the wake of reunification and remains much more developed in the eastern part of the country, where unemployment is running at twice the national average. Given Germany's decentralized political-administrative system, unemployed movements proliferated on a local basis but gradually became structured around a number of national associations, notably the Arbeitlosenverband, which is very strong in the former East Germany. Beginning in the mid-1990s, demonstrations by the unemployed in many cities brought together several thousand people. The phases of this mobilization match the various stages of a series of reforms called "Agenda 2010," which involves restrictions in social security, of retirement, sickness and invalidity insurance, and the rules regarding payment and job assignment for the unemployed.

Action peaked in 1998 and again in 2004. In 1998, tens of thousands of people turned out each month when the latest unemployment figures were published. And in the spring and summer of 2004, almost one million people—half of them in Berlin—protested in 230 cities against the most recent installment of the labor market reforms. Obviously the magnitude of the unemployed protests owes much to the extent of the reforms, which affected the whole population. In this context, the role of the unions and in particular of the Deutscher Gewerkschaftsbund (DGB) remained ambiguous, as the latter, even though it could not ignore the level of popular discontent, did not condemn the reforms. Thus, the unemployed organizations, of which about half were affiliated to a trade union body, received support.

Opposition to the reforms was so broad that it was in part beyond the control of the powerful DGB and offered militant unemployed people a relatively favorable context to express their political opinions. Notably, it tended to neutralize the stigma often attached to joblessness in Germany. These are major changes in a country traditionally characterized by its corporatist model and the efficacy of its system of management/labor negotiation, and they represent new opportunities for action by the unemployed. As in France—but without being able to count on the same popular support and the same political connections—Germany's unemployed seem to be turning toward increasingly autonomous, often eruptive forms of action reflecting the unified country's difficulty in resolving the mounting problems stemming from labor market exclusion.

This overview of the European scene offers a perspective on aspects of how the unemployed mobilize but also on the limitations of such mobilizations. High levels of mobilization correspond to unemployment peaks, even if the relationship is neither direct nor automatic. The feelings of frustration and anger generated by the spread and the fear of unemployment are aggravated by the fact that expectations in some cases have been high. The development of mutual aid and political awareness affected by such groups is a vital lever for the transition to action (Maurer 2001). This mobilization develops in regional contexts, via confrontation with local actors—usually employment agencies or municipalities—but this does not hamper its geographical expansion. When such expansion is the goal, devolved and/or decentralized political-administrative systems—of which the epitome is doubtless the federal state—seem most propitious to collective action by the unemployed (Bagguley 1991). Other specific factors play an even more decisive part.

A restrictive welfare state system would be likely to cause discontent among the unemployed and thus encourage mobilization. However, the expectations and demands of the unemployed increase in line with their rights, giving rise to correspondingly more acute frustration and protests when these are challenged and diminished. This version of de Tocqueville's law, which holds that the subjective dynamic of a social phenomenon counts more than its objective gravity, is a key element to understanding the issue. One of the configurations most conducive to unemployed mobilization is thus the association of a high level of protection with reforms intended to restrict benefits. At the same time, there is a distinction to be made concerning countries in which benefits are paid via the trade unions, a system which seems to entail better defense of the interests of the unemployed. At the same time, unions' dividedness and fragmentation generally offer greater scope for action to unemployed groups, which can play on rivalries and find room for maneuver in a host of possible alliances. The unemployed, however, run the risk of a dependency counter to their desire for autonomy and rely on a global political configuration over which they have no control: thus, the impulse to protest on the part of unemployed people has frequently been discouraged by trade unions concerned about keeping social dissent in their own hands. A significant split is now appearing between reformist unions close to governments accepting benefit cuts for the unemployed, and those, often less powerful and rooted in a culture of opposition, backing these groups.

Finally, it is necessary to underline the role of cultural and cognitive contexts in unemployed mobilization. The Younex research[7] showed that Italy is the country where

---

[7] See "Youth, Unemployment, and Exclusion in Europe: A Multidimensional Approach to Understanding the Conditions and Prospects for Social and Political Integration of Young Unemployed" (YOUNEX). This project was funded by the European Commission under the 7th Framework Programme (grant agreement no. 216122). For a presentation of the results and the methodology, see http://www.younex.unige.ch/index.html. Accessed 24 Mar 2011.

public discourse is most favorable, well ahead of the intermediate zone occupied by France and Switzerland, while Germany and Sweden stand out for their relative lack of receptiveness. A number of explanatory factors underlie these differences, among them the value set on work and the consequent stigma attached to those without jobs. This kind of consideration can play a certain part in regions influenced by Protestantism. On the whole, however, attitudes within countries indicate a support for the unemployed all the more vital in that it helps compensate, at least partly, for their political isolation in Europe and opens possible alternative strategies for challenging public opinion.

Despite the crests of mobilization, what mainly stands out is the sporadic, not to say marginal, character of actions taken. In one of the European democracies' most painful paradoxes, the most vulnerable fringe of the population is unable to organize on a lasting basis or, especially, to give structured, enduring expression to the main social ill that has been gnawing at it for decades now.

5.4 European Marches and Alter-Globalization Movements

Collective action by the unemployed has also taken on an EU dimension. The movement known as European Marches against Unemployment, Job Insecurity and Social Exclusion first demonstrated its mobilization capacity in Amsterdam on June 14, 1997, when almost 50,000 people turned out against the holding of the European Summit (Chabanet 2002). What made the event even more remarkable was the presence of demonstrators from many countries: for over 2 months, small teams of marchers had crisscrossed Europe before converging on the Netherlands and calling people into the street. Nor was the event's impact short-lived: on June 3–4, 1999, marches took place involving some 30,000 people in protests against the European Summit in Cologne. Since then, similar events have been affected by demonstrations on a smaller scale.

In the absence of a common policy for countering unemployment, the responsibility remains on individual member states, which effectively prevents any "top-down" Europeanization. The European Trade Union Confederation, for example, cannot function as a focal point for grievances because it emphasizes consultation as part of the social dialogue procedure and expresses support for EU policy. Moreover, the networks of associations capable of representing the interests of "precarious" workers at the European level are few, not very protest-oriented, and for the most part cut off from national organizations. Thus, the European Anti-Poverty Network, founded in 1990, is a kind of epistemic community that enjoys consultative status at the Council of Europe but whose capacity for action is limited and not especially protest-oriented (Haas 1992). Established in 1982, the European Network of the Unemployed, which includes most of Europe's national unemployed associations, is even less influential: lack of funds has prevented it from meeting since 1998, and it now has virtually no active existence (Royall 2002).[8]

[8] See Chap. 8 by Frédéric Royall in this volume.

Although the processions of marchers set out from a host of different points all over the EU, thus calling attention to their truly European character, the organization of the marches was largely due to a small number of leaders from the French far Left. In the mid-1990s, these activists had limited visibility and were out to get issues relating to unemployment and job insecurity onto the European agenda. The mobilization of the unemployed in each country depended mainly on the help provided by allies. As Michael Lipsky (1970: 2) noticed, "the 'problem' of the powerless in protest activity is to activate *third parties* to enter the implicit or explicit bargaining area in ways favorable to the protestors." Help from trade unions and civil society actors, the Churches in particular, was decisive in Germany—second only to France in mobilizing troops—and in the northern European countries, whose numbers, while not negligible, were appreciably less. Unemployed people from Italy helped fill out the processions and were present in greater numbers than, among others, the Belgians, Slovenians, and Spanish.

By contrast, the number of English unemployed marchers was strikingly low. Backing from England's unions was extremely limited: first, because most of them have declined considerably in strength over the last 20 years and, second, because the Trade Union Congress refused to take part, aligning itself with a Labor Party whose agenda had little to do with the claims of the unemployed. In addition, the overall loss of job security around the country had eased the employment situation and diminished still further the unemployed associations' capacity to mobilize. The fact that unemployment benefit systems were residual did not encourage protest as long as work—even when precarious—was widely available.

On the whole, then, the national makeup of the European march movement closely reflected the mobilization capacity of the unemployed in member states. However, this was not the case where unemployment provisions were most favorable but rather in the countries where, in spite of restrictive measures, the system was most generous, notably France, Germany, Finland, and Belgium. In contexts of high unemployment, it was the conjunction of these two phenomena—plus the part played by the trade unions—that explained participation by unemployed people. This participation was even more marked in countries where a significant split in the labor market, induced by structural rigidities, meant less hope of finding a job.

The main challenge facing the organizers of the marches was that of highlighting the situation of the unemployed in Europe as a political issue. In a context of limited possibilities for action, the march approach enabled groups with restricted access to power to make themselves visible and mobilize public opinion in the hope of influencing political institutions. In this perspective, the marches embodied two major, conflicting agendas: the first was long term, seeing the creation of an "alter-European" social movement as the main objective of mobilization and the actual claims of the unemployed and precariously employed as secondary. The second—and as a rule, the one put forward by unemployed association leaders and the unemployed themselves—emphasized the urgency of the situation in obtaining immediate material gains.

The tensions surrounding the goals of the movement did not prevent the marchers from seeking the same level of visibility and the support of public opinion in Europe. This organizational pattern made the marches a unique mode of *externalization of protest*: the unemployed taking part made up a transnational coalition of actors whose targeting of the EU was a means of opposing government policy in the member states.

Completely reliant on the various welfare state systems, they had no short-term expectations toward European institutions with no direct influence on their fate. Rather, they took advantage of the visibility obtained by confronting the European Council to put pressure on their national executives.

In many respects, the European marches can be seen as among the pioneer elements of the alter-globalization movement and the system of counter-summits. Nonetheless, this unemployed movement did not outlive its early success, running out of steam so quickly that by the time of the Nice summit in December 2000, its capacity to mobilize had plummeted. All that remains now is an (admittedly very active) exchange and information network on the Internet.[9] The cruel truth is that today's alter-globalization movement does little to express or represent the demands of the unemployed and, as a number of recent surveys indicate, is situated on the other side of a sociological divide.

Overall, the activists at the first European Social Forum in Florence in 2002 offer profiles far removed from those of the deprived and excluded thrown up by European integration and the globalization process. Among the former, "53% were students, 11% unemployed or underemployed people, 25% wage earners, and 7% self-employed" (della Porta 2004: 54). At the anti-G8 protests in Genoa in July 2001, the unemployed and those without job security totaled only a fraction over 10% (della Porta 2004: 52–55). Participants in the second ESF in and around Paris in November 2003 offered the extremely homogeneous image of a group with real cultural capital—69% with higher education qualifications (as against 30% for the population as a whole), of whom 51.6% held degrees from a university or a *grande école*—and in many cases a stable public-sector job (46.1% as against 10 % for the workforce as a whole) (Gobille and Uysal 2005: 107).

Far from giving a voice to the victims of globalization, alter-globalization actors express the discontentment of a fringe of "rooted cosmopolitans" (Tarrow 2001) with a rich social and cultural capital. The organizations fighting unemployment and job insecurity make attempts at involvement in the ESFs so as to benefit from the hearing they get in the public arena, but the results are meager. True, their case is stated, but diluted and stifled by the much more powerful representatives of civil society and the trade unions, who find it appreciably easier to get a hearing and gain access to the political sphere. The isolation and the position of inferiority imposed on the unemployed at national level are equally present within the European movement, which they in fact helped to found, and which is now emerging as a collective actor of steadily mounting influence (Agrikoliansky et al. 2005).

5.5 Conclusion

Our analyses and, more broadly, the whole of the literature devoted to the representation of interests in Europe, strongly suggest that the EU, even when it constitutes an alternative space for action, is not capable of substantially modifying the balances

[9] Found at www.euromarches.org

of power and the inequalities that are part of the national spaces. To a certain extent, a counterexample is provided by the unemployed, who have succeeded in mobilizing massively at EU level over the last few years, something they had not been capable of within the member states. It should be pointed out, however, that it has been much more a case of exploiting the European summits—hijacking them, so to speak, in order to take advantage of their visibility—than of benefiting from the voluntary support of EU institutions in the way the women's movement did.

Unrest among the unemployed and disquiet within European public opinion as a whole finds an outlet in sporadically emerging mobilizations that find only feeble expression in national and EU political agendas. These mobilizations take the form of either mistrust or rejection of political actors and the EU in particular—notably evident in the French "no" to the European Constitution on May 29, 2005—and the rise of far-Right populism. In other words, adequate political responses to the seriousness of the phenomena of exclusion in Europe are not forthcoming, and this is widening the gulf between a growing part of Europe's population—rendered vulnerable by economic and social difficulties—and political institutions. Nonetheless, the attribution of unemployment to European integration is largely unfounded. Unemployment issues remain for the most part the responsibility of individual member states and outcomes are extremely wide-ranging, unemployment rates being in some cases quite low. The most recent major steps in political integration—the single market of 1992, the enlargements of 1995 and 2004, and the changeover to the euro in 2001—have not had negative repercussions in this field. Nonetheless, the persistence of the unemployment problem and the mounting dangers of exclusion are seen by public opinion in Europe as priority concerns helping to undermine the credibility of national and European policies. Given its limited legitimacy, the EU is the main institutional loser here, even though the implementation of employment policies—and even more so of the fight against unemployment—remains the responsibility of the member states.

Overall, groups with scant resources suffer much more from their limited means of action and their isolation at national level than from EU ostracism. In this view of things, migrants are doubtless an exceptional case since the measures taken by the EU are aimed at drastically limiting the arrival and entry of non-EU migrants. The combination of the powerful integration models embodied by the states and the policy overlay of increasingly strict controls on entry into EU territory is a dual obstacle to their action and its Europeanization: first, because the problems migrants face remain locked into precise politico-judicial contexts, a situation not conducive to the transnationalization of mobilizations and, second, because European institutions, especially the Council, agree on the need to harmonize the mechanisms for combating the influx of refugees and immigrants. It must be stressed here that in this field the balance of power between the Commission and the Council is clearly in favor of the latter, which largely governs the possibilities for dialogue between interest groups and the publicizing of the related issues.

For migrants, the difficulties accumulate as the restrictive measures taken by heads of state and government become more effective and, in parallel, as backing from other international organizations crumbles. This situation is all the more prejudicial for them in that it has little visibility in Europe and has only marginal status on national political agendas, thus rendering inoperative the strategies for challenging public opinion used by other resourceless groups. Nonetheless, the constraints are never total or irreversible, and alternative levers for action do exist. In particular, mobilization of migrants in the member states is fueled by exchanges of information and ideas allowing for comparison between militant experiences on a European scale. Similarly, applications to the ECJ offer the glimmer of a possibility of judgments favorable to defense of their rights. The traditional attachment of democracies to the issue of human rights might also, in the long term, generate greater media attention to the fate of migrants, thereby causing shifts in opinion, a partial reaction among the ruling classes, and a substantial modification of the political formulation of those rights.

References

Agrikoliansky, É., Fillieule, O., & Meyer, N. (2005). *L'altermondialisme en France: La longue histoire d'une nouvelle cause*. Paris: Flammarion.

Bagguley, P. (1991). *From protest to acquiescence? Political movements of the unemployed*. London: Macmillan.

Chabanet, D. (2002). Les marches européens contre le chômage, la précarité et les exclusions. In R. Blame, D. Chabanet, & V. Wright (Eds.), *L'Action collective en Europe*. Paris: Presses de Sciences Po.

della Porta, D. (2004). Démocratie en mouvement. Les manifestants du Forum social européen, des liens aux réseaux. *Politix (Militants de l'altermondialisme), 17*(68), 49–77.

Gobille, B., & Uysal, A. (2005). Cosmopolites et enracinés. In É. Agrikoliansky & I. Sommier (Eds.), *Radiographie du mouvement altermondialiste*. Paris: La Dispute.

Guiraudon, V. (2001). Weak weapons of the weak? Transnational mobilization around migration in the European Union. In D. Imig & S. Tarrow (Eds.), *Contentious Europeans: Protest and politics in an emerging polity*. Oxford: Rowman & Littlefield.

Haas, P. (1992). Introduction: Epistemic communities and international policy coordination. *International Organization, 46*(1), 377–403.

Koopmans, R., Statham, P., Giugni, M., & Passy, F. (2005). *Contested citizenship: Immigration and ethnic relations: Politics in Germany, Britain, France, the Netherlands, and Switzerland*. Minneapolis: University of Minnesota Press.

Lipsky, M. (1970). *Protest in city politics: Rent strikes, housing and the power of the poor*. Chicago: Rand McNally.

Maurer, S. (2001). *Les chômeurs en action (décembre 1997–mars 1998), Mobilisation collective et ressources compensatoires*. Paris: L'Harmattan.

Monforte, P., & Dufour, P. (2011). Mobilizing in borderline citizenship regimes: A comparative analysis of undocumented migrants' collective actions. *Politics & Society, XX*(X), 1–30.

Royall, F. (2002). Building solidarity across national boundaries: The case of affiliates of the European network of the unemployed. *Journal of European Area Studies, 10*(2), 243–258.

Tarrow, S. (2001). Transnational politics: Contention and institutions in international politics. *Annual Review of Political Science, 4*, 1–20.

Valluy, J. (2005). La nouvelle Europe politique des camps d'exilés: Genèse d'une source élitaire de phobie et de répression des étrangers. *Cultures et Conflits, 57*, 13–69.

Chapter 6
Agricultural Markets and Food Riots: The European Union and Asia Compared

M. Bruna Zolin

6.1 Introduction

The current economic crisis is one of the most serious crises that the world has faced since at least the 1930s. The crisis started with the financial sector and then affected the commodity sector. The crisis began in high-income countries, but developing countries have been caught up in its wake. In fact, in 2008, the world's attention was focused on the global food crisis and, as a consequence, on global food security. By mid-2009, commodity prices had dropped substantially, but, in late 2010, for the second time in 3 years, food prices (wheat, corn, and sugar) began to soar and still remain at or above past trend levels.

In 2008, the major and relatively new drivers of high food prices could be brought back (Gilbert 2010; Mitchell 2008): the rise in oil and energy prices which affected the entire value chain of food production, the previous economic boom in some emerging countries creating increased demand for cereals mainly for meat production, bad harvests due to weather-related events (floods and droughts), competition between food and fuel, policy choices (export bans in some developing countries and biofuel subsidies in western countries), increasing urbanization (more people are becoming consumers rather than producers), general rundown in commodity stocks, dollar depreciation, and finally speculation. In 2009, prices fell due to a slower gross domestic product (GDP) growth and energy demand, increased supplies, and revised expectations. In 2010, droughts (China and Russia), frost (Mexico), and floods (Australia) affected a number of crops in different parts of the world and had a great impact on prices. The consequences of the food crisis and the extreme price volatility go far beyond economics. Achieving food security means not only ensuring that sufficient food is produced but that everyone has access to it. A basic concern for

M.B. Zolin (✉)
Department of Economics, Ca' Foscari University, S. Giobbe 873, 30121 Venice, Italy
e-mail: zolin@unive.it

B. Andreosso-O'Callaghan and F. Royall (eds.), *Economic and Political Change in Asia and Europe: Social Movement Analyses*, DOI 10.1007/978-94-007-4653-4_6,

policy makers is to understand the desirable level for food prices and the acceptable level of price volatility. Limited increases could benefit farmers, but price rises could compromise the food security of low-income consumers.

It is generally recognized that high food prices have increased world hunger because the most vulnerable social groups spend a large portion of their income on food staples. This is a serious concern because the reduction in income affects the ability to provide for basic needs and compromises the possibility to escape from poverty. The impacts of high food prices are different also in the comparison between countries with the same consumption pattern. This is, for example, the case of Vietnam compared to Bangladesh. In Vietnam, the land distribution is generally egalitarian, and a large portion of farmers produce and sell rice. In Bangladesh, few farmers have access to land, and the impact of high food prices is destructive, with consequent political and social instability.

Experts are thereby worried about food riots, and we note that they are now happening. High food prices and volatility have been among the main reasons for protests in Egypt and elsewhere in the Arab world (Algeria, Tunisia, Yemen, Iraq, Iran, Libya, and Bahrain). On January 14, 2011, Cha Eunjung posted in the *The Washington Post* that:

> Tunisian President Zine el-Abidine Ben Ali on Thursday vowed to reduce the price of staples such as sugar, milk and bread, but the pledge wasn't enough to placate the thousands of protesters who mobbed the capital, Tunis, on Friday to demand his ouster.

On February 4, 2011, *The New York Times* noted that:

> A prominent political commentator in Sana, told me that he believes Mr. Saleh will have to keep his promises this time: "The rules of the game have changed – he cannot not honor his word this time. Tunisia and Egypt have raised the bar." He thinks Mr. Saleh has six months to prove himself trustworthy. At the end of that time, revenues from his two main sources – Saudi aid and minor oil exports – will not be enough to foot the civil service wage bill, or the diesel and food subsidies. Then he will not be worrying about polite opposition politicians but more likely about bread-rioters, hungry and unmanageable, exploding into violence.

Since the food system has to provide more and "just" food and it has to secure food security in the future, this chapter explores the pressures on food prices (Sects. 6.2 and 6.3), identifies the decision that policy makers adopted in some selected Asian countries as a consequence (Sect. 6.4), with a specific focus on food aid (Sect. 6.5), and tries to suggest some sustainable key actions for policy makers (concluding remarks).

6.2 Main Drivers Affecting the Food System

The food system has experienced a strong confluence of pressures since the end of the first decade of the 2000s, driven by both supply and demand factors (Andreosso-O'Callaghan and Zolin 2010b). Volatility is frequent in agricultural markets, but it appears higher now than that prevailing before the 2008 world crisis (World Bank 2010a; Lucia et al. 2010), with a strong impact on the global food system and, when

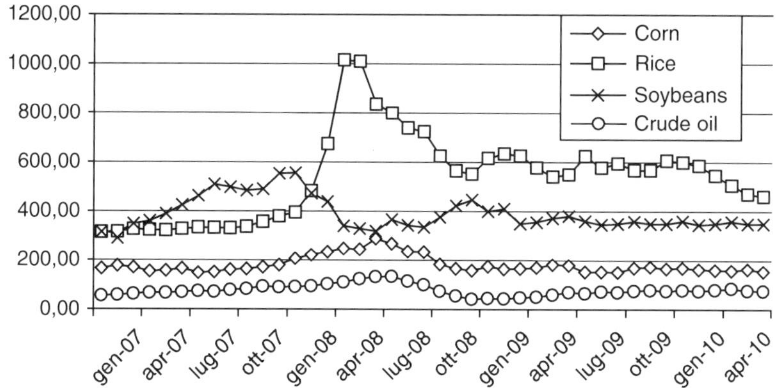

Fig. 6.1 Selected cereal and soybean prices (2007–2010) (Source: http://www.indexmundi.com/commodities/)

particularly severe, on economic and political instability. These consequences are most heavy for poor and low-income countries.

Wheat prices increased from US$200 a ton in March 2007 to US$440 between March 2007 and March 2008. Rice prices in the first month of 2008 tripled, while soybean prices increases 44% between 2007 and 2008. In the period 1985–2010, corn prices increased 21.7%, rice 51.1%, wheat 5.4%, soybeans 41.6%, and crude oil 63.7%. In the period 2007–2010, the results of the observed extreme variability are price reductions in wheat and corn (24.4 and 8%, respectively) and price increases in rice, soybeans, and crude oil (31.8, 10.1, and 8.7%, respectively) (Fig. 6.1).

In February 2011, the Food and Agriculture Organization (FAO) reported that its food price index jumped 32% in the second half of 2010, surpassing the previous record set in the early summer of 2008 when deadly clashes over food arose around the world (FAO 2011).

Decisions made now and in the foreseeable future will greatly influence food security. Surges in food prices could create inflation and expectations in wage demands. For the advanced economies, inflation impacts would be relatively soft. This is not the case for developing countries (mainly net importers of food) where the increasing prices, because of the trade-off between growth and inflation and because of Engel's law,[1] would create a severe impact.

One of the main causes of increases in food demand (and as a consequence in food prices) is the population explosion in the poorer and emerging countries. According to FAO data (FAO 2009b), the Asian population increased by 30.0% between 1985 and 2010, and it is expected to rise by another 24.5% by 2050. The highest increases are observed in the least developed countries where the Malthusian

[1] According to Engel, as income rises, the proportion of income spent on food falls. Lower-income householders spent a greater proportion of their available income on food than middle-/higher-income households. As food prices increase, the percentage spent by lower-income households is expected to increase.

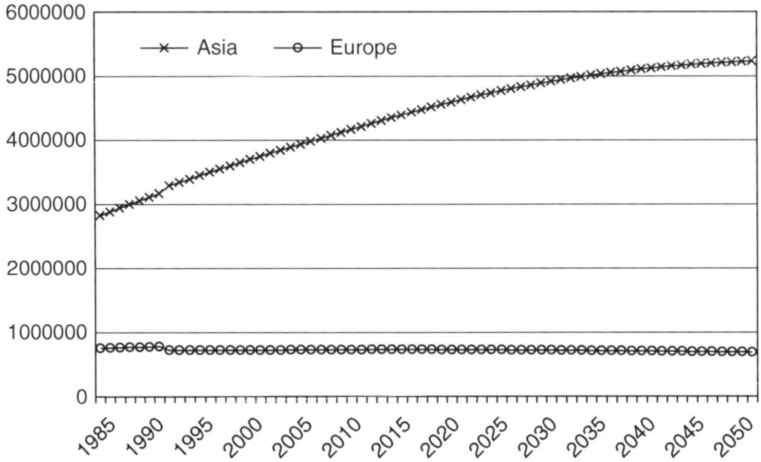

Fig. 6.2 Population in Europe and Asia, 1985–2050 (FAO estimates from 2010 to 2050) (Source: Our elaboration on FAOstat data)

theory could become a reality (Fig. 6.2). Does the specter of Malthus reappear in some parts of the world? As is well known, Malthus (2008) believed that population would increase at a geometric rate and the food supply at an arithmetic rate. This gap would lead to widespread poverty and starvation which would only be checked by natural negative events such as disease, high infant mortality, famine, war, or moral restraint. Decreasing population growth and future world food consumption trends could be affected by other demographic factors such as the increasing share of people of retirement age that generally eat less than the young or adolescents.[2]

In food consumption, different patterns exist between developed and developing countries. As standards of living increase in the developed countries, individuals tend to waste food and to eat food with a higher value added content (such as consumer-ready meals and processed food). If hunger is a crucial global issue, obesity is epidemic in the United States and in other developed countries: more than half of Americans are overweight. This is the path that the emerging countries with high-income people are following.

Though the food high prices crisis has affected all areas of the world, it is recognized that these high prices hit twofold the developing countries. On the one hand, the economic crisis becomes a food crisis with soaring prices and a dramatic impact on the poorer populations, and, on the other hand, it leads to the decline in remittances, in export earnings, in foreign direct investments, and, thus, in income. According to Engel's law, the share of income spent on food is higher in the poorer population. Households in poor countries spend 50% (or more) of their income on food and about 10% on energy. Moreover, the demand for food is quite inelastic.

[2] Patterns of food in the European Union (EU) and in Japan reflect the fact that a large part of the population is seniors.

This low income elasticity of demand for food puts in doubt the projections of the demand for food by developing countries when big income inequalities are taken into account (De Hoyos and Lessem 2008).

The basis of agricultural production is land. In traditional agriculture, more land means more income and better quality of living. The possibilities of increasing the surface of land are limited. According to the Organization for Economic Cooperation and Development (OECD) and the Food and Agricultural Organization (FAO) estimates (FAO 2009a, b; OECD–FAO 2009), 1.6 billion hectares could be added to the current arable land (about 1.8 billion hectares, Table 6.1). The largest potential is in forested land with the strong unused supply in Latin America and sub-Saharan Africa. However, strong competition exists in land use[3] such as land needed for urbanization and industrialization and for biofuel production (Andreosso-O'Callaghan and Zolin 2010a). But, increasing land use for agriculture by deforestation would accelerate soil deterioration, climate change, and loss of biodiversity. In other words, we are facing the dilemma of the tragedy of commons (Hardin 1968).

Next to land, one of the major instruments for achieving a greater output is labor. In densely populated societies (such as in some Asian countries), abundant labor is available in quantitative terms, but some limits could be envisaged in terms of quality. In these conditions, farmers often choose between alternative crops and methods of farming, bearing in mind existing norms, traditions, and, sometimes, religion which could also play a crucial role. Finally, where land is scarcer than labor, the response to demand growth is intensification.

As far as world agricultural land is concerned, it can be noted that according to FAO data (FAO 2009a), world land for primary crops has been expanded by 11 % from 1985 to 2008 (Table 6.2). In Africa it increased by 37%, South America by 26%, and Asia by 18%, while in North America, but mainly in Europe, it decreased by 4.4% and by about 36%, respectively. The largest harvested area is located in Asia. Crop production increased more than population and more than consumption. Supply decreased only in the European Union (EU), where population and consumption followed the same negative trend with lower levels (Fig. 6.3).

At world level, primary crop production increased by 37.5% from 1985 to 2008. The main actors are in Asia (+49%), Africa (+47.5%), and Central and South America. European production fell by 9%. Agricultural production has in the past 30 years increased more than the population, despite the fact that the share of agricultural workers in total employment has declined. Cereal yield showed a variation equal to 28.6 in the period 1985–2008 (Table 6.3). As far as productivity is concerned, the largest increase in productivity is visible in South America. The lowest is in Africa where productivity is 40 % lower than the world average (Table 6.3). Northern America, followed by Europe, has the highest productivity in the world.

Primary crops for human consumption increased sharply until the mid-1990s in Asia, and then, growth was slower. In Northern America and Europe, the trend is stationary, while it is continuously growing in Africa and in Central and South

[3] Other restrictions are referring to water utilization.

Table 6.1 Global agricultural land use (1,000 ha)

	1985	1990	1995	2000	2005	2008	2009
Cereals	720,199	708,474	686,392	672,693	690,104	712,226	708,495
Oil crops	174,450	184,941	208,032	222,119	253,260	259,681	261,099
Pulses	66,761	68,761	70,390	64,850	70,544	71,807	70,598
Roots and tubers	44,657	46,029	49,309	53,202	53,718	52,861	53,666
Fruits	37,694	41,148	46,321	49,063	52,698	55,012	55,607
Vegetables	29,408	31,223	36,633	44,860	50,826	53,710	54,739
Subtotal	1,073,169	1,080,576	1,097,078	1,106,787	1,171,150	1,205,296	1,204,203
Other crops	564,694	556,353	572,512	565,904	612,229	630,045	623,911
Total area harvested	1,637,863	1,636,929	1,669,590	1,672,691	1,783,379	1,835,341	1,828,114
Agricultural land total	4,758,172	4,854,606	4,925,590	4,941,012	4,915,774	4,883,697	–

Source: FAOstat, http://faostat.fao.org/site/567/default.aspx#ancor

Table 6.2 Primary crops[a]: area harvested (1,000 ha)

	1985		1990		1995		2000		2005		2008		
	1,000 ha	% on world	1,000 ha	% on world	1,000 ha	% on world	1,000 ha	% on world	1,000 ha	% on world	1,000 ha	% on world	Var. % 1985–2008
Africa	135,764	11.9	149,609	13.0	170,173	14.6	179,306	15.2	210,480	16.8	215,516	16.7	37.0
North America	135,630	11.9	126,907	11.0	126,405	10.8	129,166	10.9	125,299	10.0	129,957	10.1	–4.4
Central America	21,561	1.9	21,255	1.8	21,547	1.8	20,976	1.8	20,583	1.6	22,127	1.7	2.6
South America	87,211	7.6	87,755	7.6	88,735	7.6	94,027	8.0	111,191	8.9	118,365	9.2	26.3
Asia	484,135	42.4	504,191	43.8	546,271	46.8	550,912	46.6	574,855	46.0	591,734	45.8	18.2
Europe	250,680	22.0	238,791	20.7	190,417	16.3	177,620	15.0	178,439	14.3	184,451	14.3	–35.9
Oceania	21,014	1.8	17,504	1.5	19,846	1.7	24,446	2.1	24,559	2.0	25,503	2.0	17.6
World	1,141,061	100.0	1,150,938	100.0	1,168,270	100.0	1,181,082	100.0	1,249,514	100.0	1,291,685	100.0	11.7

Source: FAOstat, http://faostat.fao.org/site/567/default.aspx#ancor

[a]Primary crops are those which come directly from the land and without having undergone any real processing, apart from cleaning. They maintain all the biological qualities they had when they were still on the plants

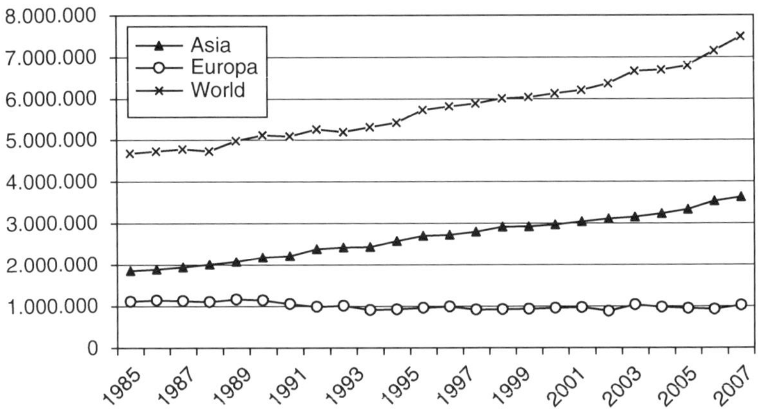

Fig. 6.3 Primary crop production trend 1980–2008 (1,000 t) (Source: Our elaboration on FAOstat data)

Table 6.3 Cereal yield (hg/ha)

	1985	1990	1995	2000	2005	2008	Var. % 1985/2008
Africa	11,413	11,761	11,099	12,700	13,373	14,130	19.2
Northern America	41,800	42,316	41,893	51,307	57,461	59,333	29.6
Central America	23,118	23,232	24,055	25,965	28,586	31,942	27.6
South America	20,825	20,042	26,199	29,810	33,372	37,725	44.8
Asia	24,848	28,095	28,989	31,106	33,668	36,100	31.2
Europe	25,083	29,016	28,737	31,611	35,180	39,615	36.7
World	25,288	27,553	27,646	30,627	32,849	35,393	28.6

Source: FAOstat, http://faostat.fao.org/site/567/DesktopDefault.aspx?PageID=567#ancor

America (Table 6.4). As far as primary crops per capita human consumption is concerned (Table 6.5), in 2007 the highest consumption was in Central America (266 kg/capita), followed by Asia (156 kg/capita), and the lowest was in Oceania. At world level, per capita human consumption from 1985 to 2007 decreased worldwide, with the exceptions of Africa and North and South America.

The comparison with the percent variation in 1985–2007 of GDP (current prices and PPP), population, and crop production and consumption (Table 6.6) shows that GDP increased more than population and crop production and consumption. The growth in population is lower than the rates of increases of crop production and consumption worldwide, except in Africa where consumption shows a value higher than production.

In Asia, the highest growth in GDP is accompanied by the highest increase in crop production, while consumption growth is at world average level. Generally, the increase in global crop production has been driven predominantly by productivity gains rather than by increased available land. In the period 1985–2007, although demand for crops increased all over the world (except in Europe) and, sometimes,

Table 6.4 Primary crop human consumption (1,000 t)

	1985		1990		1995		2000		2005		2007	
	1.000 t.	% on world	1.000 t.	% on world	1.000 t.	% on world	1.000 t.	% on world	1.000 t.	% on world	1.000 t.	% on world
Africa	74,236,090	10.4	86,816,190	11.1	100,402,681	11.7	112,357,678	12.6	129,265,481	13.7	138,022,206	14.3
Northern America	24,875,750	3.5	30,111,319	3.8	36,009,832	4.2	36,853,076	4.1	36,849,891	3.9	38,393,467	4.0
Central and South America	50,278,622	7.0	53,718,354	6.9	58,230,223	6.8	63,422,044	7.1	71,345,295	7.6	71,182,572	7.4
Asia	459,644,114	64.3	505,924,879	64.6	563,723,930	65.9	584,362,897	65.3	605,513,171	64.2	619,473,036	64.2
Europe	104,046,552	14.6	104,228,192	13.3	95,108,311	11.1	95,138,392	10.6	97,162,442	10.3	96,004,714	9.9
Oceania	1,891,000	0.3	1,975,571	0.3	2,249,723	0.3	2,196,504	0.2	2,332,472	0.2	2,495,760	0.3
World	714,972,127	100.0	782,774,506	100.0	855,724,701	100.0	894,330,590	100.0	942,468,752	100.0	965,571,755	100.0

Source: Our elaboration on FAO stat data

Table 6.5 Primary crop for human consumption (kg/capita/year)

	1985	1990	1995	2000	2005	2007	Var. % 1985–2007
Africa	134.7	137.0	139.8	138.6	141.9	144.7	6.9
North America	93.3	106.5	120.0	115.7	110.0	112.4	16.9
Central America	278.8	262.4	254.6	265.3	265.1	266.2	–4.7
South America	111.7	109.5	108.9	109.6	120.4	115.2	3.0
Asia	164.5	164.5	165.7	160.3	156.3	156.3	–5.2
Europe	139.5	136.2	130.8	131.0	133.2	131.4	–6.2
Oceania	91.2	88.7	94.7	87.3	87.1	91.1	–0.1
World	149.7	150.1	151.5	148.0	146.6	146.7	–2.0

Source: Our elaboration on FAOstat data

severe food shortages with Malthusian consequences were predicted, growth in productivity remained at higher levels so that the ability to feed an increasing world population was continuing to grow. However, it is a fact that the high food prices impact, especially on poorest households, demonstrates the inability of the current food system to protect the most vulnerable population.

6.3 Prices Crisis or Food Crisis?

According to FAO definition, food security exists when all people at all times have access to sufficient, safe, and nutritious food to meet their dietary needs and food preferences for an active and healthy life. This requires adequacy of food supply and availability, stability of supply without fluctuation or shortages from season to season or from year to year, accessibility to food or affordability, and quality and safety of food (FAO 2002).[4] The battle to defeat famine is almost as old as the world. The causes of hunger are numerous. At this moment in time, scarcity is not one of these causes. Undoubtedly, as a consequence of soaring food prices, the number of malnourished people increased. According to the World Bank (2010b), it looks as a jeopardized situation: some developing countries became net importing countries because they were convinced that they could buy food or agricultural products in the international markets at cheaper prices, while others, in the emerging country typology, have become self-sufficient in food production.

At the global level, the cost of higher food and fuel prices in developing countries during 2008 was estimated to have been about US$680 million. The estimated macroeconomic effects are increased deficit (5% of GDP), inflation, increased incidence, and severity of worldwide poverty (World Bank 2010b). The goal of the Second World

[4] Food insecurity is more pervasive than hunger. A person can be food insecure but not hungry. Undernutrition overlaps with food security because there are nonfood factors such as deficiency of or polluted water and poor health services. The food price rise had shown the incapacity of the world food system to support the most vulnerable, even if the increase and volatility of food prices appear less marked than those of the mid-1970s (Government Office for Science 2011).

Table 6.6 GDP (current prices and purchasing power parity – PPP), population, crop production and consumption, cereal area harvested and yield, variation % 1985–2007

	GDP, current prices	GDP, PPP	Population	Crop production	Area harvested for cereals	Cereal yield	Crop consumption
Africa	72.8	72.0	42.3	45.3	30.8	19.2	46.2
Northern America	70.5	69.9	22.0	18.3	−22.0	29.6	35.2
Central and South America	79.3	69.7	29.4	40.5	1.3	72.4	29.4
Asia	85.6	86.1	29.8	47.6	7.8	31.2	25.8
Europe	83.4	71.7	−3.7	−20.8	−41.9	36.7	−8.4
Oceania	81.6	71.1	28.0	17.5	16.9	13.4	24.2
World	79.2	75.3	27.5	34.5	2.6	28.6	26.0

Source: Our elaboration on International Monetary Fund, World Economic Outlook Database (for GDP), and FAOstat (for population and crop consumption)

Table 6.7 Number of undernourished persons (millions and percentage)

	1990–1992		1995–1997		2004–2006		Var. %
	millions	%	millions	%	millions	%	1990–2006
Developed countries	19.1	2.3	21.4	2.6	15.2	1.7	−25.7
Developing world	826.2	97.7	803.5	97.4	857.7	151.5	3.7
Near East and North Africa	19.1	2.3	29.6	3.6	33.8	3.9	43.5
Sub-Saharan Africa	168.8	20.0	193.6	23.5	212.3	24.3	20.5
Asia and the Pacific	585.7	69.3	528.5	64.1	566.2	64.9	−3.4
Latin America and the Caribbean	52.6	6.2	51.8	6.3	45.3	5.2	−16.1
World	845.3	100.0	824.9	100.0	872.9	100.0	3.2

Source: FAOstat, http://www.fao.org/economic/ess/ess-fs/ess-fadata/en/

Food Summit in 1996 (FAO 1996, 2002) was to reduce in half by 2015 the number of malnourished people (no more than 420 million), but over the period 1990–2006, this number increased in absolute value. At the world level, the number of malnourished people increased from 845 million in 1990–1992 to 873 million in 2004–2005, and according to FAO (FAO 2009b; World Bank 2010b), the number was estimated at 1.02 billion people in 2009. The number of hungry people, which was concentrated mainly in sub-Saharan Africa, shows only the peak of malnutrition problems, while the undernourished are concentrated in Asia and the Pacific (Table 6.7).

In other words, food insecurity is far from decreasing and hunger is the antithesis of development. Asia and the Pacific is one of the world's most dynamic regions; however, it still has a large share of people suffering from food insecurity. Within this area, India has more undernourished people than sub-Saharan Africa, but in Asia and the Pacific, food-insecure people are rarely visible because they are concentrated in remote areas (FAO 2008). The greatest problems are in Southwest Asia, and the countries with the most severe problems are Afghanistan followed by Tajikistan, the Democratic People's Republic of Korea, Mongolia, Bangladesh, Cambodia, Pakistan, Sri Lanka, India, and the Salomon Island.

So, in spite of sufficient food production, the number of food-insecure people is increasing due to the problem of soaring prices which are affected by structural and temporary problems. The main reasons for current high prices appear as temporary (bad weather, drought if not linked to climate change, and speculation), and public policies play a crucial role.

6.4 Food Riots and Policy Responses

In 2007, food riots were reported in the Indian state of West Bengal. In response, India banned the export of rice except for Basmati types of rice. In 2008, protests over the price of food took place in Indonesia, Bangladesh, and the Philippines. The recent violent food riots in Tunisia and Algeria show how political consequences can produce food shortages. These two northern African nations were considered to be very stable and without any major problems. Faced with high and rising world food prices, many countries adopted policy measures designed to reduce the impact on their domestic populations (FAO 2009a; IFPR 2008a, b; Oxfam 2008). For the poorest countries, some form of additional assistance was provided (the United Nations, the Food and Agricultural Organization, the International Fund for Agricultural Development, the European Union, and the World Food Program). The domestic measures, involving different key commodity sectors, can be classified into four broad categories: trade, production, consumption, and stock policies. Most of these policy measures were implemented for limited periods (IFPRI/CGIAR 2008).

The trade-related measures were in export and import measures (Table 6.8). Usually the export measures included export taxes and/or subsidies, export bans, and other quantitative restrictions. They were applied by net exporting countries to enhance supply on the domestic market. If an export subsidy reduces the price paid by foreign importers, taxes, bans, and quotas tend to reduce prices in the domestic market. These measures have a significant impact on the domestic market: they reduce the gains for producers, limit their supply response, and affect prices on the international markets. On the other side of developing countries which are importers, high prices increase the size of their poorest population and the level of their undernourished population. However, in the long run, higher agricultural income could help rural people to escape from poverty and to increase public and private investment. This is a summary of the history of the Common Agricultural Policy (CAP). Concerned with the elimination of food shortages after the Second World War, CAP supported agricultural prices and production, leading to overproduction and export subsidies with unfair competition toward developing countries.

China adopted raised taxes on exports and banned exports of maize and corn. For rice and soybeans, China utilized only taxes on exports to protect domestic consumers. In mid-November 2010, even before the drought began, the Chinese government imposed a wide range of price controls to contain inflation that could threaten its powerful economic growth. China is essentially self-sufficient in rice and other types of grain production for national security reasons, but it imports a large share of soybeans and wheat. Due to the drought, China increased its American wheat imports (from 31,900 metric tons in 2008 to 893,700 metric tons in 2009), a percentage equal only to 2% of the American economic output.

India banned exports for non-basmati rice, maize, and wheat. To promote imports in the domestic market, taxes on imports were reduced. These two instruments on trade (banned exports and reduced taxes on imports) were adopted by Bangladesh, Indonesia, and Pakistan. Cambodia introduced export bans, and the Philippines reduced taxes on imports.

Usually, production policies are aimed at relaunching agriculture. Among the production policies adopted as a consequence of the crisis were the control of domestic prices – to boost internal production – input subsidies, and the easing of cropland set-aside requirements targeted at promoting an expansion in production through an expansion of arable land (Table 6.9). These policies require relevant public resources, and the impact on domestic consumer prices is limited in the

Table 6.8 Trade measures

	Countries	Raised taxes on exports	Banned exports	Reduced (or eliminated) taxes on imports
Asian countries	Bangladesh	–	X (rice)	X
	Cambodia	–	X (rice)	–
	China	X (wheat, rice, maize, soybeans)	X (maize and wheat)	–
	India	–	X (non-basmati rice, maize, wheat)	X (wheat flour)
	Indonesia	–	X (rice)	X
	Malaysia	X (palm oil)	–	–
	Pakistan	–	X (wheat)	X
	Philippines	–	–	X
Other countries	Argentina	X (wheat, maize, soybeans and soybean products)	–	–
	Brazil	–	–	X (wheat, wheat flour and bread)
	Egypt	–	X (rice)	X
	Ethiopia	–		X (food grain and flour)
	Kazakhstan	X (wheat)		
	Kenya			X (bread)
	Madagascar, Nigeria			X (rice)
	Mali, Mexico, Morocco, Peru, Senegal, Islamic Republic of Iran, Congo			X
	Russian Federation	X (wheat and barley)		
	Serbia, Ukraine	–	X (wheat)	–
	Turkey	–	–	X (wheat and barley)

Source: Our elaborations on FAO data (2009a)

Table 6.9 Production measures

	Countries	Input subsidies	Expansion of cropland	Expansion of irrigation	Increasing floor price	Direct payments
Asian countries	Bangladesh	X	–	–	–	–
	China	X	–	–	X	X
	India		–	–	X	–
	Indonesia	X	–	–	–	–
	Malaysia	X	–	–	X	–
	Philippines	X	–	–	–	–
	Armenia	–	X	X	–	–
Other countries	Dominican Republic, Kazakhstan, Madagascar	X	–	–	–	–
	European Union	–	X	–	–	–

Source: Our elaborations on FAO data (2009a)

context of an open market. If not well managed, input subsidies may lead to an increase in input prices as demand for inputs increases, thus benefiting input industries more than agricultural producers.

The set-aside instrument, adopted by developed countries such as the EU members, may otherwise constrain the production response to higher prices. In the case of major exporters, such as the EU, it may also have a significant dampening effect on international prices.

Input subsidies were introduced by Bangladesh, China, Indonesia, Malaysia, and the Philippines. China made use of both higher floor prices and direct payments.

The policies to support consumers and vulnerable groups included direct consumer subsidies, tax reductions, distribution from public stocks, price consumption subsidies, public sector salary increases, and social safety net programs (Table 6.10). In Asia, one of the most popular instruments utilized was emergency food aid (Afghanistan, Bangladesh, Cambodia). Food for target groups (including students and workers) were adopted in Bangladesh, Cambodia, China, India, Mongolia, and the Philippines.

Self-targeting food-for-work programs were put in place by countries such as the Dominican Republic, Egypt, Ethiopia, Indonesia, Jordan, Lebanon, Mongolia, Morocco, the Philippines, and Saudi Arabia, which sold food at subsidized prices to targeted groups. A buffer stock scheme is an instrument for stabilizing price: commodities are bought and stored when there is a surplus and then sold from these stores when there are shortages. In a context of closed domestic markets, depending on buying and selling behavior, buffer stock policies may stabilize or destabilize domestic prices (Table 6.11). Food released from public stocks was utilized by China and India (that both, in the meantime, increased cereal stocks), while Indonesia and Pakistan also provided subsidies for staple food.

All these policies were adopted as short-term tools to fight soaring prices. These trade-related measures seriously distort international markets and act as a brake on the globalization of food markets. Due to a reduced supply, prices in the international markets increase with a strong impact on net importer countries.

The food crisis in 2008 changed some European polices in this area. In 2010, the European Commission announced its intention to sell its cereal stocks in order to stabilize the markets after a Russian grain export ban had hit world markets, sending wheat prices to 2-year highs and sparked worries of a crisis in global food supplies that could spark widespread protest. In the same year, the European Commission adopted two "communications." The first (CEC 2010a) was directed to improve the food distribution program for the most deprived persons in the EU. The objective of the second communication (CEC 2010b) was to create a common policy framework in the fight against world hunger and malnutrition with a specific priority for Africa and some parts of South Asia. In these areas, the EU would improve smallholder resilience and rural livelihoods (through efficient agricultural intensification, support for research demand, participation of civil society and farmer organizations, and improvement of the institutional conditions); support effective governance, regional agriculture, and food security policies; and provide specific assistance mechanisms for vulnerable population groups. As a consequence of the recent riots resulting from rising prices, the EU has reopened the debate on the future of CAP after 2013.

Table 6.10 Consumption measures

	Countries	Emergency food aid	Food sold at subsidized prices to targeted groups	Food programs for students	Food programs for workers
Asian countries	Afghanistan	X	–	–	–
	Bangladesh	X	–	–	X
	Cambodia	X	–	–	X
	China	–	–	X	–
	India	–	–	–	X
	Mongolia	–	X	–	–
	Philippines	–	X	–	–
Other countries	Angola	X	–		–
	Brazil, Burkina Faso, Cape Verde, Kenya, and Mexico	–	–	X	–
	Dominican Republic, Egypt, Morocco, Jordan, and Saudi Arabia	–	X	–	–
	Ethiopia	–	X	–	X
	Haiti, Liberia, Madagascar, Mozambique, and Peru	–	–	–	X

Source: Our elaborations on FAO data (2009a)

Table 6.11 Stock measures

	Countries	Food from public stock	Increased cereal stocks	Targeted and untargeted subsidies for staple foods
Asian countries	China	X	X	–
	India	X	X	–
	Indonesia	X	–	X
	Pakistan	X	–	X
	Philippines	–	X	–
Other countries	Cameroon, Ethiopia, and Senegal	X	–	X
	Saudi Arabia	–	X	–

Source: Our elaborations on FAO data (2009a)

Table 6.12 Food aid deliveries per typology (1,000 t) and share of total (%)

	Emergency		Program		Project		
	1,000/t	%	1,000/t	%	1,000/t	%	Total
1990	2,348	18.4	7,728	60.4	2,716	21.2	12,792
1995	3,505	36.1	3,993	41.2	2,200	22.7	9,699
2000	5,063	46.3	3,284	30.0	2,587	23.7	10,934
2005	4,988	62.9	1,123	14.2	1,822	23.0	7,933
2008	4,607	76.4	285	4.7	1,138	18.9	6,030
Total (1990–2008)	77,021	40.7	70,731	37.4	41,408	21.9	189,160
Var. % 1990/2008	49.0	–	–2,610.6	–	–138.7	–	–112.1

Source: World Food Program/INTERFAIS

6.5 Food Aid Policies

Food aid is a controversial issue and a point of disagreement within the agricultural trade negotiations under the World Trade Organization (WTO). The total food aid delivered has declined from 13,000 t in 1990 to 6,000 t in 2008 (Table 6.12). Food aid has various purposes. The so-called Food Aid Program is the sale in local markets of food grown in a donor country. The recipient country pays for the food with resources obtained at lower than market interest rates. In the Food Aid Project, food is provided as part of a specific project aimed at promoting agricultural or economic development or nutrition and food security. In the case of emergency food aid, food is delivered for emergency situations (e.g., war, natural disasters). As an act of humanitarian assistance, food is distributed for free.

In 1990, the Food Aid Program was the predominant form of food aid delivered, but in 2008, its weight became marginal (4.7% of the total food aid). Emergency food aid increased its share of the total food aid delivered between 1990 and 2008. It was composed mainly of cereals, with wheat accounting for 40.5% (Tables 6.13 and 6.14). Even though if it is generally distributed in difficult situations such as natural disasters and war, emergency food aid is a protection against chronic food insecurity. Its value doubled between 1990 and 2008, with its peak in 2003.

Table 6.13 Food aid per commodities (cereals/non-cereals), 1,000 t

	1990		1995		2000		2005		2008		Total	
	1,000/t	%	1,000/t	%	1,000/t	%	1,000/t	%	1,000/t	%	1,000/t	%
Non-cereals	1,150	9.0	1,334	13.8	1,538	14.1	1,177	14.8	892	14.8	24,567	13.0
Cereals	11,642	91.0	8,365	86.2	9,396	85.9	6,755	85.2	5,138	85.2	164,593	87.0
Total	12,792	100.0	9,699	100.0	10,934	100.0	7,933	100.0	6,030	100.0	189,160	100.0

Source: World Food Program/INTERFAIS

Table 6.14 Food aid: main cereals involved

	1990–2008	
	1,000 t	%
Hard red winter wheat	6,519	4.0
Maize	30,735	18.7
Rice	20,232	12.3
Sorghum	7,363	4.5
Wheat	66,666	40.5
Wheat flour	12,384	7.5
Totals	164,593	100.0

Source: World Food Program/INTERFAIS

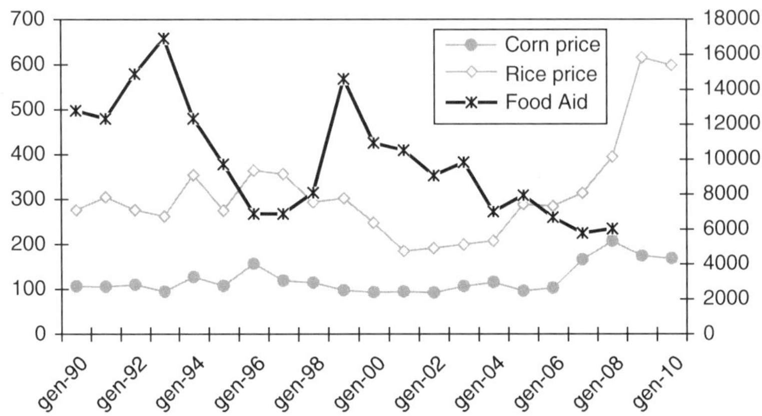

Fig. 6.4 International food aid flows (1,000 t, sx) compared to international cereal prices (USD/t, dx) (Source: Our elaboration on World Food Program/INTERFAIS and index mundi data)

Food aid policies are controversial as they are often used to support friendly or strategic countries or to reduce surpluses in some agricultural commodities and, last but not least, to promote and expand exports. They are often criticized because of their distortions on international trade, and on domestic production (Southgate et al. 2011), Bende, according to Barrett and Maxwell (2005), food aid is under the influence of specific crop lobbies, shipping industries, and NGOs. Under the World Food Program (WFP 2009), the top five donor governments in 2009 were the USA, Japan, the EC, Saudi Arabia, and Canada, respectively, and they accounted for 71% of food aid deliveries.

Figure 6.4 shows the relationship (if any) between cereal prices and international food aid flows. It can be noticed that food aid has not increased as a consequence of higher food prices and the resulting food crisis for the most vulnerable people. Even if in 2007–2008 rice, wheat, and corn prices increased dramatically, the international food aid and flows continued its downward curve.

6.6 Concluding Remarks

After years of price stability, in 2008 the prices of many staple foods experienced a dramatic surge and, then, a rapid decrease. Recently, world food prices hit a new record, driven by strong increases in the prices of wheat, corn, sugar, and oil. This event is the second price hike in less than 4 years. The public policies of developed, developing, and emerging countries are not neutral. In high-income countries, such as the EU, public subsidies acted as a disincentive in achieving an efficient global food system. If the current European efforts to reduce protectionism and its negative externalities are directed mainly by the recognition of agricultural products as public goods, it is also a fact that more attention is paid on energy issues notably on supply and cost for households. In fact, food crises are not among the main European critical problems. By contrast, in the developing and emerging countries, food crises are a major political concern. In Asia, people who are food insecure are largely dispersed in remote hidden areas. The greatest problems are located in South and Southwest Asia where 21 % of the population is undernourished. Due to the large share of income spent on food, the recent popular civil unrest and riots can be seen as a social response to high food prices. The state of emergency of the Arab world is, in fact, partly driven by the rise of food prices.

As far as higher prices are concerned, literature and international organizations (FAO 2009a, b; World Bank 2009, 2010b) are convinced that the impact on poor people and on developing countries is devastating: high prices are the source of economic and political instability. From an optimistic point of view, high agricultural prices provide additional income to farmers and, as a consequence, to the rural areas where about 75% of the world's poor are concentrated. However, higher agricultural prices affect and increase the number of poor consumers, and the gains for farmers could be less than expected. According to Ivanic and Martin (2008), bearing in mind that the poorest countries and/or persons are net consumers of food, the effects of soaring food prices on poverty, mainly for urban households, are totally negative. According to their calculations, even if farmers gain from higher food prices, on balance the total effect on poverty remains negative. Price volatility adds additional risks mainly for low-income and small farmers (prevailing in developing countries) who are not totally able to manage these fluctuations.

Faced with the crisis, countries adopted various short-term instruments. Generally, policies were delayed when the impact of the food crisis became evident. Policy makers utilized measures that increased volatility or that promoted price increases (such as biofuel policies, bans, or restrictions on exports). Food prices will certainly continue to show fluctuations (for noneconomic reasons such as manifestations of climate change, war, and breakdown of governance and economic reasons), but it is very hard to predict if and when volatility will increase or decrease. The main problems to solve are: What is the acceptable level of volatility, how to mitigate its negative effects, and which key figures have to be protected (producers or consumers)?

The rapid increase in the number of undernourished people, in spite of a supply higher than consumption, suggests that the current food system needs to be revised, bearing in mind long-term structural changes. The world population is growing (especially in China and India), but the growth is lower than in the past. Slower population growth will affect the future demand for commodities. Despite the economic crisis, some Asian emerging countries show strong increases in their GDP, in the presence of high incidences of hunger. In the meantime, t he growing standards of living in emerging countries with higher incomes and population shifts (from rural to urban) require different kinds of foods (from vegetarian diets to animal proteins) with competition in staple foods for land and water. Biofuels could expand crop demand: the energy market need is much stronger than the corn market. Some such policies have been expensive, exacerbate the rise of prices, and do not benefit those most in need. Productivity is growing only slowly, land availability is limited, and climate change effects pose other severe threats. This situation needs some comprehensive and coherent responses to be found at national and international levels, because food security is a human right.

At an international level, humanitarian assistance has to be boosted. Food aid could be reinforced (better if replaced with cash aid to buy local or regional production), but, to avoid the prevalence of national goals or lobbies (not linked to the interests of donor countries), it has to be reevaluated to see if specific targeted cash transfers could be better than food aid. The grain reserves have to be improved and bans and restrictions on exports need to be eliminated. Speculation needs to be regulated and policies promoting biofuel reassessed.

At a national level, some short-, medium-, and long-term measures could be planned (Economic and Social Commission for Asia and the Pacific (United Nations 2009)). The short-term measures have to promote access to food. People with low income have not sufficient access to food. To prevent food insecurity, governments have to boost the supply of food with social protection for agricultural production, insurance schemes, common management system (to prevent land deterioration), and productivity-related schemes. To promote physical access, specific measures on transport and logistics are needed. In the medium term, the conservation of natural resources is a key driver through revitalizing small-scale production of sustainable food, better water management, and external connections. In the long term, particular attention has to be placed on the adaptation to climate change.

References

Andreosso-O'Callaghan, B., & Zolin, M. B. (2010a). Land, biofuels and food security: Another 'impossible trinity theorem?'. In B. Andreosso-O'Callaghan & M. B. Zolin (Eds.), *Current issues in economic integration: Can Asia inspire the "West"?* Aldershot: Ashgate.

Andreosso-O'Callaghan, B., & Zolin, M. B. (2010b). Long-term cereal price changes: How important is the speculative element? *Transition Studies Review, 17*(4), 624–637.

Barrett, C., & Maxwell, D. (2005). *Towards a global food aid* (Compact Cornell University Applied Economics and Management, Working Paper). http://ssrn.com/abstract=715002. Last accessed on 7 May 2011.

Commission of the European Communities. (2010a). *Communication from the Commission to the Council and the European Parliament: An EU policy framework to assist developing countries in addressing food security challenges*. Brussels: European Commission.

Commission of the European Communities. (2010b). *Communication from the Commission to the Council and the European Parliament humanitarian food assistance*. Brussels: European Commission.

De Hoyos, R., & Lessem, R. (2008). *Food shares in consumption: New evidence using Engel curves for developing countries*. Washington, DC: World Bank.

Food and Agriculture Organization (1996, November 13–17). *Report of the world food summit*. http://www.fao.org/docrep/003/w3548e/w3548e00.htm. Last accessed on 26 Aug 2010.

Food and Agriculture Organization (FAO). (2002). *The state of food insecurity in the world*. Rome: FAO.

Food and Agriculture Organization (FAO). (2008). *The state of food insecurity in the world 2008: High food prices and food security: Threats and opportunity*. Rome: FAO.

Food and Agriculture Organization (FAO). (2009a). *The state of agricultural commodity market*. Rome: FAO.

Food and Agriculture Organization (FAO). (2009b). *Feeding the world: Eradicating hunger*. http://www.fao.org/fileadmin/templates/wsfs/Summit/WSFS_Issues_papers/WSFS_Background_paper_Feeding_the_world.pdf. Last accessed on 26 Aug 2010.

Food and Agriculture Organization (FAO). (2011). *Food price index*. http://www.fao.org/worldfoodsituation/FoodPricesIndex/en/. Last accessed on 19 Feb 2011.

Gilbert, C. (2010). How to understand high food prices. *Journal of Agricultural Economics, 61*, 398–425.

Government Office for Science. (2011). *The future of food and farming, final project report*. London: Government Office for Science.

Hardin, G. (1968). The tragedy of the commons. *Science, 68*(3854), 1243–1248.

International Food Policy Research Institute (IFPR). (2008a). *Rising food prices: What should be done?*. www.ifpri.org/pubs/bp/bp001.asp. Last accessed on 18 Aug 2010.

International Food Policy Research Institute (IFPR). (2008b). *Biofuels and grain prices: Impacts and policy responses*. http://www.ifpri.org/pubs/bp/bp001.asp. Last accessed on 18 Aug 2010.

International Food Policy Research Institute/Consultative Group on International Agricultural Research (IFPR/CGIAR). (2008). *High food prices: The what, who and how of proposal policy actions*. http://www.ifpri.org/PUBS/ib/foodprices.asp. Last accessed on 10 Aug 2010.

Ivanic, M., & Martin, W. (2008). *Implication of higher global food prices for poverty in low income countries* (Policy Research Working Paper 4594). The World Bank Development Research Group Trade Team.

Lucia, M., Andreosso-O'Callaghan, B., & Zolin, M. B. (2010, September). *Are volatility patterns changing in commodity prices?* In Proceedings of the 16th Euro–Asia International Research Seminar Corporate Social Responsibility: European and Asian Perspectives, Hiroshima, Japan.

Malthus, T. (2008). *An essay on the principle of population*. Oxford: Oxford University Press.

Mitchell, D. (2008). *A note on rising food prices* (Policy Research Working Paper No. 4682). Washington, DC: World Bank.

OECD–FAO (2009). *Agricultural outlook 2009–2018*. http://www.fao.org/es/esc/common/ecg/599/en/OECD_Highlights.pdf. Last accessed on 23 Aug 2010.

Oxfam. (2008). *The time is now: How world leaders should respond to the food price crisis*. http://www.oxfam.org/en/policy/the-time-is-now. Last accessed on 28 Aug 2010.

Southgate, D., Graham, D., & Tweeten, L. (2011). *The world food economy*. London: Wiley.

United Nations' Economic and Social Commission for Asia and the Pacific (ESCAP). (2009). *Sustainable agriculture and food security in Asia and the Pacific*. Bangkok: United Nations.

World Bank. (2009). *Global economic prospects: Commodities at the crossroads*. Washington, DC: World Bank.
World Bank. (2010a). *Food price watch. Poverty reduction and equity group*. http://siteresources.worldbank.org/INTPOVERTY/Resources/335642-1210859591030/Food_Price_Watch_May2010.pdf. Last accessed on 18 Aug 2010.
World Bank. (2010b). *Bank, donors take long-term view on food security*. http://go.worldbank.org/9STXO04330. Last accessed on 23 Aug 2010.
World Food Programm (WFP) (2009). *The international food aid system* (INTERFAIS). http://www.wfp.org/fais/. Last accessed on 21 Aug 2010.

Part II
Social Movements in a Transnational Perspective

Chapter 7
Marginalization and Transnationalizing Movements: How Does One Relate to the Other?

Pascale Dufour

From June 25 to 27, 2010, the "Mouvement des Sans Voix" (MSV) (literally, the movement of people without a voice) organized the third edition of the "Forum des Sans" (FS) (the social fora of the "withouts" or of the "have-nots") in Bamako, Mali. At the same time, world leaders were meeting in Toronto, Canada, for the G8/20 summit. The MSV was established in 2005 as an initiative of young activists from Mali, Burkina Faso, Ivory Coast, Togo, Benin, and Guinea. Its original name was Mouvement Alternative de la Jeunesse Africaine. Today, the movement is broader and is part of the No-Vox transnational network. The MSV defines itself as a movement of struggle and resistance in the defense of human rights.[1]

The FS is organized each year by the MSV. Its main aim is to discuss questions relating to marginalized and poor people and to propose alternatives to neoliberal economic policies. According to its website, "The FS is an anti-capitalist space whose aim is to create and consolidate national and supra-national links of struggles against capitalism, to develop and consolidate solidarities among peoples, sine qua non condition of emancipation."[2]

The 2010 FS was also a step toward the preparation of the World Social Forum (WSF) that took place in Dakar, Senegal, in February 2011. Without doubt, the MSV is very critical of the WSF process, and especially of some European organizations, and the MSV wished to make the world gathering in Dakar a "moment of

[1] No Vox, *Mouvement des Sans Voix*, http://afrikka.no-vox.org/spip.php?rubrique11. Last accessed on 10 June 2011.

[2] Primitivi, Mali: Forum des "sans" du 25 au 27 juin 2010 (author's translation). See http://www.primitivi.org/spip.php?article356. Last accessed on 10 June 2011.

P. Dufour (✉)
Département de science politique, Université de Montréal,
C.P 6128 – succ. Centre-ville, Montreal, QC H3C 3J7, Canada
e-mail: pascale.dufour@umontreal.ca

B. Andreosso-O'Callaghan and F. Royall (eds.), *Economic and Political Change in Asia and Europe: Social Movement Analyses*, DOI 10.1007/978-94-007-4653-4_7,

resistance of African peoples."[3] The FS could be described as a transnational event where marginalized people from diverse parts of the world gather to defend fundamental human rights, promote new rights, and discuss and exchange practices and analyses about the struggles against all forms of discrimination and domination. One of the particular targets of the FS is to promote and ensure participation of the "have-nots" (les sans) in international gatherings such as the WSF. This event is very interesting from the point of view of the transnationalization of collective action for at least three main reasons:

- Transnationalization is, in this case, different from internationalization because it does not depend on international institutions such as the United Nations, the World Bank, or the International Monetary Fund, but it is rather linked to the emergence and spread of another global social event, the WSF.
- This transnationalizing movement is driven by some of the world's most marginalized/underprivileged actors. These activists are quite different from the "rooted cosmopolitan" archetype described by Tarrow (2005): white young men, multilingual, graduate students or professional workers. On the contrary, activists from the FS are part of the "semi-invisible" described by Escobar (2008). They belong to countries (in Africa) that are not generally seen as being at the forefront of modern western history or even of social struggles, and they also represent underprivileged people in terms of the world-class struggles, as well as in terms of the world-racial struggles. Of course, it does not mean that these people are not educated or multilingual, but they are, unquestionably, coming from the South and are mostly young and black. These are not the usual characteristics of activists that we find in transnational social movements' literature.
- The FS is an ongoing transnationalization process; it is not just a big onetime event, with demonstrations or some other direct actions, but rather a process that began in 2005, and that is still alive today, testifying to its continuity.

Thus, starting from this empirical example, we would like to address a more theoretical concern in this chapter: How are the transnationalization and the marginalization processes related? As stressed in the introductory chapter of the book, we use the term marginalized people to refer to people's weak volume of political resources and subsequently to their dominated position in a certain domain of power relations (Mouchard 2010). From the literature on transnational social movements in general, we know that such processes are extremely costly, difficult to sustain, and largely ineffective in terms of direct outputs emanating from the struggles (Bandy and Smith 2005; McCarthy 1997: 245). The literature on the transnationalization of marginalized people's movements also discusses the fragility of the mobilizations of marginalized collective actors on the global scale (Giraud et al. 2005; Dufour 2009). In particular, the question of alliances with other social actors appears very

[3] Mouvement des sans Voix, *Le FSM 2011 ou la grande exhibition des réseaux*, http://www.mouvementdessansvoix.com/spip.php?article49. Last accessed on 10 June 2011.

problematic (Hmed 2007). In this context, questions arise regarding how (and why) powerless people initiate processes of transnationalization? How and why they participate in processes of transnationalization and, furthermore, why they continue to do so? Even if they are critics of the overall process, as we have mentioned is the case of the MSV for the World Social Forum, why do they choose to invest energy in these kinds of networks and events?

The main theoretical argument of the chapter is that in order to understand more accurately how marginalized people's movements and transnationalization processes are embedded, we need to open our understanding of transnationalization processes to see what the actors do when they build transnationalizing movements. In order to analyze experiences such as the FS, we propose first to consider transnationalization as a social practice of solidarities building, and second, as practices of "translation."

In the first part of the chapter, we briefly go back to the sparse literature that has examined both social movements' transnationalization and marginalized people to see what kind of explanations they have developed. In the second part, we suggest that, to reach a more comprehensive view of the phenomenon, we should also take into account two elements that have been neglected: the question of transnationalization as a solidarities-building process led by a search for recognition beyond borders, what De Sousa Santos (2005) called the work of "translation."

7.1 Studying Transnational Social Movements from Marginalized People's Point of View

Donatella della Porta and Sidney Tarrow (2005: 7) refer to transnational collective action as "the coordinated international campaigns on the part of networks of activists against international actors, other states, or international institutions." This generally accepted definition has two implications. First, it implies that the transnational aspect of collective action is defined by the presence of activists or groups belonging to more than one nation-state (the focus is therefore on the "international" or the "multinational" character of the coalitions). Second, the implication is that the target of the actions is also "international" or "multinational," and that it must possess institutional features (governmental or nongovernmental).

As we have shown elsewhere (Dufour 2009), studies that deal with the question of marginalized collective actors and that of transnational social movements can be divided into two parts. In one category of such studies, the transnationalization of marginalized collective actors could be analyzed with the same tools and theories developed for other social movements. For example, several European studies show how movements use changes in European institutions and dynamics to create new places of protest, at the European level, for their national groups or coalitions. The case of the immigration issue is a good illustration of this process (see Geddes 2000; Danese 1998; Monforte 2010). In most of these studies, transnationalization is seen as a scale shift: movements invest in another institutional level, which is transnational in the case of the European Union (or international if the analysis concerns the way movements invest in the United Nations). In particular, these studies have employed the classic boomerang effect and spiral model (Sikking 2005: 171) to explain the collective action of the unemployed in France vis-à-vis European institutions and the organization of activists from various European countries into networks. The boomerang effect and spiral model describe a series of actions that occur when activists – who are operating within a domestic opportunity structure that is generally closed, owing to repression or exclusion from the national system of representation – search for international allies from more open international political opportunity structures in order to exert a pressure on their national government "from above." The mobilizations of the unemployed in the late 1990s and the emergence of the European marches against unemployment follow this logic, at least in part (Chabanet 2002). Chabanet (2002) has demonstrated how the mobilizations against unemployment that targeted the European Union (EU) were archetypical of the externalization process described by Imig and Tarrow (2001); the EU offered an additional level of opportunity, a sounding box, compelling national states to respond to demands made at the European level.

In these studies, transnationalization of marginalized people movements is a question of collective actors' instrumental interests; transnationalization is seen by activists (and mostly leaders of movements) as a tool, a strategy, efficient to reach some external (usually national) gains, valid for the group itself. In that sense, the finality of transnationalization is outside the process of transnationalizing itself. Some groups decide to "go transnational" as they could decide to build upon or to deepen some local alliances. The answer as to how they do that is related to specific sociological mechanisms and political dynamics, as is the case for other social movements strategies.

In another category of studies on marginalized collective actors and transnational social movements, the focus is more on the effect that these new, and transnational, spaces of protest have on marginalized collective actors. For example, in the case of the so-called *alter*-globalist movement[4]:

> By joining the new anti-globalisation movement, these organisations sought to assert their legitimacy to represent the victims of neoliberal globalisation in France (…). For organisations defending marginalized people who struggled to be heard within traditional social mobilisations, the concept of anti-globalizations allowed them to take part in a potentially large-scale movement. (Desbos 2010: 230)

In this context, marginalization and transnationalization are mainly related by the spread of a Global Social Justice movement. Struggles against neoliberal capitalism have offered a radical critique of neoliberal political actions, and thus, have suggested a common frame for all collective marginalized actors. For example, in the case of Droit au logement (DAL), one of the main networks defending the right to housing for all in France, the links with the alter-globalization movement are

[4] The term "alter" is a French expression that has come to replace "anti" with respect to the globalization processes. It implies that activists are not against globalization as such but rather that they wish to promote another, noncapitalist, vision of the world.

presented as being there from the beginning of the Justice Movement from the end of the 1990s. "The emergence of DAL is characteristic of a new type of engagement, independent from traditional political parties. DAL developed a solidarity network with other organisations involved in the defence of the 'sans'" (Desbos 2010: 221). This enlargement is directly linked, by the author, to the building of the so-called alter-globalist discourse. DAL was a founding partner of ATTAC (Association for the Taxation of Financial Transactions and Aid to Citizens), one of the main alter-globalization organizations in France, and as such, it was directly concerned with the question of transnationalization from the beginning, even if the relationships between the two networks are not always easy. In that view, the dynamism of marginalized people's movements in the 1990s and 2000s is embedded in the emergence of the Global Justice Movement and the love-hate relationship that marginalized people's movements developed with it. The multiple tensions that exist between the two are seen as concrete sources of development.

Here, the answer as to why marginalized people's movements participate in transnational social movements is more a question of contingency and contextual history; how transnationalization occurs explains why it happens. Transnationalization could be chosen as a strategy by leaders' movements, but this strategy exists (or could be chosen at the time considered) because of historical contingencies and not only because of actors' interests. In this chapter, we propose another kind of answer, complementary to the two that have already been proposed in the literature. Instead of searching for interests (what are marginalized collective actors' interests in transnationalization strategy?), we explore transnationalization as a social practice. How do marginalized collective actors become transnationalized? What is the "daily activist work" that is required for transnationalization to occur and to continue? In the following section, we propose a theoretical answer, one that could lead empirical research on transnational movements and networks of marginalized people.

7.2 Transnationalization and Social forums for Marginalized People: A Process of Solidarities Building and a Work of Translation

As reported by Dufour et al. (2010), Dennis Young identified as early as 1992 major obstacles to the building of cross-border coalitions: political, cultural, and linguistic diversity, which jeopardizes the very notion of coalition as it makes agreeing on common interests arduous; the physical distance separating activists, who then require significant resources in terms of travel; economic barriers to the movement of people, goods, and information that restrict opportunities to form coalitions; and the specificities of local political contexts that determine, in part, the opportunities for local groups to act at a global level (Young 1992).

In the case we are exploring, marginalized people's movements, we could add to this list all the barriers and obstacles usually mentioned in the literature (lack of nonmaterial resources such as know-how, lack of social integration, etc.).

It is improbable that the constraints that exist for these movements locally or nationally vanish at the global scale. On the contrary, we could expect these constraints to play a major role in the transnationalizing process. If we pursue our line of inquiry, when a transnational movement continues through time, it means that marginalized people have succeeded in dealing with all these obstacles (several kinds of diversity, physical distance, economic barriers, and local political contexts). In the following text, we argue that these elements are not only obstacles but also tools upon which transnational social movements could be built. We focus on two of them: solidarities and diversities.

7.2.1 Building and Deepening Solidarities

According to the open letter, the MSV published in November 2010, the WSF in Dakar (February 2011) was to be an important step in the struggle against the capitalist system. MSV members went to Dakar because they wanted to turn the event:

> into a moment of resistance and permanent struggle of peoples from Africa, until the victory of the human being over capital. We go there to discuss together the long-term struggles, strategies and alternative perspectives to globalization. Brothers and sisters "without voices" from Africa and elsewhere, you count more than a vast army of women and men imported to Dakar by the power of networks. We should not forget the ferocity of anti-capitalist activists for a worthy and prosperous Africa. (author's translation)[5]

As Teune (2010: 3) indicated, transnational exchange is not a natural thing. Social movements' transnationalizing is always the result of a convergence, beyond national borders, of actors' differing interests and identities. If some basic sense of shared meaning is necessary to initiate transnationalization[6] or at least a basic sense of collectivity, the work of convergence implies continuous exchanges among activists, discussions, negotiations, and mutual learnings. Convergence building is thus a process in which not only solidarities among activists are created and traveled but also deepened (Devin 2004).

In other words, "the building of solidarities by actors involved in transnationalization processes goes hand in hand with the decisions made, strategies formulated, and specific mechanisms established within their respective organizations, movements or networks" (Dufour et al. 2010: 4). Activists build stronger ties among themselves in the course of their mobilizations and actions. More or less conflictual, this process

[5] Mouvement des sans Voix, *Le FSM 2011 ou la grande exhibition des réseaux*, http://www.mouvementdessansvoix.com/spip.php?article49. Last accessed on 12 June 2011.

[6] As Storm and Häse argue in their chapters in this book, the typical Western notion of collective action quite generally implies that the establishment of movement starts with (unproblematic individual) shared intentions. The Chinese notion of *guanxi* means that the decision to engage in connections with others (in a group or a movement) could also be the result of collective concerns that exist before the formation of the group (because of common past trajectories, rituality, or fixed roles).

promotes shared understandings of problems and analyses and sometimes even solutions. For example, building solidarities in the context of an alter-globalization movement translates for activists into a deepening of their shared understanding of injustice at specific moments (mass demonstrations and social fora). As Agrikoliansky et al. underlined (2005: 40), "protest events are privileged moments where injustice frames are drawn that structure the critique of globalization" (author's translation). In this sense, social fora offer a very specific context for transnational solidarities building: during 2 or 3 days, activists gather in one place and participate in workshops, conferences, discussions, debates, thoughts, exchanges, etc. Social fora are "spaces that produce solidarities" (Mésini 2009: 196) in the very nature of what they are.

Building and deepening solidarities among networks' activists means also that people will transform their perception of commonality between themselves. This is not only a question of frame connections or of necessity to find an umbrella sufficiently loose and encompassing to connect the multitude of struggles – such as the master frame for the Global Justice Movement: anti-neoliberalism (della Porta et al. 2006; Jossin 2010) – it is also a question of transnational collective identity. How could it work?

7.2.2 The Work of Translation

As Teune (2010) stresses, social movement theorists should evade a "paternalist conception of commonality" and look carefully at a "frame alignment process" (Snow et al. 1986) that occurred in transnational coalitions. Building commonality is not only a question of language (finding the words that will suit all participants) but also experiences and cognitive concepts. It is far too short to explain alignment of frames with instrumental strategies to reach certain (often seen as nonproblematic) goals on the basis of a common rationality (Smith 2002). More and more, research explores dimensions linked with the "cross-national traffic of ideas and practices," using concepts such as diffusion, translation, reception, learning (Roggeband 2007: 247). As we have seen, in the case of transnationalizing solidarities, the requirement is very high: not only do ideas and practices need to travel "well," but some commonality has to be built and deepened through time (Mohanty 2003).

In the case of social fora experiences, De Sousa Santos has identified the work of "translation" as one of the main concrete practices that sustained the process as well as one of the main challenges to face in the near future. For De Sousa Santos:

> Translation is the procedure that allows for mutual intelligibility among the experiences of the world, both available and possible, as revealed by the sociology of absences and the sociology of emergences, without jeopardizing their identity and autonomy, and without, in other words, reducing them to homogeneous entities. (De Sousa Santos 2005: 16)

In a context of multinational belongings, some concrete questions are asked in relation to: multilanguages situations, cultural misunderstandings, diversity of social struggles practices and objectives, diverging priorities, multiplicity of local constraints. For a network to manage and overcome these difficulties, translation is necessary:

> The work of translation is a work of epistemological and democratic imagination, aiming to construct new and plural conceptions of social emancipation upon the ruins of the automatic social emancipation of the modernist project. (De Sousa Santos 2005: 21)

In this specific process, "diversity is celebrated, not as a factor of fragmentation and isolationism, but rather as a condition of sharing and solidarity" (De Sousa Santos 2005: 17). We propose, as a working hypothesis, that in the case of the FS, translation, as a social practice, is at work. The FS creates a specific moment and place where such a practice is possible. We can also go further and say that if the FS continues through times, it is at least partially because this work of translation is done.

The cultural translation we are speaking of involves several steps (these steps are not linear, they overlap, but for the clarity of discussion we present them successively). The first step is the communication and expression of activists' voices. Here, the problem of languages is central as Doerr (2009) has shown. Who is able to speak, how and when? What are the consequences of direct translation by nonprofessionals on the deliberative process? Is the moment of communication inclusive or not? The second step relates to exchanges, discussions, sharing, and mutual understanding. In the case of marginalized people, it could be the time when they realize their common position of domination in their respective societies but also their fragile position in the Global Justice Movement. The third step implies a process of reappropriation of personal and collective histories and recognition of the personal and collective histories of others. As De Sousa Santos underlines (as well as Barthes 1970, and Sandoval 2000), this step is crucial: the work of translation would not be fair and complete if recognition of the histories of others (as singular as well as collective histories) is not there. Without recognition, there is no cultural translation, only a colonial process. To belong to a movement (marginalized or not) means that activists are seen by others as sharing some elements of a collective identity.

For example, to belong to women's movements means to be *recognized* as a woman by other members of the movements and by public opinion. It is also a way to be able to give some content to what it is to be a woman, which is a way to reaffirm a women's own identity. In that sense, being part of a movement is a double process in terms of recognition: a way to make his or her own individuality recognized by others (in the networks, groups, and at large) and a way to create something collective on the very content of this individuality.

In the case of marginalized people participating in social fora, this question of recognition is crucial. If they are not recognized by other social movements, they will not exist in the social forum space as marginalized people and the problem they carry with them, their claims, will not be heard and not even expressed. So, one of the first aims they put forward when they participate in social fora is to be there to be recognized as a "legitimate collective actor" that can best express the social suffering of part of the world population.[7] Recognition, in this perspective, is the process by

[7] No Vox, http://www.no-vox.org/. Last accessed on 12 June 2011.

which "epistemic injustice" is repaired: "the injustice of having some significant area of one's social experience obscured from collective understanding owing to persistent and wide-ranging hermeneutical marginalization" (Fricker 2006: 99). As Lazzeri suggests, a fight for recognition is thus a way to overcome the material conditions as the symbolic depreciation an individual or a group leave with (Lazzeri 2009: 344). In the FS, activists accept that they are at the margins of their own society. The fact to be together, as part of the FS (and the MSV) is a way to recognize others as peers and to be recognized by others as such.

The results of a successful work of translation are thus mutual learning, the empowerment of the people involved and the emancipation of the (collective and individual) subject. In the "work of translation," collective and individual positions of domination are put in context: if one is able to understand the dynamics of relationships others (who are peers) live in, he/she will also be able to better understand the social mechanism (especially domination and resistance), in which he/she lives and which defines the shared conditions of marginalized people. By naming what activists of the FS have in common, participants are also in a process of emancipation: they learn how to speak for themselves (rather than "speak by others" as Bourdieu (1982) said), and they create some space of autonomy to exist by themselves in the context of the alter-globalization field of protest. At the same time, they recognize and identify the similarities of their conditions and positions in their respective societies and are able to recognize and identify the multiplicity of their situations with all their differences. A successful translation, in this perspective, would be a process in which the existence of the transnational collective is reinforced and at the same time in which all individual, as well as groups differences, could be expressed (and recognized).

Of course, the question of recognition is not new in the literature of social movement studies (see Polletta 2008). However, the context of social fora is. Therefore, is it possible to build sustained solidarities in a context of multinational belonging? And how is it possible to go beyond national borders in the content of the solidarities and claims that were built? As the literature has shown, transnational social movements and networks face specific difficulties and barriers that are even more salient in the case of marginalized collective actors. The concrete gains they can make in transnationalizing, independently of the success or the failure of the movement as a whole, are directly linked with this work of translation.

7.3 Conclusion

If we go back to the beginning of the chapter, we have some hypothetical answers to the three intriguing dimensions we highlighted in our case study. Of course, these hypotheses will need empirical validation, which was not the aim of the chapter. We first underlined the fact that the FS is not a "classical" case of transnationalization. The process that creates the network is not a shift of scale of actions where activists "go international." We suggest that it could be a building solidarities process among peer activists from Africa and other parts of the world. The proclaimed finality of the network – to fight the neoliberal agenda – is probably not the whole story. Building solidarities beyond borders allows marginalized collective actors to exist at the global scale, as a social movement among other recognized and legitimate social movements. In other words, it could be strategically important for them simply to continue "to be there."

Second, "classic" rooted cosmopolitans do not drive this global network; activists are mainly part of the "semi-invisible" class of the world. This characteristic is probably particularly crucial for the question of recognition. Activists from the FS are at the margins of their respective societies and also of the "world systems," and their place inside the alter-globalization field of protest is very fragile. If they want to exist – and to be recognized – as such, if they want to have a voice, they probably need to pursue solidarities-building processes beyond national borders.

Third, we mentioned the question of the continuity of the network. If we agree that participation in a movement or a network such as FS and MSV is a way to reaffirm its belonging to a certain community or collective, we understand much better why people, even if they lack resources, opportunities, and even concrete results of their actions, continue to mobilize transnationally. They do so also to "ensure the conditions of reproduction of their circle of recognition, to ensure the continuity of their identity, so to ensure or to overcome the uncertainty that could change this circle, make it weaker or disappear" (Lazzeri 2009: 151, author's translation).

We argue that the concrete practice that allows activists to build and deepen transnational solidarities is translation. With the "work of translation," activists mutually recognize and understand themselves, as the same and different at the same time (what De Sousa Santos called mutual intelligibility). They develop the tools that could be used for their collective and individual emancipation. The "work of translation" is not the monopoly of marginalized people movements; it concerns all movements and networks which develop and sustain transnational ties. Nevertheless, because of their specific position, in their respective society, the "output" of this work is extremely important for them. It creates the very possibility of their individual and collective existence, for themselves as well as for the movements of others.

References

Agrikoliansky, É., Fillieule, O., & Meyer, N. (2005). *L'altermondialisme en France: La longue histoire d'une nouvelle cause*. Paris: Flammarion.

Bandy, J., & Smith, J. (2005). *Coalitions across borders: Transnational protest and the neoliberal order*. Oxford: Rowman & Littlefield.

Barthes, R. (1970). *Mythologies*. Paris: Le Seuil.

Bourdieu, P. (1982). *Ce que parler veut dire*. Paris: Fayard.

Chabanet, D. (2002). Les marches européens contre le chômage, la précarité et les exclusions. In R. Blame, D. Chabanet, & V. Wright (Eds.), *L'Action collective en Europe*. Paris: Presses de Sciences Po.

Danese, G. (1998). Transnational collective action in Europe: The case of migrants in Italy and Spain. *Journal of Ethnic and Migration Studies, 24*(4), 715–733.

De Sousa Santos, B. (2005). The future of the world social forum: The work of translation. *Development, 48*(2), 15–22.
della Porta, D., & Tarrow, S. (2005). Transnational processes and social activism: An introduction. In D. della Porta & S. Tarrow (Eds.), *Transnational protest and global activism*. Boulder: Rowman & Littlefield.
della Porta, D., Andretta, M., Mosca, L., & Reiter, H. (2006). *Globalization from below: Transnational activists and protest networks*. Minneapolis: University of Minnesota Press.
Desbos, C. (2010). Limits on the integration of the "sans" within the anti-globalisation movement: The case of Droit au Logement in ATTAC France (1998–2008). In D. Chabanet & F. Royall (Eds.), *Mobilising against marginalisation in Europe*. Newcastle: Cambridge Scholars.
Devin, G. (Ed.). (2004). *Les solidarités transnationales*. Paris: L'Harmattan.
Dufour, P. (2009). Globalization and the collective action of the socially excluded in France: At the heart of the margins? *French Politics, 7*(3–4), 316–341.
Dufour, P., Masson, D., & Caouette, D. (2010). *Transnationalizing women's movements: Solidarities beyond borders*. Vancouver: University of British Columbia Press.
Doerr, N. (2009). Language and Democracy 'in Movement': Multilingualism and the Case of the European Social Forum Process. *Social Movement Studies, 8*(2), 149–165.
Escobar, A. (2008). *Territories of difference: Place, movements, life, redes*. Durham: Duke University Press.
Fricker, M. (2006). Powerlessness and social interpretation. *Episteme: A Journal of Social Epistemology, 3*(1), 96–108.
Geddes, A. (2000). *Immigration and european integration: Towards fortress europe?* Manchester: Manchester University Press.
Giraud, B., Garcia, G., Mouchard, D., & Yon, K. (2005). La question sociale au Forum social. In É. Agrikoliansky & I. Sommier (Eds.), *Radiographie du mouvement altermondialiste: Le second Forum social européen*. Paris: La Dispute.
Hmed, C. (2007). Aux marges de l'altermondialisme: la représentation des classes populaires issues de l'immigration au deuxième forum social européen. In S. Cadiou, S. Dechezelles, & A. Roger (Eds.), *Passer à l'action: Les mobilisations émergentes*. Paris: L'Harmattan.
Imig, D., & Tarrow, S. (2001). *Contentious Europeans: Protest and politics in an emerging polity*. Lanham: Rowman & Littlefield.
Jossin, A. (2010). How do activists experience transnational protest events? The case of young global justice activists from Germany and France. In S. Teune (Ed.), *The transnational condition: Protest dynamics in an entangled Europe*. London: Berghahn Books.
Lazzeri, C. (2009). Conflits de reconnaissance et mobilisation collective. *Politique et Sociétés, 28*(3), 117–160.
McCarthy, J. (1997). The globalization of social movement theory. In J. Smith, C. Chatfield, & R. Pagnucco (Eds.), *Transnational social movements and global politics: Solidarity beyond the state*. New York: Syracuse University Press.
Mésini, B. (2009). Les Sans dans les forums sociaux. Luttes aux confins et lignes de confrontation. *Politique et Sociétés, 28*(1), 193–228.
Mohanty, C. T. (2003). *Feminism without borders: Decolonizing theory, practicing solidarity*. Durham: Duke University Press.
Monforte, P. (2010). Le secteur associatif face aux politiques européennes d'immigration et d'asile: Quels acteurs pour quels modes d'européanisation? *Politique européenne, 31*(2), 119–145.
Mouchard, D. (2010). Les mouvements sociaux, laboratoires de la démocratie. *La Vie des Idées*. http://www.laviedesidees.fr/Les-mouvements-sociaux.html. Last accessed on 24 Nov 2010.
Polletta, F. (2008). Culture and movements. *The Annals of the American Academy of Political and Social Science, 619*, 78–95.
Roggeband, C. (2007). Translators and transformers: International inspirations and exchange in social movements. *Social Movement Studies, 6*(3), 245–259.
Sandoval, C. (2000). *Methodology of the oppressed*. Minneapolis: University of Minnesota Press.

Sikking, K. (2005). Patterns of dynamic multilevel governance and the insider-outsider coalition. In D. della Porta, & S. Tarrow (Eds), *Transnational protest and global activism* (pp. 151–173). New York: Rowman and Littlefield.
Smith, J. (2002). Bridging global divides? Strategic framing and solidarity in transnational social movement organisations. *International Sociology, 17*(4), 505–528.
Snow, D., Rochford, B., Worden, S., & Benford, R. (1986). Frame alignment processes, micromobilizations and movement participation. *American Sociological Review, 51*(4), 464–481.
Tarrow, S. (2005). *The new transnational activism*. Cambridge: Cambridge University Press.
Teune, S. (2010). The transnational condition: An introduction. In S. Teune (Ed.), *The transnational condition: Protest dynamics in an entangled Europe*. London: Berghahn Books.
Young, D. (1992). Organising principles for international advocacy associations. *Voluntas, 3*(1), 1–28.

Chapter 8
Transnational Collective Action and the European Network of the Unemployed

Frédéric Royall

8.1 Introduction

Most scholars accept that when people from different countries come together to promote a cause they want to give voice to interests that find it hard to be heard in the day-to-day business of politics. A number of scholars have looked at many such types of transnational activities, but I would like to look at another – maybe less discussed – facet of this type of activity which has been described as "Europeanization from below" (della Porta and Caiani 2007). I wish to analyze the challenges of transnational collective action and the trials and tribulations of people and organizations who initiate such activities. My discussion is based on a review of developments of the European Network of the Unemployed (ENU) between the mid-1980s and the late 1990s.[1] The first section provides a brief overview of the literature on transnational collective action. The second section looks at issues related to the development of the ENU, and the third reflects on the impact of transnational collective action on the network.

8.2 Brief Overview of Research on Transnational Collective Action

Much of the literature on social movements has, as a starting point, what is perceived to be the symbiotic relations between nation states and such movements. Following Charles Tilly (1986) and Sidney Tarrow (1994/1998), many scholars argue that

[1] Fieldwork for this chapter was essentially carried out between 1993 and 2005. I interviewed and corresponded with a number of leading members of ENU and of its affiliates. I also examined the organizations' documents, circulated questionnaires, and used ethnographic observation.

F. Royall (✉)
School of LLCC, University of Limerick, Limerick, Ireland
e-mail: Frederic.royall@ul.ie

B. Andreosso-O'Callaghan and F. Royall (eds.), *Economic and Political Change in Asia and Europe: Social Movement Analyses*, DOI 10.1007/978-94-007-4653-4_8,

challengers face many obstacles when putting forward their claims because states exert a strong influence on available resources and opportunities. But today, in Europe at least, states seem to be losing their hold as primary repositories of power, and the dominant interests that are traditionally associated with them are equally in disarray (Marks and McAdam 1996).[2] New centers of conflict have emerged outside the states' control, and there is some evidence of lobbying and some protest directed at European institutions (Balme and Chabanet 2008).[3] Transnational collective action may also be becoming more common because people often look abroad to see what they have in common with others who are facing the very same types of social or economic problems or who must overcome the very same obstacles to collective action as they do.[4] Transnational collective action can take many forms. It can happen when people – or other non-state actors – diffuse ideas and practices across borders. It can occur in the case of domestication, that is, when contentious activities relate to external issues but whose actors – and the institutions they target – are local, regional, or national. It can happen in the case of externalization, that is, when people bypass national obstacles and call upon international institutions to intervene and to resolve domestic problems or conflicts. Finally, it can take place when actors cross national borders and target international institutions. In these cases, actors most often lobby the international institutions, but they sometimes also protest against them (Tarrow 1995).

Transnational collective action is not a new phenomenon – the nineteenth-century international struggle against the slave trade is a case in point – but it is perhaps far easier today for people living in different countries to contact each other simply because of the vastly improved telecommunication systems, cheap air travel, English as the international language, etc. The ease of international communication and travel in particular has helped people to compare their experiences and objectives; to see how to overcome organizational, financial, political, or cultural obstacles; and to learn how others avail of resources and opportunities for mobilization (Giugni 1998).[5]

---

[2] For a discussion of related points, see Sidney Tarrow (2001).

[3] Scholars disagree as to whether European integration has led to an increase in protest notably among the most disadvantaged/marginalized people. Studies are inconclusive. For example, Ewe Reising (1999) argues that there has been a moderate rise in protests in only some European countries. Dieter Rucht (2002) is not convinced. He feels that in the case of Germany, the Europeanization and even the globalization of protests is a myth. He underlines how difficult organizations find it to agree about what to protest against and to know if protests move from national frameworks to a European level. Other scholars doubt that social actors abandon so freely the political opportunity structures that had been so successful and move on to protest at a European level. Gary Marks and Doug McAdam (1999) in particular suggest that once nonprofessional categories establish themselves in Brussels, they try to benefit from the opportunities offered by the European Union and to lobby rather than engage in street-level protests.

[4] Donatella della Porta and Sidney Tarrow (2005: 2–3) define transnational collective action as "coordinated international campaigns on the part of networks of activists against international actors, other states, or international institutions."

[5] See Johanna Siméant (2010) for a broad discussion of issues related to research on transnational collective action.

In terms of research on the issue, transnational social movements (TSMs) have attracted a good bit of attention over the past two decades or so (Imig and Tarrow 2001; Tarrow 2000), as have the TSM organizations that are "a subset [...] operating in more than two states" (Smith et al. 1997: 43). The non-state actors that have attracted the most attention have been nongovernmental organizations (NGOs). Some authors have viewed NGOs to be specific examples of TSMs. For them, NGOs helped to promote themes of universal, consensual, and non-contentious import such as humanitarian issues, sustainable development, or third-world aid. However, NGOs are not usually considered to be social movements as such following Sidney Tarrow's (1994/1998) generally accepted definition.[6] Another problem is that TSMs were often defined so broadly that far too many types of NGOs were included as TSMs.

In an attempt to deal with some of the difficulties of this approach, a second wave of research focused on transnational advocacy/activist networks (TANs) following Margaret Keck and Kathryn Sikkink's (1998) pioneering study. TANs are "those relevant actors working internationally on an issue who were bound together by shared values, a common discourse, and dense exchanges of information and services [the main objective of which is to] change the behavior of state or of international organizations" (Ibid.: 2). Keck and Sikkink also encouraged scholars to look at less contentious forms of mobilizations and to move away from analyses of nationally based mobilizations. Although TANs' research did open interesting lines of inquiry, it is neither clear if all organizations involved with TANs are themselves transnational nor if a number of TANs that are active at an international level have national bases of support. Another problem is that it is unclear how they relate to state systems or to domestic social actors.

With the rise in contentious activities focusing on opposition to global governance and globalization since the early 2000s, much of the recent research on transnational collective action has increasingly dealt with global activism or global justice movements (GJMs) (della Porta 2006; Reitan 2007). GJM activists promote transnational solidarity and campaign on issues such as world poverty or mass unemployment. Research on GJMs has contributed to the revisions of the generalizations at the heart of studies which consider that ONGs and TANs are models for transnational collective action. A difficulty with the GJMs' approach is its western ethnocentric and prescriptive, transnational mobilization bias.

All of these areas of research opened up interesting perspectives and increased our understanding of the rise in the international relations of a range of non-state agents in recent years – including those of the unemployed – even if contentious politics continue to be framed by domestic opportunities and constraints.[7] The difficulty

[6] Social movements are "collective challenges by people with common purposes and solidarity in sustained interaction with elites, opponents and authorities" (Tarrow 1994/1998: 2–3).

[7] A number of scholars have looked at pro-unemployed protests across space and time (Giugni 2009; Reiss and Perry 2011). Summarizing recent international research on the subject, Donatella della Porta (2008) underlines a number of key findings: protests on unemployment in Europe are no more uncommon than other types of protest events by civil society actors; the unemployed

as I see it is that even though it is interesting to know if, how, and why there is a rise in the international relations of non-state actors, what is perhaps just as important is to assess the local, regional, and/or national contexts that bring about contentious activities and/or the ways that the increase in international relations affects the organizations or the people that take part in them (Chabanet and Giugni 2010: 158–161).[8] In other words, in today's world of mass communication and ease of travel, it should come as no surprise that people contact each other across borders. But what is perhaps more interesting is to investigate the various and perhaps commonplace – personal and/or organizational – reasons that people do so and the consequences of such.

With regard to the jobless, some key questions may be: What are the local social, economic, or political circumstances that push Portuguese pro-jobless organizations or people to come into contact with their Belgian counterparts? Why do they want to exchange their experiences and how do they go about doing so? How do these people actually work together across borders? How are the day-to-day tasks carried out within their transnational networks? How are decisions taken? How are collective identities forged since these people come from very different cultural, linguistic, and political backgrounds? What effects does international cooperation have on the participating organizations and/or members? In short, why do pro-unemployed organizations and people become involved in transnational cooperation/relations? But perhaps more importantly for my purposes, what is the impact of such involvement on them – their goals, their attitudes, their disappointments, and the unexpected consequences? The following analysis of the transnational experiences of the ENU is a modest attempt to address some of these issues.

8.3 The ENU as a Case Study

8.3.1 Background

The ENU was originally known as the First West European Network of Unemployed People (FWENU). Its founders first met in 1982 at a conference organized by the European Contact Group on Church and Industry (ECGCI) and met again at a conference in Brussels in 1984 where and when the FWENU was established. During the fifth FWENU annual conference in 1988 in Hanover (Germany), delegates voted to restructure the network and to draw up statutes, thus leading to the official launching of the ENU by the ECGCI in 1989 in Dublin (Ireland) during the sixth

depend on key allies such as trade unions or left-wing organizations; there are major differences between countries in terms of the intensity of the protests, the strategies used, and the actors that participate possibly because of the diverse political traditions and opportunities across the countries; and pro-unemployed protests are the most disruptive at local levels whereas protests at an international level are rare.

[8] Some scholars have looked at some of the cultural, political, and personal impact of social movements on their external environments (Kriesi et al. 1995). Marco Giugni (1998) has also highlighted the conceptual or methodological difficulties of research in this area.

annual conference. The ENU had five members in 1984, rising to eight by 1989. Over the years, a number of affiliates and associate observers joined and others left. By the time of the ENU's "demise" in the early 2000s, affiliate membership had risen to 13 and there were a number of associate observers.[9]

The ENU was only one of several pro-unemployed transnational networks set up during the 1980s. Two other such networks include the West European Network on Work and Unemployment and the Churches (WENWUC) and the European Claimants' Association (ECA). The WENWUC was established in 1986 and received financial and organizational input from mainly Protestant churches in Britain, Germany, and Holland. Over the course of its existence, it also received funding support from the Commission of the European Community to help it carry out its mission statement: international collaboration to identify the causes of unemployment, facilitation of a process of mutual learning, and the promotion of integrated approaches to address work and unemployment issues. The WENWUC withered away by the early 1990s. For its part, the ECA was established in December 1985 in Göttingen (Germany). Its main goal was to raise awareness of the social and economic effects of rising rates of unemployment in Europe. Affiliates were located in at least four European countries (Britain, Germany, Italy, and Holland), but the network depended very much on the organizational acumen of its Dutch and German founding members and on the contacts they had with a number of social activists, academics, and church leaders who provided it with financial and material support. The ECA coordinated a number of seminars in Germany and Holland in 1988 and 1989, and it also organized an international colloquium on unemployment in Maastricht (Holland) in 1989. This colloquium was to be its last major undertaking because the ECA founders were subsequently no longer in a position to raise sufficient funding.

8.3.2 Organizational Features and Objectives

When the FWENU was first set up, the founding members sought primarily to coordinate the policies and initiatives of its five affiliates with a view to defending the rights and status of unemployed people in Western Europe. Notes and leaflets from the first

[9] Over the years, some of the ENU affiliates and observers have included Bundesdachverband für Soziale Projekte (Austria); Collectif Solidarité contre l'exclusion: Emploi et revenu pour tous (Belgium); Association 29 rue blanche (Belgium); National Unemployed Centres Combine (Britain); Työttömien Valtakunnallinen Yhteistoimintajärjestö ry (Finland); Agir contre le chômage (France); Mouvement National des Chômeurs et Précaires (France); Mission Populaire (France); Arbeitslosenverband Deutchland e. V. (Germany); Association of Social and Ecological Intervention (Greece); Munkanélküliek és Álláskeresök Egyesületeinek Országos Szövetsége (Hungary); Irish National Organisation of the Unemployed (Ireland); Samenwerkingsverband Mensen Zonder Betaald Werk (The Netherlands); Ogólnopolskie Porozumienie Zwiasków Zawodowych (Poland); Centro de Apoio Desempregados (Portugal); Humlorna (Sweden); and Association de défense des chômeurs (Switzerland). Other affiliates were located in Russia and in Spain. Observing bodies regularly included the International Labor Organization, the European Trade Union Confederation, and the European Commission.

meetings refer to a number of other objectives: to compare European social welfare systems, to promote cross-national analyses of unemployment policies and their effects on unemployed people, to draw up the economic profiles of underprivileged European regions, to establish alliances with organizations active in the fight against social exclusion, to promote common objectives, to ensure that the network became a permanent and viable fixture in Europe, and to promote the dignity and identity of unemployed people.[10] In short, the founding members wished to compare and to contrast the political, social, and economic systems in Europe and to understand how unemployed people throughout Europe coped with their situation and deal with these issues. The founding members recognized the increasing influence of the European community on the economic affairs of home states, but they also claimed that the unemployed right across Europe were not benefitting fully from European construction.

Although autonomous from one another in terms of structure and action, ENU affiliates increasingly worked together toward shared political and social objectives. Many members of the affiliates were of the left of the political spectrum (Socialists, Communists, Greens, Radicals, and Christian Democrats), and so a number of them promoted “alternative” issues such as quality of life and self-reliance. The ENU’s objectives – as well as those of its affiliates – evolved over time as local, national, and international circumstances changed. For some affiliates, their main initial interest lay in urban regeneration, whereas others were more preoccupied with promoting social issues such as welfare rights. Over time, most of the affiliates became primarily concerned with issues of direct relevance to unemployed people including service-oriented objectives (better living conditions, increases in unemployment benefits, and basic income support measures) and political objectives (improved status, social change, full employment, and economic redistribution). Later, some ENU affiliates also sought to widen their organization’s and the ENU’s remit on the unemployed and to defend marginalized/disadvantaged groups in general through rights-based collective action on themes and issues such as equality, freedom, and solidarity. The themes of solidarity and equality in particular became important rallying points by the 1990s. Most of the affiliates also sought to get unemployed people – as members of a disadvantaged/marginalized social group – to become aware that they were embedded in a system which did not meet their needs and to fight for their rights. One such example was by encouraging them to participate in the Euromarches Against Unemployment – as will be discussed below – and in later years to take part in antiglobalization campaigns (Sommier 2001).

Most of the ENU affiliates were grassroots movements set up in the 1980s and early 1990s in response to the specific social and economic problems of their region or country. ENU affiliates were either very locally based organizations or national organizations with a quite limited local input.[11] For example, the German, Austrian,

[10] Author’s archives.

[11] The 1993 standing orders of the ENU stipulate that “In any country where there exists a national or co-ordinating organization of the unemployed, this body shall be the member of the ENU, and local organizations shall be encouraged to participate through that national or co-ordinating body.” In practice, very few ENU affiliates could claim to be national representatives given that most of them had no national foothold.

Irish, French, English, and Finnish affiliates were national networks of locally based organizations.[12] One of the French affiliates (Mission Populaire) was principally a national superstructure with little local presence. By contrast, some affiliates were in essence locally based organizations that had little or no representation or remit at a national level (the Belgian, Greek, Portuguese, and Spanish affiliates). In the case of the Italian affiliate, it had no role to play outside of the city of Naples. The Portuguese affiliate was the first organization of its kind in the country, and it was set up by people who had been made redundant when a local car manufacturing plant shut down. The Irish affiliate was established in 1987 by members of locally based pro-unemployment and antipoverty groups at a time of record levels of unemployment. The Greek affiliate was set up in Athens by university students who were also involved in a local Green movement.

Although the organizational structure of ENU affiliates varied from country to country, most of them shared a number of basic characteristics including a high level of flexibility in the way they operated. Thus, the ENU was above all a loosely structured network, most of whose affiliates had an aversion to formal, hierarchical, and centralized structures. A number of the affiliates also tended to view trade unions with suspicion. This is perhaps surprising, given that some ENU affiliates were themselves trade-union-supported structures (Britain, Poland). This meant that the ENU was rarely in a position to exercise authority over them, leading to significant mid- to long-term problems. The Irish affiliate, for example, was in favor of the ENU having greater ties with national or European bodies such as the European Parliament or the European Trade Union Confederation, whereas the Greek, Belgian, and Portuguese affiliates cherished their independence and wished to avoid all forms of collaboration with official bodies – national or international – because they wanted to be at liberty to criticize employment and unemployment policies. By the early 1990s, ENU leaders tried very hard nonetheless to forge alliances with many national and international bodies and people.

ENU affiliates took vastly different approaches to their membership. The Greeks, for example, had no formal rules. People simply joined and left rather informally. The English and the Irish, by contrast, had formal membership procedures. The German, Irish, and Finnish organizations became increasingly organized and professional in outlook. Since these three affiliates were themselves networks of locally based groups in their own countries, they had a greater number of supporters and registered members than, for example, the Association 29 rue blanche – one of the Belgian affiliates – that was simply a local women's rights organization. Membership figures also varied across the affiliates. People joined and left as their personal, social, and economic circumstances changed. All in all, most ENU affiliates were only loosely structured organizations in which members came and went at will, decisions were taken collectively, and hierarchy was frowned upon.

---

[12] The English organization was a special case. It came into existence following an initiative of the Trade Union Council (TUC) in the 1980s but subsequently moved very much away from TUC control. One of its main problems was deciding whether to organize on a national basis or to keep up its links with the TUC.

8.3.3 ENU Development

The ENU developed in three main phases. A first phase stretches from 1982 to the mid- to late 1980s: the consolidation phase. Not well known by the general public, its financial resources limited, and lacking in international support structures, the FWENU struggled to survive. The turning point came about at the third FWENU conference in Hanover in 1986 where it "became obvious that to be able to work together effectively we have to have a basic infrastructure."[13] Following the conference, a secretariat was established in Holland.

A second phase began as of the late 1980s and saw the French and the Irish affiliates play an increasingly important role in pushing through policy measures and in bringing a greater level of organizational coherence to the ENU. Paul Abela of Mission Populaire – the French affiliate – was president in the late 1980s and secretary in the early 1990s. Mike Allen – chief executive of the Irish National Organisation of the Unemployed (INOU) – became ENU's secretary in 1989 – 2 years after the INOU joined the ENU – a post he held until 1994. The French and Irish affiliates also strove to improve the exchange of information within the network, to coordinate the network's international initiatives, and to lobby members of European institutions. In short, they tried to promote transnational "identities" or "solidarities" to a far greater scale than had been the case with the ENU to date.

But also of importance is that the ENU of that phase also sought to address a number of internally generated and seemingly trivial but nonetheless fundamental obstacles to transnational cooperation and mobilization. Some examples of these difficulties are included in a letter from Mike Allen to his French counterpart, Paul Abela.[14] In the letter, Mike Allen alluded to the fact that ENU's work was being impeded by petty quarrels and misunderstandings. Just as importantly, many ENU affiliates often simply could not communicate in each others' language. During the annual conferences, for instance, ENU delegations were usually broken up by language group – Spanish, French, Dutch, German, and English – to discuss issues. The groups subsequently presented summaries to the rest of the delegates as best they could.[15] But Allen also pointed out in his letter that when the ENU leadership communicated with each other in English, for instance, they used terms whose meaning was not always clear because of the limited linguistic skills of some of the officers. Allen also referred to the fact that the ENU's cultural diversity led too often to deep misunderstandings and, at times, wariness of each others' positions: "the differences between our countries are so great that it is hard to find specific solutions we can all agree on."[16] So, problems of communication and the issue of lack of trust between the ENU and some of its affiliates posed key challenges.[17]

[13] Protocol of the 6th Congress of the ENU, Dublin (Ireland), 1989, p. 3.

[14] Letter, October 20, 1988. Author's archives.

[15] The 1993 standing orders finally addressed this issue. "The official languages of the network shall be Spanish and English and the language of the host country."

[16] Letter, October 20, 1988. Author's archives.

[17] In 1994, for example, the ENU secretary indicated that measures were afoot to try to resolve problems of the lack of trust between the Portuguese affiliate and the ENU. Secretary's Report, 1994 annual conference, Kerkrade (Holland).

Complications also arose because affiliates could not or would not implement the decisions taken during ENU annual conferences. For example, four ENU affiliates did not have the financial or organizational capacity to follow through on decisions taken at the Glasgow annual conference in 1991 – the organization of protests in member states in support of the ENU's "week of action against unemployment." Some affiliates simply chose not to hold the week of action because they did not agree with this activity even though the motion had been approved via democratic procedures.[18] Affiliates also suffered from ongoing financial problems. Indeed, the ENU depended almost exclusively on the subsidies it received from the European Commission to organize its annual conferences, whereas its daily activities depended more often than not on the goodwill or on the financial support that its affiliates provided.[19] The INOU was particularly adept in this regard as it had established close ties with the Irish trade union movement, whereas the Greeks were penniless. Other key challenges related to affiliates' disagreements with respect to the importance of setting up alliances as discussed above or ENU's objectives. The Spanish and Danish delegations – whose representatives were anarchists in the main – were confirmed Euroskeptics who wanted the ENU to be anti-European and to promote an alternative economy, whereas critical Europeanists of the Irish delegation wanted the ENU to lobby European institutions to help bring about a consensual change to various European programs.[20]

The ENU's third and most dynamic phase started toward the mid-1990s. This phase was also to lead to the network's ultimate "demise."[21] Prior to the mid-1990s, the ENU was essentially a network whose affiliates hailed from a number of European countries, as discussed above. It had a constitution, statutes, and democratic procedures. But it often found it hard to initiate collective action at a European level. "We need to prove to ourselves that we can co-ordinate international actions such as the 'day or action'. The current level of joint action is so low that we will be ignored."[22]

From the early to the mid-1990s, the ENU's principal activity was to organize annual conferences during which delegates got to know each other better, met in seminars to compare and contrast the situation of the unemployed in their countries, debated national and European employment and unemployment policies, and issued press statements. ENU annual conferences were also the occasion for delegates to

[18] Interview of Mike Allen, October 13, 1994.

[19] Financial dependency sometimes led to major problems. One example is what occurred during the 1994 Kerkrade (Holland) annual conference. An observer from the International Labor Organization attended sessions and contributed to the debates. At one point, Danish delegates criticized him strongly, and the observer felt compelled to leave the conference. His departure caused some disquiet as many delegates feared that this could lead to funding problems for the following year.

[20] On the various approaches that protesters have taken vis-à-vis the European integration project, see Donatella della Porta and Caiani (2007).

[21] The last ENU annual conference took place in Glasgow (Scotland) in 1998.

[22] President's report to the 1993 annual conference.

agree on the date for the annual ENU "week of action against unemployment." The ENU was present – at least in name – at a European level, but its mobilizing capacity was stunted because it faced a host of obstacles as already described: decentralized structures, weak decision-making processes, inadequate ongoing funding, internal bickering, and the political, geographical, cultural, and linguistic diversity of its membership.

The ENU truly began to take a more active mobilizing role at a transnational level following external intervention. Instrumental in this respect were the roles and activities of the organizers of the European Marches Against Unemployment – the Euromarches.[23] An invitation to the ENU to participate in the Euromarches was provided to the ENU executive by the French affiliate in October 1995 just prior to the ENU annual conference in Graz (Austria).[24] Euromarches organizers hoped the event could take place in the spring of 1997 and could bring together up to 100,000 people in Brussels. ENU delegates in Graz discussed the proposal and agreed to participate in the organization of the marches subject to receiving further information from the French coordinating organization – Agir ensemble contre le chômage (AC).[25] The date and ultimate destination of the Euromarches (Amsterdam) were finalized in spring 1996.[26] ENU agreed to support the resolution during the Ennis (Ireland) conference in October 1996, and the Euromarches took place in the spring of 1997. Marchers started off from a number of European locations and set out for Amsterdam to arrive in time for the June European Community Intergovernmental Conference.

The fact that the Euromarches did take place was in no small part due to the key role played by Christophe Aguiton[27] and many of his principally far-left colleagues in AC. It was also a result of the particular social and political circumstances in France at that time. By the late 1980s, the French political establishment had become largely discredited since it had been unable to find solutions to a number of social and economic problems including the rise in "new poverty." This situation helped to shape what has been labeled an "autonomous space" that allowed civil society actors to play a more active role in the country's social and political affairs (Mathieu 2007). With the French political establishment in mayhem, dissident, left-wing political and social leaders became more involved in a number of civil society organizations, including the four main pro-unemployed organizations that were set up between the late 1970s and the early 1990s. These activists gave the emerging pro-unemployed organizations the political and mobilizing know-how they clearly lacked. In time,

---

[23] For an analytical summary of the Euromarches, see Chabanet (2002, 2008).

[24] Draft proposal. October 1995. Author's archives.

[25] Agir ensemble contre le chômage is a French pro-unemployed organization particularly active in the French marches.

[26] The decision was taken in Turin on March 28, 1996, at a meeting attended by Italian, Spanish, French, and German non-ENU pro-unemployed activists.

[27] Christophe Aguiton was an emblematic figure of French pro-unemployed organizations in the 1990s and a cofounder of AC.

these types of organizations worked together toward shared political and social objectives, and they came to participate in a number of protest events at national and local levels to deal with the day-to-day problems unemployed people encountered and to demand increases in unemployment benefits and, more widely, for a rise in the various basic income support measures. By the mid-1990s, French pro-unemployed organizations had participated in a number of major protest events such as the occupation of unemployment benefits offices and marches on Paris in 1994. They had also participated in a major national, trade union-led strike in 1995. This 1995 strike in particular helped unite the organizations as the leaders met on a regular basis and often reached agreement on common strategies (Aguiton 2000). Thus, the French leaders brought something special to the ENU: relevant social capital and key political and organizational skills.

But even though the ENU had agreed in principle to participate in the Euromarches, there were still a number of issues that needed to be resolved. One such issue was related to the appropriate institutional levels for lobbying or protest activities.

> One way to overcome this is may be to combine demands and concerns of European and national character, to provide, in each country, points or reference for demands which can be readily formulated and built in a mass way (sic).[28]

The fact that ENU affiliates were very different from one another from structural, political, and cultural perspectives was also problematic. For example, how could the organizations agree on a unified platform: should protesters demand job sharing or other measures?

> One answer might be to create – at European level – a radical statement on the denunciation of unemployment and its consequences, a critique of European policies which exacerbate the situation, and in fairly general terms on proposals on job creation, reduction in working time, the aim of full employment, the fight against job insecurity etc., and to leave it then to national level to add the detail of the demands. (sic)[29]

Other issues of concern were of a more practical nature. For instance, would the affiliates be able to organize marches that could last up to 3 months? Some members feared that not all of the affiliates had the required experience or expertise to organize such an event. Concern was also expressed that some affiliates would not be in a position to foster a spirit of European solidarity or "identity" around the Euromarches.

> Such marches, if they are to have any purpose, cannot be just groupings of national marches, they need a European identity, which means propaganda material, logos, speakers ready to go from one country to another, staff, a central location for at least minimum co-ordination, European finance etc. (sic)[30]

The ENU was quite keen to help organize the Euromarches, but it was also conscious of the difficulties that participation in the events would have on its

---

[28] Draft of a *European Appeal for a Major Initiative Against Unemployment* contained in a letter from Christophe Aguiton to the ENU. April 24, 1996. Author's archives.

[29] Ibid.

[30] Ibid.

affiliates once the decision was ratified. They worried therefore that if delegates did not find solutions to the general and specific problems highlighted above, then the dynamic of this European cooperation process was in danger of floundering.

Despite these fears, the Euromarches took place and the media gave them favorable coverage (Chabanet 2002: 475–476). Instrumental in this success story was the long and patient work of the main organizers. The organizers used their organizational skills and newfound contacts across Europe to full advantage and became rather adept at diffusing its message throughout a number of European countries.[31] But the Euromarches were also a success because the ENU took an active part in them. Indeed, one of the key reasons why the French organizers looked to the ENU for help was because the ENU had affiliates in many European countries, a situation that would help to diffuse information about the marches and, more generally, about the plight of unemployed people.

An unintended consequence of the ENU's participation in the Euromarches, however, was that a major shift in power was now in train. As the marches slowly became a type of transnational network in its own right, it came to compete with the ENU for the allegiance of unemployed people and pro-unemployed organizations throughout Europe.[32] National and international social and political circumstances had in fact changed very much over the years, and Euromarches organizers adapted to them far quicker and with far more success than their ENU counterparts.

Another explanation for the turn in fortunes relates to the fact that very early on, the ENU leadership felt that the network was in danger of floundering if urgent measures were not taken to bring structure and coherence to the way it operated. ENU leaders had spent a good deal of time and effort to secure the network's viability and to change the affiliates' aversion to formal, hierarchical, and centralized structures. They drafted a constitution, wrote statutes, created a secretariat, and established a political office. This was done at much cost in the sense that some colleagues now became "enemies" and also in the sense that some leaders had worked so hard for the ENU that it had weakened their status in their home organizations, forcing some to reconsider their position in the network. By contrast, the Euromarches readily adopted the prevailing model of the AC – the French organization – an occasional informal and leaderless gathering of individuals and groups to express grievances and to organize public actions. The Euromarches never really forced members to act in one way or another.

The two organizations were also very different in terms of their goals and strategies. Many Euromarches participants saw the European Community in a negative way and linked it with the rise in global capitalism. Equally important is that the Euromarches took campaigning activities to a level that the ENU was never willing or able to take. Protests were an integral part of the Euromarches' repertoire of

[31] Later, some Euromarches organizers became key activists in transnational antiglobalization campaigns.

[32] The Euromarches still exist as such. See http://www.euromarches.org/. Last accessed 14 Aug 2010.

action whereas the ENU increasingly looked to lobbying various European institutions. Since the Euromarches regularly used more visible forms of protest than the ENU, the media also tended to focus on them rather than on the ENU.

The fact that the ENU faded as of the mid-1990s and that this "demise" coincided with the rise of the Euromarches may well be because some ENU affiliates were no longer able or willing to follow the ENU leadership. When some of the more radical ENU affiliates saw how the Euromarches network was operating and the media success it had, it brought back to the fore some of the ideological and strategic differences that they had had with some of their more reform-minded and centralizing ENU colleagues. These were the very issues that the ENU leadership had sought desperately to overcome and to a certain extent had succeeded in doing. In the short term, internal tensions within the ENU rose to the surface and set in train processes that slowly undermined the network's mid- to long-term viability.

8.4 Discussion

Let me try to summarize and to briefly explain some of the main points that I have raised.

8.4.1 The Activists and the Organizations

I have not provided sociological depictions of the main ENU leaders, nor have I presented an exhaustive sociological overview of how and why these main ENU activists invested their time and energy in this network.[33] It appears clear, nonetheless, that most of the ENU leadership had the required cultural and social capital that enabled them to become involved in such an endeavor.[34] For example, one of the main leaders of the German affiliate had a doctorate in sociology, and he had been well immersed in the social and political affairs of the German Democratic Republic. Most of the leading Finnish or Irish leaders had a university degree, and they had had a long involvement in their countries' trade union movement. Some of the French leaders had close links with ecumenical or the trade union movements. Even the leading Spanish or Greek members' heavy involvement in far-left, anarchist, or

[33] For an interesting discussion of what can be entitled a microsociological theory of engagement, see Doug McAdam (1982). McAdam argues that social actors normally follow a defined three-stage pattern: they oppose dominant social values; they structure alternative practices that are diffused in socializing networks bigger than the movement itself; they become involved in larger layers of society. In this final stage, social actors draw closer to social norms and lose their subversive character. It would appear that ENU affiliates have passed through the three phases.

[34] There are only very few biographies or personal reflections of some of the main ENU actors. See, for example, those of the Irish, Dutch, or German actors: Mike Allen (1998), Jo Bothmer (1991), and Klaus Grehn (1994).

autonomist political movements helped them to develop a discourse of anticapitalism and to forge working ties with their ENU colleagues. But the key activists also became involved in ENU affairs because of a quite a number of cultural, personal, or ideological reasons.[35]

With regard to the organizations, none of the ENU affiliates had any international experience prior to joining the network, but this is hardly surprising. Perhaps more interesting though is the various organizations' local or regional raison d'être, and how this helps to explain their involvement in the diffusion of information and in the collection of resources at a European level. ENU affiliates developed as a result of more or less local events or circumstances: a local factory closing in the Portuguese case or students wishing to promote alternative lifestyles in the case of the Greek affiliate. In fact, the Spanish or the Greek affiliates were not very important entities in their home country – at local, regional, or national levels. The Spanish organization in particular was simply a collection of individuals – anarchists – who vehemently denounced all types of authority. Its extremist political tendencies militated against its participation in mainstream networks in Spain. Its leaders did not recognize the legitimacy of Spain and claimed that they were representatives of the nations of the Spanish state, much to the amusement and, often, to the annoyance of other ENU affiliates. For such radical and politically marginal organizations in their home countries, participating in the ENU could be considered as no more than an attempt by them to justify their existence and importance to their immediate environment back home.[36] Other more politically moderate affiliates had quite different local or regional bases or organizational raison d'être. In the case of the Irish affiliate, for instance, ENU participation was a way for it to target the EU in order to apply pressure on its own government to change social and economic policies. Later, as domestic circumstances changed, the INOU wanted to be considered as an expert interest group in unemployment affairs in Ireland and, if possible, at the European level. So what most of the affiliates really wanted was to deal with very local – and more rarely – regional, or national issues. None had a truly international vocation, and most of them only became involved in the ENU by chance: they heard about it, contacted it, were invited to become an observer, and subsequently joined it. Participating in the network was a means to an end: local or national recognition and kudos vis-à-vis their competitors at home. Key objectives of the network were to publicize their grievances and to oblige national governments to resolve them.

8.4.2 Cooperation or Conflict and Misunderstanding?

The ENU was established as a network to promote the interests of the unemployed in Europe, and international cooperation was at the heart of the initiative.

[35] For example, some people established links across borders for linguistics of trade union affinities, as in the case of the Irish and the English.

[36] In fact, one of the Spanish delegates – Manolo Sáez – was ENU president in the early 1990s.

Let us take the case of the ENU annual conferences. The annual conferences allowed most of the affiliates the opportunity to avail of the financial resources that they would not have had otherwise at their disposal. Since the vast majority of ENU business was conducted during these conferences, European Community funding allowed delegates to travel abroad, to come into direct, face-to-face contact with foreign colleagues, to exchange their views in an often frank manner, and to widen their circle of allies. These annual, face-to-face encounters were instrumental in helping to create a type of collective "identity," at least for the attending delegates. ENU annual conferences facilitated mutual respect and learning and allowed delegates to become part of a greater space and to defend the interests of the unemployed and to speak out on their behalf. These are positive outcomes of ENU participation.

But this transnational initiative also had a downside including conflicts and/or misunderstandings. One example of this is that as the ENU developed, clear patterns of division of labor emerged. Very early on some of the more social-capital-endowed members took active roles in the ENU and thereby helped the network to develop and to present a coherent discourse (as an international network). This meant that these active members marginalized – however unwittingly – other members. The latter group became increasingly bitter, resentful, and wary of the ultimate motives of the ENU leadership. One key example is that when the Euromarches came to the fore, some of the ENU affiliates that were actively supporting the marches were able to compare, negatively, the way the ENU was operating (increasing centralization) compared to the Euromarches' way of operating – the occasional informal and leaderless gatherings of individuals and groups to express grievances and organize public actions.

The ENU developments highlight, therefore, that the network was founded upon extremely fragile alliances. By attempting to centralize its affairs, the ENU leadership alienated a number of its affiliates. But did it really have any other choice but to try to become a permanent fixture so as to defend the interest of the unemployed at a transnational level? One option was to continue along its affiliates' initial aversion to formal, hierarchical, and centralized structures, but clearly not all affiliates or leaders saw that this as a viable option.

8.5 Conclusion

The ENU's development highlights a number of interesting issues when assessing organizations' and people's involvement in transnational networks of this type. Participation may lead to positive results in the sense that people increase the number of professional contacts and even become friends, that they push forward issues that are close to their heart, and that they succeed in changing other people's lives for the better. But there may also be some unexpected negative consequences: tension, lack of trust, bitterness, jealousy, etc. The experiences of the ENU underline the difficulties of bringing about the transnational collective action of weakly resourced people.[37] In this respect, I would like to conclude by highlighting two points. The first is that ENU affiliates faced very different types of constraints within their country, and they tried to overcome them as best they could. For example, the stigmata attached to unemployment was not the same in England, Belgium, or Portugal and may well explain the differences in the intensity of pro-unemployed mobilizations between countries or even the organizations' involvement in the ENU (Chabanet and Royall 2009). The second point is that ENU affiliates emerged in vastly different social, political, cultural, and historical contexts. Despite the fact that they may have shared the same objective goal – the eradication of unemployment – they really did not have the same grievances nor did they face the same opposition. This obviously was a factor in the intensity of their short- to long-term commitment to the ENU as local, national, and international circumstances changed.

References

Aguiton, C. (2000, June 9–10). *Les syndicats français après décembre 1995*. In Conference: France 1995: Turning Point or Tremor?. London: French Institute.

Allen, M. (1998). *The bitter word*. Dublin: Poolbeg.

Balme, R., & Chabanet, D. (2008). *Collective action and European democracy*. New York: Rowman & Littlefield.

Bothmer, J. (1991). Unemployment is not a fate. *International Journal of Sociology and Social Policy, 11*(1), 68–80.

Chabanet, D. (2002). Les marches européens contre le chômage, la précarité et les exclusions. In R. Blame, D. Chabanet, & V. Wright (Eds.), *L'Action collective en Europe*. Paris: Presses de Sciences Po.

Chabanet, D. (2008). When the unemployed challenge the European Union: The European marches as a mode of externalization of protest. *Mobilization, 13*(3), 311–322.

Chabanet, D., & Giugni, M. (2010). Les conséquences des mouvements sociaux. In O. Fillieule, É. Agrilоliansky, & I. Sommier (Eds.), *Penser les Mouvements Sociaux: Conflits sociaux et contestations dans les sociétés contemporaines*. Paris: La Découverte.

Chabanet, D., & Royall, F. (2009). Economic recession and the mobilization of the unemployed: France and Ireland compared. *French Politics, 7*(3/4), 268–293.

della Porta, D. (2006). *The global justice movement: Cross-national and transnational perspectives*. New York: Paradigm.

della Porta, D. (2008). Protest on unemployment: Forms and opportunities. *Mobilization, 13*(3), 277–295.

della Porta, D., & Caiani, M. (2007). Europeanization from below? Social movements and Europe. *Mobilization, 12*(1), 1–20.

[37] Virginie Guiraudon (2001: 179–180) argues that in the case of migrants' associations at the European level, "they have been better able to avail themselves of a discourse of transnationalism than to either forge working ties with their supposed constituencies or positively affect EU policies in their favor […] European integration provides them with only weak weapons of the weak" (Guiraudon 2001: 179–180).

della Porta, D., & Tarrow, S. (2005). Transnational processes and social activism: An introduction. In D. della Porta & S. Tarrow (Eds.), *Transnational protest and global activism*. Boulder: Rowman & Littlefield.
Giugni, M. (1998). The other side of the coin: Explaining cross-national similarities between social movements. *Mobilization, 3*(1), 89–105.
Giugni, M. (Ed.). (2009). *The politics of unemployment in Europe: Policy responses and collective action*. Aldershot: Ashgate.
Grehn, K. (1994). *Arbeitslos in Deutschland*. Munich: Knaur.
Guiraudon, V. (2001). Weak weapons of the weak? Transnational mobilization around migration in the European Union. In D. Imig & S. Tarrow (Eds.), *Contentious Europeans: Protest and politics in an emerging polity*. Oxford: Rowman & Littlefield.
Imig, D., & Tarrow, S. (2001). *Contentious Europeans: Protest and politics in an emerging polity*. Lanham: Rowman & Littlefield.
Keck, M., & Sikkink, K. (1998). *Activists beyond borders: Advocacy networks in international politics*. Ithaca: Cornel University Press.
Kriesi, H., Koopmans, R., Duyvendak, J., & Giugni, M. (1995). *New social movements in Western Europe: A comparative analysis*. London: UCL Press.
Marks, G., & McAdam, D. (1996). Social movements and the changing structure of political opportunities in the European Union. *West European Politics, 19*(2), 249–278.
Marks, G., & McAdam, D. (1999). On the relationship of political opportunities to the form of collective action: The case of the European Union. In D. della Porta, H. Kriesi, & D. Rucht (Eds.), *Social movements in a globalizing world*. London: Macmillan.
Mathieu, L. (2007). L'espace des mouvement sociaux. *Politix, 77*, 131–153.
McAdam, D. (1982). *Political process and the development of black insurgency, 1930–1970*. Chicago: University of Chicago Press.
Reising, E. (1999). United in opposition: A cross-national time-series analysis of European protest in three selected countries, 1980–1995. *Journal of Conflict Resolution, 43*(3), 317–342.
Reiss, M., & Perry, M. (Eds.). (2011). *Unemployment and protest: New perspectives on two centuries of contention*. Oxford: Oxford University Press.
Reitan, R. (2007). *Global activism*. London: Routledge.
Rucht, D. (2002). The EU as a target of political mobilization: Is there a Europeanisation of conflict? In R. Balme, D. Chabanet, & V. Wright (Eds.), *L'action collective en Europe*. Paris: Presses de Sciences Po.
Siméant, J. (2010). La transnationalisation de l'action collective. In O. Fillieule, É. Agrikoliansky, & I. Sommier (Eds.), *Penser les mouvements sociaux: Conflits sociaux et contestations dans les sociétés contemporaines*. Paris: La Découverte.
Smith, J., Chatfield, C., & Pagnucco, R. (Eds.). (1997). *Transnational social movements and global politics: Solidarity beyond the state*. New York: Syracuse University Press.
Sommier, I. (2001). *Les nouveaux mouvements contestataires à l'heure de la mondialisation*. Paris: Flammarion.
Tarrow, S. (1995). The Europeanisation of conflict: Reflections from a social movement perspective. *West European Politics, 18*(2), 223–251.
Tarrow, S. (1998/1994]). *Power in movement: Social movements and contentious politics*. Cambridge: Cambridge University Press.
Tarrow, S. (2000). La contestation transnationale. *Cultures et Conflits, 38–39*, 187–220.
Tarrow, S. (2001). Transnational politics: Contention and institutions in international politics. *Annual Review of Political Science, 4*, 1–20.
Tilly, C. (1986). *The contentious French*. Cambridge: Harvard University Press.

Part III
National Examples

Chapter 9
The British and French Hunger Marches of the 1930s: An Exclusive Mode of Protest, a Cultural Transfer, and a Fulcrum of Success

Matt Perry

9.1 Introduction

If the hunger marches remain a key signifier of 1930s Britain, in France such protests of the unemployed barely register in present-day political culture (Perry 2007; Kingsford 1982). This chapter will compare the hunger marches associated with the British and French unemployed protest movements of the 1930s. These movements are comparable on several grounds. First, regarding socioeconomic conjuncture, both movements occurred in advanced industrial states during the global economic slump of the 1930s. Secondly, connected through the transnational networks of the Communist International (Comintern) and its affiliates such as the Red International of Labour Unions (RILU) and the International Workers' Relief, Communist Parties played a disproportionate role in animating the *Comités des chômeurs* (committees of the unemployed) and the National Unemployed Workers' Movement (NUWM) (Croucher 1990; Hayburn 1983). This is not to say that there were no non-communist-inspired protests. Both countries provide notable examples that have persisted in the collective memory. In France, the Saint-Nazaire to Nantes march and, in Britain, the Jarrow Crusade were, despite their importance, exceptions rather than the norm (Aremors 1983; Perry 2005). Finally, both movements confronted the unemployed subject, with all its peculiarities of social position, identity, and patterns of collective action. In other circumstances, their mobilization has been described as "improbable," "unprecedented," "fragile," and even "miraculous" (Chabanet 2002; Bourdieu 1998; Paugam 1998; Pierru 2007).

M. Perry (✉)
School of Historical Studies, University of Newcastle,
Armstrong Building, Newcastle upon Tyne, NE2 4HH, UK
e-mail: matt.perry@ncl.ac.uk

B. Andreosso-O'Callaghan and F. Royall (eds.), *Economic and Political Change in Asia and Europe: Social Movement Analyses*, DOI 10.1007/978-94-007-4653-4_9,

9.2 Comparing the Exclusive Mode of Unemployed Protest

Having established clear grounds for comparison, it is necessary to clarify questions of methodology, conceptual categories, and line of approach. From a conceptual perspective, social movement analysis would seem to be a fitting center to this comparative undertaking. This approach provides a conceptual toolbox – protest event analysis, repertoire of protest, cycles of contestation, resource mobilization, and political opportunity structure – conducive to the comparison of these movements (Tarrow 1998[1994]). Methodologically, this study takes a historical approach basing itself on extensive archival research and familiarity of the secondary literature in both comparators. The departure point for comparison will be a particular form of unemployed protest: the hunger march. This provides a convenient focus for wider temporal, spatial, and movement comparisons of these two protest histories (della Porta 2002).

There are good reasons for starting with the hunger march. It is the only form of collective action that is exclusively a mode of *unemployed* protest; other social groups do not embark upon hunger marches (though admittedly this is partly a semantic question, given the significance attached to "hunger"). Other species of protest within the repertoires of these unemployed movements, such as the street demonstration or eviction fight, are shared with those of other social groups and labor movements. Furthermore, the hunger march has distinctive characteristics that give it a pivotal part within repertoires of unemployed protest movements. Beyond its place in protest repertoires, the hunger march crucially provides a convenient unit of analysis that is both measureable and offers insights into cultural, linguistic, and transnational processes.

Three features of comparison between the French and British hunger marches in the interwar period are striking. First, the French hunger march is a late arrival. The first British national hunger march of this period took place in 1922. There were seven British hunger marches, possibly more, before the first French hunger march in 1932 between Oyonnax and Nantua (in the department of Ain). The Oyonnax to Nantua march neither claimed the title of hunger march nor did it feed into a cycle of protest beyond the isolated comb manufacturing town of Oyonnax.

The second noticeable difference between British and French hunger marches is their spatial orientation. While there were three hunger marches to Paris (December 12, 1932, November 18–December 2, 1933, January 12, 1935), there is no French national hunger march in the sense of the British ones. Only the Lille to Paris march of 1933 might arguably be considered a national march. Thus, the French hunger marches were a largely regional phenomenon unlike their British counterparts. The regional rather than the national arena renders the French hunger march less persistent in national political culture. Once the less visible provincial hunger marches are taken into account, the French movement does not seem so inconsequential in comparison with the British movement as is sometimes assumed (Reiss 2007).

There were 19 hunger marches in France and 28 in Britain (nine were national hunger marches). Whereas in France the regional hunger march was the norm, in Britain, regional hunger marches principally resulted from a shift in tactics in 1933 when marches took place in 17 localities including notably Lancashire, Durham, Edinburgh, Glasgow, Kent, Cornwall, and Northumberland. Over 1,000 took part in the Scottish march to Edinburgh, 800 in the Yorkshire march, and 150 in the Nottinghamshire march.[1] The provincial hunger march was part of the NUWM's tactical flexibility and indicated its innovation across the repertoire of unemployed contestation. It also highlighted the different structures of the movements themselves. The British movement had its own national structures, with intermittent national newspapers, a National Administrative Council, regular national conferences, and a national leadership, including the recognized chief of the NUWM from its early days onward, Wal Hannington. The French movement had nothing of this sort. There were on three occasions national conferences of the unemployed (September 1933, November 1936, November 1937), but no permanent national organization existed. At times the Paris regional movement substituted for a national center calling conferences that attracted provincial delegates. However, it is hard to talk of a French national unemployed movement. It was rather a collection of local and regional movements with varying network structures. They were often connected to a regional center sometimes radiating from a regional newspaper for the unemployed. This was the Parisian model that Nord and the Saint-Étienne regional movements followed with greater success than the original. Many French committees of the unemployed existed in relative isolation and had a rather ephemeral existence. Except on the rare occasion of a national conference, national communication among French unemployed activists was therefore conducted by default through the *Confédération Générale du Travail Unitaire* (CGTU) or the *Parti Communiste Français* (PCF) and their press. Partly this was a function of the industrial geography of France with its major industrial areas far-flung across the French hexagon (the mouth of the Seine, the Paris region, Nord-Pas-de-Calais, Lyons-Loire, Marseilles, the mouth of the Loire, Alsace-Lorraine). Britain being more compact – and its industry more so still – made for more cohesive national structures and for national hunger marches.

Thirdly, cross-country comparison of hunger marches provides insights into protest cycles. The chronology of hunger marches suggests very different cycles of contestation in Britain and France, though examination of hunger marches alone is an inadequate guide to this. In both cases, hunger marches mark key thresholds in the most significant phases of protest. The comparative pattern of hunger marches in Britain and France underlines a wider lack of synchronicity between their protest cycles. The differences were at their greatest between 1920 and 1931. During these years, continuous national organization existed in Britain in the shape of the NUWM, whereas this was not true of any locality in France. The cycles of unemployed

[1] NUWM NAC Report, August 26–27, 1933, p. 2.

protest over the longer time frame reflect in part scales and cycles of unemployment. However, they were also subject to a host of other variables not least political opportunity structures connected to the social policy regarding the unemployed (Bagguley 1992). In France, a weak pulse of protest appeared in 1921 and 1927, with strong protest cycles developing in 1931–1932 and late 1933–1935 (and 1940–1941 in Paris alone). Within this, there were very considerable local and regional variations in terms of repertoire, intensity, and chronology. From a British perspective, protest cycles occurred in 1919–1922 and 1931–1936, with peaks of protest activity in late 1932, early 1935, and late 1936.

The place of the hunger march within cycles of protest also underlines the spatial characteristics of the two movements. Protest cycles were more local or regional in character in France than Britain. Although the NUWM was never a genuinely nationwide organization, having considerable regional unevenness, there was nevertheless a much greater national synchronicity to protest. In France, there were a series of local or regional cycles of protest. For example, the Parisian movement reached its peak in March 1932 and never recovered to that point. It was in the provinces – in the Pas-de-Calais and Nord area in 1934–1935, Saint-Étienne in 1932 and 1934, and Ardennes in early 1935 – that witnessed more impressive collective action on the part of the unemployed. On several occasions, there were highly localized or short-term protest cycles often out of step with more general trends such as the march from Oyonnax to Nantua in April 1932 or the Méru to Beauvais hunger march on Christmas day 1934. The greater local specificity of protest cycles in France can in part be explained by the decentralized and nonmandatory nature of social provision for the unemployed in that country.

From a temporal perspective, these protest cycles were obviously limited in both countries to periods of mass joblessness. However, they did not rise and fall in a simple way with the unemployment rate. While unemployment in Britain fell steadily from early 1933 onward, there were significant peaks of protest after that point. In France, similarly, unemployment remained persistently high after the autumn–winter of 1935, but protest was largely absent.

Finally, hunger marches seemed to extend the cycles of protest of the unemployed, on occasion initiating or sustaining protest cycles slotting in alongside other forms of protest. The French cycles of protest during 1934 and 1935 appeared to have an extended duration after the hunger march had been added to the repertoire of contestation. In the Nord-Pas-de-Calais area, the most impressive regional movement witnessed the most sustained cycle of contestation: from the return of the Lille to Paris hunger march in December 1933, the Calais riot of January 5, 1934, local hunger marches to sub-prefectures in February and April 1934, the regional hunger march to Lille in October 1934, and then a wave of occupations of the mayor's offices at the year's end. This connected sequence of events poses an interesting question about the relationship between the hunger march and other activities of the movements of the unemployed.

9.3 The Hunger March as the Fulcrum of Successful Mobilization

Study of the French and British movements of the unemployed reveals a largely shared repertoire of protest and for that matter non-protest activity. Appendix 9.3 outlines the characteristics of these forms and categorizes them in terms of their transgressive or non-transgressive quality. They constituted a spectrum from moderation to militancy. Such a procedure is admittedly problematic because, with a number of protest forms, transgression is determined by the political context, namely the permissive or hostile attitudes of the authorities: central and local government as well as the different levels of police forces. Thus, notwithstanding its spectacular, ritual or symbolic dimensions and the moral limits that rioters observe, a riot is clearly always transgressive. At the other end of this moderate-militant spectrum, in the context of democratic polities, cooperative or self-help activity is non-transgressive, operating within the law and publicly sanctioned moral codes, whatever the ideological inflections of such activity. Between these poles, the demonstration occupies an intermediary position contingent upon circumstance: both the behavior of the participants and the attitudes of the authorities. A further problem with this procedure is that these actions do not stand in isolation from one another but interact in complex sequences. Indeed, this was precisely the object of the hunger march for communists who circumstances permitting would have preferred, until 1934 at least, more militant forms of mass mobilization.

The hunger march occupies a particular location in this typology of modes of unemployed protest, and it is this characteristic that provides the key to its historical importance. The hunger march was the closest of all intermediate protest forms to the moderate and non-transgressive category. In other words, it was perceived as less threatening to the authorities than demonstrations, which were based on unlimited numbers and whose goal was mass mobilization. Unlike a relief strike, it could mobilize small minorities and be successful. From the point of view of the movement, the hunger march required a considerable amount of preparation, an investment of time and resources. It was far from spontaneous and has considerable costs; appreciation of its benefits was therefore a necessary precondition for a hunger march. From the perspective of the authorities, the hunger march was difficult to repress as the French authorities found when they tried to ban the 1933 Lille to Paris march. The organizers were able through cat-and-mouse tactics to march in twos and threes and thereby circumvent the ban. In part, this was because it was difficult to provide a legal basis for its repression. British Home Secretary Sir John Gilmour chaired a cabinet committee to discuss the possibility of banning hunger marches in November–December 1932, going so far as formulating a draft bill but ultimately deciding against it on legal advice (Turnbull 1973).[2]

[2] TNA CAB 27 497 Attorney General's Memorandum, December 2, 1932.

A careful scrutiny of the hunger march reveals that it is actually constituted by a chain of other protest forms. A hunger march ideal type might be viewed as a cycle of contestation in itself, consisting of a particular sequence and repertoire of protest: petitioning, send-off demonstration, a daily cycle of marching between locations and evening public meetings, a reception demonstration in its ultimate destination, and the presentation of a petition. In practice, the hunger marches often diverged from this model. The send-off demonstrations of the 1933 Lille to Paris hunger march were banned, so the send-off demonstrations were canceled as part of the organizers' subterfuge. In addition, there were only occasional evening public meetings usually hosted by Communist municipalities. If hunger marches did not always match to this ideal type, each constituted particular configurations of protest repertoires. They also took place within and connected into longer waves of contestation. Where the 1933 French march was concerned, there had been a long hiatus of unemployed protest. The NUWM's 1932 hunger march occurred against a backdrop of rioting in Belfast and Birkenhead and as many as 39 demonstrations in such places as West Ham and North Shields.[3] On the march itself, clashes with the police broke out in Stratford-upon-Avon and in Hyde Park.

As our typology of transgressive protest forms indicates (Appendix 9.3), the hunger march entails a particular relationship between the protest organizers and the authorities that is especially favorable to mobilization in the face of state hostility. However, the hunger march also possesses a symmetry with the dynamics of unemployed agency. Several historians and political scientists have tried to judge the propensity of the unemployed to undertake collective action (Bagguley 1992; Chabanet 2002; Perry 2005; Pierru 2007). It is extremely difficult to establish sustained organizations of the unemployed. Patterns of social conflict differ very significantly from employed workers. From a historical perspective, social recognition of unemployment is late and contested. Notions of individual responsibility, free market economics, and the undeserving poor masked the emergence of unemployment. Unemployed protest often therefore takes the form of a contest for recognition. Activists both sides of the Channel came to realize the fit between the hunger march and the unemployed subject. Charles Tillon, reporting shortly after the Lille to Paris hunger march, noted how the hunger march revitalized the regional networks of unemployed committees in the Nord and in the Paris region because it matched the unemployed "state of mind," putting practical demands that were beyond the horizons of municipal politics. Regarding claims to recognition, the hunger march was popular with the unemployed because it showed the unemployed were not "lazy" (Goffman 1963). Given the fragility of unemployed protest, Tillon observed how the hunger march was a form of action that was able to draw solidarity from a broad spectrum of opinion within the labor movement.[4] Reinforcing this point in another report, the organizers of the

[3] NUWM NAC Minutes, December 3–4, 1932, pp. 3–8.

[4] ADSSD 3Mi6 107 Tillon's report, January 7, 1934.

Lille to Paris march understood this mode of protest's location as a potential fulcrum of successful mobilization of the unemployed:

> The hunger march to Paris, the first important experience of mass unemployed struggle for a part of the country, was a necessary action, a precious experience and has advanced the movement of the unemployed and contributed to the highlighting of their battle. But this act ought to be valuable from a revolutionary perspective, if it is not an end in itself, but a starting point for a movement in preparation for further stages of more intense and wider battles.[5]

9.4 The Hunger March as a Cultural Transfer

It is apparent from cross-country comparison of hunger marches that the British and French movements existed within quite distinctive political cultures of contentiousness with regard to unemployment. Thus, from the vantage point of the 1970s, march leader Charles Tillon noted:

> Breaking the silence and humility of the unemployed required an army of hunger to take to the streets. The French workers' movement did not possess the power of the English famed unemployed marches (Tillon 1977: 170).

Comparison between British and French movements has not only been a retrospective one but also a contemporaneous feature. As early as 1927 during the PCF leadership's previous turn toward the unemployed, they explicitly drew on the British experience.[6] The cultural discrepancy was greatest where the hunger march is concerned, which might be considered a specific repertoire deficit for the early French movement. As we shall see, the British unemployed movement helped French militants frame an understanding of unemployed protest (Johnston and Noakes 2005). There is plenty of evidence that the NUWM understood the paramount significance of this mode of protest. For instance, it recorded the impact of its 1934 hunger march; thus:

> The NAC [National Administrative Council] declares that the organizing of the Hunger March and the Congress does down as the biggest thing ever done by our movement. It made the working-class United Front a living reality. It roused the whole country on [sic – the question] of the unemployed as it has never been roused before. It was certainly the finest piece of organizational work that our Movement has ever carried out.[7]

There were a host of other subtle transfers and exchanges between these movements. Most obviously, these were transmitted within the Comintern, which constituted a latter-day Tower of Babel. Transmission took place through international conferences, international days of struggle against unemployment, literature

---

[5] Institut d'Histoire Sociale (CGT) Comité Régional des Chômeurs de la RP "Bilan de la marche", in *Bulletin: Après la Marche de la Faim*, January 25, 1934, p. 6.

[6] ADSSD 3 Mi 6 30 PCF Central Committee minutes, January 13, 1927.

[7] NUWM NAC Minutes, April 7–8, 1934, p. 3.

(notably International Press Correspondence, pamphlets, and the RILU Magazine), comparisons, and injunctions based on the successes of elsewhere. British and French activists were not alone in this process but, despite these multilateral exchanges, the hunger march was fundamentally a transfer from Britain to France. During the Third Period (1928–1934), the RILU and the Executive Committee of the Communist International (ECCI) became concerned with unemployed protest.[8] In 1930–1932 in particular, these bodies instructed affiliates to agitate among the unemployed. The RILU organized two international conferences on the question. At the time when the RILU and the ECCI stressed the need to mobilize this social group, French and British communists found themselves in very different positions: the NUWM was already a well-established movement, whereas there was no movement to speak of in France.

Irrespective of the late arrival of mass unemployment to France in late 1931, French representatives participated in earlier forums redirecting the work of communist organizations toward the jobless. The Dusseldorf conference on unemployment held on February 2, 1930, designated March 6 an international day of struggle against unemployment [*journée de lutte internationale contre le chômage*].[9] The communist-led trade union confederation, the CGTU, was charged with forging the new movement of the unemployed. When discussing the Comintern's international day of struggle, the PCF political bureau was very well aware of France's exceptional position. Nevertheless, it went ahead with the protest. On the day, its slogans were sectarian and abstract. The result was a fiasco.[10]

The lack of headway with the unemployed troubled the PCF political bureau. The priorities of the international communist movement, rather than contact with the unemployed, prompted this concern. The French communist leadership remained silent on the subject until the fifth congress of the RILU. In light of RILU criticism, Comintern favorite Maurice Thorez, who had been appointed General Secretary in July 1930, intervened at the following PCF political bureau. He insisted on the urgency of initiating an unemployed movement. Confusion reigned among the PCF leadership about unemployment insurance, the relationship between the workplace and the unemployed, and the current state of unemployed organization. But French communist leaders clearly understood that the ECCI expected them to establish a movement of the unemployed and that peculiarities of their national situation would not be considered mitigation for failure to do so.[11]

By February 25, 1931, the second international day of struggle against unemployment, joblessness had begun to rise in France. The campaign for the day of action reveals considerable resource mobilization on the part of the French communist

---

[8] Communism and the International Situation: *Thesis on the International Situation and the Tasks of the Communist International*, Adopted at the Sixth World Congress of the Communist International, 1928.

[9] *International Press Correspondence*, February 4, 1930, p. 100.

[10] F7 13307 *Journée* of March 6, 1930.

[11] ADSSD 3 Mi 6 57 PCF BP minutes, September 22, 1930.

movement, but this was not sufficient in itself to result in effective protest. On the day, as the Seine departmental police report noted, the communists were foiled at every assembly point. It observed: "Order was maintained; the physiognomy of the street was not changed at any time; transport functioned normally; the freedom to work was assured. Nowhere was there a demonstration."[12] The costs of mobilization were high. In all 188 arrests were made, of which 21 were foreigners who were likely to be deported.

Despite communist resource mobilization, the day's agitation proved disappointing, no doubt in part because the level of unemployment was by no means comparable with elsewhere in Europe. An acrimonious apportioning of blame dominated the next Central Committee of the Unemployed of the Paris Region [*Comité Central des Chômeurs de la Région Parisienne*, CCdC(RP)] delegate meeting. The chair of the CCdC Monceaux started to complain about the general apathy of the unemployed, and the Confederal Bureau of the CGTU replaced him with Lucien Monjauvis (secretary of 20th region of the CGTU).

The next transnational opportunity to communicate the means to build an effective movement of the unemployed to France was the Prague conference about unemployment of September 1931. German communist Walter Ulbricht accentuated this communicative function in his presidential address, indicating the necessity that "exchange of experience made at this conference be taken as a basis for a concrete working plan for every country."[13] He outlined the Comintern/RILU's key demands, its principal fighting methods, and organizational approaches. Both British and French Communists were represented at this conference. Whereas longstanding leader of NUWM Wal Hannington was the British delegate, the French representative was Benoît Frachon, the general secretary of the *Confédération Générale du Travail Unitaire*, who was to have minimal personal involvement in the French movement of the unemployed. Believing the NUWM's position to be a barrier to mass involvement, the Comintern polemicized against the leadership of the NUWM because Hannington insisted upon a fee-paying membership organization (Campbell and McIlroy 2008). Instead, recognizing the universal weaknesses of communist efforts among the unemployed, the Comintern touted the German model, of which Ulbricht's presidency of the conference was emblematic. Frachon reported to the conference about the movement in France and noted that the conference provided French comrades with "the opportunity of learning from the experience of comrades in other countries where there has long been widespread unemployment."

If the conference report underlines the transnational exchange of ideas and of practical experience to assist the building of unemployed movements, the lessons were not as useful as participants might have assumed. What would have been most helpful to French communists would have been an understanding of the nature of unemployed agency, realistic expectations, and the most effective protest or organizational strategies and tactics. Instead, catastrophism informed the conference's

[12] AN F7 13541 police report, February 25, 1931.

[13] *International Press Correspondence*, October 30, 1931, p. 1018.

view of the international prospects for unemployed movements. An "army" of 35 million unemployed was anticipated in the following year. Such language encouraged an underestimation of the difficulties of mobilizing the unemployed. The message about the forms of collective action was ambiguous. The mass demonstration was "no doubt [...] the chief weapon available to the unemployed," and Ulbricht unhelpfully conflated the hunger march and the mass demonstration. He also deployed voluntaristic rhetoric to argue that communists were "lagging behind" the opportunities that the "hunger army of the unemployed" offered for militant action. The conference organizers insisted on the establishment of links between the unemployed and employed workers. This might be reasonable enough in the abstract but might confuse the need to build distinct organizations of the unemployed themselves in a context where trade unionists were often skeptical about their workless colleagues who might be equated with a lumpenproletarian rabble. Even in Hannington's rather brief report, there was no mention of the hunger march tactic, despite the fact that he had already led three national marches.[14]

The sheer impracticality of the conference's perspectives was less of a problem where significant movements already existed such as in the British, German, or Czech cases. However, the French delegates had no such luxury. Indeed, from the perspective of the embryonic French movement of the unemployed, the conference could be considered a missed opportunity for learning the most appropriate strategies and for establishing realistic expectations. In this sense, the Comintern did not provide a straightforward means of communication between activists in unemployed movements. These failings notwithstanding, the conference did impress a sense of urgency upon the French delegates and an awareness, even if an unrealistic one, of the possibilities of mass protest.

The Comintern and RILU's approach continued in similar vein in the months after the Prague conference.[15] The 12th plenum of the ECCI in late 1932 resolved that the shortcomings with unemployed movements were that they had not implemented the Prague decisions.[16] Ironically, the Communist International pushed the PCF leadership hardest on this question in the relative absence of the unemployed. By the time mass unemployment emerged in France, the ECCI had abandoned both its strategy of *journées* against unemployment and its strongest prioritization of unemployed mobilization had passed. Thus, significant multi-organizational resource mobilization, movement structure building, and an unfavorable conjuncture characterized the first phase of efforts to build a movement in France. However, the exploration of the limits of earlier strategies created conditions conducive for a transfer from the vibrant culture of unemployed protest in Britain to the French context.

Whereas references to foreign hunger marches in the press of the French *Comités des Chômeurs* were relatively rare and are not sufficient to explain the translation of

---

[14] *International Press Correspondence*, October 30, 1931, p. 1007–1008.

[15] *RILU Magazine*, 1932, pp. 499–507.

[16] *RILU Magazine*, 1932, pp. 937–938.

the hunger march into the French idiom, this was not the case with the PCF daily, *L'Humanité*. The crucial crossing point of the hunger march into the consciousness of French militants appears to be *L'Humanité's* reporting of the British hunger march of 1932.[17] These reports played the function of demonstrating the possibility of significant unemployed mobilization, its repertoire of action, and its very language.

The historiography has overlooked the obstacles within French political culture to the emergence of a successful unemployed protest movement. Apparently low levels of French unemployment provide a ready-made answer, closing further consideration. Without ignoring this latter feature, though the scale of French unemployment has seriously been underestimated, it is worth considering the cultural dimension. A survey of French newspapers discloses the absence of the phrase "hunger march" prior to 1930 from the political lexicon (Appendix 9.1). This term only entered the French language via reporting of foreign hunger marches, principally the British, but also the German and American, marches. Thus, the first use of the term in *Le Temps* was in 1930; in *Le Petit Parisien* and *Le Figaro*, it was in 1932. Even then appearances were rare. To the French bourgeois press, it was a term to be treated with skepticism. Its use recognized the legitimacy of the protest given hunger's connotation of injustice. Hence *Le Temps* talked of the "so-called hunger march" ["*soi-disant marche de la faim*"] when writing on the US hunger march.[18] Much of the mainstream press failed to employ the term at all, either in domestic or international contexts.

The presence of the hunger march in the French language and a practical appreciation of its constituent parts should not be assumed. Unlike the semiotic equation between the hunger march and the unemployed movement in Britain, other signifiers were more likely to identify the movement at the time and subsequently. The slogan "bread and work" appeared widely in the press and has persisted over time (Guitard 1933: 96). The unemployed demonstration turned riot of March 8, 1883, that Louise Michel led had chanted "*Du pain, du travail*" ["Bread and work"] (Perry 2000). The movement of the 1930s was also more likely to be identified through the *comités des chômeurs* than with its hunger marches. It was far from the case that protest against unemployment itself was alien to the French labor movement. It was rather that French political culture provided its own reference points: the insurrections of Lyonnais silk workers of 1831 and 1834, the discourse initiated by the utopian socialists Charles Fourier and Flora Tristran of the right to work, the June days of 1848 against the closure of the national workshops, and the contemporary campaign for the 40-h week. In contrast, British traditions of unemployed *self-activity* had a pedigree stretching back to the Blanketeers, the West End riot in 1889, and most significantly the hunger marches such as that from Leicester to London in 1905 (Beerbühl 2011; Reiss 2011; Vernon 2007: 22). Thus, French frames of opposition to unemployment (given the absence of a discourse of the hunger march) did not specifically address the question of how the unemployed might engage in collective

[17] *L'Humanité*, September 24–October 29, 1932.

[18] *Le Temps*, June 7, 1930.

action in the same way. To most French men and women, therefore, the concept of the hunger march was an unfamiliar one. *L'Humanité* was the key broker for this cultural import, facilitating a unilateral flow of mobilizing know-how. In late 1932, *L'Humanité* familiarized its readers with the British repertoire of protest. This reporting had two particular characteristics. First, it introduced the hunger march, and, secondly, it showed how this had the potential of connecting to a more militant repertoire of action.

International networking facilitated the function that *L'Humanité* played in the French reception of the concept of the hunger march. Thus, on October 15, 1932, French Communist Party deputy and *L'Humanité's* foreign affairs editor Gabriel Péri spoke at a committee against war rally at the Friends' Meeting House in London. Alongside the deputy for Argenteuil, an Irish communist O'Donnell and British Communist Party general secretary Harry Pollitt described the barricades of the rioting jobless in Belfast to loud applause.[19] Thus, the protests of the unemployed intersected with other communist-inspired movements (the Amsterdam-Pleyel movement) to which the French Communist Party were much more central. It was in the context of the riots of the unemployed in Belfast, Liverpool, North Shields, and West Ham that *L'Humanité* took greater interest in the hunger march of 1932 (particularly when it too clashed with the police in Stratford-upon-Avon and at Hyde Park). The newspaper featured photographs of both the devastation on the streets of Belfast and the hunger march. The Scottish delegation, the entry into London, and the platform at the Hyde Park demonstration all appeared on *L'Humanité's* front page. Its coverage of the British march was substantially greater than that of the US or the German hunger marches.

Prior to late 1932, the foreign hunger marches were often not reported as such. For instance, the 1922 hunger march was termed the *marche des chômeurs*.[20] The "Ford Hunger March" of March 1932, although reported in the French Communist newspaper, was not termed a hunger march. After 1932, the paper's interest in the hunger marches was transformed. There were a reasonable amount of coverage of the February 1934 national hunger march and even coverage of the Lancashire hunger march of 1933. It seems that the NUWM's 1932 hunger march was a turning point in the imagination of the French movement. The hunger march established itself as central to the repertoire of the French unemployed movement. The terms *marche de la faim* and *marche sur Paris* (march on Paris) were used interchangeably for the one-day affair of December 22, 1932. The *marche de la faim* was deployed more systematically with the Lille to Paris march which was much closer to the British model of a hunger march. This *marche de la faim* acted as a practical tipping point. In the years 1934 and 1935, following on from the Lille to Paris hunger march, there were hunger marches across the French provinces as can be seen from Appendix 9.2. The hunger march had also pervaded the language of the French unemployed movement to the extent that, for instance, the newspaper of the Ardennes Union of Committees of the Unemployed was given the title of *La Marche de la Faim*.

[19] *L'Humanité*, October 16, 1932.

[20] *L'Humanité*, November 18, 1922.

Was this cultural transfer then simply a question of language or a matter of semantics? The special term – hunger march – conveyed a comprehension of the special nature of this form of collective action, more specifically its complex aggregate character as an amalgamation of other protest forms. The word alerted organizers to the model used abroad, particularly in Britain, and implied a realization that this required careful resource-intensive preparation. The use of this initially alien term highlighted a new understanding of a method that worked elsewhere and that was suited to the particular dynamics of unemployed contestation. It signified an appreciation of the hunger march's strategic place in the repertoire of protest and its facilitation of more militant forms of collective action. It signaled the possibility of greater success in the building of movements of the unemployed.

In sum, the hunger march's crossing of the Channel resulted from an entangled matrix of circumstance. Mass unemployment, conducive political opportunity structures, top-down solicitation from the leading communist party and union bodies, political resources, and external pressure from the Comintern all came together. But these provide an inadequate explanation without the addition of the cognitive-cultural dimension: the appreciation on the part of French communist activists of what a hunger march entailed and how it might help an unemployed movement achieve its aims. This final dimension was diffused from British experience via *L'Humanité* to the grassroots of French communism with the British hunger march of 1932 and the Lille to Paris march of 1933 being critical moments in this process.

9.5 Conclusions

Clearly, the French and British unemployed protest movements of the 1930s share key features. Although the British movement became engrained into the political culture and collective memory to a far greater extent than the French movement, they do have a perhaps surprising degree of symmetry when it comes to the repertoire of collective action. Despite differences of social and economic geography, of cycles and intensity of unemployment, and of welfare policies, both movements had to confront the unemployed subject. Neither the Comintern's voluntaristic metaphor of the army ready to march into battle nor the descent into despair apparent to the visiting ethnographers in the distressed Austrian village of Marienthal adequately captured the realities of efforts to mobilize the unemployed (Jahoda et al. 1972).

This study has probed the most obvious aspect of unemployed protest: the hunger march. Given the visual seductiveness of the hunger march and its privileged place in representations of the protests of the 1930s, historians have peered beyond this to a rich range of activity that could be missed if the hunger march monopolizes our understandings of unemployed protest. For instance, historians have stressed the significance of advice and representational work on behalf of the unemployed (Stevenson and Cook 1994: 178).

Yet this study put the question slightly differently: What happens if we compare the hunger marches of two unemployed movements? And how do the hunger marches interact with other forms of protest in cycles of contestation? A subtle, mediated, but nonetheless vital, transnational connection was discovered between the British and French unemployed movements with regard to the hunger march. The British unemployed helped to reframe French unemployed protest. The British hunger march of 1932 was critical to French activists learning of a new language of protest. After the assimilation of this insight, the Lille to Paris hunger march was then a catalyst for its diffusion across France.

This reexamination of the hunger march in comparative context has reasserted the significance of this form of protest. Its effect in both countries was to connect together a complex sequence of protest forms and to extend protest cycles where otherwise they would be more disconnected, localized, short-term and, from the point of view of the activist, dispiriting. Herein lies a further reason why those who participated in these movements privileged the hunger march in their own narratives. In sum, this investigation of the hunger march has disclosed its uniqueness as a mode of unemployed protest on three grounds: as an exclusive mode of unemployed protest, as a transfer from British to French unemployed protest culture, and as the fulcrum that extended the temporal and spatial range of unemployed cycles of contestation.

9.6 Appendices

Appendix 9.1 The Appearance of "*Marche De La Faim*" in French Newspapers

Newspaper (time span)	Date (occasions)	Context
Le Figaro (1854–1942)	1932 (3)	Belfast hunger march (?)
		British hunger march
		Paris hunger march
	1933 (1)	Belgian hunger march
La Croix (1880–1944)	1931 (2)	Bulgarian hunger march
		US hunger march
	1932 (4)	US hunger march
		Dublin hunger march
	1933 (1)	Darmstadt hunger march
	1934 (1)	Dives hunger march
Le Petit Parisien (1876–1939)	1932 (3)	Viennese hunger march
		US hunger march
		Berlin hunger march
L'Humanité (1904–1944)	1930 (1)	Dortmund hunger march
	1932 (4)	British hunger march
		US hunger march
	1933 (2)	Berlin hunger march
		Lancashire hunger march
Le Temps (1861–1939)	1930 (1)	Berlin hunger march

Source: Gallica

Appendix 9.2 French Hunger Marches, 1932–1935

Date	Hunger march
April 9, 1932	Oyonnax to Nantua march, Ain
December 9, 1932	Paris hunger march
June 27–28, 1933	Saint-Nazaire to Nantes hunger march
November 18–December 2, 1933	Lille to Paris hunger march
December 3, 1933	Tarnos to Ondres hunger march
January 4, 1934	Dives-sur-Mer to Caen hunger march
February 4, 1934	Valenciennes hunger march, Nord
February 10, 1934	Saint-Étienne hunger march, Loire
February 23, 1934	Cambrai hunger march, Nord
April 6, 1934	Croismare to Lunéville hunger march
April 18, 1934	Douai hunger march, Nord
April 20, 1934	Rouen hunger march
April 22, 1934	Avesnes hunger march
October 15–19, 1934	Nord regional hunger march to Lille
November 21, 1934	Neuves-Maisons to Nancy hunger march
December 15, 1934	Alès to Nîmes hunger march
December 25, 1934	Méru to Beauvais hunger march
January 12, 1935	Paris hunger march
February 22–23, 1935	Ardennes hunger march to Charleville
April 7, 1935	Pont L'Abbé to Quimper hunger march
April 24–26, 1935	Somme hunger march to Amiens

Appendix 9.3 Repertoires of Action of the Unemployed

Activity form	Characteristics
(a) Transgressive repertoire of activity (militant)	
Riot	Transgressing legal or public constraints on behavior often challenging property and the forces of the state in a violent manner
Occupation	Physical seizure of local site of power, property or production
Eviction protest	Militant transgressive challenge to the prerogatives of landlords. Often involving physical challenges to bailiffs or the police. Challenging property rights and social standing of landlords. Highly localized
(b) Intermediary repertoire of activity	
Relief strike	Withdrawal of labor of those on public schemes to provide work for the unemployed. This is often framed within trade union notions of wages and conditions and the negative associations with compulsory labor connected with the poor law or authoritarian regimes
Demonstration	Protest of unlimited numbers connected to more or less formal claim-making. Depending on the context of the stance of the authorities either transgressive or non-transgressive. Physical and symbolic contestation of public space

(continued)

Appendix 9.3 (continued)

Activity form	Characteristics
Hunger march	Distinctive form of protest for the unemployed. Formalized protest involving small numbers, formalized process of claim-making often through petitioning and delegations. Considerable organizational resources and planning required. Important spatial dimension as the protest takes place over an extended route or routes
(c) Non-transgressive repertoire of activity (moderate)	
Public meeting	Open public claim-making and planning forum
Petitioning/letter writing	Moderate form of claim-making activity focusing on the public authorities
Representation	Defensive usually non-transgressive claim-making for individuals within welfare or legal structures
Cooperative or self-help activity	Non-transgressive moderate activity to provide assistance to unemployed peers. Sometimes there is an unclear boundary between this and charitable activity on behalf of the unemployed

References

Association de Recherches et d'Etudes du Mouvement Ouvrier de la Région de Saint-Nazaire (Aremors). (1983). *Saint-Nazaire et le mouvement ouvrier de 1920 à 1939*. Saint-Nazaire: Aremors.

Bagguley, P. (1992). Protest, acquiescence and the unemployed: A comparative analysis of the 1930s and the 1980s. *The British Journal of Sociology, 43*(3), 443–461.

Beerbühl, M. S. (2011). The March of the Blanketeers: Tragic failure or pioneer of unemployed protest. In M. Reiss & M. Perry (Eds.), *Unemployment and protest: Two centuries of protest*. Oxford: Oxford University Press.

Bourdieu, P. (1998). *Acts of resistance: Against the new myths of our time*. Cambridge: Polity.

Campbell, A., & McIlroy, J. (2008). The National Unemployed Workers' Movement and the Communist party of Great Britain revisited. *Labour History Review, 73*(1), 61–88.

Chabanet, D. (2002). Les marches européens contre le chômage, la précarité et les exclusions. In R. Blame, D. Chabanet, & V. Wright (Eds.), *L'Action collective en Europe*. Paris: Presses de Sciences Po.

Croucher, R. (1990). Communist unemployed organisations between the world wars. *Archiv für Sozialgeschichte, 30*, 590–591.

della Porta, D. (2002). Comparative Politics and Social Movements. In B. Klandermans & S. Staggenborg (Eds.), *Methods of social movement research*. London: University of Minnesota Press.

Goffman, E. (1963). *Stigma: Notes on the management of spoiled identity*. Englewood Cliffs: Prentice Hall.

Guitard, P. (1933). *Le Chômage*. Paris: Maurice d'Hartoy.

Hayburn, R. (1972). The police and the hunger marches. *International Review of Social History, 17*(2), 625–44.

Hayburn, R. (1983). The national unemployed workers' movement, 1921–36: A re-appraisal. *International Review of Social History, 28*, 279–295.

Jahoda, M., Lazarsfeld, P., & Zeisel, H. (1972). *Marienthal: The Sociography of an unemployed community*. London: Tavistock.

Johnston, H., & Noakes, J. (2005). Frames of protest: A road map to a perspective. In H. Johnston & J. Noakes (Eds.), *Frames of protest: Social movements and the framing perspective*. Lanham: Rowman & Littlefield.
Kingsford, P. (1982). *The hunger marches 1920–40*. London: Lawrence and Wishart.
Paugam, S. (1998). La révolte des chômeurs: Un mouvement sans précédent. *Magazine Littéraire, 365*, 73–76.
Perry, M. (2000). *Bread and work: The experience of unemployment 1918–39*. London: Pluto.
Perry, M. (2005). *Jarrow crusade: Protest and legend*. Sunderland: Sunderland University Press.
Perry, M. (2007). *Prisoners of want: The experience and protest of the unemployed in France, 1921–45*. Aldershot: Ashgate.
Pierru, E. (2007). Mobiliser 'la vie fragile': Les communistes et les chômeurs dans les années 1930. *Sociétés Contemporaines, 65*, 113–146.
Reiss, M. (2007). Marching on the capital: National protest marches of the British unemployed in the 1920s and the 1930s. In M. Reiss (Ed.), *The Street as stage: Protest marches and public rallies since the nineteenth century*. Oxford: Oxford University Press.
Reiss, M. (2011). From Poor Relief to Politics: The Protest of the Unemployed in the 1870s and 1880s. In M. Reiss & M. Perry (Eds.), *Unemployment and Protest: Two Centuries of Contention*. Oxford: Oxford University Press.
Stevenson, J., & Cook, C. (1994). *Britain in the depression: Society and politics, 1929–1939*. London: Longman.
Tarrow, S. (1998[1994]). *Power in movement: Social movements and contentious politics*. Cambridge: Cambridge University Press.
Tillon, C. (1977). *On chantait rouge*. Paris: Laffont.
Turnbull, M. (1973). Attitude of government and administration towards the 'Hunger Marches' of the 1920s and 1930s. *Journal of Social Policy, 2*, 131–142.
Vernon, J. (2007). *Hunger: A modern history*. London: The Belknap.

Chapter 10
Comparing Mobilizations Against Three Social Reforms in the 2000s in Belgium

Jean Faniel

10.1 Welfare State "Activation" and Social Mobilizations

In 1999, the Flemish and French-speaking Liberal, Socialist, and Green parties formed a coalition government. One of the government's aims was to turn the Belgian social protection system into a so-called *active* welfare state (Matagne 2001). This plan was mainly promoted by the Flemish Socialist Party (SP.A) and clearly inspired by the policies of British Prime Minister, Tony Blair. In that vein, this government and its successor implemented three major reforms: changes in subsistence income, in unemployment procedures, and in the early retirement scheme.

10.1.1 Reforming Minimum Subsistence Income

In 2001, the SP.A Minister of Social Integration proposed to reform the eligibility criteria for the minimum subsistence income, known as the "minimex." The minimex was allocated to people with limited financial resources who were not entitled to social security benefits such as unemployment insurance. The minimex – set up in 1974 in order to replace the system of public assistance based on the principles of charity – concerned roughly 80,000 people in the early 2000s. A number of minimex recipients were poor and socially excluded people, many of whom were prevented from receiving unemployment benefits. The main points of the reform were the requirement for applicants to do a training course or to accept any type of employment, even if the job did not meet the criterion for "suitable" employment

J. Faniel (✉)
Centre de recherche et d'information socio-politiques (CRISP), Place Quetelet 1A, B-1210 Brussels, Belgium
e-mail: j.faniel@crisp.be

B. Andreosso-O'Callaghan and F. Royall (eds.), *Economic and Political Change in Asia and Europe: Social Movement Analyses*, DOI 10.1007/978-94-007-4653-4_10,

commonly used for unemployment insurance. Applicants were also required to sign a "social integration contract" with public authorities committing themselves to taking appropriate steps to find employment.

Several organizations speaking on behalf of poor people and a number of trade unions publicly opposed the minister's proposal. They indicated their disappointment that the minister had not consulted them and also criticized the reform itself (Faniel 2006a). French-speaking Green party (Écolo) ministers prevented the government from ratifying the proposal until such time as the Minister of Social Integration had made a number of minor changes. The organizations most opposed to the reform underlined that it focused mainly on labor market access for socially excluded people, that it forced people to accept any kind of employment, and that this situation would have implications for all salaried workers whose standards of employment would also suffer. The trade union movement did not share these reservations, and union confederations approved a revised version of the proposal.

There are three reasons that explain the union confederations' position. First, union confederations have few contacts with minimex recipients and thus do not feel committed to defend their cause. Second, the Flemish sections of the unions were well disposed toward the active welfare state discourse, whereas their French-speaking counterparts were much more reluctant to accept this shift in paradigm. The rate of unemployment being higher in French-speaking regions, the issue of job creation is very important for unions in these areas. By contrast, Flemish sections saw the active welfare policies as a useful tool to help integrate workers into the labor market and to increase employment levels. Thirdly, the fact that Flemish leaders of the Socialist union (ABVV/FGTB) and those of the SP.A have close ties also ensured that opposition to the reform was weak. The ABVV/FGTB[1] is generally seen as more radical than the Christian confederation (ACV/CSC)[2] or the Liberal trade union (ACLVB/CGSLB)[3] – both of which are dominated by their Flemish sections.

Although several organizations continued to criticize the revised version of the minister's proposal, they did not manage to stop the reform being passed into law in 2002.

10.1.2 *Reforming the Tracking Procedures on the Unemployed*

Following the 2003 legislative election, the Liberal and Socialist parties formed a new coalition government, thus leaving aside the Flemish and French-speaking Green parties. In January 2004, the new SP.A Minister of Employment proposed to

[1] Algemeen Belgisch Vakverbond/Fédération générale du travail de Belgique (General Labour Federation of Belgium).

[2] Algemeen Christelijk Vakverbond/Confédération des syndicats chrétiens (Confederation of Christian Trade Unions).

[3] Algemene Centrale der Liberale Vakbonden van België/Centrale générale des syndicats libéraux de Belgique (General Confederation of Liberal Trade Unions of Belgium).

reform the system for tracking the unemployed. The official purpose of the bill was to provide unemployed people with extra help in finding employment. Since then, claimants who have been out of work for a certain length of time (15 months for people under 25 years of age and 21 months for people of other age groups) are required to report to the National Employment Office (NEO) for one-to-one interviews at which time he/she is required to show that he/she has been actively seeking work (Faniel 2010a). The reform changed in a fundamental way the philosophy underlying unemployment insurance in Belgium. Henceforth, the unemployed are not only required to be available for work, but he/she must also show proof that he/she has been actively seeking work. Should the interview highlight problems, then the claimant is required to take specified steps to address this issue. Subsequent interviews are to be organized to assess compliance with the conditions stipulated in the personalized contract. Should the subsequent interviews prove to be unsatisfactory, the claimant is subject to a penalty which may result in forfeiting his/her unemployment insurance.

Soon after the minister proposed to reform the system for tracking the unemployed, some of the organizations that had mobilized against the 2001 minimex reform roundly criticized this proposal. Christian and Socialist union confederations also opposed such a reform (Faniel 2005, 2012). The links between the Belgian union confederations and the unemployed make them particularly sensitive to issues related to joblessness and to that of the unemployed. For historical reasons, most unemployed Belgians are trade union members – currently in excess of 80% – and they receive benefits via their union. Trade unions act therefore as payment agencies (Vandaele 2006; Faniel 2009, 2010a, b), and their relationship with the unemployed is mainly characterized by that of service provision. Although unions represent workers – including those who are unemployed – in the official bodies that manage social security, unions have been reluctant to mobilize the unemployed as such and to defend specially their interests. Nevertheless, since the dramatic rise in the rate of unemployment as of the mid-1970s, a few union-based groups of the unemployed were created at local levels (Faniel 2006b). The organizations that had mobilized in 2001, the union-based groups of unemployed, and the Walloon wing of the Socialist union now also opposed the new tracking procedures and pointed out that the unemployed could be forced to accept any kind of job to avoid sanctions. They also claimed that the proposal would relieve the State and private companies from their responsibility in job creation or to provide support for the unemployed. The opponents of the bill also indicated that it would have repercussions for people currently in employment. By contrast, the national leaders of the Socialist and Christian union confederations requested that the government change the bill slightly so as to soften its impact. These approaches by various sections of the trade union movement – some strongly opposing, some more conciliatory – led to tensions within the movement itself. Once again, the divergent views of the Flemish and the French-speaking union sections as well as the close ties of some Flemish leaders with the minister's party help to explain these differences within the union confederations. Backed by some Green Members of Parliament, now in opposition, the organizations, the union-based groups of the unemployed, and the Walloon wing of the Socialist union initiated protest actions including demonstrations and symbolic occupations of public buildings. National union officials lobbied the government, but they did not encourage their members – especially people in employment – to reject the proposal.

In time, the minister changed a few minor points of the proposal, especially those related to the frequency of the interviews and to the date when the new measures were to take effect for each age group.[4] Moreover, unions received subsidies from the regional governments to help the unemployed prepare for their interviews with the NEO and to hire staff to help their members during the interviews. Although the above-mentioned organizations and union sections continued to criticize the philosophy behind the reform, the national union confederations approved the revised project which came into effect in July 2004.

10.1.3 Reforming the Early Retirement System

In 2005, the government decided to make swinging cuts in early retirement opportunities, emphasizing (as did other governments in the European Union at that time) the need to tackle the rising cost of the country's aging population and the requirement to increase the rate of employment among people over the age of 55 (Moulaert 2006). Confronted with major restructurings occurring in a number of industrial sectors in the 1970s, unions and management worked out early retirement arrangements. They offered people who had been in employment for a relatively long period of time the opportunity to retire early, thus freeing up jobs for younger people. These types of measures had the advantage of attenuating the social costs of collective redundancies, which is one of the reasons why employers were interested in them and even more so in times of economic recession. The early retirement packages usually consisted of a NEO allowance payment and an employer's supplemental payment.

While employers accepted the 2005 reform – as they had backed the minimex and unemployment reforms – unions rejected it. The Socialist ABVV/FGTB called for a 1-day general strike, the first in 12 years. Three weeks later, as the government refused to withdraw or to amend its project, the three union confederations joined forces and organized a second 1-day general strike. A major demonstration took place in Brussels with between 80,000 and 100,000 participants. Clearly, the ACV/CSC and ACLVB/CGSLB rank and file succeeded in forcing their union leaders to oppose the government's plan and to join the strike actions led by the ABVV/FGTB. Once again, the reform of the early retirement arrangements had various impacts

[4] In the first year, the new procedures were introduced for unemployed people up to 30 years of age. In 2005, the tracking procedures were extended to unemployed people up to the age of 40. Since 2006, they apply to all unemployed people up to the age of 50. A review of the system was to be carried out in 2007.

across regions. While in Flanders, employers railed against a labor shortage and the fact that many older workers were leaving the workforce, in a region such as Wallonia – where unemployment rates remained particularly high especially for young people – the idea of forcing older people to remain in employment seemed even more surprising. Nevertheless, workers from all regions pointed to the increasingly difficult working conditions and to the difficulties these conditions provoke, especially for older workers. Hence, trade unions all over Belgium sought to ensure that employees continued to be entitled to retire before the age of 65, at least in the heavy industry sectors. The mobilizations against the reform thus involved not only early retirees but also a great number of unionized people then currently employed.

Despite the protests, the government made only minor changes to the project before ratifying it. Unlike the reforms of the minimex and of the system for tracking the unemployed, the reform of the early retirement system referred only to a general framework and it left room for further negotiations between unions and management on issues surrounding the reform (e.g., the age groups or the types of professions that would still be entitled to avail of early retirement arrangements). The fact that the mobilization against the 2005 reform was not successful does not appear therefore to have had major consequences when compared to the consequences of the failed mobilizations in 2001 and in 2004. In 2005, some categories of workers were still entitled to retire early.

10.1.4 Crises, New Issues, and More Mobilizations

As in other European countries, a growing number of actors claimed that Belgium had to reform its retirement scheme in order to ensure financial sustainability. But successive governments were reluctant to address this issue. Several reasons explain such a state of affairs. In 2005, the reform of the retirement scheme was a politically sensitive issue given the level of mobilization against it. Moreover, unions and management are still poles apart on this issue as are the Socialist and Liberal parties, coalition partners since 1999.[5] Over the past number of years, Belgium has also had to face a number of political and economic crises. On the political front, Belgium is unstable owing to the tensions between Flemish and French-speaking parties on institutional matters. At an economic level, Belgium has also had to deal with the financial and economic crisis in the fall of 2008, and the government was forced to come to the financial aid of the country's main banks. Many companies including several major multinationals such as General Motors and Carrefour downsized or simply closed down their Belgian operations. Early retirement arrangements were

[5] Between December 2007 and December 2011, the SP.A was in opposition at the federal level, but the French-speaking Socialist Party (PS) stayed in government.

often used to soften the social consequences of the redundancies, even in contradiction to the 2005 reform. Belgium's political and economic difficulties thus contributed to impede the debate on the reform of the retirement system.

Along with the general rise in unemployment, the economic situation also contributed to renew the opposition of the Walloon sections of the Socialist union against the tracking procedures on the unemployed set up in 2004. The Walloon wing of the ABVV/FGTB stressed that capitalists were responsible for the financial and economic crisis and refused to accept that the unemployed should suffer the consequences: initially by being (or remaining) unemployed, then by being sanctioned by the NEO when unable to get a job. Since 2008, the Walloon wing of the ABVV/FGTB and its local sections organized several small demonstrations as well as so-called flash mobs. They urged the government to change the tracking procedures reform, and they sought the support of the local communities who had to bear an increasing financial burden to subsidize the minimex applicants who were not entitled to unemployment insurance. However, the tracking procedures modified in 2004 first remained unchanged and in 2012 even were extended to the unemployed up to the age of 58.

10.2 Explaining the Different Levels of Mobilization: Actors and Alliances as Focal Points

The contention in this chapter is that the strength and the impact of any mobilization depend on its internal features as well as on the context in which it takes place. It is, therefore, necessary to look both at the features of the organizations involved in a "movement" as well as at – what scholars refer to as – the political opportunity structure (POS). Tarrow (1998 [1994]: 85) depicts a POS as "dimensions of the political environment that provide incentives for people to undertake collective action by affecting their expectations for success or failure." It is extremely important to look at any mobilization's POS so as to identify the contextual factors of the political processes.

Tarrow (1998 [1994]: 86) identifies four salient changes that can facilitate the rise of a social movement and influence its success: "The opening up of access to participation, shifts in ruling alignments, the availability of influential allies, and cleavages within and among elites." The three mobilizations presented above show the central role played by the trade union movement in Belgium. The more trade unions were involved in the protests – very few in 2001, some in 2004, a considerable number in 2005 – the bigger and more visible the protests, and the more the protestors managed to obtain (albeit minor) concessions from the government. For the civil society organizations that mobilized in 2001 and 2004, the unions appeared to be "influential allies," that is, powerful actors with whom it was necessary to form alliances in order to strengthen their mobilization.

It is thus crucial to focus on the role of trade unions in protests, to take into account the unions' capacity for mobilization, to identify the issues that are likely to attract the attention of the unions, and to assess the conditions under which unions agree to form alliances with other organizations. But it is also necessary to look at the features of the other social actors involved in the protests listed above, in order to understand the specific dynamics of each of these mobilizations. Hence, the commonly described features of so-called new social movements and their relationships with trade unions will be dealt with.

10.2.1 *Trade Unions as Influential Actors*

For a number of reasons, union density in Belgium is greater than 50 %, one of the highest rates in Europe (Faniel 2010b). Union membership has also continued to grow despite high levels of unemployment. This is due to the fact that most of the jobless Belgians are union members or people who join unions in order to receive benefits (Vandaele 2006). Unions in Belgium are well grounded in the private and public sectors, and union confederations take part in many official advisory bodies: social security or various social and economic bodies. Along with the employers' confederations, union confederations negotiate national and sector-specific agreements that the Minister of Employment may recognize legally. Historically, the three Belgian union confederations developed links with political parties, thereby influencing relations at times. Political parties have sought to improve the position of the unions (especially of the union confederation ideologically close to them), and the unions have sometimes been reluctant to challenge decisions made by ministers of the same ideological leaning.

Although unions are major political and social actors in Belgium, globalization and neoliberalism have undermined their position and they have lost some of their influence over the past decades. Nonetheless, unions still have the capacity to rally their members when dealing with specific issues (e.g., the 2005 mobilization against the reform of the early retirement system). But such a capacity for mobilization does not always ensure that the government will listen and do as they are told. Moreover, the unions do not consider that every issue deserves the same level of attention.

Generally speaking, trade unions aim to represent and to defend class-based interests, but they often promote the interests of their "core" rank and file, that is, full-time, manual, skilled, white, male workers who are employed in large companies and who have secure jobs. "As a corollary, those in lower-skilled jobs with insecure labor market positions – and notably, women and migrant workers or those from ethnic minorities – have in most countries, and for much of the time, been marginalized within trade unionism: their interests not only neglected but rendered almost invisible" (Hyman 2001: 30–31). The unemployed could also be usefully added to Hyman's list (Ness 1998; Richards 2000; Faniel 2009) as well as the people excluded from unemployment insurance, such as the Belgian minimex recipients.

Trade unions are bureaucratic organizations as well. Union leaders defend workers' actions, but they also put a check on them so as to make protests manageable (Mills 1948) and to ensure "their" organization's stability. Through collective bargaining, union leaders are also influenced by employers and state representatives (Hyman 1971, 1975) and may be forced to accept major concessions so as to be seen as "responsible" actors. Moreover, since many union leaders are part of the "core" membership, they are likely to defend the interests of the "core" rank and file to the detriment of the more "marginal" workers, especially the unemployed and the socially excluded.

Finally, many unions have developed close links with political parties (Valenzuela 1992; Slomp 1996). When allied political parties are in office, the special relationship may ensure that unions reach their objectives through legislation. But unions can also become a government vector, ensuring that unpopular reforms are put in place while reducing the likelihood of protests.

10.2.2 Trade Unions and NSMs

Beside unions, many organizations are active in a number of social and cultural arenas. Their influence and their relationship to unions and to the state vary greatly. Some authors focus on the interactions between trade unions and organizations, often described as "new social movements" (NSMs) (Bellal et al. 2003; Tartakowsky and Tétard 2006; Faniel 2006a).[6] NSMs' members are often depicted as being different from unions' members (Pakulski 1993). Membership of NSMs is not based on the production process but rather on so-called new issues that are not specifically linked to particular social classes such as gender, peace, the Third World, and poverty. NSMs are also considered to function according to different criteria compared to unions (Offe and Wiesenthal 1985: 214–15). Unions are described as well-structured organizations where decision-making processes are highly formalized. Conversely, NSMs are seen to be more flexible gatherings of people where the rank and file are more closely involved in the decision-making process, but where defections can cause a greater level of instability.

Unions and NSMs do not have the same goals. Normally, unions are often described as organizations that seek to change society from economic and political standpoints.[7] It would also appear that unions have become less radical in the sense that they no longer seek to overturn the economic system, and that they have come to accept the capitalist status quo. NSMs are, therefore, seen to be more radical than trade unions on social or cultural issues but not necessarily on economic or political issues. Cohen (1985: 664) argues that NSMs are different from unions in that they dispense

[6] The appropriateness of the term is not discussed here.

[7] This assertion focuses on the original conceptions of the trade union movements of the Socialist, Communist, or Anarchist traditions. Such a view does not take into consideration other tendencies such as Christian or business unions.

with "revolutionary dreams in favor of the idea of structural reform" and that they promote "a defense of civil society that does not seek to abolish the autonomous functioning of political and economic systems – in a phrase, self-limiting radicalism." Some authors point out that NSMs and trade unions share common points characterized by complementarity and competition (Tartakowsky and Tétard 2006). At a micro-sociological level, people are often involved in both types of organizations at the same time, leading to interpersonal links and facilitating exchanges.

These differences reflect to a large extent the variety of the positions in civil society, especially between NSMs, on the one hand, and trade unions, on the other. But NSMs and unions, as they are portrayed in this section, are stereotypes. Such schematic views can thus seem oversimplified, and one has to view the above-mentioned features with some caution.

10.3 Three Mobilizations, Three Political Processes

Each of the three reforms described in the first part of this chapter led to collective action involving NSMs and/or trade unions. But the features and the intensity of the mobilizations have been quite different: public claims, two 1-day general strikes, and demonstrations ranging from 200 activists to approximately 100,000 protesters. How is it possible to explain such differences according to the analytical framework discussed above?

10.3.1 Different Social Groups

One way of assessing the differences is by looking at the people who are targeted by the reforms. There were approximately 80,000 minimex applicants in 2001, 485,000 registered unemployed people in 2004, and 110,000 early retirees in 2005. Clearly, these numbers alone cannot explain the differences since there were four times more unemployed people than early retirees, but the 2005 protests involved many more people than the number of those that opposed the 2004 reform of the tracking procedures. Another possible way of assessing the differences is by looking at the people who benefited from the reforms. Minimex beneficiaries often face personal problems such as homelessness, poverty, or social exclusion. From a resource mobilization theory's perspective, these minimex beneficiaries should be politically quiescent. This comment also applies to the unemployed, but because a country has high levels of unemployment, this does not mean that the unemployed will mobilize (Chabanet and Faniel 2011). On the contrary, early retirees are not normally considered to be socially excluded. Rather, they are seen to be people likely to have an experience of union activism. By participating in trade unions, they can make their unions more aware of their worries. So, the numbers belonging to and the profiles of the three social groups can account for only part of the differences in the level of mobilization.

One way of resolving this issue is by looking at the people directly involved in the mobilizations. The demonstration that took place in 2005 brought together between 80,000 and 100,000 people, almost as many people as the total number of early retirees (110,000). Such large-scale mobilizations rarely involve all members of a social group. Indeed, most of the demonstrators were not early retirees but people in employment. This demonstration was coupled with the second of the 1-day general strikes, thus enabling people in employment to join the protest event. These people went on strike because they wanted to ensure that they too could retire before the age of 65. They also protested so as to fight against youth unemployment. The objective of youth employment seems to be in contradiction with the government's desire to keep people at work for a longer period of time, since people over the age of 50 are seen to compete with young people on the labor market. A key point that explains the intensity of the mobilization against the 2005 reform is, therefore, that the public at large saw the issue at stake as being highly sensitive. There were far more people affected or concerned by the changes compared to the number of people then benefiting from early retirement arrangements.

This is not the case for minimex recipients and for the unemployed. People in employment rarely considered that what was happening to minimex recipients and to the unemployed affected them. This was not the case for the early retirement scheme. Moreover, very few minimex recipients participated in the mobilization against the 2001 reform. This mobilization was thus initiated by organizations that acted on behalf of minimex recipients, but without the support of unions or of people in employment. The 2004 mobilization also involved very few of the people targeted by the reform and, therefore, only several hundred unemployed people mobilized – less than 1 % of the registered jobless. But in 2004, there were more unions and employed people involved in the protest than in 2001, thus showing a greater level of public support. The 2004 mobilization was thus initiated by organizations acting on behalf of the unemployed, by organizations made up of unemployed people, and by some union sections. Let us now turn to the reasons that led to the collective action of a number of organizations in 2001, 2004, and 2005 and at the alliances they set up with other actors and especially trade unions.

10.3.2 Different Allies

The mobilization against the 2005 reform of the early retirement system mainly involved the union confederations. Initially, these confederations negotiated with employers and the government with a view to reforming the early retirement arrangements. The mobilization took place because the Socialist confederation and, later, the Christian and Liberal unions wished to put pressure on the government when it became clear that negotiations were taking a turn the unions wished to avoid.

In 2001 and in 2004, the union confederations' national leaders approved, more or less readily, the proposed reforms, and the confederations did not participate in the mobilizations. Hence, the organizations that challenged the reforms could not lean on the union confederations and on unions' capacity for action – lobbying, demonstrating, and organizing strikes. In 2004, the associations that criticized the reform of the tracking procedures, the union-based groups of the unemployed, and the Walloon wing of the ABVV/FGTB mobilized, but on a weak footing. Moreover, the Walloon wing of the ABVV/FGTB was put in a difficult position as the national confederation had already accepted the reform.

In 2001, almost no union section mobilized against the reform of the minimex. Hence, organizations were on their own to defend minimex recipients, often seen as socially excluded people, rather than as former or potential employees. As pointed out in the second part of this chapter, the issue of poverty is more likely to be of concern to NSMs than to unions. These organizations tried to gain the support of unions by highlighting the effects that the 2001 reform could have on the labor market. Scholars refer to this as a type of frame extension (Snow et al. 1986).[8] By becoming involved in the organizations, union activists helped them to conceptualize the issues of employment and of social security. Such a type of collaboration illustrates the links between NSMs and unions at a micro-sociological level. But union activists and the organizations failed to gain the support of the union confederations as such, thereby depriving them of influential allies. They also were not able to depend on the politically quiescent minimex recipients to support the mobilization. In the end, a good number of the organizations who had signed a petition rejecting the reform did not even take part in the demonstrations, thus illustrating one of the features of NSMs: the possibility of a lack of commitment.

In the previous section, the key issues of the reforms and the social reactions they brought about were looked at. In this section, another important element that explains the different levels of mobilization against the three reforms was analyzed: the capacity for mobilization of the social groups concerned by the reforms and their likelihood of getting the support of influential allies. The issue of whether influential allies come to the help of social groups depended essentially on how they viewed the reforms. As pointed above, trade unions are key actors in Belgium, so it is necessary now in turn to analyze their positions on the reforms.

10.3.3 Varying Union Positions

One key point in understanding the varying union positions on the reforms relates to the very characteristics of trade unions as discussed in the second section of this chapter.

---

[8] According to Snow et al. (1986: 472), a process of frame extension occurs when a social movement tries "to extend the boundaries of its primary framework so as to encompass interests or points of view that are incidental to its primary objectives but of considerable salience to potential adherents. In effect, the movement is attempting to enlarge its adherent pool by portraying its objectives or activities as attending to or being congruent with the values or interests of potential adherents."

The three reforms were proposed by Flemish Socialist members of the federal government. The close relationships between the SP.A and some leaders of the Socialist union confederation made these union leaders more amenable to the reforms. More broadly, the leaders of the three union confederations shared the views of the government on the urgency of reforming the Belgian welfare state.

Nevertheless, the three social groups targeted by the reforms are quite different, and they all have specific relationships with unions. For example, union representatives have very few contacts with minimex recipients, and the views of senior management of the union confederations on the 2001 reform were dictated by their technical and political understanding of the issue. The rank and file exerted no pressure on them to consider other options.

Since a good number of unemployed people are union members in Belgium and since local unions are aware of the day-to-day difficulties of the unemployed, the union confederations mobilized to a greater extent in 2004. However, the reform was proposed by an SP.A minister and was based on active labor policies that many union leaders considered to be acceptable policies. Moreover, trade unions, especially professional federations, prioritize the defense of their members in employment and pay less attention to the interests of the unemployed. For these reasons, the national confederations – with a number of dissenters – accepted a revised version of the reform of the tracking procedures. However, the Walloon sections of the ABVV/FGTB adapted their strategy when it became clear that the government would pass the reform into law. They mobilized to force regional authorities to free public subsidies that could be used by the unions to hire representatives that could help their jobless members during NEO interviews. Although they failed to stop the reform of the tracking procedures, unions did strengthen their organizational structures because they had mobilized.

The 2005 reform of the early retirement arrangements was relevant to the trade union membership for several reasons. First, 86 % of the people already benefiting from these arrangements are union members. Second, the reform was of direct interest to people in employment – the core trade union membership – who may wish to avail of early retirement provisions. Moreover, unions act as payment agencies for early retired members and for the unemployed. The 2005 reform implied that early retirement arrangements would be progressively eliminated. Ultimately, this would threaten the unions' position. The 2004 reform did not have the same consequences for their position toward the unemployed since the reform did not seek to end the unemployment scheme itself or to withdraw benefit payments. Hence, union leaders were more reluctant to accept the 2005 reform compared to the 2004 reform, and they also faced rank-and-file pressure to mobilize strongly against the 2005 reform. Since the political and institutional channels proved to be ineffective, direct confrontation was inevitable even for the Christian and Liberal union confederations whose leadership initially wished to avoid it. Union confederations thus dedicated major resources to collective actions against the reform, unlike what happened in 2004 or in 2001, when unions barely participated in the protests.

10.3.4 New Mobilization Against the Tracking Procedures on the Unemployed

In June 2010, the ABVV/FGTB congress adopted a resolution against the tracking procedures on the unemployed. Since 2008, several Walloon sections of the Socialist union have mobilized against the procedures through lobbying, demonstrations, and flash mobs. Both contextual and internal reasons explain why the Socialist union decided to initiate collective action once again on this issue.

In the fall of 2008, a financial and economic crisis hit the Belgian economy. Due to its industrial configuration, Flanders soon became the Belgian region most heavily affected by the economic and social consequences of the crisis. Unemployment grew more rapidly in Flanders compared to the Walloon region or to Brussels. Although the rate of joblessness clearly remains at a lower level in Flanders than in the other two regions, with the growth in unemployment in Flanders, it was felt that Flemish public opinion toward unemployment could change in the short term – the unemployed would no longer be regarded as lazy and responsible for their plight.

Equally important is that the Flemish Socialist Party, which promoted the 2004 reform, was no longer in government as of December 2007. Until December 2011, the Minister of Labor was a member of the Center and the Socialist trade union consequently no longer hesitated to challenge the minister's policies. Changes at the economic and political levels could thus become an opportunity for the Walloon sections of the ABVV/FGTB to convince their Flemish counterparts to do away with the tracking procedures on the unemployed as introduced in 2004 or, at least, to suspend them as long as high rates of unemployment persisted. Moreover, unions used the public subsidies earmarked for recruitment to help the unemployed prepare for NEO interviews. These representatives of the unions defend the interests of the unemployed by informing members about the new procedures, helping them prepare for the interview, challenging NEO controllers that try to force the unemployed to accept any job, etc. The representatives thus made union officers and the wider public aware of the ways the reform affected unemployed people on a daily basis. The representatives also collaborated with some of the organizations that had mobilized in 2004. Finally, Thierry Bodson, one of the very few union officers that had opposed the 2001 and the 2004 reforms, became General Secretary of the Walloon wing of the ABVV/FGTB in May 2008. His status made him more sensitive to the preoccupations of socially excluded people and also aware of the effects their worsening situation could have on people in employment. At a local level, he received the support of other newly appointed union officers who themselves had been worried about the situation of the jobless. Together, they organized a number of local mobilizations against the tracking procedures. However, the new wave of protests had little effect and the tracking procedures introduced in 2004 were still in effect in 2011 and even strenghtened in 2012.

10.4 Conclusion

The Belgian federal government introduced three major welfare state reforms in the 2000s. This chapter sought to explain the reasons for the differences in the intensity of the mobilizations that arose in opposition to the reforms. Its conclusions are that the differences are of four main types. First, differences lie in the nature of the reforms and, subsequently, in the social groups affected by them. A second reason for the differences lies in the capacity of these social groups to initiate collective action. A third reason refers to the capability of the same social groups to form alliances with other organizations. Finally, differences emerge with respect to the attitudes of the labor movement toward government reforms because trade unions are influential actors in Belgian society, at least with respect to their capacity to mobilize. This last point is more broadly related to the country's social, political, and economic contexts as contexts influence the positions of union confederations.

Although the focus was on the Belgian case in a very specific period, this study can shed some light on the importance of comparative research. Comparing different mobilizations across time in a single country helps scholars to better understand mobilizations' characteristics and similarities. In the case of Belgium, the three mobilizations did not really form a single cycle of protest as defined by Tarrow (1998 [1994]: 153–68). The mobilization by some organizations against the 2001 minimex reform enabled them to gather around the same goals and to compare notes on issues related to social protection and to employment. By 2004, this sharing of experiences had become quite useful, allowing the organizations to consider in a more informed way the means by which to challenge the reform of the tracking procedures on the unemployed. The organizations widened their circle of allies – especially with some union sections – leading to a greater level of opposition to the 2004 reform compared to that of the 2001 reform. The mobilization against the reform of the early retirement system in 2005 cannot really be compared with the two other protest events. It would probably have taken place even had the other two events never occurred. But this assertion can only be verified by a comparative study across time.

This chapter also stressed the importance of looking at the various categories of actors involved in a collective action so as to understand who mobilizes, when, and on what issues. This is to be considered in a broad sense and would include analyzing the alliances established between the various social groups (including the alliances between NSMs and trade unions). This case study shows that the perceptions of the reforms can also encourage specific social groups to mobilize even if they are not directly or personally concerned by the issue at stake, as in the case of people in employment who had to deal with the changes to the early retirement arrangements or in the case of the organizations that mobilized against the 2001 minimex reform. Conversely, the lack of social, organizational, or economic resources can hamper the mobilization of so-called poor people, hence their tendency to seek alliances with influential actors.

To this extent, it is important to explore the specific features of trade unionism and to look at the elements that influence the positions of union confederations, especially in countries where the labor movement remains a key social and economic actor. Such a perspective requires looking – among other things – at the characteristics of the core rank and file, at the bureaucratic tendencies of the unions, at unions' links with the capitalist system and at its effects on their ideology, and at unions' relationships with political parties. It is also quite important to take into account the relationship between trade unions and other social movements such as NSMs. Finally, this chapter stressed the dynamic nature of collective action. Although the 2004 mobilization did not manage to block the reform of the tracking procedures on the unemployed, a new wave of protest actions against these procedures was initiated in 2008. Both contextual factors (including the financial and economic crisis) and the internal dynamics of a main actor (the Walloon wing of the Socialist union) explain the reemergence of a struggle that appeared to have been resoundingly defeated several years earlier.

References

Bellal, S., Berns, T., Cantelli, F., & Faniel, J. (Eds.). (2003). *Syndicats et société civile: Des liens à (re)découvrir*. Brussels: Labor.

Chabanet, D., & Faniel, J. (2011). The mobilization of the unemployed: A recurrent but relatively invisible phenomenon. In M. Reiss & M. Perry (Eds.), *Unemployment and protest: New perspectives on two centuries of contention*. Oxford: Oxford University Press.

Cohen, J. (1985). Strategy and identity: New theoretical paradigms and contemporary social movements. *Social Research, 52*(4), 663–716.

Faniel, J. (2005). Réactions syndicales et associatives face au 'contrôle de la disponibilité des chômeurs'. *L'année sociale, 2004*, 133–148.

Faniel, J. (2006a). Les relations entre syndicats et associations en Belgique: Le cas de la réforme du minimex. *Recherches Sociologiques et Anthropologiques, 37*(1), 123–141.

Faniel, J. (2006b). L'organisation des chômeurs dans les syndicats. *Courrier Hebdomadaire du CRISP, 1929–1930*, 5–76.

Faniel, J. (2009). Belgian trade unions, the unemployed and the growth of unemployment. In M. Giugni (Ed.), *The politics of unemployment in Europe. Policy responses and collective action*. Aldershot: Ashgate.

Faniel, J. (2010a). Belgium: Unemployment insurance caught between pressure from Europe, regional controversy and fall-out from the crisis. In F. Lefresne (Ed.), *Unemployment benefit systems in Europe and North America: Reforms and crisis*. Brussels: IRES-ETUI.

Faniel, J. (2010b). Caractéristiques et spécificités des syndicats belges. In É. Arcq, M. Capron, É. Léonard, & P. Reman (Eds.), *Dynamiques de la concertation sociale*. Brussels: CRISP.

Faniel, J. (2012). Inside or outside trade unions? The mobilization of the unemployed in Belgium. In D. Chabanet & J. Faniel (Eds.), *The mobilization of the unemployed in Europe. From acquiescence to protest?* New York/Basingstoke: Palgrave Macmillan.

Hyman, R. (1971). *Marxism and the sociology of trade unionism*. London: Pluto Press.

Hyman, R. (1975). *Industrial relations: A Marxist introduction*. London: Macmillan.

Hyman, R. (2001). *Understanding European trade unionism: Between market, class and society*. London: Sage.

Matagne, G. (2001). De l' 'État social actif' à la politique belge de l'emploi. *Courrier Hebdomadaire du CRISP, 1737–1738*, 5–79.

Mills, C. W. (1948). *The new men of power: America's labor leaders*. New York: Harcourt, Brace and Co.
Moulaert, T. (2006). Le Pacte de solidarité entre les générations. *Courrier Hebdomadaire du CRISP, 1906–1907*, 5–68.
Ness, I. (1998). *Trade unions and the betrayal of the unemployed: Labor conflicts during the 1990s*. New York/London: Garland.
Offe, C., & Wiesenthal, H. (1985). Two logics of collective action. In C. Offe (Ed.), *Disorganized capitalism*. Oxford: Basil Blackwell.
Pakulski, J. (1993). Mass social movements and social class. *International Sociology, 8*(2), 131–158.
Richards, A. (2000). Trade unionism and the unemployed in the European Union. *La Lettre de la Maison française d'Oxford, 12*, 153–181.
Slomp, H. (1996). *Between bargaining and politics. An introduction to European labor relations*. Westport: Praeger.
Snow, D., Rochford, B., Worden, S., & Benford, R. (1986). Frame alignment processes, micromobilizations and movement participation. *American Sociological Review, 51*(4), 464–481.
Tarrow, S. (1998 [1994]). *Power in movement: Social movements and contentious politics*. Cambridge: Cambridge University Press.
Tartakowsky, D., & Tétard, F. (Eds.). (2006). *Syndicats et associations en France. Concurrence ou complémentarité?* Rennes: Presses Universitaires de Rennes.
Valenzuela, S. (1992). Labour movements and political systems: Some variations. In M. Regini (Ed.), *The future of labour movements*. London: Sage.
Vandaele, K. (2006). A report from the homeland of the Ghent system: The relationship between unemployment and trade union membership in Belgium. *Transfer, 12*(4), 647–657.

Chapter 11
Employment Status and Political Participation: Does Exclusion Influence the Protest Behavior of the Young Unemployed?

Marco Giugni and Jasmine Lorenzini

11.1 Introduction

This chapter examines the relationship between employment status and the political participation of young people.[1] We focus more specifically on the impact of long-term unemployment on the political participation of youth. We aim to determine whether exclusion from the labor market deters the potential that youngsters have for political participation and therefore for taking part in the democratic process. This is all the more important in the light of the often stressed political alienation of young people (Bay and Blekesaune 2002; Dalton 2009). On a broader level, this implies questioning the relationship between an important dimension of social exclusion and political exclusion.

However, being excluded from the labor market is not the only form of exclusion, albeit a very important one in contemporary western society. Other forms exist as well and might add up to exclusion from the labor market in erecting barriers to the political participation of young unemployed. Here we will consider three such forms of exclusion. Firstly, unemployment most obviously can lead to economic exclusion, that is, a lack of financial resources as well as a feeling of not having the means to conduct the life one would like (Rantakeisu et al. 1999). This form of exclusion can be mitigated by the existence of a social protection net, be it the state, charity organizations, or the family, but it arguably is the first obstacle one faces in the case of unemployment. Second,

[1] Results presented in this chapter have been obtained within the project "Youth, Unemployment, and Exclusion in Europe: A Multidimensional Approach to Understanding the Conditions and Prospects for Social and Political Integration of Young Unemployed" (YOUNEX). This project is funded by the European Commission under the 7th Framework Programme (grant agreement no. 216122).

M. Giugni (✉) • J. Lorenzini
Département de science politique et relations internationales, Université de Genève,
40 Boulevard du Pont d'Arve, CH-1211 Geneva 4, Switzerland
e-mail: marco.giugni@unige.ch

B. Andreosso-O'Callaghan and F. Royall (eds.), *Economic and Political Change in Asia and Europe: Social Movement Analyses*, DOI 10.1007/978-94-007-4653-4_11,

as various studies have shown (Ervasti and Venetoklis 2010; Hammer 2003; Winkelmann and Winkelmann 1998), the loss of a job might push the unemployed in a funnel of exclusion from various layers of social life and weaken social bonds (Castel 2000; Paugam 2009). For example, friendship circles shrink, social activities diminish, and involvement in civic or other kinds of associations becomes more sporadic. Thus, unemployment might have a negative impact on the amount of social capital at the disposal of young unemployed people. Since social capital has been repeatedly shown to be a major resource, both for finding a job (Granovetter 1973) and more generally for the social and political life of people (Almond and Verba 1963; Coleman 1988; Lin 2001; Portes 1998), such a loss may prove very detrimental for young unemployed people. Third, unemployment might also lead to political exclusion. By this we refer to a diminishing political involvement of young unemployed. This may include, for example, a lower degree of interest in politics, less trust in political institutions such as the government or the parliament, and a weaker feeling of political efficacy. These aspects reflect a long-standing tradition in political science (Almond and Verba 1963; Verba et al. 1995). In addition, recent work has shown how political involvement might depend strongly on the social capital stemming from associational involvement, both in general (Baglioni et al. 2008; Li et al. 2005; Maloney and Rossteutscher 2007; Maloney and Van Deth 2010) and for specific groups such as immigrants (Morales and Giugni 2011), hence suggesting that the three dimensions of exclusion with which we are dealing are interrelated in some way.

In brief, the questions we are addressing in this chapter are the following: Does the employment status have an impact on the political participation of young people and, in particular, on their engagement in protest, social-movement kind of activities? To what extent do forms of exclusion – other than exclusion from the labor market – play a role in this regard? Specifically, do economic, social, and political exclusion affect the potential for young unemployed people to engage in political activities? These questions will be addressed empirically through an analysis of the results of a random survey of young long-term unemployed and a control group of regularly employed youth conducted in the context of a European Union-funded project on youth, unemployment, and exclusion in Europe. The survey was conducted in several European cities. This chapter focuses on Geneva, which is the city in Switzerland with the highest unemployment rate. The data includes various indicators of political participation such as engagement in different kinds of political activities (including protest activities), allowing us to examine the impact of different types of exclusion (economic, social, political), and various sociodemographic characteristics of respondents which we use as control variables (sex, age, nationality, education).

11.2 Employment Status and Political Participation

The effects of employment on political participation can be studied from different angles. Some scholars have done so looking at the effects of employment on political participation through socialization (Gaxie 2002). During the last decade, a revival of socialization studies have appeared which no longer address the question of the persistence of political socialization but rather try to understand how youth become socialized politically, where and how they develop political interest, trust, and other political attitudes sustaining political activities (Hooghe 2004; Sapiro 2004). Much focus has been given to primary socialization in the family (Muxel 2001; Percheron and Meyer 1993) and secondary socialization throughout school and higher education (Michon 2008; Torney-Purta et al. 2004). A fewer number of scholars have worked on the process of political socialization through employment as an agent of secondary socialization. In this case, employment is treated as a sphere of life in which, through socialization processes, people acquire certain understandings and practices of the world in which they live, and this helps them to form political opinions and influences their political behaviors.

Other studies focus on the capabilities and competencies useful for political participation that can be acquired in the workplace through working experiences (Brady et al. 1995; Pateman 1970; Schur 2003; Sobel 1993). In this regard, we can distinguish between the spillover model and the civic skills model (Adman 2008). The spillover model assumes that participation in the workplace offers opportunities to learn how to participate and to develop roles related to social and political participation (Pateman 1970; Sobel 1993). According to this model, participation supports participation, that is, involvement and responsibilities in the workplace have an impact on political participation (Sobel 1993). Moreover, participatory mechanisms in the workplace offer opportunities to develop a sense of political efficacy (Adman 2008: 118). The civic skills approach argues that people participate when they have resources (e.g., time, money, civic skills), when they have psychological predispositions toward engagement (e.g., interest in politics, concern with public affairs, belief that engagement can make a difference, perception of shared interests), and when they are recruited (e.g., by voluntary associations, by individuals) (Brady et al. 1995: 271). Schur (2003) tested this model, focusing specifically on those variables that can be related to employment. Her findings show that income, recruitment, and civic skills (which include the ability to communicate and to organize) have all an impact on political participation. Most importantly, the author shows that employed people participate more than unemployed people (on all activities except voting).

A recent review of the literature presents expected political attitudes and behaviors of the unemployed: high abstention levels in elections, high proportions of extreme right- or left-wing voting, and a low degree of trust in political institutions (Chabanet 2007). Thus, we would expect an overall low level of political participation of the unemployed as compared to regularly employed people. However, the effect of unemployment on political attitudes and behaviors has been shown to be contingent upon the socioeconomic status (Scott and Acock 1979). Since the impact of unemployment is not the same across social groups, we should analyze unemployment by taking into account other dimensions of the individuals' social life. This would allow us to study the impact of unemployment on political participation.

Students of social movements have sometimes examined the collective action by the unemployed, not only showing their difficulty to organize and mobilize but also pointing to a rather unstructured form of mobilization (Bagguley 1991, 1992; Chabanet 2008; Faniel 2004; Royall 1997). Thus, their political participation seems to oscillate between apathy and radicalism, also as a result of varying institutional and organizational conditions (Baglioni et al. 2008; Berclaz et al. 2004; Giugni 2008; Zorn 2010).

Scholarly works also exist on the individual engagement in protest activities by the unemployed. They are particularly important for our present purpose as we also focus on individual participation. For example, Maurer and Pierru (2001) have looked at the individual factors explaining engagement in protest activities. Their research was based on qualitative interviews and examined both people who participated in protest activities and others who did not in order to understand what explains their mobilization or lack thereof. They found that unemployed people mobilize when they are already politicized and socialized to political engagement through their family or through their professional background, when they are isolated or marginalized and enter the organizational world in search for material and human support which leads them to taking part in protest with little or no political motivation, and for individual reasons, to express their discontent, lacking political socialization and a political vision.

While there is a substantial body of literature on the political involvement of the unemployed, especially if we include research on collective action and protest activities, work focusing on young unemployed people is sparser. Some studies have compared unemployed to employed youth, finding predispositions toward violent and illegal actions on the part of the former (Breakwell 1986; Clark 1985). However, these studies focus on attitudes rather than behaviors. Other works have shown that, while being interested and open toward radical actions, young unemployed people display a lower affiliation to political groups such as parties and social movements than employed youth. Banks and Ullah (1987) have studied political attitudes and voting behaviors of young employed and unemployed people. They found overall low levels of interest and involvement in politics for youth, tending toward apathy and resignation, but little difference between employed and unemployed youth. Similarly, Bay and Blekesaune (2002) found that, beyond a specific political marginalization of young unemployed, youth in general are little interested in politics. Nevertheless, young unemployed were found to be less satisfied with the way democracy works and in particular with the authorities' failure to solve problems relating to unemployment (Banks and Ullah 1987). As for political engagement, young unemployed are predicted to be either marginalized from political participation or engaged in radical activities.

One of the limits of these studies is that it is difficult to ascertain whether regularly employed people are different from unemployed people from the start, as stated by Schur (2003). Some studies have questioned the direction of the relationship between employment and political participation as well as the very existence of the relationship. Cohen and Vigoda (1999), for example, have found that political participation can explain attitudes and behaviors in the workplace, reversing the relationship between the two variables. To solve this puzzle, Adman (2008) has tested the effect of work on political participation with panel data. The effect found in cross-sectional analyses does not hold when one takes into account the temporal ordering of events (first being involved in a specific workplace setting, then participating politically).

11.3 The Survey

Our analysis is based on a telephone survey carried between February and October 2010 on a representative sample of young long-term unemployed and precarious youth, plus a control group of regularly employed youth. All three groups include people aged between 18 and 34 residing in the canton of Geneva, Switzerland. Long-term unemployment is defined as having been without a job for at least 1 year, and regularly employed youth are people that have an open-ended contract since at least 1 year. Here we focus on unemployed and regularly employed youth. The sample size for these two groups is, respectively, 301 and 317. The data was retrieved as part of the EU-funded project "Youth, Unemployment, and Exclusion in Europe: A Multidimensional Approach to Understanding the Conditions and Prospects for Social and Political Integration of Young Unemployed" (YOUNEX). This project aims to provide new knowledge on the causes, processes, and perspectives for change related to social and political exclusion of unemployed youth. It provides an integrated approach to the study of unemployment effects on youth exclusion from social and political spheres. It does so through a design that has three main components: a multidimensional theoretical framework integrating different explanatory factors, a comparative design including countries with different institutional approaches to unemployment, and an integrated methodological approach based on multiple sources and methods. The survey is one such methods.

Table 11.1 shows the sociodemographic composition of the two groups in the sample, indicating whether cross-group differences are statistically significant. We look in particular at four variables: sex, age, nationality (Swiss/foreigners), and level of education. These variables are then entered as controls in the regression analyses below. As we can see, unemployed and regularly employed youth do not differ systematically on all these aspects. Specifically, we observe, firstly, that the gender composition is virtually the same in the two subsamples, with nearly half of the respondents being of each sex. In other words, gender does not discriminate between youth having a job and those who do not have one. Second, concerning age, we distinguish between three age categories: 18–24, 25–29, and 30–34. We decided to include respondents up to the age of 34 in the survey in order to take into account youth as a transition period, one in which individuals enter the labor market, gain financial independence, live on their own, and start their own family (Van de Velde 2008). Looking at the figures, there are some differences in the distribution of age across the two groups. In particular, there is a slightly higher proportion of the oldest age category among those who have a regular job. In other words, unemployed youth tend to be a bit younger than regularly employed youth. These differences, however, are not significant. Third, we find a higher percentage of foreigners among the unemployed. The difference, in this case, is statistically significant. Thus, nationality seems to be a discriminating factor between employed and unemployed youth. Although some other factor such as education might explain this difference, this should not surprise us as holding Swiss citizenship is a resource to be used on the labor market. Fourthly, there are also differences, this time statistically significant,

Table 11.1 Sociodemographic composition of the sample by employment status (percentages)

	Unemployed	Employed	Cramer's V
Sex			n.s.
Men	50.5	51.4	
Women	49.5	48.6	
Total	100%	100%	
N	301	317	
Age			n.s.
18–24	21.6	18.6	
25–29	32.2	29.0	
30–34	46.2	52.4	
Total	100%	100%	
N	301	317	
Nationality			.108*
Swiss	50.0	59.9	
Foreigners	50.0	40.1	
Total	100%	100%	
N	301	317	
Level of education			.217***
Not completed compulsory schooling	3.4	1.3	
Primary level	26.7	13.7	
Secondary level	47.6	47.1	
Tertiary level	21.6	35.6	
Second stage of tertiary level	0.7	1.6	
Total	100%	100%	
N	301	317	

*$p<.05$; **$p<.01$; *** $p<.001$

across the two groups with respect to education. Overall, the unemployed have a lower level of education. In particular, there are more unemployed people who have stopped school after the primary level and fewer who have reached the tertiary level of education than expected. Nevertheless, we should stress that in our sample, 22% of the unemployed have a tertiary level of education and have been unemployed for 1 year or more.

11.4 Political Participation Among Unemployed and Employed Youth

Do young unemployed people participate less or, on the contrary, more than regularly employed youth? To answer this question, Table 11.2 shows participation in five kinds of political activities as well as the overall participation by employment status. Political participation is measured following a standard approach consisting

Table 11.2 Political participation by employment status (percentages)

	Unemployed	Employed	Cramer's V
Contacting activities	17.3	13.6	n.s
Group activities	3.3	1.3	n.s
Consumer activities	56.5	58.7	n.s
Protest activities	22.6	18.3	n.s
Any political activity	63.5	65.0	n.s
N	301	317	

Note: Contacting activities include contacting politicians, contacting government officials, contacting media, and contacting solicitor/judicial body. Group activities include working in a political party, working in another political group, and donating money to a political organization. Consumer activities include sign a petition, boycott products, and deliberately buy certain products. Protest activities include wear or display a badge, participate in demonstration, participate in illegal actions, and participate in violent actions. Any political activity includes all the above-mentioned activities except voting
$^{*}p<.05$; $^{**}p<.01$; $^{***}p<.001$

in asking respondents to mention whether they have made use of one or more of a number of political activities in the past 12 months.[2] These questions were used to distinguish between four main types of participation: contacting activities (contact politicians, government officials, the media, a solicitor, or judicial body), group activities (work in a political party, work in another political group, donate money to a political organization), consumer activities (sign a petition, boycott products, deliberately buy certain products), and protest activities (wear or display a badge, participate in demonstration, participate in illegal actions, participate in violent actions).[3] In addition to these four types of participation, we created a more general indicator of participation in any political activity (corresponding to having answered yes to any one of the activities mentioned).

Overall, the differences across the two groups are not statistically significant for any of the four kinds of political activities, nor for the overall political participation.

---

[2] The political activities are the following: contacted a politician; contacted a national or local government official; worked in a political party; worked in a political action group; worn or displayed a badge, sticker, or poster; signed a petition; taken part in a public demonstration; boycotted certain products; deliberately bought certain products for political reasons; donated money to a political organization or group; taken part in a strike; contacted the media; contacted a solicitor or a judicial body for nonpersonal reasons; participated in an illegal action (e.g., blockade, building occupation); and participated in a violent action (e.g., violent demonstration, physical attack).

In our analyses, we exclude participation in strikes as we are working on groups of youth with different employment status, not all of them having the same opportunities to take part in strikes. In particular, the unemployed have lower chances of having taken part in a strike.

[3] These four types reflect in part the typology of political participation proposed by Teorell et al. (2007). We factor-analyzed the response items in order to confront this typology with our data. The factor analysis yielded four main factors, but some of the items did not correspond to their classification. We therefore adapted the typology to our present purpose.

Yet, we can have a closer look at the figures in spite of this lack of statistical covariation. We see, first, that, if any, young unemployed make more often use of contacting activities than regularly employed youth. This would point to an interpretation of the relationship between employment status and this kind of activities stressing the mobilizing role of being excluded from the labor market. Again, however, the difference is not statistically significant, and, therefore, we cannot conclude that being unemployed leads to more participation of this kind. Second, group activities are by and large the less often adopted by both groups. This is understandable, knowing that this form of participation is quite demanding in terms of commitment, energy, and time spent doing this kind of political activities. Most importantly, once again no significant difference can be observed across the two groups. Third, the two groups are more or less equally active with regard to consumer activities. Unlike, for example, group activities, these are a kind of political activities that do not require a strong engagement, which explains why they are the most frequently used among the five types. Fourth, and most importantly for our present purpose, the young unemployed are slightly more often involved in protests activities, but, as for all other forms of participation, no significant difference can be observed across the two groups.

In sum, our findings suggest that unemployed and employed youth basically do not differ in terms of their use of different kinds of political activities, be contacting, group activities, consumer activities, or protest activities. This can also be seen in the percentages for engagement in any political activity, our indicator of overall political participation: youngsters who are excluded from the labor market participate virtually as much as those who hold a regular job. Thus, the employment status does not seem to have a direct impact on the political participation of youth. We need therefore to turn to other forms of exclusion to see whether they exert some kind of influence in this regard, namely, economic, social, and political exclusion. Before we turn to this point, we examine the extent to which unemployed and employed youth are excluded on these three counts.

11.5 Economic, Social, and Political Exclusion Among Unemployed and Employed Youth

The loss of a paid job and, more generally, being excluded from the labor market potentially has a number of consequences on other spheres and types of exclusion. Here we wish to investigate the extent to which unemployed youth are worse off in terms of economic, social, and political exclusion as compared to regularly employed youth. Table 11.3, which compares the two groups on these three counts, provides an answer. Of course, there are many ways to capture the concepts of economic and especially social and political exclusion. Before we have a look at the figures, we need therefore to explain how we have operationalized the three forms of exclusion.

Table 11.3 Degree of exclusion by employment status (means)

	Unemployed	Employed	*T*-test
Economic exclusion	4.18	2.23	15.84***
Social exclusion	4.83	4.39	4.27***
Political exclusion	6.35	5.88	2.75**

† <.10; *p<.05; **p<.01; ***p<.001

To define economic exclusion, we rely both on objective and subjective aspects. More precisely, we created an index based on three aspects. The most obvious objective indicator of economic exclusion is income. Although people who do not dispose of earnings from their working activity are likely to face financial difficulties, their degree of exclusion in economic terms might vary from one individual to the other due to the existence of other sources of revenue. This is particularly true for young people, who can often receive the support from their family. Borrowing money is another objective indicator of economic exclusion. If one is forced to borrow money, regardless from whom, she or he can be said to be economically more excluded. Finally, we also take into account the subjective dimension of economic exclusion, namely, the feeling one has about her or his own income. To do so, we use a variable measuring the degree to which one feels that she or he can live comfortably with the available income: the less one feels comfortable, the more she or he is economically excluded.

Social exclusion is a long-standing concept in sociology and in the social sciences more generally. Here we rely on an equally well-known scholarly tradition that stresses the role of social capital for political participation (Coleman 1988; Lin 2001; Portes 1998). This has an individual and a collective dimension. From a collective point of view, it refers to those properties of organizations, such as networks, norms, and trust, facilitating action and cooperation among people (Putnam 1993, 2000). From an individual point of view, it comprises the actual or potential resources related to having a durable set or relations of mutual recognition (Bourdieu 1986). In brief, since we are dealing here with individual-level data, social capital refers to the "ability of actors to secure benefits by virtue of membership in social networks or other social structures" (Portes 1998: 6). Thus, the resources one can draw from being embedded in social networks are a crucial feature of social capital, which in turn can be considered as a measure of social inclusion. Such resources can stem from two kinds of networks: interpersonal relations or involvement in voluntary associations. Accordingly, we look at these two aspects in our definition and operationalization of social exclusion. Specifically, we created an index comprising three aspects: the size of the circle of close friends young unemployed people have (the number of friends), the intensity of their social life (the frequency of social gatherings), and whether or not they are members, of voluntary associations (associational membership).

To grasp political exclusion, finally, we draw from another long-standing scholarly tradition, namely, the study of political behavior. Since at least the seminal works of Campbell et al. (1960) and Almond and Verba (1963), research has long shown the impact of political attitudes on political participation and behavior. In particular, predispositions and orientations toward politics, the institutions, and one's own role in the political system largely contribute to the political inclusion or exclusion of people, hence young unemployed people also. Following this perspective, we use three indicators to measure political exclusion: the interest young unemployed people have in politics, their trust of the core political institutions of a democratic country (the executive, legislative, and judiciary powers), and the feeling of political efficacy.

We can now look at how these three forms of exclusion vary across the two groups. The comparison is based on mean values on each of the three dimensions (on scales from 0 to 8 for financial and social exclusion and from 0 to 10 for political exclusion). The differences are statistically significant on all three counts, thus suggesting that the employment status matters for these different forms of exclusion. To begin with, we find that young unemployed people are much more excluded economically than regularly employed youth. This type of exclusion has by and large the strongest effect. This comes as no surprise, as lacking a paid job has serious implications on one's sources of revenue. The other two forms of exclusion, however, are more interesting.

The degree of social exclusion varies across the two groups. The difference is less important than for economic exclusion, but it is statistically significant. Specifically, the mean value is significantly higher for the unemployed. This suggests that the lack of a regular job leads youngsters to social exclusion and isolation. On the one hand, the circle of close friends becomes narrower, and the willingness to engage in social activities decreases. On the other hand, involvement in collective enterprises such as voluntary associations becomes less attractive, and unemployed youth tend to retreat from public life. That said, the difference, albeit significant from a statistical point of view, is not very strong. After all, we are dealing with a population of youngsters, who are in a phase of their life in which friendship and social contacts play a particularly important role.

Finally, we observe a statistically significant difference between the two groups concerning political exclusion. Young long-term unemployed people are also politically more excluded than regularly employed youth. However, the difference between the two groups is quite small. In fact, this result is not surprising once we consider the rather homogeneous distribution of the respondents with regard to political participation. Indeed, political participation can be considered as the behavioral dimension of political inclusion, whereby political interest, trust, and confidence represent its attitudinal dimension. The fact that young unemployed people display little difference in comparison to employed youth with regard to political exclusion is therefore consistent with the observation that they are politically as active as the regularly employed youth.

In sum, unemployed and employed youth differ significantly in terms of economic, social, and political exclusion. However, while on the economic dimension the difference reflects expectations as regards the impact of employment status, the smaller differences on the social and political dimensions suggest that long-term unemployment may have only a limited impact on the social and political exclusion of young long-term unemployed.

11.6 The Impact of Economic, Social, and Political Exclusion on Protest Activities by Unemployed Youth

The final step in our analysis consists in assessing the impact of the three forms of exclusion on political participation, with a specific focus on protest activities, which are the typical social-movement kind of political involvement. To do so, we conduct a multivariate regression analysis of the effect of the three indexes of exclusion as well as a number of controls (sex, age, nationality, and level of education) on the use of protest activities by young unemployed people. We first enter each form of exclusion and the controls in the analysis separately, starting from economic exclusion (model 1), then social exclusion (model 2), and finally political exclusion (model 3). Then we present a full model including all three variables and the controls (model 4). The coefficients shown are odds ratios. Values above 1 indicate a positive relationship between dependent and independent variables (if statistically significant), while values below 1 indicate a negative relationship.

Table 11.4 shows the results of this analysis. If we look at the full model, economic exclusion and social exclusion have a statistically significant effect on the dependent variable. The measure of economic exclusion is not significant in the partial model, but becomes so in the full model. Thus, both economic and social exclusion have an impact on the use of protest activities by young unemployed people. However, the direction of such an impact varies across types of exclusion. The indicators of economic exclusion display a positive effect, meaning that the more one is economically excluded, the more she or he is likely to engage in protest activities. This suggests that economic deprivation due to unemployment might lead the young unemployed to mobilize in order to ask for the intervention of political authorities to solve the problem. In a way, this result could be interpreted as supporting, at the individual level, breakdown or grievance theories of collective action (see Buechler 2004; Useem 1998 for reviews), which point to the fact that deprived people are more likely to engage in protest activities.

The effect of social exclusion points to the opposite direction. In this case, being socially excluded leads to less rather than more protest behavior. Thus, youth who are socially isolated in terms of friendship, social life, and associational involvement suffer from a deficit of political involvement, at least in terms of engagement in protest activities. As far as associational involvement is concerned, this is in line with studies showing that membership in voluntary associations provides migrants with social capital that spills over into political participation (Berger et al. 2004; Eggert and Giugni 2010; Fennema and Tillie 1999, 2000; Jacobs et al. 2004; Morales and Pilati 2011; Tillie 2004; Togeby 2004). These studies show that the more an immigrant is a member of voluntary associations, the more she or he participates politically. In this perspective, this is not so much related to the individual skills or resources one can develop in associations, but has something to do with the social capital generated by such an organizational affiliation. The mechanism would be found in the creation of social trust through associational involvement which in turn would bring to higher levels of political trust and participation (Jacobs and Tillie 2004). Furthermore, interpersonal networks and social activities might equally be

Table 11.4 Effects of forms of exclusion on protest (odds ratios)

	Model 1	Model 2	Model 3	Model 4
Forms of exclusion				
Economic exclusion	1.13	–	–	1.41**
Social exclusion	–	.75**	–	.69**
Political exclusion	–	–	.87	.88
Controls				
Man	1.81	1.59	1.65	2.01*
Age	1.02	.99	.96	1.00
Swiss	2.29**	2.09*	2.13*	2.61**
Level of education	1.02	1.02	1.23	1.28
Pseudo R^2 (Nagelkerke)	.08	.10	.13	.21
N	265	295	267	233

*$p<.05$; **$p<.01$; ***$p<.001$

important as sources of social capital not only to find a job but also to become politically engaged. In other words, the more unemployed and precarious youth are socially integrated (in terms of associational involvement and in terms of interpersonal relations), the higher their social capital and the more likely their participation in protest activities.

Finally, political exclusion does not seem to have an impact on the political participation of young unemployed, at least as protest is concerned. While this might be considered at odds with political engagement, it suggests that participation in collective action does not necessarily diminish when one has little interests in politics, a low trust in political institutions, and a weak feeling of political efficacy. In fact, as the political behavior literature has repeatedly shown, these kinds of political attitudes are very important when it comes to electoral participation or some other kinds of conventional political engagement (Campbell et al. 1960; Dalton 2006; Nie et al. 1979; Verba and Nie 1972; Verba et al. 1995), but perhaps less so to explain protest behavior.

As a way to testing whether political exclusion has an impact on other forms of participation, we ran a logistic regression on voting in a model including the same covariates as in the one concerning protest activities (results not shown). We found that political exclusion reduces the chances that young unemployed people engage in this kind of political activities (odds ratio of .72, significant at the 1 % level).[4] Thus, political exclusion reduces participation in institutional forms such as voting but has no effect on extrainstitutional forms such as protest. To some extent, this is in line with previous research on the political consequences of youth unemployment, which expected to find either political apathy or political radicalism among young unemployed (Bay and Blekesaune 2002; Breakwell 1986; Banks and Ullah 1987).

[4] This additional analysis was conducted on a smaller sample (135 respondents) as we had to exclude those who do not have the right to vote. It is worth noting that neither our indicator of economic exclusion nor the one of social exclusion yield a statistically significant effect on voting.

We controlled the effect of the three types of exclusion by a number of sociodemographic characteristics. Two of them are statistically significant (full model). On the one hand, men are more likely to be involved in protest activities than women. This probably reflects a more general gendered pattern of political participation whereby women tend to participate less than men, although the gender gap is no longer a systematic trait in western societies, at least in electoral behavior (Schlozman et al. 1999; Verba et al. 1997). On the other hand, the young unemployed who have Swiss citizenship also participate more. This is in line with recent studies showing that, other things being equal, noncitizens and more generally migrants often withdraw from political participation (Morales and Giugni 2011). Age and education have no effect. The latter result is particularly surprising as the general literature on political participation has long stressed the importance of education and human capital as a resource to be used in politics (Verba et al. 1995).

11.7 Conclusion

In this chapter, we inquired into the impact of the employment status on the political participation of youth. We have focused in particular on the propensity of young long-term unemployed people to engage in collective action and, more specifically, in protest activities. The empirical analysis proceeded in three main steps. First, we examined the extent to which young unemployed and youth with a regular job differ not only in terms of sociodemographic characteristics but above all in terms of their political engagement. Concerning the latter aspect, which is the one of interest here, we found that the two groups do not differ significantly on all the four broad forms of participation considered (contacting, group activities, consumer activities, and protest activities), nor do they differ on the indicator of overall political participation. Thus, at least in the case of Geneva, the employment status and, more specifically, being unemployed does not seem to have a direct impact on the political participation of youth, perhaps because of an already relative apathy of the latter in general. Second, we focused on three kinds of exclusion that may arise from being unemployed (economic, social, and political) and looked at whether young unemployed and regularly employed youth differ in this regard. Here we found that the two groups differ significantly on all three counts, young unemployed being more excluded on all three counts, but the difference is greater on the economic dimension than on the social and political dimensions. Third, we zoomed in on the sample of young unemployed people in order to test for the effect of three kinds of exclusion on their propensity to engage in protest activities. Two forms of exclusion have a statistically significant effect on the use of protest activities: economic exclusion and social exclusion. However, while economic exclusion encourages the young unemployed to be politically active, social exclusion seems to deter political participation, at least as far as protest is concerned. We also found political exclusion to make voting less likely.

In conclusion, it is worth stressing one important implication of our study relating to the impact of social exclusion on the use of protest activities. Our measure of social exclusion includes three aspects: the number of friends, the frequency of social gatherings, and associational membership. All three aspects can positively influence participation by yielding important resources that can be put to use in political behavior. Social capital can be seen as one such resources.

The concept of social capital has become fashionable in recent years in various research fields (see Lin 2001; Portes 1998 for overviews), including the study of political participation. The mainstream literature linking social capital to political participation has stressed the role of voluntary associations as crucial for the production of social capital. In this perspective, which goes back at least to Tocqueville's analysis of American democracy and was reinvigorated in particular by the work of Putnam (1993, 2000), there is a positive relationship between associational life and democracy (Paxton 2002). Another theoretical tradition has also looked at the impact of people's involvement in voluntary associations on political participation and behavior, specifying the mechanisms linking the latter to the former. The civic voluntarism model (Verba et al. 1995), for example, points to the important role played by involvement in associations for increasing the level of civic skills, political efficacy, and political knowledge. In a similar fashion, recent work has shown more specifically the benefits that people can draw from their involvement in voluntary associations for their political involvement (Baglioni et al. 2008; Maloney and Rossteutscher 2007; Maloney and Van Deth 2010).

If we put our findings in this perspective, we can conclude that, just as the social capital stemming from the associational involvement of migrants may lead people who are excluded from citizenship (in a broad sense) to be politically more active (see Morales and Giugni 2011 for a recent assessment), membership in voluntary associations may create social capital spurring the political participation of youth excluded from the labor market. Thus, youngsters who find themselves unemployed will benefit from being members of voluntary associations and therefore be more inclined to engage politically, both in general and more specifically in protest activities. This, of course, should also apply to regularly employed youth, at least following scholarly writing in this field. However, one might the impact of associational membership on political participation to be stronger for unemployed and precarious youth as this might compensate for the lack of resources and motivations stemming from their situation of social exclusion.

References

Adman, P. (2008). Does workplace experience enhance political participation? A critical test of a venerable hypothesis. *Political Behavior, 30*, 115–138.

Almond, G., & Verba, S. (1963). *The civic culture: Political attitudes and democracy in five nations*. Princeton: Princeton University Press.

Bagguley, P. (1991). *From protest to acquiescence? Political movements of the unemployed*. London: Macmillan.

Bagguley, P. (1992). Protest, acquiescence and the unemployed: A comparative analysis of the 1930s and the 1980s. *The British Journal of Sociology, 43*(3), 443–461.

Baglioni, S., Baumgarten, B., Chabanet, D., & Lahusen, C. (2008). Transcending marginalization: The mobilization of the unemployed in France, Germany, and Italy in a comparative perspective. *Mobilization, 13*(3), 323–335.
Banks, M., & Ullah, P. (1987). Political attitudes and voting among unemployed and employed youth. *Journal of Adolescence, 10*, 201–216.
Bay, A.-H., & Blekesaune, M. (2002). Youth, unemployment and political marginalisation. *International Journal of Social Welfare, 11*, 132–139.
Berclaz, M., Füglister, K., & Giugni, M. (2004). États-providence, opportunités politiques et mobilisation des chômeurs: Une approche néo-institutionnaliste. *Revue suisse de sociologie, 30*, 421–440.
Berger, M., Galonska, C., & Koopmans, R. (2004). Political integration by a detour? Ethnic communities and social capital of migrants in Berlin. *Journal of Ethnic and Migration Studies, 30*, 491–507.
Bourdieu, P. (1986). The forms of capital. In J. Richardson (Ed.), *Handbook of theory and research for the sociology of education*. New York: Greenwood.
Brady, H., Verba, S., & Schlozman, K. L. (1995). Beyond SES: A resource model of political participation. *American Political Science Review, 89*, 271–294.
Breakwell, G. (1986). Political and attributional responses of the young short-term unemployed. *Political Psychology, 7*, 575–586.
Buechler, S. (2004). The strange career of strain and breakdown theories of collection action. In D. Snow, S. Soule, & H. Kriesi (Eds.), *The Blackwell companion to social movements*. Malden: Blackwell.
Campbell, A., Converse, P., Miller, W., & Stokes, D. (Eds.). (1960). *The American voter*. New York: Wiley.
Castel, R. (Ed.). (2000). *Les métamorphoses de la question sociale: Une chronique du salariat*. Paris: Fayard.
Chabanet, D. (2007). Chômage et exclusion sociale: L'échec européen. *Politique Européenne, 21*, 157–187.
Chabanet, D. (2008). When the unemployed challenge the European Union: The European marches as a mode of externalization of protest. *Mobilization, 13*(3), 311–322.
Clark, A. (1985). The Effects of unemployment on political attitude. *Journal of Sociology, 21*, 100–108.
Cohen, A., & Vigoda, E. (1999). Politics and the workplace: An empirical examination of the relationship between political behavior and work outcomes. *Public Productivity and Management Review, 22*, 389–406.
Coleman, J. (1988). Social capital in the creation of human capital. *The American Journal of Sociology, 94*, 95–120.
Dalton, R. (Ed.). (2006). *Citizen politics: Public opinion and political parties in advanced industrial democracies* (4th ed.). Washington, DC: CQ Press.
Dalton, R. (2009). *The good citizen: How a younger generation is reshaping American politics*. Washington, DC: CQ Press.
Eggert, N., & Giugni, M. (2010). Does associational involvement spur political integration? Political interest and participation of three immigrant groups in Zurich. *Swiss Political Science Review, 16*, 175–210.
Ervasti, H., & Venetoklis, T. (2010). Unemployment and subjective well-being. *Acta Sociologica, 53*, 119–139.
Faniel, J. (2004). Chômeurs en Belgique et en France: Des mobilisations différentes. *Revue internationale de politique comparée, 11*, 493–506.
Fennema, M., & Tillie, J. (1999). Political participation and political trust in Amsterdam: Civic communities and ethnic networks. *Journal of Ethnic and Migration Studies, 25*, 703–726.
Fennema, M., & Tillie, J. (2000). Civic community, political participation and political trust of ethnic groups. *Connections, 24*, 26–41.
Gaxie, D. (2002). Appréhensions du politique et mobilisations des expériences sociales. *Revue Française de Science Politique, 52*, 145–178.
Giugni, M. (2008). Welfare states, political opportunities, and the mobilization of the unemployed: A cross-national analysis. *Mobilization, 13*, 249–258.

Granovetter, M. (1973). The strength of weak ties. *The American Journal of Sociology, 78*, 1360–1380.

Hammer, T. (2003). *Youth, unemployment and social exclusion in Europe: A comparative study*. Bristol: Policy Press.

Hooghe, M. (2004). Political socialization and the future of politics. *Acta Politica, 39*, 331–341.

Jacobs, D., & Tillie, J. (2004). Introduction: Social capital and political integration of migrants. *Journal of Ethnic and Migration Studies, 30*, 419–427.

Jacobs, D., Phalet, K., & Swyngedouw, M. (2004). Associational membership and political involvement among ethnic minority groups in Brussels. *Journal of Ethnic and Migration Studies, 30*, 543–559.

Li, Y., Pickles, A., & Savage, M. (2005). Social capital and social trust in Britain. *European Sociological Review, 21*, 109–123.

Lin, N. (2001). *Social capital*. Cambridge: Cambridge University Press.

Maloney, W., & Rossteutscher, S. (Eds.). (2007). *Social capital and associations in European democracies: A comparative analysis*. New York: Routledge.

Maloney, W., & Van Deth, J. (Eds.). (2010). *Civil society and activism in Europe: Contextualizing engagement and political orientations*. London: Routledge.

Maurer, S., & Pierru, E. (2001). Le mouvement des chômeurs de l'hiver 1997–1998: Retour sur un 'miracle social'. *Revue Française de Science Politique, 51*, 371–407.

Michon, S. (2008). Les effets des contextes d'études sur la politisation. *Revue Française de Pédagogie, 163*, 63–75.

Morales, L., & Giugni, M. (Eds.). (2011). *Social capital, political participation and migration in Europe: Making multicultural democracy work?* Basingstoke: Palgrave.

Morales, L., & Pilati, K. (2011). The role of social capital in migrants' engagement in local politics in European cities. In L. Morales & M. Giugni (Eds.), *Social capital, political participation and migration in Europe: Making multicultural democracy work?* Basingstoke: Palgrave.

Muxel, A. (Ed.). (2001). *L'Expérience politique des jeunes*. Paris: Presses de Sciences Po.

Nie, N., Verba, S., & Petrocik, J. (1979). *The changing American voter*. Cambridge: Harvard University Press.

Pateman, C. (Ed.). (1970). *Participation and democratic theory*. Cambridge: Cambridge University Press.

Paugam, S. (Ed.). (2009). *La disqualification sociale: Essai sur la nouvelle pauvreté*. Paris: Presses Universitaires de France.

Paxton, P. (2002). Social capital and democracy: An interdependent relationship. *American Sociological Review, 67*, 254–277.

Percheron, A., & Meyer, N. (Eds.). (1993). *La socialisation politique*. Paris: Armand Colin.

Portes, A. (1998). Social capital: Its origins and applications in modern sociology. *Annual Review of Sociology, 24*, 1–24.

Putnam, R. (1993). *Making democracy work: Civic traditions in modern Italy*. Princeton: Princeton University Press.

Putnam, R. (2000). *Bowling alone: The collapse and revival of American community*. New York: Simon & Schuster.

Rantakeisu, U., Starrin, B., & Hagquist, C. (1999). Financial hardship and shame: A tentative model to understand the social and health effects of unemployment. *British Journal of Social Work, 29*, 877–901.

Royall, F. (1997). Problems of collective action for associations of the unemployed in France and in Ireland. In R. Edmonson (Ed.), *The political context of collective action: Power, argumentation and democracy*. London: Routledge.

Sapiro, V. (2004). Not your parent's political socialization: Introduction for a new generation. *Annual Review of Political Science, 7*, 1–23.

Schlozman, K. L., Burns, N., & Verba, S. (1999). 'What happened at work today?': A multistage model of gender, employment, and political participation. *Journal of Politics, 61*, 29–53.

Schur, L. (2003). Employment and the creation of an active citizenry. *British Journal of Industrial Relations, 41*, 751–771.

Scott, W., & Acock, A. (1979). Socioeconomic status, unemployment experience, and political participation: A disentangling of main and interaction effects. *Political Behavior, 1*, 361–381.
Sobel, R. (1993). From occupational involvement to political participation: An exploratory analysis. *Political Behavior, 15*, 339–353.
Tillie, J. (2004). Social capital of organisations and their members: Explaining the political integration of immigrants in Amsterdam. *Journal of Ethnic and Migration Studies, 30*, 529–541.
Teorell, J., Torcal, M., & Montero, J. (2007). Political participation: Mapping the terrain. In J. van Deth, J. Montero, & A. Westholm (Eds.), *Citizenship and involvement in European democracies: A comparative analysis*. London: Routledge.
Togeby, L. (2004). It depends… How organisational participation affects political participation and social trust among second-generation immigrants in Denmark. *Journal of Ethnic and Migration Studies, 30*, 509–528.
Torney-Purta, J., Barber, C., & Richardson, W. (2004). Trust in government-related institutions and political engagement among adolescents in six countries. *Acta Politica, 39*, 380–406.
Useem, B. (1998). Breakdown theories of collective action. *Annual Review of Sociology, 24*, 215–238.
Van de Velde, C. (Ed.). (2008). *Devenir adulte: Sociologie comparée de la jeunesse en Europe*. Paris: Presses Universitaires de France.
Verba, S., & Nie, N. (1972). *Participation in America: Political democracy and social equality*. New York: Harper & Row.
Verba, S., Schlozman, K. L., & Brady, H. (1995). *Voice and equality: Civic voluntarism in American politics*. Cambridge: Harvard University Press.
Verba, S., Burns, N., & Schlozman, K. L. (1997). Knowing and caring about politics: Gender and political engagement. *Journal of Politics, 59*, 1051–1072.
Winkelmann, L., & Winkelmann, R. (1998). Why are the unemployed so unhappy? Evidence from panel data. *Economica, 65*, 1–15.
Zorn, A. (2010). *The welfare state we're in: Organisations of the unemployed in action in Paris and Berlin*. Doctoral dissertation in Political Science, European University Institute, Florence.

Chapter 12
Practical Uses of Administrative and Cultural Categories Across the Field of Pro-Gypsy Activities in France Today: Activist Constructions and Adaptations to Political Categorizations

Anne-Cécile Renouard

12.1 Introduction

The nature of Gypsy and pro-Gypsy activities relates to official definitions and self-definitions of what it is to be a "Gypsy," a "Roma," or a "traveler."[1] It is also related to the ways that activists and institutions deal with Gypsy-related issues. These key issues are at the crossroads of a number of other issues such as economic and social marginality, limits imposed on the free movement of people, as well as cultural specificity. In the past, Gypsy groups have been reluctant to join political and civil society organizations such as trade unions and political parties. Consequently, their interests have not been well supported in political spheres even if some organizations have emerged and have been active for quite a considerable period of time.

[1] The term "Gypsy" is used here in a generic way regardless of normative social uses. In France, the term has no pejorative connotation compared to the situation in many other European countries. I refer to the term "travelers" or "traveling people" – "Gens du Voyage" in French – when I point to groups that are administered officially as "travelers" according to the 1969 and 2000 French laws. The 1969 law focuses on the administrative status of persons with no fixed residence who exercise traveling activities. The 2000 law deals with the local regulation of the stationing of travelers in cities. Different standards are set up for collective housing areas of groups of travelers according to the size of the cities. The creation of parking areas ("aires de stationnement des gens du voyage") is compulsory in cities of over 5,000 people. The travelers are defined by their residence and professional status only, and almost all of them are French citizens.

A.-C. Renouard (✉)
Political Science, University of Strasbourg, 7 Rue de l'Université, Strasbourg, France
e-mail: ac.renouard@hotmail.fr

B. Andreosso-O'Callaghan and F. Royall (eds.), *Economic and Political Change in Asia and Europe: Social Movement Analyses*, DOI 10.1007/978-94-007-4653-4_12,

The objective of this chapter is to compare the issues of delegation, Gypsy participation, and Gypsy voice(s) in a context of relative social, economic, and political exclusion. The pro-Gypsy collective actions discussed in this chapter are underpinned by reference to the paradigm of framing processes.[2] I use frames analysis as a theoretical tool to assess the emergence of a Gypsy voice in France. I also refer to discursive opportunities that suggest that collective expressions do not progress in a linear fashion over time. They may also not be favorable to organizations. All depends on the ways organizations approach and define Gypsy interests or issues.

From an institutional point of view, Gypsies in France have been classified according to the administrative category of "travelers" or "traveling people" – "Gens du Voyage" – following the implementation of the 1969 law regulating the free movement of people who exercise traveling activities (defined as professional activities that are undertaken outside a person's residence on public highways or outdoor markets, via door-to-door selling, or for the purpose of selling goods or providing services).[3] From this administrative point of view, the legislation targeting travelers represents a legal framework related to the practical living conditions of these people, on the one hand, and for the claims and activities of pro-Gypsy and pro-traveler activists, on the other hand. Following from this, I consider that official depictions and categories represent key aspects of the symbolic and institutional rules that activists must address and that the ambiguities of group delimitation or problem definition are part of the building of a discourse in the pro-Gypsy organizations under study here. In doing so, I address the relational work of definitions of the groups by activists, and I do not engage in an essentialist definition of groups based on objective characteristics such as origins (Indian origin), language, etc. In other words, the types of activities that pro-Gypsy organizations initiate are constrained by the legal definitions of what it is to be a Gypsy, whether these organizations accept the definitions or not. Two series of questions arise from this. A first is the extent to which these discursive processes relate to how the group is defined and to the sociology of the actors. A second question is the extent to which these discursive processes relate to the expectations that the actions which are initiated can succeed.

This chapter focuses on the discursive practices and strategies that have been used by pro-Gypsy and Gypsy activists that claim to act on behalf of Gypsies' interests. It questions the extent to which these activities have renewed the official and political definitions of Gypsy-related issues. The chapter is organized in the following way. The first part considers the extent to which the organizations' discourses restrict or enable their access to political and institutional resources for collective action. The second part considers the structure of cleavages and conflicts in the field of pro-Gypsy activities and the possibilities for alliances.

---

[2] See Snow and Benford (2000) for an overview of theoretical and empirical applications of frames analysis.

[3] The 1969 law introduced the category of "travelers" thereby replacing the administrative category of "nomads" that had been put in place in 1912. This law will be repeatedly referred to in the developments of this chapter as "the 1969 law."

12.2 Organizations, Group-Building, and Repertoires of Action: Diverging Resources for Gypsy- and Traveler-Related Issues

My argument in this section is that collective action is restricted or facilitated by the ways an organization's interests and claims interact with the dominant interpretations of the issue of travelers.

First of all, I wish to make explicit the differences between the so-called objective definitions, frames or discourse building, and the underlying representations. I use the term "Gypsy" here on the basis that activists often use it as an explicit reference to people and groups that share a number of cultural or anthropological features. The term "Gypsy" is not used as such by the administration and localities that officially focus on traveler groups on the basis of criteria such as housing (caravan) and way of life (nomadism). The term "Gypsy" is often implicit when used by institutions when dealing with travelers. I do not engage in an objective definition of Gypsies, but I focus rather on the social uses of various terminologies and definitions of various groups: the uses of various terminologies such as Gypsies, Roma, travelers, "Roms," "Manouches," and "Gitans"[4] among activists exemplify symbolic struggles for the "right" approach to Gypsy issues and political struggles to being recognized as "Gypsy representatives." Leaving aside the anthropological features of some groups, I consider here that the Gypsy category is a multifaceted category in as far as it points to different groups and different public issues according to which activists and institutions refer.

The discourse on behalf of Gypsies is understood not only by reference to the degree of criticism of the categories that the institutions target, namely, travelers, but also by reference to the organizations' internal activities for a "constituency," for grassroots members. When the organizations are structured on membership and have grassroots support, activists and members bridge institutional framings and their own grassroots' needs and claims. Following from this, framing processes are thus a key aspect of mobilization processes on which I focus attention here (Snow and Benford 2000). I analyze these processes as they relate to official issues: official and institutionalized labels are legitimate frames to define social reality and, thereby, to influence and to limit the possibilities of describing and acting on social reality (Bourdieu 2001). For this purpose, I wish to recall briefly the ways Gypsy groups have been dealt with in public policies.

---

[4] The term "Roma" refers to various groups according to contexts. One such context is the political construction of the Gypsies as a minority according to ethnic criteria. This view is supported by many Gypsy activists in Europe and considered as such by European institutions (Council of Europe and the OSCE). The term also refers to this one subgroup among Gypsies – the other subgroups being Sinti – Manouches, and Gitans. This view is based on migration patterns across Europe. The term "Roma" is used here according to media and political denominations of the Romanian and Bulgarian (Gypsy) immigrants that are governed by French immigration laws and by the European Union transitory regime for Romanian and Bulgarian citizens in their access to the labor market in particular.

12.2.1 *Public Frames and Policies*

Gypsies are generally perceived and defined collectively by reference to age-old representations and stereotypes such as nomadism, marginality, cultural difference, or illicit behavior. In France, the term "Gypsy" is usually seen as having cultural or ethnic connotations and cannot thus be seen as valid from an official point of view. This is because in France, citizens are defined in relation to common interests. The specificity or the characteristics of a group are only recognized in a private capacity. This cultural approach to travelers as Gypsy groups, and therefore as an ethnic group, in France underlies the institutional and political context although the official definition targets travelers.[5] France has dealt with Gypsies – generally seen to be nomadic people – by reference to an administrative category entitled "Gens du Voyage" (travelers). Beyond the common "traveler" label, travelers are a heterogeneous group characterized by different patterns of movement, motivation, size, or social/community networks (Bizeul 1993). The criteria included in the French 1969 law refer more to a negative definition than to specific characteristics, although Gypsies as a collective entity are implicitly understood to be the "ethnic" component of the traveler category.

The traveler category introduced in 1969 was a continuation of the nomads' status of 1912, in which the groups were issued an individualized, domestic passport that included some 15 anthropological measures and that described in detail family links. This passport is the embodiment of an administrative regime that targets specific activities and living conditions while registering anthropometrical data. This legislation is a key marker when considering later developments in France whereby organizations – structured in part on ethnic or cultural criteria – have been recognized by state institutions these past 20 years with respect to the administration of the movement of people. In 1969, a new law came into effect superseding past legislation. The 1969 law established a new administrative organization to deal with the same groups exercising traveling activities and to target persons "of no fixed abode and residence." The status of travelers is divided into three categories according to (1) professional status evidenced by official registration of commerce and (2) sources of regular income. The final category focuses in particular on individuals who "do not practice traveling commercial activities" (i.e., have no official commercial registration) and who have "no regular resource for securing normal conditions of existence," which generally defines the groups with the most precarious status of all traveler groups. These people must abide by specific administrative requirements: registration, access to civil rights (vote), freedom of movement – compulsory police visa, etc. This is the very category of travelers that is predominantly represented in the collective action for and by travelers and Gypsies.

[5] See Robert (2000) and Cossée (2004) for analyses of parliamentary debates in the preparation of a traveler-related law in 2000 and a security law in 2002–2003.

But in addition to this administrative status applied to the above-mentioned specific professional and residence situations, the traveler label is to a great extent an interpretative and a subjective label: those who define themselves as travelers do not necessarily travel and have the administrative status of travelers, whereas those who are legally travelers are quite diverse as far as way of life, ethnic origin, subjective sense of belonging, condition of housings, or economic marginalization are concerned. Thus, all travelers are not Gypsies. The traveler category is in part an administrative and legal category with practical effects on daily life; for some people, it is more a cultural category which they identify with. Identification with the traveler culture and way of life is sometimes affirmed or hidden by the same person in different social contexts, depending on the costs (stigmatization) and advantages of presenting oneself as a traveler (Bizeul 1993). This point underlines that Gypsy-related issues are not based purely on cultural or ethnic criteria. When building group identities and claims-making, Gypsy and traveler organizations deal with various social and cultural aspects of the traveler category.

12.2.2 *Pro-Gypsy Activities and Their Legacy*

In addition to the administrative and legal constraints, it is also important to review briefly the background of pro-Gypsy and pro-traveler mobilizations in France dating from the 1960s and the 1970s. Scholars have noted two trends.[6] A first trend refers to the establishment of an international movement in support of a Gypsy group called Roma (self-definition by Gypsy activists). This was carried out by transnational activists and based on ethnicity (of Indian origin, Romani language and culture) and organized at a European level. Most of these activists were themselves Gypsy migrants living in France. A second trend refers to French Gypsies' and travelers' problems as a result of the application of the 1969 law. These activists contested the discriminatory nature of the law as applied to Gypsies and travelers. Many of the activists were French travelers and some of them Gypsies. They were in competition with social workers' networks, and they criticized public institutions as well as social work organizations that were deemed to reproduce the official discourse on assimilation and that generally excluded Gypsies or travelers from the collective discussions regarding these social problems. Both movements were mainly led by Gypsies and travelers who aimed to enhance the participation of Gypsies and to build a "Gypsy voice" that would oppose that of non-Gypsy activists.

[6] See Liégeois (1976) and Cossée (2004).

12.2.3 Collective Identity and Group-Building

When looking at the organizations' definitions of one group and one social problem, we must address the question of their resonance with official issues and the possibility for organizations to have their claims publicized through institutional channels of discussion. Here, I refer to studies on discursive opportunities that analyze mobilizations and discourses within symbolic domains of a polity and not only an institutional one (political institutions and structures).[7] The symbolic aspects of mobilizations can be analyzed by comparing the repertoires of action and the types of discourse by various organizations, which will be addressed below. Regarding the concept of discursive opportunities, I wish here to consider more specifically sectoral discursive opportunities related to the mobilizations' area of claims.[8] In this study, the area of claims relates to cultural particularities of groups (itinerant way of life or caravan housing), ethnicity (stressing one's origin and identity), social and economic difficulties (access to the labor market, to education), and segregation in rights implementation (subcategory among French citizens for travelers; subcategory among Europeans for the Romanian and Bulgarian Roma). These aforementioned areas of claims are quite heterogeneous regarding the groups, and their administrative and legal status, nationality, and ethnic origin. But the groups they target are sometimes bundled together as Gypsy or Roma by some activists.

Collective action strategies and repertoires must be analyzed alongside the delimitation of the group and the construction of the organizations' issues. For example, some activities target Gypsies as a homogeneous cultural group and sometimes claim for the recognition of specificity in the traveling way of life. It is important to consider the model of citizenship in which collective action takes place. The expressions of cultural difference on a collective basis are not equally legitimized in national contexts and are considered to be particularly restricted in France according to the principle of universalism, by which citizens are defined as members of a political community, irrespective of their differences. The cultural approach to Gypsy-related and traveler-related issues does not account for the goals and actions that are most often sought out. In discourse, Gypsy or Roma identity is often officially promoted as the recipients French travelers, French Gypsy groups (such as Manouches and Gitans), and also Roma immigrants from Eastern Europe. In practice, organizations usually target the group of travelers who fall within the scope of the laws on residence, regular resources, and traveling habits. Many of their activities relate to the social and legal aspects of this group's living standards. Most organizations only deal with the problems of so-called Roma (immigrant Gypsy groups) as an afterthought.

[7] Discursive opportunities may be defined as follows: "which collective identities and substantive demands have a high likelihood to gain visibility in the mass media, to resonate with the claims of other collective actors, and to achieve legitimacy in the public discourse" (Koopmans et al. (2005: 19)).

[8] See examples of Swiss and French migrants in Giugni and Passy (2006) and Irish travelers in Royall (2010).

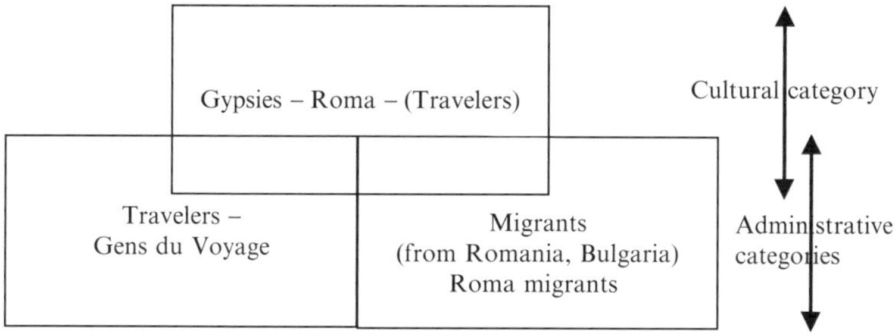

Fig. 12.1 Activist framing categories and types of categories

The following examples are typical of the approaches used by activists and organizations' members to deal with Gypsy and traveler issues in the French context. The first and most widespread approach refers explicitly to the principle of universalism and to a definition that is as inclusive as possible: travelers and Gypsies are French citizens and are thus entitled to full civil and social rights. Inclusive claims are expressed for French travelers: equality before the law and equal treatment by administrations. Such inclusive and legal claims are also made for foreigners, for Roma immigrants (denunciation of a transitory derogatory status for accessing the labor and housing markets). Part of this approach is based on arguments related to the legal provisions targeting travelers that are denounced as discriminatory. In such a situation, the legal reference is a discursive "repertoire of legitimation" (Mouchard 2003). The second approach focuses on the cultural specificity of both French and migrant Gypsy groups. This approach focuses on the recognition of different ways of life and of cultural specificity, and it lies in a shared culture. The third and final approach insists on the discriminatory ways that institutions treat Gypsy groups, directly as a cultural group, or indirectly as nomads. This argument relates to demands for acknowledgment of special treatment by institutions (and more particularly the discriminatory policies in France toward nomads during the Second World War, for example).

Most organizations use the first two repertoires of inclusiveness and cultural specificity in their discourse. Discrimination-related strategies are used together with the approaches of either inclusiveness (legal discrimination) or cultural specificity (cultural discrimination). Figure 12.1 represents a simplified scheme of the various categories used by pro-Gypsy and pro-traveler activists (Roma migrants are studied here only as far as they are included as Gypsies by pro-Gypsy activists).

These trends are key aspects of the Gypsy and pro-Gypsy activities insofar as they impact very much upon the types of actions that can be initiated and the political actors that can be targeted: not only as discursive assets or obstacles but also as support for different purposes and repertoires of action. From a sociological point of view, if we try to assess which kind of activists use one argument or the other and one group definition or the other, we can outline the following observation: cultural arguments tend to be more often used within organizations targeting Gypsies as a common and homogeneous group than within pro-traveler organizations, whereas the legal argumentation is used in both kinds of organizations but is the main approach within pro-traveler activities. Organizations that promote Gypsy culture are made up in a major way by Gypsies and more particularly Gypsy migrants with relatively high cultural capital. Pro-traveler organizations are quite heterogeneous as far as cultural origin and education are concerned. The former are not structured as grassroots organizations, whereas the latter are organized as providing services (of a social and religious nature) to their beneficiaries.

12.2.4 Group-Building and Repertoires of Action

Social movement theory has demonstrated the variety and development of repertoires of collective action over time and its contextualization in political and social relationships. Since the nineteenth century, collective action has been characterized as being predominantly national and autonomous (Tilly 1986). But as discussed in the chapter, my argument is that the repertoires of action that can be mobilized are limited by the kinds of claims and the framing strategies of the organizations. Keeping in mind the dominant and official norms and categories, I argue that the possibilities of access to political and institutional actors are restrained by and related to these very institutional norms. If activists target and criticize these norms, then I assess that they are more likely to fight these norms with legal and administrative instruments than through political contacts.

Activists can target official norms in two main ways: (1) by contesting the existing derogatory aspects of legislation and (2) by agitating for the enactment of new legislation. If we compare activists' symbolic processes for the Roma in Finland or the Roma and Sinti in Italy (Renouard 2010), actors in France have to deal with traveler legislation which produces practical effects on many segments of the Gypsy or traveler population. In Finland, Gypsy activists' claims initially focused on public institutions' attempts to assimilate Gypsies. These activists denounced what they referred to as the "illegitimate non-Gypsy representatives of Gypsies'/Roma's interests." In Italy, activists addressed the issue of nomadism which was the main frame of analysis of the situation of the Roma and Sinti. However, some activists questioned the extent to which this issue was an appropriate way to tackle the problems of Gypsies, feeling that more appropriate ways were the fight against discrimination or for education. In France, by contrast, activists predominantly focus on the effects produced by norms, representations, and administrative procedures.

Because I stress the administrative framework as a cognitive and legal framework to the issue of Gypsies in France, legal strategies are considered of particular importance here. There are several reasons for this. Firstly, many organizations have used legal strategies and invested in legal resources in recent years: legal counselors' assistance to individuals, law suits in cases of law implementation or discrimination, attempts for a wider circulation of information on jurisprudence among activists, etc. In these cases, the legal sphere may become a public place for widening the discussion toward institutions (Israël 2009). It is therefore interesting to look how claims are build in legal argumentation. Finally, groups access the political and institutional actors and procedures with difficulty because of their relative exclusion or distance from the public arena. They also have difficulty of access because culture-related or community-related claims cannot easily resonate with public actors. Legal strategies, therefore, become important in the system in order to have individual rights secured (for instrumental gains) and in order to question the limits of legal and institutional treatments of categories of population such as travelers (for symbolic gains). These strategies bring to mind some of the mobilizations of the "have-nots" in France in the 1990s in which actors such as the unemployed or undocumented migrants criticized and questioned the institutional norms and procedures to which they were subjected on a daily basis by recourse to the courts (Mouchard 2003). Activists' legal action in this context is both instrumental and symbolic. Symbolically, traveler or Gypsy individuals and groups are claimed as full members of society.

The actions that activists initiate are mostly related to the travelers' category as discussed earlier in this chapter. The claims can be usefully divided into two main categories. First of all, claims are used to ensure that the 1969 and 2000 laws are enforced. Activists have recourse to the courts to ensure that a number of public bodies meet their legal obligations. Some of these actions have been successful. With such positive outcomes, the legal legitimacy is reverted against institutions for law infringement (Israël 2009) which in turn reinforces the position of organizations and finally the cause that activists stand up for.

Activists in a number of organizations also engage in lobbying to have the laws changed on the basis that they are contrary to the principles enshrined in the French constitution and specifically with respect to the equal treatment of all citizens. Derogatory status applied to the travelers in many aspects of daily life and civil rights are denounced (restricted access to voting rights for travelers, special procedures of expulsion of travelers when stationing temporarily in communal places). Some of these claims are cultural claims whereby it is requested that their cultural features such as caravan housing and related housing rights are recognized.

Normally, organizations have taken legal actions separately and not collectively. But similarly, activists of various organizations emphasize the advantage of legal actions as a possible means of defense of the group (several members of organizations insist on their aim to "make laws").

In the 2000s, the issue of the fight against discrimination came to be more widely discussed publicly as a result of European Union directives in 2000 relating to discrimination, and it was institutionalized through the creation of an independent administrative body in 2004 in France, the HALDE.[9] Besides administrative litigation, the politicization of discrimination opened up new institutional and symbolic

---

[9] HALDE (Haute Autorité de Lutte contre les Discriminations et pour l'Égalité – the High Authority for the Fight against Discrimination and for Equality) is a national administrative body that monitors cases of discrimination.

opportunities to many disadvantaged groups and minorities and to travelers and Gypsies in particular. This also gave pro-Gypsy activists more opportunities to avail of legal recourse. The principles of law such as equal treatment and equality before the law have also been a discursive resource so that Gypsies and travelers are placed on an equal footing with other citizens, by focusing on common features and common status rather than on differences. The traveler issue was politicized within HALDE: reports were submitted to public authorities[10] and were published; individuals and Gypsy organizations called upon HALDE to investigate litigious matters. These actions resulted in administrative adjustments to legal texts and in a preventive use of traveler-related discrimination publications in contacts between administrative bodies and individuals. Through the establishment of expert groups within HALDE, activists were consulted and recommendations were published in line with some of pro-traveler organizations' arguments about discrimination.

This brief overview of the discursive and practical actions of pro-Gypsy and pro-traveler organizations points to the fact that successful outcomes arise when universalist arguments and legal strategies focusing on travelers are combined. Cultural mobilizations are comparatively less successful, because they are symbolically less legitimate. These developments point to the fact that discursive choices are not only important in themselves as determined by structural factors but also that these choices are not equally converted into means of mobilizations and repertoires of action.

12.3 Cleavages and Alliances: Structuring Lines of the Field of Pro-traveler and Pro-Gypsy Activities

In the previous section, the argument focused on the ways activists' discourses and actions discussed and criticized official approaches to the issues of Gypsy and traveler groups. Whereas the legal and administrative framework for travelers has been an opportunity for action through the legal system, cultural claims and protests on the basis of cultural or ethnic discrimination have been less successful for the activists engaged in these actions.

To what extent therefore can the types and outcomes of participation or of mobilization be linked to discursive strategies and to their discursive contexts? In a general situation where activities are mainly carried out by organizations – even if some protest events take place outside an organizational framework within small groups – I question the importance of the individual and collective resources of the different organizations.

[10] Deliberation n° 2009–316, September 14, 2009.

McCarthy and Zald (1977: 1218) define a social movement organization as "a complex or formal, organization which identifies its goals with the preferences of a social movement [...] and attempts to implement those goals." I focus here on organizations because they are centralizing resources for mobilization and for the diffusion of information of a legal and administrative nature in the main. Érik Neveu (2002: 10) defines collective action as "an intentional 'acting together' in a process of claims, defense of a material interest or a 'cause.'"

Organizations that deal with travelers and Gypsies do not have the same goals and grievances. To what extent then can we speak of a traveler or a Gypsy "cause" or of traveler or Gypsy common interests? In general, pro-Gypsy and pro-traveler activities refer to legal procedures. The definition of problems and needs as ethnic and cultural issues for Gypsies and travelers is quite restricted, whereas the ethnic approach to Gypsy issues is quite common in other countries.[11] Peter Vermeersch (2006) has analyzed the mobilization and political strategies of Gypsy/Roma activists in the Czech Republic, Slovakia, and Hungary since the early 1990s. He found that activists' strategies differed greatly in terms of ethnicization and integration into mainstream politics. But, as a whole, the ethnic frame was mobilized – though to various extents – within the three countries.

In France, the issue of travelers is set by the regulation of traveling activities and of the circulation of travelers. Many of the populations under this administrative status are supervised by social assistance structures, given that a considerable number of travelers are socially and economically disadvantaged. Social assistance has been provided in education, access to social and civil rights, employment, housing, and some social work organizations have also taken part in the management of the parking areas for travelers, etc. Local social, political, and administrative actors are thus involved in travelers' issues and also build discourses related to Gypsies and travelers. Among the organizations under study, some social professionals have competed with pro-Gypsy and Gypsy activists when speaking on behalf of Gypsy interests, and some have long considered travelers to be needy people who required to be integrated according to mainstream standards, that is to say assimilated (Liégeois 1983).

The space of pro-Gypsy activities is divided along several categories: profession, religion, or community belonging. There are five federations of associations, generally made up of associations involved in social and administrative assistance. Federations build up claims and strategies mostly toward regional and national levels of administrations. The field of pro-Gypsy activities has been partly structured on an opposition between some professionals in social work and nonprofessionals, mostly Gypsies, since the 1970s. The latter made claims for a Gypsy voice and denounced the institutional approach by social workers to the traveler issue as assimilative and paternalistic in its objectives. They emphasized the legitimacy of being a Gypsy and a traveler to act as spokespersons for the populations (Cossée 2004). These arguments of legitimation or disqualification according to the belonging of spokespersons to

[11] In the case of Finland, see Renouard (2010). In the case of Central European countries, see Vermeersch (2006).

traveler groups took place in a context of the nonparticipation of travelers in the discussion on traveler problems. Some of the social workers were conveying in part the official definition of traveler problems, which Liégeois explains as being partly the result of social work organizations' dependence on public funds (Liégeois 1983). The qualified and professional actors had often more resources in terms of cultural capital and administrative know-how than traveler and Gypsy activists, who were then "dispossessed" (Bourdieu 1981) of the expression of their views and needs. This professional divide is an analytical simplification of the positions and oppositions, as social work professionals had not just one single approach to traveler groups and issues. Another kind of opposition between activists has been the religious or secular structure of organizations: how could collective claims and objectives be legitimized by religious motivations, and to what extent did religious practice and Gypsy and traveler identity overlap?

The following is a brief overview of the main organizations. The ASNIT (Association Sociale Nationale Internationale Évangélique Tsigane) defends the interests of evangelical members of the international mission, Life and Light. Its activities revolve around social assistance and religion. By organizing religious events and coordinating the traveling routes and stops of large numbers of groups from one religious place to the other, members of this organization have come to collaborate with national and local civil servants. They are generally considered to represent the interests of travelers. Membership to this organization is based upon religion, thus theoretically excluding travelers and Gypsies who are atheists or who belong to non-Christian faiths. The other federations are not religious even though one has a Catholic name (ANGVC – Association Nationale des Gens du Voyage Catholique). UFAT (Union Française des Associations Tsiganes) was created in 2008, but many of its member associations and prominent activists have been involved in secular Gypsy organizations and have undertaken a number of legal and lobbying activities. The Voix des Rroms deals with the promotion of Gypsy culture and defends the rights of all Gypsies, travelers, and Roma irrespective of nationality. Only one organization is made up of and led by a majority of non-Gypsy individuals: FNASAT – Gens du Voyage (Fédération Nationale des Associations Solidaires d'Action avec les Tsiganes et Gens du Voyage) brings together many local social work associations dedicated to travelers whose members are predominantly social workers. Finally, pro-Roma migrant organizations and human rights organizations are more or less active in publicizing Gypsy issues, and when they do, they work with the non-Gypsy FNASAT.

When looking at the structure of membership and belonging (McCarthy and Zald 1977), most organizations provide services (social and administrative assistance) to their members; social work organizations as professional organizations are not structured on membership but apply social policies locally. Membership is of a social and cultural nature; those with administrative difficulties related to the traveler status often turn to the organizations for social and administrative services.

There are various resources that support organizations' activities such as the number of members and activists' competence and expertise (Offerlé 1998).

Resources are of various kinds from one organization to another. The number of grassroots members as well as their motivations for membership vary greatly between the organizations. Evangelical organization can rely on a large support of religious grassroots' members, and most of them are Gypsies (a low estimation is 30,000–60,000; evangelists claim to have 100,000 members in France – figures cited in Garo 2005). Pastors are recruited from the Gypsy community and get special training (Garo 2005). As spokespersons, they present the group's needs to the public authorities that are involved in the organization of traveling and stops for religious reasons. For example, they plan the routes of groups several weeks in advance (some groups of 200 caravans often travel together which needs some planning) and contact every locality where these groups intend to stop so as to organize in advance the needs of the stationing areas. By organizing this, pastors are seen as community representatives by Home Office civil servants and mayors, because they are travelers and help solve practical problems of groups' movements. They help organize, control, and anticipate the circulation of large numbers of groups, which are difficult issues, both at an administrative and political local level.

The other organizations do not mediate between authorities and the people they would claim to represent, and do not act as such representatives. They have a more limited grassroots base (a few hundred) – based mainly on providing social and administrative services – and their resources consist mainly in individual and organizational competences used for expertise, legal action, and administrative support.

Pro-Gypsy activities are organized according to the organizations' areas of specialization and professional competences. They are also structured to a certain extent along cultural or ethnic lines. But these activities also have a political significance. The process of legitimation of self and disqualification of others is not only a matter of legitimacy and representativeness. Organizations compete to be recognized by institutions as experts and try to establish political contacts to influence the debate related to travelers (e.g., parliamentary debates, contacts with the senior civil servants).

If organizations are structured along the lines of institutional legitimacy and official recognition, they also wish to work together. Aside from the issue of representativeness, travelers and professionals (social workers) have sought to adopt common views on issues such as the legal status of travelers (perceived as discriminatory). One such collective action is cognitive, and it regards the communication and the diffusion of information. Professionals have tried to establish procedures and to circulate information among travelers and between organizations, regarding discrimination (the diffusion of the works of the HALDE administration), and decisions of the justice system related to travelers. Other kinds of collective action are lobbying and challenging local or regional authorities about the local problems facing travelers.

Pro-Gypsy organizations have come to cooperate and build alliances, sometimes also with non-Gypsy organizations, as when traveler and migrant issues were politicized and ethnicized by institutions (as during parliamentary debates of a law on internal security in 2002–2003 in which travelers were ethnicized as Gypsies and

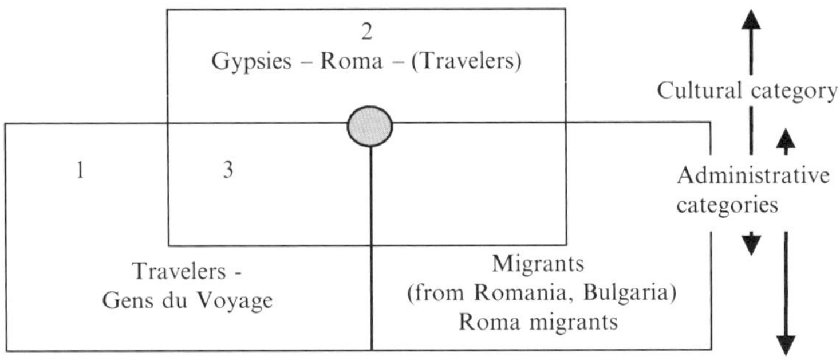

Fig. 12.2 Activist categories and common framing structures

described collectively as outlaws, see Cossée 2004).[12] By targeting both Roma migrants and travelers in 2010, the French President brought together two different legal categories, one based on profession and residence (travelers) and the other based on nationality and residence length (Romanian and Bulgarian citizens residing in France over 3 months), whereby he asserted a common ethnic belonging of these different groups (gray spot in Fig. 12.2). Against the institutional discourse of ethnicization, traveler populations and organizations and pro-migrant organizations counterframed jointly this discourse as stigmatizing. These organizations created joint platforms, expressed common political positions, and organized demonstrations. These discourses and actions can be graphically located (see Fig. 12.2) at the intersection of administrative and cultural issues whereby traveler and Gypsy issues are addressed together through the frame of stigmatization and discrimination (space defined by point 3 and the gray spot), whereas these very organizations generally undertake actions separately in space 1 for travelers or in space 2 for Gypsies (named as Roma by activists). The discursive and practical alliances of traveler, Gypsy, and migrant organizations proposed alternative views and counterframing to the political effects of these institutional discourses.

12.4 Conclusion

The recent activities of pro-Gypsy organizations – such as lobbying central or local authorities, engaging in legal action, or disseminating information – have been more or less successful. Several organizations have developed legal action as a major strategy and have thus obtained legal gains with regard to discrimination and law

[12] In a famous case in 2010, the French President, Nicolas Sarkozy, referred to the "problems caused by some of the travelers and foreign Roma."

enforcement, but Gypsy-related and traveler-related issues are not only legal matters, they are also political issues (e.g., administrative control of circulation). The collective action studied here has been analyzed from the perspective of categorization and interest-building that activists and members of organizations undertake. Institutional categories are official frames that shape the ways activists can build claims. But these strategies of labeling and framing are also expressions of a highly divided field of activities, in which organizations have different membership support, separate targets, and activities beyond a single traveler or Gypsy label.

Is it therefore possible to speak of a pro-Gypsy space of activities from an activist perspective, or is this field not predominantly defined by the very political categorization processes? One can assume that alliances on a cultural or ethnic basis are answers to political and institutional approaches to a "Gypsy issue" as problematic, and that these alliances are facilitated by discourses perceived as stigmatizing. For most activists, daily administrative and social problems are at least as much addressed as sensitive as the issues of identity.

References

Bizeul, D. (1993). *Nomades en France. Proximité et clivages*. Paris: L'Harmattan.

Bourdieu, P. (1981). La Représentation politique. Eléments pour une Théorie du Champ Politique. *Actes de la Recherche en Sciences Sociales, 36–37*, 3–24.

Bourdieu, P. (2001). *Langage et Pouvoir Symbolique*. Paris: Le Seuil.

Cossée, C. (2004). *Tsiganes et politiques: Vers quelle représentation? Représentation politique et mouvements minoritaires en France et en Hongrie*. Doctoral Theses, Université Paris, 8, Paris.

Garo, M. (2005). Les Rroms et les organisations évangéliques: Entre culte religieux et stratégie 'politique'? *Hérodote, 119*, 81–94.

Giugni, M., & Passy, F. (2006). *La Citoyenneté en débat. Mobilisations politiques en France et en Suisse*. Paris: L'Harmattan.

Israël, L. (2009). *L'Arme du Droit*. Paris: Presses de Sciences Po.

Koopmans, R., Statham, P., Giugni, M., & Passy, F. (2005). *Contested citizenship: Immigration and ethnic relations: Politics in Germany, Britain, France, the Netherlands, and Switzerland*. Minneapolis: University of Minnesota Press.

Liégeois, J.-P. (1976). *Mutation Tsigane*. Brussels: Complexe.

Liégeois, J.-P. (1983). *Tsiganes*. Paris: Maspero.

McCarthy, J., & Zald, M. (1977). Resource mobilization and social movements: A partial theory. *The American Journal of Sociology, 82*(6), 1212–1241.

Mouchard, D. (2003). Une ressource ambivalente: Les usages du répertoire juridique par les mouvements de 'sans'. *Mouvements, 29*(4), 55–59.

Neveu, É. (2002). *Sociologie des Mouvements Sociaux*. Paris: La Découverte.

Offerlé, M. (1998). *Sociologie des groupes d'intérêt*. Paris: Montchrestien.

Renouard, A.-C. (2010). The emergence of the cause of Gypsies in Finland and Italy. In D. Chabanet & F. Royall (Eds.), *Mobilising against marginalisation in Europe*. Newcastle: Cambridge Scholars Publishing.

Robert, C. (2000). Le Discours sur les 'gens du voyage' dans les enceintes parlementaires. *Recherche Sociale, 155*, 7–25.

Royall, F. (2010). Mobilisations and demobilisation in the traveling community. In D. Chabanet & F. Royall (Eds.), *Mobilising against marginalisation in Europe*. Newcastle: Cambridge Scholars Publishing.

Snow, D., & Benford, R. (2000). Framing processes and social movements: An overview and assessment. *Annual Review of Sociology, 26*, 611–639.

Tilly, C. (1986). *The contentious French*. Cambridge: Harvard University Press.

Vermeersch, P. (2006). *The Romani movement. Minority politics and ethnic mobilization in contemporary Central Europe*. New York: Berghahn Books.

Chapter 13
Challenges of Social Engagement: NGO Work in the People's Republic of China

Birgit Häse

13.1 Reform Policy and Grassroots Engagement in China

For more than a decade, Chinese and Western media alike report on various forms of collective action in China. Examples are strikes in large enterprises for higher pay and better working conditions, peasants' protests against illegal taxes and land confiscations, urban home owners' protests against the demolition of their houses, public protests by laid-off workers and pensioners against late payment of their state aid and pensions, respectively, as well as the rise of different NGO activities in fields like environmental protection, health care, education, and poverty alleviation. This illustrates that the formerly omnipresent socialist party state has vacated social spaces which it had exclusively occupied before the beginning of the reform era in the 1980s. It further implies that the state-citizen and the intercitizen relationships are in a process of being negotiated anew. In the following, the question will be highlighted of how individuals can act according to personal and/or societal needs within the authoritarian Chinese state which predominantly suspects privately organized forms of collective action and therefore tries to restrict them. For this, I shall refer to NGO work as a special form of social engagement and shall describe selected NGOs. These case studies will further support Carsten Storm's arguments developed in Part I of this book, namely, that collective action in contemporary China tends to be state-affirmative and that it is legitimated on moral grounds.

Western research on social movements tends to stress their potential to initiate and support not only social change but to even foster forms of democracy (Medina 2007). For China, one recent, very prominent but also rare example which supports this understanding of the term is the Charter 08 movement (*lingba xianzhang* 零八宪章)

B. Häse (✉)
Centre for East Asian Studies, Technische Universität Dresden, Dresden, Germany
e-mail: Birgit.Haese@tu-dresden.de

B. Andreosso-O'Callaghan and F. Royall (eds.), *Economic and Political Change in Asia and Europe: Social Movement Analyses*, DOI 10.1007/978-94-007-4653-4_13,

(Link 2009).[1] By this wording, the initiators and signers of the petition deliberately referred to the Czechoslovakian Charter 77 to voice their call for political change and human rights in China. Like their East European predecessors, they demanded the end of one-party rule and the implementation of democracy in China as the sole guarantee of freedom and development. They all shared the same fate: they were harassed by the government authorities and denounced as criminals. Liu Xiaobo, who is one of the most prominent signatories of this Charter and an internationally well-known human rights activist, was imprisoned in December 2008. Under charge of having incited subversion of state power, Liu was sentenced to 11years' detention and an additional 2years' deprivation of his political rights in December 2009. However, for his courageous and nonviolent engagement for human rights, he was honored with the Nobel Peace Prize in December 2010. This provoked a fierce reaction by the Chinese government which defended its own judgment of Liu as being a lawfully sentenced criminal. Consequently, neither was Liu released from prison to accept his prize nor was his wife Liu Xia allowed to leave the country to receive it on her husband's behalf.

Once again, since the violent crackdown of the students' movement in 1989, the government's attitude has clearly been setting the limit for officially tolerated social movements. These movements are accepted – although not always welcomed – as tools of channeling social demands as long as they are not classified as undermining social stability and protesters are engaged in what can be called "opportunistic troublemaking tactics" (Chen 2007: 277) meaning that the protesters are acting inherently within the system. But once this line is crossed and social stability is thought of as being at risk, the government strikes back. The problem here is that the dividing line between accepted and subversive social movements is blurred and solely subject to local as well as national governments' decisions.

Nevertheless, the reform policies inaugurated in the 1980s have sustainably affected the relationship between the state and its citizens and hence also have their impact on the various forms of collective action in China. First of all, in a longer process, the state has increasingly redefined itself as a national one instead of being class related; revolutionary masses were turned into citizens. However, the prevailing construction of the state as a society consisting of party *and* people results in lasting reservations against new forms of collective action in terms of interest groups, NGOs, or whoever else constructs him/herself in opposition to the party and/or the society. Identity pattern and state propaganda employing notions of harmony and a harmonious society (*hexie shehui* 和谐社会) are strengthening reservations against noncooperative collective action while at the same time an increasing individualism gains momentum. Individuals, however, are realizing that they have personal interests that can be shared with other individuals and that cooperation and self-organization enhance the chances of making an impact. The state's continuing withdrawal from interference in the

[1] See Charter 08, *Lingba xianzhang* 零八宪章, www.charter08.com/chinese/charter08book.pdf. Accessed 17 Jan, 2011.

private lives of its citizens since the beginning of the reform era opens up spaces for the individual to engage in various forms of collective action driven by either individual or public interest or a mixture of both. This, certainly, is a step toward collective action.

Seen from a governmental perspective, potential popular resistance can be channeled into various forms of cooperation. This is especially true for the huge number of protests by (migrant) workers or farmers whose rights have been severely violated by local officials and/or managers who often are also influential enough to undermine the protesters' attempts to receive justice and/or compensation.[2] The equally large numbers of petitions handed in at higher administrative levels up to central government level in Beijing do show that there is still belief in the moral and judicial integrity of the state. This belief is even more surprising when taking into account the unofficial and violent aggression against petitioners.[3] In other words, many protesters (still) tend to locate the responsibility for injustices and deficiencies at local and individual levels and thus as a result of individual misbehavior of particular individuals within companies and community administrations.[4] The vast number of similar experiences are not (yet?) perceived as being fundamentally structural or systematic problems, at least not by critical levels of the populace.

Whether caused by the huge number of scandals in addition to effects of globalization and costs of the economic transformation, the state has lost much of its trustworthiness. But as Storm has previously argued in Chap. 4, this does not result in a general rejection of state power by social activists. Instead, new spaces for individual forms of social engagement have been used imaginatively. Reform policy has thus led

[2] For issues concerning rural, workers', and ethnic protests, see Froissard (2009), Rocca (2009), He (2009), and Chen (2007).

[3] According to a report by Human Rights Watch (2009), local authorities do often violently prevent protesters from handing in petitions by incarcerating them unofficially in so-called black jails (*hei jianyu* 黑监狱) and depriving them of any access to legal protection.

[4] This is also true for the most recent protests in the southern village of Wukan, Guangdong province. In September 2011, the protests arose out of the village officials' illegal selling-off of collective land to private investors. The conflict escalated in December 2011 after one of the newly elected village representatives died in custody in unknown circumstances. As a consequence, party officials and police forces were chased out of Wukan, followed by armed forces besieging the village. However, the villagers were eager to define their protests as being only directed against the corrupt local bureaucracy and not against the party in general. In fact, they declared their support for the party on various banners. Unlike many times before in other parts of the country, the Wukan protests were not suppressed violently. Instead, provincial senior officials acknowledged the legitimacy of the villagers' demands and promised to reinvestigate the situation, and the villagers subsequently ended their public protests. They received further support by Premier Wen Jiabao who stated that the government must protect land rights. In summary, the Wukan protests do illustrate impressively that people are well aware of their rights, are willing to stand up publicly for them, but also that they understand that conflicts like these are locally based. The protests also illustrate the fast-growing contradictions between economic development and social stability. Because Guangdong's provincial officials decided in favor of the latter, the conflict was settled peacefully. It remains to be seen whether this serves as a model for resolving future conflicts. On these points, see Fähnders (2011). See also Hornby (2012).

to a new development in collective action in China, most notably in organizational, operational, and functional dimensions. Additionally, an increasing number of collective actions are by non-Chinese, who are thus international actors in China.

13.2 The Chinese NGO Framework

On the one hand, social groups are emerging which are connected by shared personal likings: groups meeting in parks for dancing, singing, playing chess, or doing exercises, for instance (Ma 2006: 113–116). The vast Internet blogging sphere on topics like fashion, cars, traveling, etc., is the e-form of this informal kind of social engagement. Typically, these groups are just loosely connected and not formally organized, without official registration or membership. However, they resemble Western social clubs and societies in their provision of social activities that are free from any state or party interference.

On the other hand, associations which are devoted to public interests are emerging. An impressive example of affirmative forms of collective action is offered by the Chinese NGO sector. NGO engagement spans very diverse fields like health care, education, poverty alleviation, environment protection, and judicial assistance to name but a few. Mostly, NGOs act in realms the state has vacated or cannot reach. They offer a variety of social services to those in need and to those whose needs have been neglected by government agencies. It is not an exaggeration to state that those excluded from society because of prejudices, illness, age, gender, poverty, lack of knowledge, or of access to resources now find an NGO which cares and helps.[5]

Like in Western countries, NGO work in China is based on individual concern that translates into collective activity. Unlike in the West, large parts of the NGO sector in China are closely monitored and regulated by the state. This has led to a sector organized very differently from its Western counterparts. Simplifying the complex organizational structures described in various studies on NGOs in China (Ma 2006; Lu 2009; Schwartz and Shieh 2009), we can roughly differentiate between officially organized NGOs (*guanban* 官办) and those of a popular nature (*minban* 民办). The former are initiated by the government and receive government subsidies (= government organized NGO = GONGO). The latter are initiated by private citizens (Lu 2009: 5), are referred to as "grassroots NGOs," and rely completely on each NGO's abilities to raise funds.

In order to secure control over the fast-growing NGO sector, the Chinese government has adopted several regulations concerning what they call "popular organizations" (*minjian zuzhi* 民间组织). Thereby, a framework was established that offers legal guidelines which define and regulate the administration of NGO work although it

[5] Only recently acknowledged are new forms of entrepreneurial organizations as examples of collective action. It has to be stated, however, that these organizations represent the winners of social transformation who are a privileged group within society (Guiheux 2009).

complicates the registration process. "Popular organizations" are divided into three categories: social organizations (*shehui tuanti* 社会团体, *Regulations* 1998a), private nonenterprise units (*minban fei qiye danwei* 民办非企业单位, *Regulations* 1998b), and foundations (*jijinhui* 基金会, *Regulations* 2004). Of these three categories, only the last one concerning foundations applies to international NGOs (*Regulations* 2004, art. 6.4). Furthermore, each popular organization has to register with the relevant national or local department of the Ministry of Civil Affairs (*Regulations* 1998a, art. 6, 1998b, art. 5, 2004, art. 6). Foundations also have to register with the tax authorities although they will receive tax benefits (*Regulations* 2004, articles 14 and 26). Consequently, if international NGOs do not want to register with this Chinese state agency and/or the tax offices – which might violate their founding principles – they cannot register as popular organizations at all (Yin 2009: 523–525). This lack of legislation is quite a burden for international NGOs because they can only operate in a legal gray area if they are not forced into illegality altogether.

To further the government's control over popular organizations, every NGO that wants to act in a legally secured environment has "to place itself under the "professional management" of a state organ with responsibilities in its area of work" (Lu 2009: 29). This results in a dependency best described by the often used image of the management unit as the "mother-in-law" of the NGO. The government has thus established dual registration and control processes for NGOs that tend to "over-bureaucratize" their work in order to keep it under state control.[6]

NGO work is further restricted by what Deng (2010) called the "one NGO per sector requirement." This refers to the *Regulations*' 1998a, article 13.2, and 1998b, art. 11.3, respectively, which prohibit registration in all those cases in which a social organization or private nonenterprise unit is already "active in the same or similar area of work" (ibid.). While the "same area" might still be quite easy to define, "similar area" is a rather vague term that opens up a lot of space for arbitrary inventions by the supervising government agencies.[7] The Beijing-based NGO Stars and Rain 北京星星雨教育研究所 (*Beijing xing xing yü jiaoyu yanjiusuo*), for instance, that offers schooling for autistic children and training to their parents[8] could not

[6] In November 2011, Guangdong's Ministry of Civil Affairs issued a new *Draft* (2011) to simplify NGO registration in its province. It states that from July 1, 2012 onward, "professional management units" (*yewu zhuguan danwei* 业务主管单位) will be downgraded to so-called "professional guidance units" (*yewu zhidao danwei* 业务指导单位). Hence, NGOs will not need these units anymore but will be allowed to register directly with the respective provincial or local departments of the Ministry of Civil Affairs. See *Draft* (2011) *Yangcheng wanbao: Jin yibu peiyu fazhan he guifan guanli shehui zuzhi fang'an* (羊城晚报:进一步培育发展和规范管理社会组织方案 Yangcheng Evening News: Draft on further developing and standardizing the management of social organizations. www.gzmz.gov.cn/zmhd/mtgz/201111/11292.html. Last accessed 6 Feb, 2012.

[7] In the aforementioned *Draft* (2011), Guangdong's Ministry of Civil Affairs also lifts this restriction and will allow "numerous NGOs in the same area of work (*yi ye duo hui* 一业多会)" in the province. We have to wait and see whether Guangdong's approach to simplify the NGO-registration process will serve as a guide for the national Ministry of Civil Affairs.

[8] For all information concerning the NGO, see www.guduzh.org.cn. Last accessed 8 Aug, 2010.

register as a popular organization because the China Disabled Persons' Federation (*Zhongguo canjiren lianhehui* 中国残疾人联合会) does work within the broad field of offering services for disabled people already, although no services concerning autism are part of its portfolio (Beindorf 2008: 14). Despite Stars and Rain's self-definition as an NGO, it therefore had to register as a private profit-making unit with the Bureau of Industry and Trade and is thus subject to taxation.

Last but not least, successful NGOs are not allowed to expand beyond the locality they are registered in the first place (*Regulations* 1998a, art. 19, 1998b, art. 13).[9] Hereby, the government creates quite isolated NGO units with well-established working ties with government agencies but at the same time prevents them from setting up regional or even national networks beside and alternatively to those of party and state. This might have been caused by what I would like to call the *Falun gong* (法轮功) aftermath: By the end of the 1990s, the government and party had been shocked by this religious movement's level of organization which not only reached various strata of society but was active in all parts of the country and could easily activate its members through internal channels. All this happened unnoticed and therefore uncontrolled by the government and party. *Falun gong*'s independent organizational structure was perceived as dangerous for and by the government and party and was one of the reasons, among others, for the movement being banned in the summer of 1999.

In summary, all these regulations point to one fundamental difference between NGO work in Western countries and China. While the former legitimize their actions by underlining their independence from any power interference from outside, this is not true for the latter. According to the Chinese regulations mentioned above, it has to be stressed that "no fully autonomous NGO can lawfully exist in China" (Lu 2009: 29).

But more often than not, the existing regulations are experienced as insurmountable restrictions by NGO activists. Therefore, a lot of domestic as well as foreign NGOs at grassroots level choose to work without registration. Their work is mostly initiated by individual concern and further morally legitimized by social needs. Therefore, these unregistered NGOs are even tolerated by government and party alike without whose unofficial consent NGO work is nearly impossible. But this also means that a lot of NGOs are actually acting illegally and from a very vulnerable position. Due to their lack of legal security, they can be banned without any further explanation once their good conduct is questioned.[10] Nevertheless, scholars estimate that approximately 1–1.5 million unregistered domestic and between 1,000 and 2,000 international NGOs work in China (Deng 2010). These high numbers of illegal NGOs highlight, first, that Chinese society is obviously in need of the services they offer, second, that the Chinese government accepts this, and, third, that the government tolerates them even though, up to now, it has not found the way to legalize them.

---

[9] Only foundations are exempted from this restriction.

[10] It has to be noted, however, that the *Interim Measures for Banning Illegal Non-Governmental Organizations* (2000) do not mention any content-related reasons for the banning but only administrative measures to regulate the banning process.

In this context, Deng (2010) mentions an unpublished "internal document" that formulates the so-called three 'no' guidelines, that is, "no recognition, no banning, no intervention" (ibid.) as a framework for the government's attitude concerning illegal NGOs. These guidelines, which I had no chance to verify and which had been developed as early as 1988 for local use in Shanghai, have been applied nationwide thereafter. Deng criticizes these guidelines as actually manifesting "an absence of policy" and points to inherent problems like the lack of financial supervision of illegal NGOs, their susceptibility to corruption and fraud, and their lack of transparency concerning working and management issues, etc. While these reservations are surely justified, it has to be emphasized, however, that legal NGOs can experience similar problems. Their being controlled by the Civil Affairs' departments and external management units does not automatically prevent mismanagement and corruption. Here, we have to keep in mind that the Communist Party and the government do control the control units; sometimes they are even the same staff. The government's and the party's basic requirement for all NGO work is that their activists are true to the main social-political aim, that is, to foster social stability and contribute to the establishment of a harmonious society. No matter whether NGO work is legal or illegal, once it is perceived as affecting sensitive social and/or security issues and thus ignoring state interests, it will be banned.[11]

Despite all the bureaucratic obstacles mentioned above and a generally vulnerable position in cases of illegality, domestic as well as international NGO work is prospering in China. The lack of independence of Chinese NGOs does not necessary result in a lack of autonomy, although the autonomy NGOs are able to practice is not automatic but just granted by their respective "mother-in-law" institutions. Lu (2009) describes Chinese NGOs as experiencing various kinds of "dependent autonomy" which might, if lucky, offer them "a high degree of de facto autonomy" (ibid.: 48).

[11] Administrative pressures experienced by legal NGOs working on the sensitive issue of HIV/AIDS are but one recent example. Often registered as private for-profit units, these NGOs' income is subject to taxation, although taxes are reduced for donations. However, whether or not a donation is declared correctly is open to negotiation between the NGOs and local tax offices. Even if it is cleared in favor of the NGO, the whole process illustrates one means of officially harassing NGO work. Further harassments include additional tax audits, fire prevention tests for NGO offices, the banning of conferences and workshops, and the confiscation of published material. All this aims at hindering regular NGO work and has happened to Wan Yanhai 万延海 and his NGO, for instance. Wan is one of the most prolific and outspoken Chinese HIV/AIDS activists. In 1994, he established his first NGO called Aizhixing 爱知行. After it was shut down in 2002, he opened up the Beijing-based Aizhixing Institute of Health Education (*Beijing ai zhi xing jiankang jiaoyu yanjiusuo* 爱知行健康教育研究所). In 2005, he was forced to rename the NGO and to delete any reference to AIDS and health education. He reregistered it under the name of Beijing Zhi'aixing Information and Counseling Center (*Beijing Zhi'aixing xinxi zixun zhongxin* 北京知爱行信息 咨询中心). However, it did not escape official attention. Furthermore, Wan's activities and his linking of HIV/AIDS with human rights issues have made him a target of state harassment. Together with his family, he left China for the United States in May 2010 when state pressure became unbearable (Wong 2010; Grayson 2011). As of January 2011, the NGO's website (www.aizhi.net) can no longer be accessed.

One of her outstanding examples is the China Youth Development Foundation which was set up as an NGO by the Central Committee of the Communist Youth League. The foundation's best known project is Project Hope (*xiwang gongcheng* 希望工程) launched in autumn 1989 and directed to offering schooling to poor children in China's remote areas. As a typical top-down GONGO, the foundation experiences minimal interference by its foster institution, that is, it had the opportunity to employ its personnel independently (Lu 2009: 30–35). At the same time, the foundation can use the vast Youth League organizational structure as well as its networks which ease its actual work.

To explain further the opportunities and problems for NGO work at the grassroots level in China, I relate to two NGOs, a Chinese and an international one, in more detail below.

13.3 Affiliated NGO Work

The first is the Beijing University's Center for Women's Law Studies and Legal Services (*Beijing daxue faxueyuan funü falü yanjiu yu fuwu zhongxin* 北京大学法学院妇女法律研究与服务中心, hereafter: Law Center). This NGO was set up by Guo Jianmei 郭建梅 and others under the auspices of Beijing University's Department of Law in 1995. Guo Jianmei, born in Henan province in 1960, graduated from that very department in 1983 and had been head of the Law Center from 1995 onward (Guo 2010). Formally, the Law Center was never officially registered with the Ministry of Civil Affairs but was affiliated to Beijing University. This status implied complete dependence on Beijing University's decisions, with all its implied negative consequences. But affiliation to a state university also means that the university acts as the professional management unit. This resulted in an exemption from any taxes and the possibility of receiving national as well as international donations – here from the Ford Foundation, among others – through a bank account opened up by the financial administration of the very university. Affiliation thus implies advantages as well as dependencies.

As the first public interest organization on legal affairs in China, the Law Center's main purpose had been to provide free legal aid to women. This included the setting up of telephone hotlines, the implementation of workshops and conferences to promote awareness of gender discrimination and gender motivated violence, the setting up of the China Public Interest Lawyers' Network (*gongyi lüshi wangluo* 工益律师网络), and, last but not least, the offering of pro bono litigation. Since its establishment, the Law Center has handled more than 3,000 cases, defending poor women against common arbitrary and personal violence. One more recent example is the case of a hotel masseuse in Hubei province, who in self-defense killed a county official who tried to rape her (Li 2010). The Law Center's lawyers defended the woman successfully, and the murder charge was dismissed. Cases like this one had been reported nationwide and contributed to the good reputation of the Law Center.

For her efforts, Guo Jianmei was awarded the American Global Women's Leadership Award in 2007, the French Simone de Beauvoir Prize for Women's Freedom, and the American Woman of Courage Award, the latter two in 2010.

However, despite or because of its public successes, on March 25, 2010, Beijing University posted a note on its website stating the disbandment of four of its affiliated organizations, the Law Center being the most prominent among them. Officially, the disbandment is justified by the Law Center's lack of academic orientation (Zhang 2010). In a statement published on the Law Center's website and entitled "Goodbye, Beijing University" (Guo et al. 2010), the Law Center's work is defended and its commitment to Chinese society as well as its accordance with actual politics is underlined by assuring its appropriateness with actual state politics and a notion of morality:

> For the nation, it [that is the Center, B.H.] has made positive contributions towards a socialist harmonious society; for our clients, it represents warmth and hope; for NGOs and our partners, it is a comrade-in-arms fighting for the rule of law and civil society in China; for the public, it represents the conscience of our society and the spirit of law; and for every member of the organization, it is our common home. (Guo et al. 2010)

Although an official reason for the disbandment of the Law Center is given, its reference to mere formalities and the fact that the leading authorities had been able to ignore these formalities for 14years open up space for speculating on additional reasons. It might well be that the complex relationship between the two unequal partners had turned sour. Personal sensitivities on both sides are leastways imaginable. Furthermore, Beijing University might also have thought that the Law Center's work crossed the line between what might be called morally "good" and "bad," meaning that the Law Center's activities went beyond the scope Beijing University can accept as being in accordance with actual politics and with the concept of building up a harmonious society. It is conceivable that for Beijing University's authorities, the Law Center's work is dealing with the darker side of society and must therefore be stopped.

Moreover, in his blog on NGO work in China, the researcher Shawn Shieh has pointed to an increase in restrictions faced by NGOs which are active in legal and/or HIV/AIDS areas in 2010 (Shieh 2010). This implies that the state obviously regards these two issues as quite sensitive ones. Thus, NGO work concerning these two topics is at the mercy of its respective management units which have to decide whether the work can still be tolerated or whether it already violates the state policy. This reasoning might have influenced Beijing University's decision as well. The reasons for the Law Center's disbandment may thus be manifold. But it highlights the core problem of dependent autonomy: this concept only offers an insecure position because dependent autonomy is just granted but not assured and can therefore be withdrawn at any time. However, this is the actual legal framework for NGO work in China and seems to be the exact position the Chinese state wants for it.

Following the disbandment, Guo Jianmei and her team set up a new organization which is now called Beijing Zhongze Women Legal Consultant and Service Center (*Beijing zhongze funü falü zixun fuwu zhongxin* 北京众泽妇女法律咨询服务 中心).

It started work in April 2010 and describes itself as being a nonprofit popular organization (*gongyixing minjian zuzhi* 公益性民间组织). Until the end of 2010, all web postings were signed "Former Beijing University's Center for Women's Law Studies and Legal Services." Since January 2011, the new organization is available online by using the former Law Center's homepage: www.woman-legalaid.org.cn.

13.4 International Engagement Within the Chinese NGO Sector

My second example is the work of AIDS-Waisenhilfe China e.V. (AIDS Orphans Aid China e.V., hereafter: Orphans Aid) registered in Germany as a charity. It was founded in 2004 by students and staff of Cologne University's Department of Modern China Studies which is still its operating address.[12] It is the result of a student's research project concerning HIV/AIDS in China in general and the consequences following the scandal of hospitals transmitting HIV through tainted blood donations in central China at the beginning of the 1990s in particular (Winkelmann and Schaffer 2005).[13]

At that time, local health authorities had encouraged many of the poorer peasants to donate blood plasma which was then sold nationally and internationally. The authorities paid very well for the donations thereby attracting large parts of the population able to work. The blood left over from the plasma-separation process was not screened for health risks but mixed and reinjected in all those sharing the same blood group, thereby infecting large parts of the donors with the HIV virus.[14] This scandal was covered up by the authorities for quite some time so that those infected could easily infect others until the blood plasma donation centers were officially closed at the end of the 1990s. Today, officials admit that 250,000 former blood plasma donors are infected with HIV. However, unofficial estimations are that there are up to 1 million infected people within the donors group. In some villages up to 60% of the whole working population fell ill, with high death rates especially among the parents' generation. This resulted in the emergence of so-called AIDS orphans, children who have lost one or both parents due to AIDS without necessarily being infected themselves. The official number of AIDS orphans is 80,000 out of whom only a bit more than 10% receive state aid.[15] Belonging to the lowest stratum within the villages' hierarchies, being traumatized by the loss of their parents, relying on grandparents or having no family at all, and being stigmatized by the parents'

---

[12] All information concerning the charity was taken from its website http://en.aidswaisen.de.

[13] Much has been published on HIV/AIDS in China. For more recent studies connected to NGOs' engagement in this realm in China, see Kaufman (2009) and Wan et al. (2009).

[14] Specific to the blood plasma donation process, plasmapheresis, is the procedure whereby after the plasma is separated from the blood, this very blood is returned to the donor in a sterile circle to help the body quickly rebuild plasma. As the blood needs approximately 48 h to replace the plasma, the donation process can be repeated after 3 days. See www.donatingplasma.org.

[15] *AIDS-Waisen Hilfe e.V.* (2010), unpublished material of the charity.

illness and therefore being excluded from their respective villages, these children form a very vulnerable group.

The Orphans Aid charity uses the donations it collects to better these children's future. It is engaged in Fuyang city, Anhui province. Most importantly, it supports 170 children by providing them with a monthly allowance of between 100 and 200 renminbi (approximately 9–19 euros) which is paid directly to the children. Aimed at enabling these children to attend primary and middle schools to better their future prospects, this money has to be spent exclusively on living expenses and education costs, including tuition fees. Additionally, the charity provides equipment for schools – desks and chairs – helps building children's activity centers with playgrounds, books, toys, places to do homework, etc., and last but not least, offers training sessions on HIV/AIDS for teachers, local authorities, and volunteers. Just recently, some of the most successful pupils passed their high school entrance examinations and are further supported by Orphans Aid. With school fees being quite high, this commitment tended to exceed the charity's funds. However, due to its successful cooperation with the Education Bureau of Jieshou County, these fees will be waived in one district from summer 2011 onward.[16]

All this can only be realized by relying on international as well as local forces. As a German charitable society, Orphans Aid is a nonprofit organization; it is allowed to raise funds and is not taxable in Germany. Between 2005 and 2008, it worked closely with Save the Children UK, an international NGO which had a local branch in Fuyang, among others. Save the Children's offices in Beijing, Kunming, and Urumqi are officially registered as foreign-owned enterprises (Yin 2009: 539).[17] One of Fuyang's Save the Children's local staff members was paid by Orphans Aid and reciprocally implemented its projects. Official Chinese partners are the local branch of the Women's Federation and the Education Bureau of Jieshou County mentioned above.

However, due to the global financial crisis and the losses suffered by the British pound in the foreign exchange market, Save the Children UK had to withdraw from its engagement in Anhui province. As this was not an option for Orphans Aid, Save the Children UK used its local connections and introduced Orphans Aid to a local NGO called Pugongying Aid Center for People with Disabilities in Fuyang City (*Fuyang shi Pugongying can zhang renshi hu zhu xiehui* 阜阳市蒲公英残 障人士互助协会, hereafter: Pugongying) with which it shared a good working relationship.[18] Pugongying is a NGO which is registered as a social organization. In accordance with the *Regulations* (1998a, art. 6), Pugongying's professional management unit is the Association of Disabled People of the City of Fuyang (*Fuyang shi can zheng ren lianhehui* 阜阳市残症人联合会), and it is registered with the local branch of the

[16] Ibid.

[17] See also www.savethechildren.org.cn/index.php/en/about-us/faqs. Accessed 22 May, 2011.

[18] All information concerning Pugongying, dandelion in English, is taken from the NGO's website www.pgyxh.com/index.asp.

Ministry of Civil Affairs. Formerly, it concentrated its work solely on disabled people. Since 2009, it has broadened its scope by cooperating with Orphans Aid which finances the salary of one of Pugongying's staff members and which shares its office and transport costs. Pugongying, on the other hand, is looking after the children supported by Orphans Aid, and it distributes the money among them.[19]

On March 1, 2010, a new obstacle for international NGO work in China was put into effect by the government. The State Administration of Foreign Exchange promulgated the *Notice on Issues Concerning the Administration of Foreign Exchange Donated to or by Domestic Institutions* (*Notice* 2009), thus regulating the bank transfers between national and international NGOs for the first time. On the one hand, the *Notice* favors state organs which do not have to register at all (*Notice* 2009, Appendix II). It especially complicates the financial procedures for those NGOs in China which are registered as enterprises because additional documents proving the nonprofit status of the partners have to be provided. On the other hand, the formal establishment of guidelines regulating donation transfers offers the possibility of officially designating donations as such so that no taxes are required for these payments to social organizations. But the usual problems with notices and guidelines in China apply here as well: the document itself is vaguely formulated, thus offering a number of possible interpretations. It has also confused the national NGO world and its international partners. This was also true for Pugongying and Orphans Aid. Although the former is properly registered, uncertainties arose for some months during 2010 whether additional documents would have to be presented or whether the donation transfer might have continued as before, which finally proved to be the case. Although the two examples presented here are subjectively chosen, they nevertheless explain the framework within which NGO work in China actually takes place.

13.5 Conclusion

NGO work in China clearly illustrates the transformation of Chinese society during the decades determined by reform policies. The state's withdrawal from offering all-embracing social services to its populace is met by an increasingly diverse society that recognizes its various requirements as well as the state's inability to answer them. However, this is experienced quite ambivalently by social groups: engagement is valued as a social necessity, yet also as a chance for NGO work which thus contributes to the establishment of a civil society that engages itself for its rights and duties.

Furthermore, the Chinese NGO sector reflects constant negotiations between state and citizens. While the authoritarian state is suspicious of individual engagement and

[19] See www.aidswaisen.de. Accessed 18 Aug, 2010.

strives to control it as much as possible, it has to admit, however, that its resources are limited. The state's responsibility therefore shifted from offering extensive social services to providing a legal framework accompanied by hidden guidelines which serve to support and regulate social engagement. In turn, ample opportunities are thus provided to citizens to engage in groups and to serve social needs. In this context, parallel forms concerning the legitimacy of acting occur. The state carries out its constitutionally legitimized power of control. Social engagement is legitimized by the state's legal framework and furthermore by social needs thereby becoming morally legitimized as well. Options of societal participation are thus created which empower those who take part. Due to the legal framework provided by the state, this engagement and empowerment is restricted to a local one in order not to challenge overall state power and legitimacy. Additionally, NGO activists themselves understand their engagement as an affirmative one set out to serve the state which is, after all and not only rhetorically, still perceived as a morally legitimate power.

References

Beindorf, S. (2008). *Stars and Rain – Beispiel für eine sich entwickelnde Zivilgesellschaft in der VR China?* Bonn: Rheinische Friedrich-Wilhelms-Universität. www.eu-china.net/web/cms/upload/pdf/materialien/stars-and-rain-beindorf_08-09-29.pdf. Last accessed 27 July, 2010.

Chen, X. (2007). Between defiance and obedience: Protest opportunism in China. In E. Perry & M. Goldman (Eds.), *Grassroots political reform in contemporary China*. Cambridge: Harvard University Press.

Deng, G. (2010). The hidden rules governing China's unregistered NGOs: Management and consequences. In *The China Review, 10*(1), 183–206.

Fähnders, T. (2011, 18 Dec). Hinter den Barrikaden von Wukan. In *Frankfurter Allgemeine Zeitung*. www.faz.net/aktuell/politik/ausland/china-hinter-den-barrikaden-von-wukan-11570401.htm. Last accessed 10 Jan, 2012.

Froissard, C. (2009). The rise of migrant workers' collective action: Toward a new social contract in China. In K. E. Kuah-Pearce & G. Guiheux (Eds.), *Social movement in China and Hong Kong: The expansion of protest space*. Amsterdam: Amsterdam University Press.

Grayson, C. (2011). Wan Yanhai's statement on Chinese government crack-down on NGOs. In *Asia Despatch*. www.asiadespath.com/2011/01/wan-yanhais-statement-on-chinese-government-crackdown-on-ngos/. Last accessed 25 Jan, 2011.

Guiheux, G. (2009). Justifying the new economic and social order: The voice of a private entrepreneur. In E. G. Kuah-Pearce & G. Guiheux (Eds.), *Social movement in China and Hong Kong: The expansion of protest space*. Amsterdam: Amsterdam University Press.

Guo, J. 郭建梅 (2010). Guo Jianmei 14 nian de gongyi lüshi licheng 郭建梅 14 年的公益律师历程 [Guo Jianmei's 14 years as public interests lawyer]. www.woman-legalaid.org.cn/detail.asp?id=1357. Last accessed 16 Aug, 2010.

Guo, J. et al. 郭建梅及其团队的声明 (2010). Biele, Beida 别了北大 [Goodbye, Beida]. www.woman-legalaid.org.cn/detail.asp?id=1089. Translated by Human Rights in China: *Statement of Guo Jianmei and her team: Goodbye, Peking University*, http://www.hrichina.org/public/contents/press?revision_id=173547&item_id=173519. Last accessed 2 Aug, 2010.

He, B. (2009). Social protests, village democracy and state building in China: How do rural protests promote village democracy? In E. G. Kuah-Pearce & G. Guiheux (Eds.), *Social movement in China and Hong Kong: The expansion of protest space*. Amsterdam: Amsterdam University Press.

Human Rights Watch. (2009). *An alleyway to hell: China's abusive 'black jails'*. www.hrw.org/de/reports/2009/11/12/alleyway-hell-0pdfdocumentChina1109web_1. Last accessed 16 July, 2010.

Interim Measures. (2000). Qudi feifa minjian zuzhi zanxing banfa 取缔非法民间组 织暂行办法, No. 21. http://yongzhou.mca.gov.org/article/zcwj/200912/20091200047500.shtml. *Interim measures for banning illegal non-governmental organizations*. www.fairylaw.com/lawyers/Print.asp?ArticleID=631. Last accessed 24 Jan, 2011.

Kaufman, J. (2009). The role of NGOs in China's AIDS crisis: Challenges and possibilities. In J. Schwartz & S. Shieh (Eds.), *State and society responses to social welfare needs in China. Serving the people*. London: Routledge.

Li, R. (2010). Lawyer recovers from setback in women's rights. In *South China Morning Post*. www.scmp.com/portal/site/SCMP/template.printACopy/pagerintacopy/vgnextoid=4b33e080a6809210VgnVCM100000360a0a0aRCRD. Last accessed 6 June, 2010.

Link, P. (2009). China's Charter 08. In *The New York Review of Books*. www.nybooks.com/articles/22210. Last accessed 4 Feb, 2010.

Lu, Y. (2009). *Non-governmental organizations in China: The rise of dependent autonomy*. London: Routledge.

Hornby, L. (2012, 15 Jan). Chinese premier Wen takes aim at land seizures. In *Reuters Beijing*. www.reuters.com/article/2012/01/15/us-china-land-reforms-idUSTRE80E0K620120115. Last accessed 8 Feb, 2012.

Ma, Q. (2006). *Non-governmental organizations in contemporary China. Paving the way to civil society?* London: Routledge.

Medina, L. F. (2007). *A unified theory of collective action and social change*. Ann Arbor: The University of Michigan Press.

Notice. (2009). Guojia waihui guanliju guanyu jingnei jigoujuanzeng waihui guanli you guan wenti de tongzhi 国家外汇管理局关于境内机构捐赠外汇管 理有关问题的通知, No. 63. www.safe.gov.cn/model_safe/laws/law_detail.jsp?ID=80303000000000000,24&id=4. Translated by Orange King: *Notice of the State Administration of Foreign Exchange on issues concerning the administration of foreign exchange donated to or by domestic institution* www.iccsl.org/pubs/Notice_of_the_State_Administration_of_Foreign_Exchange_20100226.pdf. Last accessed 25 May, 2010.

Regulations. (1998a). Shehui tuanti dengji guanli tiaoli 社会团体登记管理条例. No. 250. http://cszh.mca.gov.cn/article/zcfg/200804/20080400013543.shtml. Translated by Zhang, Y., & Young, N.: *Regulations for registration and management of social organizations* (Peoples Republic of China, State Council Order No. 250). www.worldbank.org.cn/english/content/Social_organizations.pdf. Last accessed 17 Jan, 2011.

Regulations. (1998b). Minban fei qiye danwei dengji guanli zanxing tiaoli 民办非企业单位登记管理暂行条例," No. 251. Translation provided by the Ministry of Commerce (MOFCOM): *Provisional regulations for the registration administration of people-run non-enterprise units*. http://tradeservices.mofcom.gov.cn/en/b/1998-10-25/44329.shtml. Last accessed 25 Jan, 2011.

Regulations. (2004). Jijinhui guanli tiaoli 基金会管理条例. No. 400. www.mca.gov.cn/article/zwgk/tzl/200711/20071100003953.shtml. Translated by Weldon, J.: *Regulations for the management of foundations*. www.usig.org/countryinfo/china.asp. Last accessed 24 Jan, 2011.

Rocca, J.-L. (2009). 'Old working class' resistance in capitalist China: A ritualised social management (1995–2006). In E. G. Kuah-Pearce & G. Guiheux (Eds.), *Social movement in China and Hong Kong: The expansion of protest space*. Amsterdam: Amsterdam University Press.

Schwartz, J., & Shieh, S. (Eds.). (2009). *State and society responses to social welfare needs in China. Serving the people*. London: Routledge.

Shieh, S. (2010). Why the chill in the air for NGOs? http://ngochina.blogspot.com. Last accessed 2 Aug, 2010.

Winkelmann, C., & Schaffer, W. (Eds.) (2005). *Task force: HIV/AIDS in China und Südostasien. Aktueller Stand der Epidemie und Projektansätze für die Entwicklungszusammenarbeit*. www.aidswaisen.de/images/dokumente/taskforce-bericht.pdf. Last accessed 21 Aug, 2010.

Wong, E. (2010). AIDS activist leaves China after government pressure. In *The New York Times*. www.nytiimes.com/2010/05/11/word/asia/11beijing.html. Last accessed 10 May, 2010.
Wan, Y., Hu, R., Guo, R., & Arnade, L. (2009). Discrimination against people with HIV/AIDS in China. In *The Equal Rights Review, 4*, 15–25.
Yin, D. (2009). China's attitude towards foreign NGOs. In *Washington University Global Studies Law Review, 8*(3), 521–543.
Zhang, H. (2010). Legitimacy of a legal centre. In *Global Times*. http://special.globaltimes.cn/2010-05/531143.html. Last accessed 2 Aug, 2010.

Chapter 14
The Suicide Problem in Contemporary Japanese Society: Its Economic and Social Backdrop and Religious Reactions

Michiaki Okuyama

14.1 A Profile of a Young Social Activist

This chapter reflects on social and economic exclusion in contemporary Japan. It is also the story of a young social activist whose outspokenness and writings have exerted some influence on this area. His career and activities illustrate recent developments surrounding the Japanese society and economy.

After finishing the course work at the Graduate Schools for Law and Politics of the University of Tokyo, Makoto Yuasa (b. 1969-) did not choose his career in the legal arena, nor in the official bureaucracy, nor in any leading company. He instead chose to continue the social activity in which he had become involved in 1995 as a graduate student. This activity involved providing support to people on the streets with neither a job nor housing. In 2001, he started to organize the Moyai Independent Life Support Center, a nonprofit organization to provide counseling for socially and economically excluded people and to provide for their empowerment. In addition, he became more and more involved in campaigning through his publications and speeches in highlighting the problems of poverty. He published several books criticizing the existence of poverty and the lack of policies to properly address the problem. His 2008 book, entitled *Han hinkon* [Against Poverty], won a prize given by a leading newspaper company, the Asahi Shimbun Company (the Osaragi Jirō Prize for Criticism) (Yuasa 2008). At the end of the same year, 2008, arising out of the global financial crisis of 2007, there was a sudden surge in Japan in the number of people who were deprived of both their job and home. Yuasa was one of those who tried to use this social crisis as a chance to have ordinary citizens realize the reality of what was going on in Japanese society.

M. Okuyama (✉)
Nanzan Institute for Religion and Culture, Nanzan University, 18 Yamazato-cho, Showa-ku, Nagoya 466-8673, Japan
e-mail: mokuyama@nanzan-u.ac.jp

B. Andreosso-O'Callaghan and F. Royall (eds.), *Economic and Political Change in Asia and Europe: Social Movement Analyses*, DOI 10.1007/978-94-007-4653-4_14,

The details about the conditions surrounding Japanese workers will be explained below in this chapter, but a general image of them, as caught by Yuasa, is as follows. A typical client who comes for counseling is someone who works in an unstable environment, is not covered by the social security service, and lacks strong family ties. Atomized people are kept away from access to social support lines that actually exist. The presence of such people shows the recent increase in laborers working on an irregular basis and the fragility of their social ties. On the other hand, if a person wants to get a job on a regular basis, he or she needs to perform at a higher than adequate level to prove his or her ability for the post, which may lead to overwork, and in some cases to death from overwork. The shrinking of the labor market and then the deregulation of employment conditions in the 1990s caused an increase in the number of part-time workers. The older age group of these part-timers – which is actually the age group to which Yuasa himself belongs – are now coming into their forties, without securing an economic basis stable enough to manage a household. These irregular laborers are thus sometimes characterized as not being able to get married or to have children. There seems to be no option for them except either overwork or poverty.

Because of his increasing social presence, Yuasa's requests and claims to the government had a better chance of being heard, especially after the change of government in 2009 from the Liberal Democratic Party to the Democratic Party of Japan. The Democratic government immediately appointed Yuasa as an advisor to the Cabinet Office to deal with the poverty issue. And then in March 2011, the Cabinet Secretariat appointed him as a Head of the Office of Coordination of Volunteer Workers for the 2011 earthquake,[1] the worst natural disaster in modern Japan comprising of a huge earthquake and tsunami that occurred on March 11. This natural disaster and subsequent destruction of the Fukushima 1 Nuclear Power Plant took the lives of 14,013 people (in addition to the 13,804 people still missing) and gave rise to the forced evacuation of 135,906 people by April 20, the date when the statistics of all the local governments were finally taken into consideration after a confusion of over 1 month.[2] These appointments show that Yuasa's social activities have been appraised as important, reflecting his dedication for over 15 years to the poverty issue. How much he can make use of his earlier experiences in social activities is now on trial under the present situation of the unexpected crises of Japanese society and economy.

In the course of these activities, Yuasa co-authored and published a booklet in 2010 with Yasuyuki Shimizu entitled *Yami no naka ni hikari o miidasu: Hinkon jisatsu no genba kara* [To Find a Light in the Dark: From Sites of Poverty and Suicide] based on their discussions addressing the relationship between poverty and suicide and its social background (Shimizu and Yuasa 2010). Shimizu (b. 1972-) is a former NHK [Japan Broadcasting Corporation] director and after leaving the position of director, he organized in 2004 a nonprofit legal corporation called Lifelink

[1] In Japan, this is referred to as the "Great Eastern Japan Earthquake."

[2] As of June 2012, the police report 15,861 dead and 2,939 missing.

dedicated to prevent suicides. Yuasa and Shimizu have been cooperating with each other over the past few years, and this joint effort to tackle the issues illustrates the existence of overlapping areas between poverty and suicide. If we pay close attention to the aforementioned options of overwork or poverty, we can understand that both options can give rise to suicides in the worst cases. Thus, we need to consider the whole picture comprising poverty, overwork, and suicide.

This critical social situation has forced the Japanese people to deal with these social and economic problems, and especially to care for those people potentially inclined to attempt suicide, and those who have lost loved ones by suicide. Religious people have also started to face the problems in their own ways. This chapter reviews the economic and social situations surrounding precarious life in contemporary Japanese society and contextualizes religious people's recent approaches to the suicide problem against that backdrop.

14.2 Suicide as a Key Issue in Contemporary Japan

14.2.1 30,000 Suicides Per Annum

From the end of World War II, for most of the time until 1975, Japan had in excess of 15,000 suicides per year, although with a higher number for some years (e.g., from 1954 to 1960 over 20,000 per year) and lower for other years (e.g., from 1964 to 1969 barely 15,000 per year).[3] From 1976 to 1997, the number exceeded 20,000 per year, and in 1998, the number of suicides suddenly jumped to 30,000 in a country of approximately 120 million, which has continued until today. The 2 years 1997 and 1998 were the years when bankruptcies of major companies in banking and insurance shocked Japanese society. According to the latest statistics in 2009, the number of suicides (32,845) was over six times more than the decreasing number of those killed in traffic accidents (4,863).[4] This means that approximately 90 suicides occur every single day. A comparison of the rate of suicides among the general population roughly shows that Japan (approximately 24 suicides per 100,000 people) follows Belarus, Lithuania, Russia (over 30) and Kazakhstan and Hungary (between 24 and 30) and is followed by Guiana, Ukraine, South Korea, Slovenia, and Estonia (over 20).

There is a big difference in the number of suicides between sexes. The majority of Japanese suicides reported nowadays are males in their 30s to 60s. The number

[3] Basic data about Japanese suicide can be obtained in the *White Paper on the Measures Against Suicide* published annually since 2007 by the Cabinet Office of the Japanese Government (Naikakufu 2010). The following description is based on the data therein.

[4] For reference, the number of homicides (including attempted homicides) has gradually decreased in recent years from 1,530 in 2003 to 1,067 in 2010.

of female suicides has not changed much and has stayed at between 5,000 and 10,000 throughout the past 60 years. Thus, the vicissitude can be attributed mostly to male suicides. The rate of male suicides per 100,000 population was high around 30 from 1954 to 1958 and then between around 25 and 30 from 1983 to 1987, but mostly between 15 and 25 throughout the years until 1997. Since 1998, it has been over 35, whereas the rate of female suicides since 1998 has kept steady at barely 15. We will return below to this gender difference in suicide numbers.

It should be noticed that all the above numbers are ones officially confirmed as suicide based on reports by the police or medical doctors, and there are far higher numbers who died in ambiguous or suspicious circumstances. In addition, it is said that the number of accomplished suicides is very small compared to the number of those attempted. In the report about suicide in 2010 published by the National Police Agency, the purported reasons for committing suicide were specified in 74.4% of all suicides. Although overlapping, approximately 50% had some health problem (including mental health problems), 23.5% had some economic or livelihood problem (including multiple debt), and 14.2% had some problem related to family, to name only the three main reasons. It is often reported that over 80% of suicides have suffered from mental illness, but since the number of psychiatrists in Japan is small, and consulting a psychiatrist is not common in Japan, it is very likely that the number of those who received special mental treatment is very much limited.

Recently, the so-called postvention has become more recognized along with the importance of the prevention of suicide. The former includes care for the bereaved family members and for those others outside of the family who were close to and intimate with the person who died. People who have happened to come across a suicide or people who have to deal with suicide in the course of their job (e.g., medical workers) also sometimes need special care after their encounter (Kawanishi 2009: 63).

The Japanese government had not been very active in tackling the suicide problem but finally started to address it for the first time in 2001 with the provision of necessary financial measures. Basic legislation was passed only in 2006, and thereafter the government has continued consistently to address this problem.

14.2.2 Poverty Made Visible in 2008

Since the rise and fall of the suicide rate mostly corresponds to the rise and fall rate of unemployment, the importance of the economic factor in suicide rates is very obvious (Takahashi 2006: 13). After the end of World War II, Japanese society has been characterized as relatively egalitarian where the gap between the rich and the poor was small compared to other countries. But this does not mean that the problem of poverty did not exist. Even when one did not pay attention, the problem has always existed, though probably in a somewhat hidden manner.

Following the economic boom in the late 1980s called the "bubble economy," a number of new economic measures were introduced, mainly through deregulation, to respond to the neo-liberalist global market. These measures included restructuring the former system of employment and the decrease in personnel expenditures. Thus, companies came to be able to hire and fire their workforce more easily in response to business trends, and they were also able to reduce the burden of social security that had been shouldered by them for regular workers. One catchy word at this time was the "self-responsibility" of each individual. This meant that an individual's plight should be attributed to personal capability and effort, not to social factors.

After the collapse of the economic boom, in the 1990s, Japan in economic depression was partly characterized by deflation, by the shrinking of the labor market, and by an increase in irregular style of employment. In 2010, one third of the workforce, that is, nearly 17 million people out of the total of 51 million employees, were part-time or short-term fixed workers, or workers sent by temporary employment agencies. In the case of female workers, the majority were such irregular employees. Currently, over 10 million people only earn less than 2 million Yen (about US$24,000) per year.

During the half century after the end of the war, the number of people covered by the social security system in the form of livelihood assistance tended to decrease until 1995. Since then, the number started to rise and almost doubled by 2009. The number of people on social security in 2010 was nearly 1,990,000, although it was estimated that this system should only provide assistance to less than 20% of those really in need of public support. It is sometimes reported that people are discouraged from applying for social security because of the strict procedures at the welfare office. And then there came shocking news coverage from 2006 and onward that some people who had been refused support were later discovered dead from starvation or had committed suicide.

Against this backdrop, several new words have often been heard that refer to the recent economic situation in Japan, such as the "working poor," "kakusa shakai," and "haken giri." The "working poor" are workers who can only get irregular-style employment and barely earn a living at subsistence level. "Kakusa shakai" means a society with a visible or growing gap between high and low strata of society. And "haken giri" means dismissing those workers sent from temporary employment agencies.

Especially after the 2008 bankruptcy of Lehman Brothers bank, legally dubious dismissal of workers who had been employed on an irregular basis occurred on a large scale. A great number of those dismissed people lost their place to live, in addition to their job, because employers had rented housing for these people as long as they were working with them. Suddenly, in the winter of 2008, ordinary people in Japan noticed the presence of a large number of jobless and homeless people in their society. Thus, the issue of poverty in Japanese society has become a pressing problem in recent years. The new government led by the Democratic Party of Japan that took office in 2009 is finally starting to grasp the reality of this domestic poverty.

Under the new government, the Ministry of Health, Labor and Welfare made public in October 2009 the poverty rate (after taxes and transfers) for the first time in the postwar years, which was over 15% as of 2006. A report by the Organisation for Economic Co-operation and Development (OECD) shows that the poverty rate for one-parent families in Japan around the same period was 58.7%, which was almost double the mean rate of the OECD countries, at 30.8%. The report notes that a majority of those one parents are employees but their work may be irregular or low paid. The report also shows that the poverty rate for children younger than 18 years of age is relatively high, at around 14%. It is astonishing that Japan is the only major OECD country that has higher poverty rates after taxes and benefits than before taxes and benefits, and this shows the obvious dysfunction of the present public welfare system in Japan.

14.2.3 Worsening Employment Conditions

In this section, we will look at the public welfare system in general in Japan and in particular at the following four areas: (a) livelihood assistance for needy families, (b) unemployment benefits, (c) health insurance, and (d) public pensions. Especially in the last decade, it has turned out that the major systems in all these four areas are not functioning well because of various factors surrounding current Japanese society, including a decreasing birth rate and a rapidly aging population.

To take one anecdote, according to recent news coverage in the summer of 2010, local governments nationwide noticed that hundreds of elderly people were missing and that it had not been officially ascertained whether they were alive or dead.[5] On the other hand, there have been around 1,000 men and women without identification found dead every year in the past 10 years or so, who probably will account for some part of those missing people. These people must have been totally excluded both from the present welfare system and from any family and social networks.

Since unstable conditions of employment can lead people into downward spirals, economic trends can be regarded as one of the important background reasons for the erosion of social stability. The basic facts about employment in Japan until around 1980 are summarized as follows (Itō 2010: 99 ff.). Standard regular employees were male, while female employees were regarded as limited-term workers until they had married or had children. The salary system for male employees was calculated so as to cover the family living costs. Subsequently, the salary for part-time or short-term female workers, who returned to the job market after their child care, was fixed so as to supplement the main salary earner, and as supplement, the tax exempt amount of their salary was set relatively low. This tendency caused a number of inequalities

[5] These missing people are not the objects of searches by the police under request by the family members of someone missing. According to the police statistics, there are currently around 80,000–90,000 requests to the police to search for someone missing in Japan. Most of those missing are found, whether alive or dead, but several thousand people have remained missing every year.

between men and women in the workplace that still apply today. The ratio of the number of male workers to female workers is approximately 3:2. In addition to the gap in the number of male and female workers, there is a gap between the salary for men and that for women, which is also approximately 3:2.

Since the mid-1980s, a series of deregulation policies were introduced into the employment system. One of the main ideas behind this deregulation was to increase flexibility in recruiting the workforce. Under this approach, the scope for temporary work was broadened to cover more and more types of industry. After several revisions of the regulations governing temporary work, the manufacturing industry, following other industries, was allowed to hire temporary staff in 2003. In the meantime, the number of temporary workers increased from 1.7 million in 1999 to almost 4 million in 2008. Temporary workers can easily be dismissed, and many of them really were dismissed after the Lehman Brothers shock. Now, ordinary people have gradually begun to understand the reality about the deregulation in employment conditions since 1980s.

14.2.4 Overwork and Mental Diseases

The harsh situation of the workplace in Japan is well illustrated by a couple of terms related to death that have been in common use in the past 20 years or so. So-called karōshi is the first term to be mentioned. This means "death from overwork" and it has become a common phenomenon after being categorized as such since around 1990.[6] From around 1,600 applications for legal compensation arising from the death from 2003 to 2007, around 750 cases were judged as "death from overwork" where the workplace was deemed responsible for the death. Among the deaths from overwork, "suicide driven by overwork" has also been recognized as such in the past 10 years or so and is now called "karō jisatsu" or "karō jishi" in Japanese. Among 730 applications for legal compensation for suicide driven by overwork from 2003 to 2007, in approximately 274 cases, workplace conditions were held responsible for the deaths (Kumazawa 2010: 19).

Problems related to work have already been mentioned above as a possible reason for suicides. Even when there was no obvious physical overwork, some suicides can be attributed to either mental stress related to work or harassment in the workplace. These three factors – overwork, mental stress related to work, and harassment in the workplace – may overlap and also may be related to some additional factors (Kawahito 2006: 93 ff.). According to statistics, since the early 1990s, working hours in general have gradually decreased. The reality is, however, that there is a division of labor, in a sense, where an increasing number of workers work shorter and shorter

[6] The first legal advice provided by lawyers in relation to death from overwork was done by telephone in 1988 (Kumazawa 2010: 16).

hours, while another increasing number of workers work as long as ever (Kumazawa 2010: 29 ff.). Makoto Kumazawa (Ibid.: 333–334) points out that a main cause of death from overwork and suicide driven by overwork is the long working hours that each individual worker needs to undertake because of the heavy workload and responsibility allotted to him or her under the assessment system based on meritocracy. This overload sometimes obliges people to work overtime without payment.

Mental depression has been increasingly identified by clinical diagnosis as a consequence of unsatisfactory working conditions. According to the statistics issued by the Ministry of Health, Labor and Welfare, the number of patients with mood (affective) disorders including manic-depressive psychosis showed a steep increase from 1996 to 2005. The number of inpatients per day per 100,000 people increased only from 18 to 22, whereas the number of outpatients increased from 30 to 60.

Takashi Amagasa, a psychiatrist who examined 22 cases of work-related suicide, highlights the following: (1) in addition to overwork over a long period of time,[7] some change related to a personal relationship occurred 5–18 months before the suicide was reported; (2) all suicide victims are assumed to have suffered from depression 2 weeks to 8 months before suicide; and (3) half experienced some trouble, accident, or failure, and several experienced physical disorders, but no one in these 22 cases consulted a psychiatrist or a psychosomatic doctor (Amagasa 2007: 5).

Regarding mental depression as a factor explaining suicide, one point in relation to the gender difference needs to be mentioned. Male suicides far outnumber female suicides, but female patients with depression outnumber males. Some psychiatrists explain this phenomenon as follows. Women can control and suppress their impulse to kill themselves at a critical moment (which explains the high number of unsuccessful female attempts). On the other hand, men are more independent and self-contained and do not share their problems with others, including psychiatrists or psychotherapists. Men also tend to use more impulsive and violent means of committing suicide that cannot be stopped easily (Takahashi 2006: 15; Kawanishi 2009: 49–50).

The influence of media and the Internet on recent suicides have often been noted. One phenomenon is the so-called suicide cluster. Well-known examples in contemporary Japan include over 30 suicides following a young popular singer's suicide in 1986 and more recent group suicides of those brought together through the Internet. In the latter cases, someone planning suicide uses the Internet to post his or her intention to commit suicide and to call out for anonymous suicide companions who would not have known each other before the Internet posting. Then they would go somewhere together and commit suicide together, only sharing their intention to die but without actually knowing each other well (Takahashi 2006: 56–57 and 64–66). Committing suicide by family as a whole has sometimes happened in Japan but nowadays this new type of group suicide has become a somewhat well-known phenomenon.

[7] In nine cases where documents show the working hours of those who committed suicide, 11–16 h work per day for over 3 months before the suicide was recorded.

In addition, some websites sometimes post detailed instructions for ways of killing oneself painlessly and without causing too much trouble to those who will find and need to take care of the dead body. In 2008, a method of committing suicide by using hydrogen sulfide appeared on the Internet and was cited as causing around 1,000 deaths within the year. These phenomena are mostly related to suicides of younger people, which require further detailed study.

14.3 Understanding Japanese Suicide

Japanese culture is sometimes characterized as one where suicide is situated as one of its normal elements. Words related to Japanese suicide as "hara-kiri" (seppuku) [stomach cutting] or "kamikaze" have been heard more frequently in Western languages than many Japanese people would expect. In some respects, Japanese suicide seems to be understood as one way of taking responsibility positively and, as such, respected to some extent. This is especially so in the recent years with the emphasis on "self-responsibility."

A number of famous and influential social figures, including musicians, actors, and politicians, committed suicide for some reason or another not only historically but also in contemporary times. Novelists (such as Ryunosuke Akutagawa [who died in 1927 at the age of 35], Yasunari Kawabata [Nobel Prize winner in literature in 1968, died in 1972 at the age of 72], and Yukio Mishima [died in 1970 at the age of 45], to name just three) also committed suicide.

A number of academic works have been published on Japanese suicide from a historical or sociological perspective both in Japan and abroad. Hirofumi Yamamoto, a specialist on Japanese history during the Tokugawa period, published a book entitled *Seppuku* in 2003 (Yamamoto 2003). This book has a subtitle, "How the Japanese take responsibility." Based on a study about the samurai's way of taking responsibility through killing himself by driving a sword through his stomach, Yamamoto explicates the structure of the warrior's society, the loyalty toward superiors in its hierarchy, and the mechanism of pressing responsibility onto inferiors in the organization. Yamamoto is critical of the last point, suggesting that this mechanism has survived in some organization-oriented Japanese companies of today.

One example of European understanding about Japanese suicide is Maurice Pinguet's detailed study entitled *Voluntary Death in Japan* (the French original was published in 1984). By introducing the phrase "voluntary death" tinged with a Latin connotation reminiscent of Cato the Younger's death, Pinguet argues against both condemnatory interpretations about Japanese suicide by early modern Christian missionaries and its pejorative interpretations by modern philosophers. Pinguet pays attention to earlier studies on suicide, including Émile Durkheim's classical sociological study. One point Durkheim insisted on in his *Suicide* published in 1897 is that if a society or a collective group is sufficiently cohesive and integrated so as to attach individuals to it, it will prevent their isolation that could result in committing suicide (Durkheim 2006: 417). In reaction to this understanding of the role of society in preventing suicide, Pinguet thinks that Japanese society, especially companies (rather than trade unions that Durkheim discussed), seems to fit Durkheim's theory. According to Pinguet, "[s]olidarity, based on the company, does exist and it does have a job to do: in particular, in preventing suicide" (Pinguet 1993: 30). This judgment might have been true to some extent at the time of the publication of Pinguet's book, but the situation has changed a great deal since then. It was originally published more than 25 years ago and thus cannot take into consideration the economic, social, and psychopathic-inducing circumstances surrounding Japanese suicides nowadays.

Nevertheless, Pinguet's attempt to make sense of Japanese suicide historically is very enlightening. Starting with the mythological classics, he reviews the long course of suicidal deaths in Japan, narrated either in literary history or in political history. Thus, he deals in his last chapters with both "kamikaze" attacks in World War II and several suicides of military leaders after the war, on the one hand, and Mishima's death in 1970, on the other hand.

Another thing worth mentioning is Pinguet's slightly Orientalist attitude toward Japanese culture. The following citation shows that he comes to the Japanese case with a somewhat idealistic understanding of it:

> By hearkening to the voices of far-off centuries in an alien culture, can we lend an ear to a discourse other than our own, which can perhaps restore to suicide the dignity of a voluntary death? [...] [E]vidence from Japan's past will help us to grasp not the illusion which may foster the act, but the truth that it institutes. If we cease to view voluntary death as either a sin or a symptom, we shall cease to see it as a passive yielding to temptations and impulses, and start to see it as the deliberate choosing of one solution among many, or an ethical gesture linked to principles and values. [...] A different ethic will help us comprehend truths which will remain forever beyond the range of the suicide theory bequeathed to us by the nineteenth century. (Pinguet 1993: 26–27)

Despite the idealistic limitation, however, there seems to be an insight that we can learn from Pinguet's study. We can get an idea of what he means by "voluntary death" in the Japanese history in the following citations:

> Death by chance – from an accident or an illness – may be easier, but it is all the more harrowing because it is meaningless. It is voluntary death which can take on meaning, and even if such meaning is not apparent on the first analysis (and there are some suicides whose motives are crazy and entangled), we can still feel its presence, and we know if we remain patient and attentive the act will at last speak for itself. (ibid.: 4)
>
> Christians saw suicide as a crisis in man's relationship with the divine will. The deed was seen as one of metaphysical revolt, and so was not subject to the moral responsibility which would have given it meaning within the human world. [...] In Japan, suicide was never divorced from ethics: it was and remained a voluntary death, a moral act – reasoned, deliberate, part of the here and now. You could understand why it had been done and find out who was really responsible. What you would find would be a lucid and completely human truth; whereas the doctors of the West, right up to the nineteenth century, would find only mania, melancholy and – alienation. (ibid.: 173)

Pinguet's understanding may seem to be too intellectual, but nevertheless we can assume, as he argues, that suicide can be filled with some meaning or morality by those who kill themselves. For the bereaved family members or friends close to the dead, however, the meaning or morality of the death may not always be that clear or convincing. The task is for those left behind by those who kill themselves.

14.4 Counteractions Against Contemporary Suicide

This chapter has described the circumstances surrounding suicide in contemporary Japan. Under the serious situation of a continuing high Japanese suicide rate, a number of measures have been taken both at the national and local governmental level and at a social level to address the problem, mobilizing various specialists in medicine, psychiatry and psychology, social work, education, law, the police, etc. Since the passing of the first legislation in 2006 to respond to the high number of suicides,[8] the government has continued to take comprehensive countermeasures to deal with this problem. In addition to the measures taken under the previous governments, the new government led by the Democratic Party started a campaign against suicide in 2009. The present Cabinet Office has established the Cabinet Office Director General for Policies on Cohesive Society, which tackles specifically the suicide problem as well as some dozen other issues. How these countermeasures can attain the goal – its simple and clear sign being the decrease in number of suicides – is, however, yet to be seen.

On the level of society in general, a number of religious groups also have started to tackle the problem of suicide, mobilizing priests, believers, and counseling specialists for this matter. Religions have traditionally had their own way of treating death, taking care of the dying and accompanying the bereaved family members and those others who were close to that person. Religious people and organizations are now required to understand the present issues surrounding suicide, to become engaged with those in trouble and pain, to revivify their traditional ways of dealing with death in a contemporary way, and to devise new methodologies for addressing the complexities surrounding suicide.

In the field of counseling provided by religious groups, specialists have tried to face the contemporary problem of suicide. In Japanese Christian groups, counseling activities started relatively early, following the example of their Western counterparts. A research group was founded in 1970 (which was later reorganized as the Japanese Association for Suicide Prevention in 1983) under the leadership of a Catholic medical doctor and the official in the health department of the Tokyo metropolitan government, Yoshirō Masuda (Saitō 2009: 100–101). Around the same time, a telephone helpline called "Inochi no Denwa" [the telephone for life] started in Tokyo in 1971 under the influence of the Samaritans, a British charity, growing to 50 call centers nationwide. Inochi no Denwa now includes around 7,000 telephone counselors and received over 726,000 calls in 2008.

[8] Under current Japanese law, committing suicide is not an issue dealt in the penal code system. However, inducing or assisting another person to commit suicide is prescribed as illegal.

In Buddhism, taking ritual care for the dead, where death has been either natural or unnatural, has been one of its traditional tasks in Japan. It has also undertaken as its special task the so-called grief care for the bereaved family members at the funeral of their beloved one and along the follow-on ritual processes that sometimes will continue for over a generation. The recent high number of suicides has caused some Buddhist priests to focus on this problem squarely, although it may look a little belated.

Japanese Buddhism contains several different traditional organizations, and each currently provides its own particular assistance. One well-known example of this is the Hongwanji subbranch of Jodo Shin Buddhism (True Pure Land School). This organization started to take action against the suicide problem in 2007 first by collecting information and conducting research. At the level of individual priests, a couple of grassroots on-site activities have followed. Some priests formed networks to tackle the issue together, sometimes interdenominationally. The activities of one group organized in Tokyo in 2007, called "Bouz Sanga" [sangha with Buddhist monks] in short, include (1) a confidential letter exchange on the matter of suicide, (2) meetings for sharing experiences between those who lost their beloved one, and (3) performing a special memorial service annually for the suicide dead.

In Kyoto, under the initiative of a Jodo Shin priest and with the cooperation of the Hongwanji head temple, a consultation center, apparently nondenominational, was opened in 2010. They have established a telephone helpline, and their activities are growing. One of their ambitious projects is to organize a course for training voluntary telephone counselors and peer supporters for grief care work. They have started this course in the summer of 2010, and the beginning looks promising.

On a nationwide level, since 2002 research institutes that belong to religious organizations in Buddhism, Christianity, and new religious groups have held annual interreligious colloquia to discuss theoretical or practical issues. Based on a 2009 colloquium that focused on the suicide problem, they organized an interreligious working group devoted to this issue with the understanding that it presents proposals to consider from religious perspectives. This ongoing interreligious project makes it clear that the suicide problem is the one that religious people and organizations need to face seriously.

From a Buddhist perspective, it will be difficult to give a definite answer to some questions related to suicide. In the Shin Buddhist teaching, whether a dead person can be reborn in the Pure Land is one of its critical questions. Yoshiyuki Takeda, a priest in Shin Buddhism and a member of their Studies and Researches Center, shares his personal views about suicide in his essay (Takeda 2009: 123). He explains that if the dead person had faith in Amitabha Buddha when dying, this person will be reborn in the Pure Land. He adds, however, that whether the dying person had faith or not cannot be known by others, which means that we cannot know whether this person will be reborn. According to Takeda, all he can say is that he believes in Amitabha Buddha's making a vow to save even the one who committed suicide, and in Amitabha Buddha's presence here and now, sharing the grief of those who lost a beloved one.

14.5 Conclusion

It is impossible to enumerate all the reasons for a person to commit suicide. Some must also be overlapping. It is difficult to understand fully the complexities surrounding the problem, which must extend from an individual psychological level in personality to social and economic levels in the country. It is true that the March 2011 gave a tremendous shock to Japanese society and culture, but its aftermath and the lingering aftereffects of the Fukushima 1 Nuclear Power Plant explosion cannot yet be clearly seen. People's solidarity and endurance may help to prevent suicide in accordance with the perspective of Durkheimian sociology, but unfortunately it could happen that a long lingering process of recovery and rebuilding could discourage some survivors from maintaining and persevering such will.

In the era of over 30,000 suicides, some religious people, especially in Buddhism, have actually started to face it together with others of the same good will. That religious people take counteractions to social and economic problems only after the problems occur can be criticized with good reason, because their reactions are a "symptomatic treatment" at best. That is, they are taken up only after some symptom appears and do not really go into the etiology of the problem. If so, these counteractions do not address the present Juggernaut system of national or international society and economy with their flaws. Quietly listening to those in suffering and patiently being together with them can be one way of facing the problem, while raising one's voice and taking action to realize a better world can be another.

In the post-2011 earthquake period, however, even the counteractions characterized as symptomatic treatment will have a substantial effect. After they started to deal with the suicide problem in Japan in the past few years, religious people and groups are now facing a further challenge. There will be a need to see for a number of years to come whether they can tackle this new crisis in Japanese society, collaborating with other social sectors or social activists like Makoto Yuasa and cooperating with citizens of good will to get voluntarily engaged in altruistic activities.

References

Amagasa, T. (2007). Suicide and depression among workers in Japan. *Journal of Japanese Scientists, 42*(7), 4–9.

Chiaki, K. (2009). *Jisatsu Yobōgaku* [Studies on the prevention of suicide]. Tokyo: Shinchō-sha.

Durkheim, É. (2006). *On suicide* (trans: Robin, B.). London: Penguin Books.

Itō, S. (2010). *Koyō Hōkai to Shakai Hoshō* [Collapse of employment and social security]. Tokyo: Heibonsha.

Kawahito, H. (2006). *Karō Jisatsu to Kigyō no Sekinin* [Suicide from overwork and the responsibility of companies]. Tokyo: Junpōsha.

Kawanishi, C. (2009). *Jisatsu Yobōgaku* [Studies on the prevention of suicide]. Tokyo: Shinchō-sha.

Kumazawa, M. (2010). *Hatarakisugi ni Taorete: Karōshi, Karōjisatsu no Kataru Rōdōshi* [Pulled down by overwork: A history of laborers who died from overwork or committed suicide driven by overwork]. Tokyo: Iwanami Shoten.

Naikakufu. (2010). *Jisatsu Taisaku Hakusho* [White paper on the measures against suicide]. Tokyo: Naikakufu [Cabinet Office of the Japanese Government].
Pinguet, M. (1993). *Voluntary death in Japan* (trans: Morris, R.). Cambridge: Polity Press.
Saitō, Y. (2009). *Jisatsu Kiki to Sono Kea* [Crises of suicide and the care for them]. Tokyo: Kirisuto Shinbunsha.
Shimizu, Y., & Yuasa, M. (2010). *Yami no naka ni hikari o miidasu: Hinkon jisatsu no genba kara* [To find a light in the dark: From sites of poverty and suicide]. Tokyo: Iwanami Shoten.
Takahashi, Y. (2006). *Jisatsu Yobō* [The prevention of suicide]. Tokyo: Iwanami Shoten.
Takeda, Y. (2009). Sōryo to shite Jishi ni Mukiau: Shakaiteki Mondai to shite no Torikumi [How I face suicidal death as a Buddhist monk: Tackling the issue as a social problem]. *Gendai no Esupuri, 501*, 116–124.
Yamamoto, H. (2003). *Seppuku: Nihonjin no Sekinin no Torikata* [Seppuku: How the Japanese take responsibility]. Tokyo: Kōbunsha.
Yuasa, M. (2008). *Han Hinkon* [Against poverty]. Tokyo: Iwanami Shoten.

Chapter 15
Constructing and Controlling People's Power from the Grass Roots: Philippine Social Movement Activism in a Historical Perspective

Dominique Caouette

The Philippines represents a fascinating and singular case of collective action in Southeast Asia. Rooted in the long struggle against the Marcos dictatorship (1972–1986), the country has been recognized and renowned in the region for its citizen's protest and organizations. In fact, a quick survey at the range of regional organizations reveals the significant presence of Filipino activists. At the same time, the Philippines is lagging behind regionally in terms of its development index and socioeconomic equity and in deepening its democratization. How can one understand such level of collective action and social movement organizing? What does this tell us in relation to broader political struggles for democracy, political participation, and left politics? How have the end of the Cold War and the succeeding era of rapid economic globalization impacted on the form, type, and range of collective action in the Philippines?

This chapter addresses these questions arguing that one can understand and explain such extraordinary level of social organizing by examining the specific conditions under which a whole generation of activists came about, namely, the constitution of the large and multisectoral social movements led or influenced by the Communist Party of the Philippines (CPP) and its umbrella organization, the National Democratic Front (NDF). Over the years, the CPP-led revolutionary movement has demonstrated both a skillful understanding of political opportunities and political struggles combined with a highly instrumentalist approach to social mobilization (Putzel 1995; Abinales 1996; Rutten 2008). Since the early 2000s, the ideologically orthodox CPP has ventured into new experiments such as electoral participation and setting up a legal electoral party, *Bayan Muna*. Finally, the CPP through its legal mass organizations has successfully inserted itself within the antiglobalization movement while continuing to be rooted in rural areas, given its Maoist strategic line, with the New People's Army (NPA) launching tactical offensives from time to time.

D. Caouette (✉)
Département de science politique, Université de Montréal,
CP. 6128, Succ. Centre-ville, Montréal, QC H3C 3J7, Canada
e-mail: dominique.caouette@umontreal.ca

B. Andreosso-O'Callaghan and F. Royall (eds.), *Economic and Political Change in Asia and Europe: Social Movement Analyses*, DOI 10.1007/978-94-007-4653-4_15,

In this chapter, I try to show that the CPP armed revolutionary movement persists because it has the defining elements of a social movement. The revolutionary movement responds to political opportunities in a way that ensures its survival. In fact, contrary to arguments that the movement has been dogmatic, the review of its past has shown that it has been very flexible, not only in terms of its tactics, as many have already pointed out, but at the level of its theory. It is elastic enough that almost any change domestically and internationally can be explained and located within the grand revolutionary narrative. The revolutionary movement's frame of action is both interpretative (explaining reality) and action-oriented (it offers a way to act). Its framework is also quite voluntaristic and presents itself as *infallible*. The revolutionary movement also generates a collective identity, the "national democrat," through a series of protocols and courses that can be mass reproduced and easily understood but also witnessed in the guerrilla battlefield. Not surprisingly, new urban-based recruit or international solidarity activists all make "field visits" to the guerrilla zones, during vacations or "exposure tours."

The chapter also suggests that part of the limited impact of the revolutionary movement on structural change can be accounted for by a double process. On the one hand, there is the gradual taming and pacification of social protest through a procedure of institutionalization and polarization of collective action into two camps: an orthodox clandestine armed revolutionary movement linked to a series of legal and sectoral people's organizations and reformist and institutionalized social movements constituted around nongovernment and political parties. On the other hand, there is persistence and resilience of the neo-patrimonial Philippine state that has managed to block structural changes, maintain networks of patron-client relations and nepotism, and oftentimes coop and divide social movements and grassroots collective action (Caouette 2011; Quimpo 2008). This double dynamics challenges understandings of democratization and social movement perspectives that would assume that the "thickness" and density of social organizing may bring about structural change toward a greater quality and a reduction in social marginalization.[1]

15.1 Developing a New Collective Action Frame: The Noisy 1960s

This section examines the genesis of the CPP, its emergence and adoption of a Marxist-Leninist-Maoist ideology, and its protracted people's war strategy. With the formation of the CPP, a new armed revolutionary movement with its own repertoire of collective action emerged. In particular, it is essential to examine numerous front and sectoral legal organizations that would eventually dominate and capture much of the collective action in the Philippines during the Marcos dictatorship (1972–1986). In the process, a whole generation of social movement activists was trained and is now responsible for a large segment of collective action, social movement organizations, and nongovernmental

[1] See, for example, Jonathan Fox (1994), Karl and Schmitter (1991), Kitschelt (1992), and Putnam (1993).

organizations (NGOs) that still occupy a central place in Philippine civil society organizations (Hilhorst 2003; Clarke 1998). This communist revolutionary movement also sought to distinguish itself from the Partido Komunista ng Pilipinas (PKP) – the first communist party established in the Philippines and pro-Soviet – bringing about a new syntax and grammar of revolutionary struggle in the Philippines.

The formative years of the revolutionary movement were crucial on four counts: (1) a particular "repertoire of collective action" was gradually created as a syncretic mixture of various forms of protest; (2) a self-defined identity of the "national-democratic activist" was constructed; (3) a body of ideological theoretical writings relatively accessible and easily communicated to others was developed; and (4) a particular organizational form of revolutionary movement, comprised of a vanguard political party, a guerrilla organization, and a set of social movement organizations, was established.

The early origins of the CPP-led revolution can be traced back to the late 1950s and early 1960s with the emergence of new forms of student radicalism. This new radicalism is usually associated with the creation in 1959 by José Maria Sison and his wife, Juliet de Lima-Sison of the Student Cultural Association of the University of the Philippines (SCAUP) (Abinales 1984; Weekley 1996a and b, 2001; Sison 1989). Although the SCAUP was not initially Marxist and rather "libertarian and nationalist" (Nemenzo 1984a: 44), it nonetheless provided a focal point for organizing. While its activities revolved around literary critiques and discussions of Philippine nationalist writers, it provided a new organizational forum to discuss what were thought as critical views of Philippine history. Another impetus for forming the SCAUP was a reaction against the religious-based student associations.[2] As Abinales explains, "student politics by the time Sison entered UP [University of the Philippines] in 1956 was characterized by the growing tension between the student *politicos*, then headed by Greek-lettered fraternities, and a powerful Christian lobby group organized around the UP Student Catholic Action" (Abinales 1992: 13).

The organizational capacities of Sison and other members of the SCAUP became a key factor in the emergence of more militant student organizations. In an interview, Juliet de Lima-Sison recalled how this strong sense for an organizational form was important at the time:

> The problem then was there was an anti-organization tendency among intellectuals. Everyone was reading Milovan Djilas' *The New Class* and Koestler's *The God That Failed*. People felt that organizations were stifling. But José said that we could not do anything until we got organized.[3]

[2] In one of his studies of the student movement, Abinales points out that "[I]t was the ideas of Recto which appeared to have inspired Sison to transcend the narrow confines of the sectarian controversy and to lead him to form an association in 1959. This association, although evolving from the continuing dispute among sectarians and liberals, was also an initiator of a new type of student involvement – that which bred nationalist sentiments among them" (Abinales 1984: 19). See also Abinales (1988).

[3] Quoted in Chapman (1987: 71). Francisco Nemenzo made similar observations about Sison: "He was shy at times and not very articulate in big crowds. But in one-on-one debates and in small groups he was very persuasive. He had enormous patience with people and would spend hours trying to convert them to his side. He was something of a dreamer but he was a great organizer" (quoted in Chapman, Ibid: 70).

However, as several observers have noted before, if not for the Committee on Anti-Filipino Activities (CAFA), the SCAUP would not have been able to achieve the necessary profile to become a focal point of organizing. As Nemenzo noted, the McCarthy-style investigations of CAFA "had the effect of rousing the irascible academic community and providing SCAUP its first experience in mass action" (Nemenzo 1984a: 45).[4] This first mass action was a successful protest on March 14, 1961, in front of the Philippine Congress attended by many SCAUP members. This mass action eventually forced the CAFA committee to abandon its investigation at the UP.[5] The protest also significantly raised SCAUP's credibility among students and increased its membership.[6] As SCAUP expanded, international events helped fuel student activism. As Nemenzo noted:

> The impetus in their political awakening came from international events, particularly the Cuban Revolution, the murder of Patrice Lumumba, the deepening of the US involvement in Vietnam, the leftward swing of Sukarno's government in Indonesia and, after 1966, the Cultural Revolution in China. (Nemenzo 1984b: 74)[7]

During those years, the UP became the intellectual center where student activists and writers were able to discover and learn about Marxism. Sison and a group of members of SCAUP also became more familiar with Marxist literature.[8] It was around this period, that Sison established links with the PKP. By then, the PKP, having been at its lowest in terms of membership and militancy a few years before, was in the process of reconstruction. The single-file policy had created a great deal of inertia and complicated the rebuilding process (Nemenzo 1984a: 39–42). The aging PKP the aging PKP leadership did not fail "to perceive a new public

[4] See also Chapman (1987: 71) and Abinales (1992: 15).

[5] For Sison, the demonstration was highly significant: "The anti-CAFA demonstration drew 4,000 students and young instructors who went up to the halls of Congress and literally scuttled the CAFA hearings. This demonstration would be of signal importance. It marked the end of a long period of quiescence and stultifying reaction in the 1950s and the beginning of the resurgence of the progressive mass movement" (Sison with Werning 1989: 12).

[6] In his classic *Philippine Society and Revolution* (hereafter referred to as PSR) initially drafted in 1970, Sison went so far as to say that "This mass action marked the beginning of a cultural revolution of a national-democratic character after more than two decades during which the bourgeois reactionary gang of the Lavas surrendered initiative to the reactionaries" (Sison 1979: 46).

[7] See also Abinales (1984: 22) and Jones (1989: 22).

[8] According to Nemenzo, Sison and others with the assistance of an Indonesian postgraduate student based at the University of the Philippines initiated a small Marxist study circle within the SCAUP. The same student was also instrumental in facilitating the connection between Sison and the PKP (see Nemenzo 1984a: 45). In his autobiographic interview with German Rainer Werning, Sison mentioned that he traveled to Indonesia early in 1962 after receiving a scholarship to study Indonesian language and literature in Jakarta. Before traveling, Sison had been the general secretary of the Philippine-Indonesian Friendship and Cultural Association. He returned to the Philippines later that year and he joined the PKP later in December (see Sison with Werning 1989: 15, 44, and 202). Since 1938, the PKP had merged with the Socialist Party of the Philippines, but after WWII, as Saulo points out, "the party came to be known simply as the Communist Party of the Philippines" (1990: 28).

mood, especially in the exertions of young nationalists beginning to march in the streets against 'US imperialism' and so saw the possibility of infiltrating nationalist groups and annexing them to a new version of the united front" (Chapman 1987: 72).[9] In December 1962, the PKP invited Sison to join the party (Weekley 1996a: 22). Soon after, Sison became the secretary head of the youth section.

15.1.1 Sison's Rise as a Social Movement Entrepreneur

The early 1960s were formative and decisive years for Sison. In 1961, his first collection, *Brothers and Other Poems,* was published. In March 1963, he worked with others to launch a new left-wing nationalist magazine – *Progressive Review* – that he edited. This involvement led him to become familiar with "the struggle for national liberation, democracy, and socialism of the Asian, African, and Latin American peoples and countries."[10] However, the key event in the emergence of a new revolutionary movement was the founding of the *Kabataang Makabayan* (KM or Patriotic Youth) on November 30, 1964.[11] Nemenzo has noted that the "PKP provided the main bulk of KM's original membership with young peasants from Central and Southern Luzon, mostly children of MASAKA members" (Nemenzo 1984b: 45).[12] Yet, the student members usually received most of the media attention (Chapman 1987: 73). Because KM wanted to be perceived as a "mass organization" or perhaps because it was thought necessary for students to break certain elitist attitudes, the "KM national council arranged occasional excursions to the MASAKA villages" (Nemenzo 1984a: 46).

PKP Youth Section Secretary Sison, along with other student leaders, played a central role in organizing and leading KM. According to American journalist William Chapman, what made KM significant was that it constituted the "first and

---

[9] See also Nemenzo (1984a: 45) and "Bart," interview with author, Angeles City, March 16, 1995.

[10] Sison with Werning (1989: 28). Chapman (1987: 73) has described the *Progressive Review* as "a popular left-wing journal devoted to Marxism and nationalism. Its editorial reflected the party's new enthusiasm for a popular front united for battle against the twins devils of 'neo-colonialism' and 'feudalism'."

[11] The date was not accidental. As Weekley has pointed out, "KM was founded on 30 November 1964, the 101st anniversary of the birthday of *Katipunan* leader Andres Bonifacio" (Weekley 1996a: 22). This detail was originally mentioned in Lachica (1971: 178). In fact, Sison stated in his opening speech "No more propitious day than this can be chosen to found Kabataang Makabayan. Today is the 101st birth anniversary of Andres Bonifacio, the Great Proletarian Hero, who in the vigor of his youth led the secret society of Katipunan and mobilized the patriotic forces that generated the Philippine revolution of 1896 – the Revolution which smashed Spanish colonialism throughout the archipelago" (Kabataang Makabayan 1965: 2).

[12] According to "Bart," a former PKP cadre based in Angeles City, MASAKA was organized to take advantage of a provision in the land reform act passed in the 1960 that guaranteed peasants the right "to organize themselves" (interview with author, Angeles City, March 16, 1995). MASAKA was the acronym for *Malayang Samahang Magsasaka* or Free Association of Peasants.

most successful attempt to unite urban middle-class radicals with peasant groups" (Chapman 1987: 73). He believed that, in many ways, KM became "the model for the much broader National Democratic Front" established 9 years later (Ibid.: 73).[13]

KM played a key role in forming and training a new generation of activists that initially helped reinvigorate the PKP.[14] KM discussion groups were established in which students read and analyzed Marxist writings. At the time, it was Mao Tse-tung's writings and the Chinese Cultural Revolution that exerted the greatest interest among this new generation of activists.[15] It is likely that Sison had some exposure to Chinese literature during his stay in Indonesia.[16] Sison has acknowledged the appeal the Chinese revolution and its international position had for young Filipino activists:

> China's militant anti-imperialist stand and advocacy of armed struggle went along well with the strong anti-imperialist and anti-colonial wave of armed struggle in Asia, Africa, and Latin America. China was therefore a source of inspiration to the Filipino revolutionaries, including myself (Sison 1989: 29).

In fact, as Filipino professor of Asian Studies, Armando Malay, explains:

> As in the Western countries, a certain amount of faddist ostentation attended the gestative period of Maoism in the Philippines. Mao jackets, caps, and badges became status symbols, worn as so many political statements denoting either adherence to Marxism-Leninism-Mao Tse-tung Thought, or a recent visit to the People's Republic, or better yet, both. (Malay 1984: 48)

In many ways, what Sison, other radicalized students, KM, and the *Progressive Review* were doing was to locate the Philippines within the global context of student radicalism and activism of the day. The Vietnam War, which had direct connections

---

[13] In fact, early in the program of KM, it is written that: "It is the chief task of the Filipino youth and its vanguard organization, Kabataang Makabayan, to assist in the achievement of an invincible unity of all national classes and forces to push further the struggle for national liberation in all fields, economic, political, cultural, and military, against the single main enemy, American imperialism" (Kabataang Makabayan 1965: 14).

[14] Some of the elected members of the first KM national council would eventually become key personalities and members of the central committee of the reestablished Communist Party of the Philippines, among them are José Maria Sison, Nilo Tayag, and Carlos del Rosario. See Katabaang Makabayan (1965: back cover).

[15] In fact, it was Mao's works that "gave this new consciousness a theoretical form" (Nemenzo 1984a: 49).

[16] In the early 1960s, China was interested in developing its own network of support to communist parties. Peter Van Ness wrote that during the 1958–1965 period "Peking began to stake out its own geographical areas of interest on the international scene – among the communist parties and communist governments of Asia and the non-communist countries of the Third World – and to seek closer economic relations with the industrialized countries of Europe and Japan" (Van Ness 1970: 14). Armando Malay (1984: 45) explains that in 1964 "the Partai Komunis Indonesia (PKI) issued a call for the creation of rival parties in those countries where the existing communist parties (CPs) were under the control of 'revisionists', i.e., communist loyal to the Communist Party of the Soviet Union in the latter's intensifying ideological conflict with the Chinese party. [...] The PKI's call, in so many words, telegraphed the Chinese party's intention to organize an international network of fraternal like-minded parties that would compete with the Soviet bloc for hegemony of the international communist movement."

with the American military bases in the Philippines, played a key role in symbolizing "imperial power" (Abinales 1988: Chapter 3; Abinales 1984; Chapman 1987: 74). The occasional killings of Filipinos around the American army bases in the Philippines combined with the "arrogant" American dismissal of these killings offered excellent opportunities for KM to spearhead and organize protest activities against "US imperialism": "Overnight, paltry demonstrations outside the US Embassy mushroomed into huge affairs attended by tens of thousands of students, workers, and intellectuals" (Jones 1989: 21). Francisco Nemenzo, Jr., who was at the time teaching at the University of the Philippines, mentions that the student movement expanded beyond the school campuses: "It did not stay as a purely student affairs, but spilled out of the universities and generated a broad popular movement" (Nemenzo 1984a: 48).

The key feature was how student protest linked itself to a broader range of social movement and eventually played a leading role. Early on, Sison and student leaders and members of the PKP saw how student protests in the Philippines could be "attached" to global developments:

> The student unrest, the black revolt and the worker strike movement in the United States also had an inspiring effect on students in the Philippines. Filipino students were glad to see US imperialism being opposed on its home ground. The student mass actions in Western Europe also had some strong impact on the Filipino students. They thought and felt that they were in strong solidarity with their counterparts in the United States and Western Europe. (Sison 1989: 29)

Equipped with "theoretical tools" that seemed the most advanced at the time, and with a sense of being with "the times" of protest, KM leaders, including Sison, were able to develop an "organizational package" that had the power of linking the present with the past, while creating a new and attractive path to channel the energies of the radicalized students.[17]

15.2 Merging the New with the Past: Marxism, Maoism, and Nationalism

The key juncture in the genesis of the CPP revolution was the period between the creation of the KM in late 1964, and the founding congress of the reestablished CPP in late 1968–early 1969. It was during that period that José Maria Sison and his followers sought to link their activism of the 1960s with the past struggles of Filipino

[17] KM saw itself having a definite role to play in developing and modeling such an organizational package. In his report to the second KM congress, Sison stated, "The Kabataang Makabayan is the training ground for uncompromising leaders in the national-democratic movement. It is also the spearhead of a vigorous propaganda movement and the initiator of mass actions that bring to the consciousness of the broad masses of our people the need for a basic national-democratic change" (Sison 1967a: 4).

revolutionary heroes of the turn of the century, the early struggles of the PKP, and the Filipino nationalists of the 1950s.[18]

By the mid-1960s, KM was part of the broader resurgence of student activism and youth activism in the Philippines. But more importantly, KM activists managed to reach out to a wider spectrum of social sectors. First, through their PKP connections, they fostered links between urban middle-class students, urban poor, and peasant youth who were members of MASAKA (Chapman 1987: 73).[19] Second, they connected also with workers. Sison became the vice-president of the "new" party-sponsored *Lapiang Manggagawa* (LM), or Workers' Party. Third, they linked up with those supporting Filipino nationalism, joining the Movement for the Advancement of Nationalism (MAN): "a primarily middle-class organization of nationalists earnestly intent on purifying the Philippines by purging it of foreign influences" (Chapman 1987: 73).[20] Chapman's description of Sison's activities illustrates well those hectic years: "Sison was at his peak as organizer, planner, and committee-room politico, fashioning new front groups and scheming to bend them to his and, at first, the party's purposes" (Chapman 1987: 73).[21] For "Bart," a former PKP cadre and MASAKA organizer, Sison's major achievement at the time was in organizing the petty bourgeoisie: "Sison did a good job at organizing the ultra-radical petty-bourgeoisie cadres."[22] A high point of this organizing was a demonstration that took place on January 25, 1965, in front of Malacañang (the Philippine president's residence), Philippine Congress, and the US Embassy. It was a significant event in that it brought together the various PKP's legal organizations.[23]

[18] Weekley (1996a: 19) makes a similar argument in her dissertation writing that besides the strong voluntarist orientation of the reestablished CPP, "Also important in the process of legitimizing the new party was the assertion that the new democratic revolution was the right and proper heir to the 'unfinished' nineteenth century revolution against the Spanish and the American colonisers."

[19] At that point, the PKP was interested in expanding its network of mass bases and was experiencing a new surge of dynamism. As Nemenzo has noted, "the fall of Jesus Lava [PKP Chairman] in May 1964 reanimated the party. Freed from the terrible burden of hiding the most wanted fugitive in the country, the provisional secretariat pushed through the first stage of the reconstruction program which aimed at creating a network of legal mass organizations as instruments of the parliamentary struggle" (Nemenzo 1984a: 40). Sison also saw this outreach as a key contribution of KM. This was explicitly stated in Sison's report to the Second National Congress of KM: "The Kabataang Makabayan should, therefore, as it has done, assist in the organization of peasant unions fighting for land reform and in the organization of labor unions fighting for their immediate economic demands while carrying forward their historic mission of leading the masses of our people towards genuine national freedom and democracy" (Sison 1967a, b: 3).

[20] Abinales suggested that MAN was in fact "envisioned as a legal united front body that would formally re-establish the PKP's ties with other groups and individuals" (Abinales 1992: 18).

[21] In his introduction to *Struggle for National Democracy*, history professor and nationalist Filipino writer, Teodoro Agoncillo, embarked on a similar description of Sison's busy life: "Much of the effectiveness of Sison derives not only from his broad, progressive outlook, but also from his analytical method, his grasp of the historical significance of events and movements, and more importantly, from his direct involvement in political mass actions" (Agoncillo 1967: viii).

[22] Interview with author, Angeles City, March 16, 1995.

[23] As Abinales noted, "Peasant organizations teamed up with workers and student groups to undertake the first show of force by the Philippine Left since the Huk debacle" (Abinales 1988: 8–9).

KM was also becoming a national youth movement, establishing chapters in provincial universities, colleges, and even high schools. Sison and KM leaders were invited to deliver keynote addresses all over the country. In 1967, a collection of speeches and articles written by Sison entitled *The Struggle for National Democracy* was published (Sison 1967a, b). Two things are most striking about this collection. One is the sheer number of "speeches and talks" delivered by Sison from 1965 to 1968 that reveal the growing network of mass and sectoral organizations being established.[24] The second is what Teodoro Agoncillo, chair of University of the Philippines' Department of History and important Philippine nationalist historian, wrote when he established a parallel between Sison and Philippine national hero and member of the first Propaganda movement, José Rizal:

> José Ma. Sison is the most harassed and maligned youth today, but he refuses to be cowed into silence by those who, having power in their hands and heads have chosen to play the roles of Captain Tiago and Señor Pasta of Rizal's novels [...] Sison is starting what may be termed the Second Propaganda Movement. (Agoncillo 1967: vii)[25]

Sison and other KM leaders had an ability to combine and package various themes of Philippine past nationalist struggles and a capacity to convince others that KM and emerging "national democratic" organizations were the contemporary embodiments of past nationalist struggles, namely, the Filipino unfinished revolution of the *Katipunan* and the economic nationalism of the 1950s. They also provided a national dimension to the emerging movement.[26]

15.3 Surfing on the Wave of Protest

By the late 1960s, there was a growing wave of social protest in Manila. Calls ranged from demands for greater democracy and clean elections, constitutional reform, and national democratic revolution. Politically heterogeneous, demonstrators were students, peasants, and workers and some sectors of the middle class.[27] However, it

---

According to Sison, it included "mainly the forces of Lapiang Manggagawa (Workers' Party), the Malayang Samahan ng Magsasaka, Kabataang Makabayan, student organizations, and a group of patriotic businessmen headed by Alejandro Lichauco and Antonio Araneta, Jr." (Sison 1989: 35).

[24] For Sison's own description of this period, see his interview with Werning (Sison 1989: 32).

[25] José Rizal is the best-known Filipino writer and a national hero who wrote two key novels that are often seen as marking the birth of Filipino nationalism and to have contributed to the emergence of the Independence movement. Making such parallel is thus of significance because it gave a great deal of legitimacy and popular appeal to Sison's writings and activism.

[26] As briefly described earlier, Katipunan was the name of the organization of Filipinos who fought a war for national independence against Spain. This was the first nationalist uprising in Southeast Asia. See Weekley (1996a: 16) and Alvarez (1992: 4).

[27] See, for example, Starner (1970), Wurfel (1988), and Abinales (1988). As Bonner noted, "In some measure the students were mimicking, somewhat belatedly, their counterparts in France, Japan, and the United States. The vast bulk of the demonstrators knew little of Marx or Mao" (1987: 78–79).

was the students and the youth who were the most vocal and started to demonstrate regularly in the streets of Manila.[28] As Rocamora noted, "[A]t this time when the CPP was relatively new it had to compete with social democrats, the old revisionist party and various other groups for the right to guide the rapidly expanding popular movement" (Rocamora 1983: 10).

The "First Quarter Storm" was a turning point in student and mass protest in the Philippines.[29] It began on January 26, 1970, when an anti-Marcos demonstration was violently dispersed. In the morning, mass organizations from various political formations (Christian left, PKP-led and CPP-led organizations) held public rallies in different locations. In the afternoon, they marched and converged toward the Philippine Congress where Marcos was to address both the Congress and Senate to deliver his "State of the Nation" address (Nemenzo 1984b: 83). When Marcos and his wife Imelda were about to leave the Philippine Congress, the angry students tried to approach them. However, the police moved on the demonstrators. Bonner described this confrontation as follows:

> When the first couple stepped outside after the president delivered his state of the nation address in January 1970, they were met by 20,000 jeering students, workers, and peasants. The mob pelted them with a papier-mâché replica of a crocodile, rocks, and bottles. It was a shocking occurrence, the first time since independence that a Filipino leader, let alone the president, had been so disgraced. (Bonner 1987: 77–78)[30]

The police repression galvanized the students (Nemenzo 1984a: 83; Lacaba 1982; Pimentel 1989: 52–60). As "Otavalo" (a pseudonym), a member of the moderate

[28] An interesting analysis of the resurgence of student activism can be found in a document entitled "The Diliman Declaration" produced as a result of the "Student Power Assembly of the Philippines." The declaration, approved on March 9, 1969, locates the student resurgence within the broader international context of student activism: "Student power is a world wide phenomenon. It is most felt where injustice and poverty prevail in the midst of wealth and excess. The French revolt against an archaic educational system sparked the general strike that paralyzed a nation and almost ended the Gaullist regime. American students occupied their universities to protest the unholy alliance of the academe with the objectives of a racist society and warfare state. The Red Guards of Peking initiated the massive Cultural Revolution in order to renew the revolutionary vigor of the Chinese people. In Italy, Indonesia, Germany, Japan, and Korea, the students have joined the workers and peasants to bring about changes in government and society" (Student Power Assembly 1969: 1).

[29] *Ang Bayan*, the CPP official publication, did not fail to heighten the significance of January 26, 1970. In a Special Release, it stated, "The militant January 26 demonstration on the real state of the nation is a great milestone not only in the revolutionary student movement but also in the broad revolutionary mass movement. […] The militant January 26 demonstration sets the keynote for more massive and more combative mass actions in the city during the current decade of the 1970. It represents a higher degree of development of the entire mass movement that unfolded during the previous decade of the sixties" (Ang Bayan 1970: 1).

[30] Nick Joaquin has described metaphorically the significance of the demonstration: "The 70s exploded when a papier-mâché crocodile was hurled at the President as he emerged from Congress after addressing it on the state of the nation. The state of the nation was presented more vividly than in his speech by the riot in the streets that afternoon. The volcano had turned active" (Joaquin 1988). Joaquin echoed a KM January 28 statement that stated, "[T]he true state of the nation was better presented by the student demonstration than Marcos' speech" (Kabataang Makabayan 1970a: 1).

National Union of Students of the Philippines (NUSP), recalls, "We organized the January 26th, 1970 demonstration which was infiltrated by the KM which took the micro and then things exploded. The NUSP supported a reform line, non partisan."[31] A second mass demonstration was organized 4 days later on January 30 to protest police repression.[32] The "indignation rally" attracted about 15,000 students. Again, there were two different approaches adopted by the student movement:

> We [moderate student organizations] planned for another demonstration on January 30 and we were able, about 20 student leaders, to get in and have a dialogue with McCoy [Marcos], in which he said that he would not negotiate with a son of a grocer [referring to a Edgar Jopson, one of the student leaders]! While we were inside, the KM assaulted Malacañang.[33]

This time, the violence was worse. Chapman wrote that the demonstrators stole "a fire truck to batter through the main gates of Malacañang Palace" (Chapman 1987: 81). Soon after, the police responded by opening fire "at the nearby Mendiola Bridge and before the night was over four students were slain martyrs and scores of others were wounded" (Chapman 1987: 81).[34] This time, however, demonstrators had come better prepared and were responding to police with homemade Molotov cocktails, stones, and whatever could be thrown. The "Mendiola Battle" lasted about 12 h.

For Nemenzo, that demonstration remembered as the "Battle of Mendiola" was particularly important as it "set the style of mass activism in the succeeding two years" (Nemenzo 1984a: 83; Lacaba 1982). "Otavalo," a student activist at the time, recalls the event brought out significant divergence of views within the student movement: "[A]fter the event, there was division within the movement between Jerry Montemayor who remained non-Marxist and the more engaged and radical elements."[35] The CPP and NPA sought to lead and take advantage of this growing militancy. On February 8, Amado Guerrero, CPP chairman, and Commander Dante, head of the NPA, cosigned an 11-page manifesto suggesting that:

> There is nothing more reasonable and urgent now than to turn our grief into revolutionary courage and to forge the most militant national democratic unity against US imperialism, feudalism and bureaucrat capitalism for which the Marcos puppet reactionary regime serves as the blood thirsty hatchet man.[36]

---

[31] Interview with author, Manila, February 28, 1995.

[32] In its January 28 statement, KM called for "more vigorous and militant and direct democratic actions" while denouncing the action of "pseudo-left elements" in trying to prevent "the upsurge of the people's revolutionary movement" (Kabataang Makabayan 1970a, b: 2).

[33] Interview with author, Manila, February 28, 1995.

[34] See also Jones (1989: 39). For her part, reviewing historical records, Weekley specified: "one hundred and fifty-seven were wounded by police and military personnel, and hundreds were arrested" (1996a: 38).

[35] Interview with author, Manila, February 28, 1995.

[36] Guerrero and Dante (1970: 1). In the same statement, they forewarned of more demonstrations and protests: "The militant mass demonstrations of January 26 and 30–31 are certainly a further development of the protest actions of the previous decade. They are also the harbinger of a more turbulent revolutionary storm in the current decade of the seventies" (Ibid.: 2).

The largest riot since Independence was followed the next day by another demonstration in front of the American Embassy. The angry crowd started throwing Molotov cocktails. Stones shattered windows. Activists pulled out the US seal from the entrance gate. Soon, the demonstrators were forced to retreat when the US marines' security detachment started to throw tear-gas grenades (Bonner 1987: 78; Jones 1989: 39). These 5 days of rallies marked the beginning of the "First Quarter Storm." During the next 3 months, protest rallies and teach-ins on various university campuses were organized, including the famous barricading and seizing of the UP campus, renamed for the occasion, the Diliman Commune. Twice during this period, Marcos invoked the possibility of Martial Law (Bonner 1987: 79). The period between January 1970 and September 1972 was particularly important because it saw the increasing polarization of the student movement and intense struggles among various factions within. As "Otavalo" recalls, "[B]eginning in 1971, there were two factions within the students movement, the moderate and the radical. Up to 1972, there were always two rallies."[37]

During this process of student radicalization, many forms of contentious collective actions were emerging: violent demonstrations, industrial strikes, "parliament of the streets," the "Diliman Commune," etc. (Nemenzo 1984b: 67).[38] During this process of greater student radicalization, NPA guerrillas became folk heroes to many students. Filipino writer Nick Joaquin understood the broader significance of these events:

> *Demo* and *activist* passed into the language and created historic dates (January 26 and 30) and a fearful geography: Gate 4 of the Palace, Mendiola Bridge and University Row, Plaza Miranda and the underpass roof employed as demo stage, Plaza Ferguson and the Embassy, San Luis and the Luneta and the Agrifina Circle. The demonstrator developed a lifestyle. Early in the year, when the nights were cold, he marched in turtleneck; at year's end he waded in bell-bottom (or "elephant's paw") pants. His original weapons were gravel and placard; after the initial riots the use of molotov and pillbox became prevalent, provoked by firepower. The demo itself became stylized into various actions: picket, long march, living theater, people's tribunal, parliament of the street. The cry against imperialism, feudalism, and fascism turned into a chanted refrain: "Makibaka, huwag matakot!" [Fight, Have no Fear]. (Joaquin 1988: 344)[39]

[37] Some of the more reformist student leaders would eventually agree on the national-democratic line and strategy proposed by the CPP: "We formed our own core group and learned about PSR on our own. Edjop already sounded like a Nat-Dem [meaning a supporter of the national democratic line]. What we were trying to do is to distinguish between the Nat.Dem. political line and the ideological line. We accepted the political line without accepting the ideological line. […] Our group [NUSP] finally decided to accept the Nat.Dem. political line but not the ideology in August 1972" (interview with author, Manila, February 28, 1995).

[38] Bonner has written that a secret report produced by the American State Department on these protests noted that the activists were essentially denouncing the deep social inequalities, that were probably some of the greatest in Southeast Asia (Bonner 1987: 79).

[39] For an example of this type of "standardized" slogan, see Kabataang Makabayan 1970a, b statement entitled "Ibunsod Ang Malawakang Pakikibaka Laban sa Imperyalismong Amerikano, Katutubong Piyudalismo at Burokrata-Kapitalismo!" (Kabataang Makabayan 1970a, b).

In today's social movement jargon, one could argue that a new repertoire of collective action was then emerging with its own modularity.[40]

15.3.1 Seizing the Momentum

The "First Quarter Storm" was significant as well because it was the juncture when "the CPP seized the initiative from the blundering PKP and absorbed the new radical forces that spontaneously emerged" (Nemenzo 1984b: 67). Whereas the PKP was very cautious and made its existence as "discreet" as possible, the CPP was very open on its plan and intention to carry out and win a "people's war":

> In public marches and demonstrations they [CPP sympathizers and activists] would unfurl red flags, shout revolutionary slogans, and glorified Commander Dante and the NPA. CPP publications were freely circulated and communist ideas were discussed with little inhibitions in the teach-ins conducted its mass activists. (Ibid: 41)

Following the "First Quarter Storm," the CPP rapidly expanded its network of mass organizations, especially among the students. Within less than a year and a half, six different student organizations were established at the UP. For each of those founding congresses or first national assemblies, Sison sent a message to be read at their opening.[41] First attempts to develop and build a united front were also ongoing. According to Sison, the Movement for a Democratic Philippines (MDP) was conceived at the time as "the new united front organization, directing and coordinating the various mass organizations and the mass actions during the First Quarter Storm of 1970 and during the entire 1970–72 period" (Sison 1989: 37).[42]

---

[40] Modularity is here defined following Tarrow (1998 [1994]: 33) as "the capacity of a form of collective action to be utilized by a variety of social actors, against a variety of targets, either alone, or in combination with other forms."

[41] Such regular pattern also reveals how of certain "standardization" was taken place. Here are these events, all organized at the University of the Philippines – Diliman campus, except for one held at the Sampaloc University Center: January 3–21, 1971: first national congress of Samahang Demokratiko ng Kabataan (SDK); March 26–28, 1971: first national congress of the League of Editors for a Democratic Society (LEADS); March 29, 1971: first national assembly of a Movement for a Democratic Philippines (MDP); August 7–8, 1971: first national congress and workshop of the Nagkakaisang Progresibong Artista-Arkitekto (NPA, Union of Progressive Artists and Architects); December 12–13: third national congress of Kabataang Makabayan(KM or Patriotic Youth); December 18–19, 1971: first national congress of Panulat para sa Kaunlaran ng Sambayanan (PAKSA, Literature for People's Progress); and March 18–19, 1972: first national congress of Makabayan Kilusan ng Bagong Kababaihan (MAKIBAKA or Free Movement of New Women) (see Sison 1972). In addition to these student and youth organizations, other sectoral mass organizations that were also established during that period are Katipunan ng mga Samahang Manggagawa (KASAMA – Federation of Labor Unions), Pambansang Kilusan ng mga Manggagawa ng Pilipinas (PAKMAP – National Workers' Movement of the Philippines), Katipunan ng Kabataang Demokratiko (KKD – Federation of Democratic Youth), Kapisanan ng mga Gurong Makabayan (KAGUMA – Association of Patriotic Teachers), and the Christians for National Liberation (CNL).

[42] Starner (1970: 24) made a similar remark in her 1970 article: "Tactically, we are told, the KM and its numerous chapters dominate the MDP (Movement for Democratic Philippines), an umbrella organization formed earlier this year to co-ordinate student, worker, and peasant activities."

While mass organizations were being organized and protests were increasingly frequent, the NPA was becoming increasingly popular both in the countryside and in urban areas.[43] In Manila, especially in university and college campuses, NPA commander Dante Buscayno and other NPA commanders were becoming local heroes and legends.[44] Scores of activists of the "First Quarter Storm" would eventually join the NPA and the CPP and live underground.[45] The declaration of Martial Law in 1972 by President Marcos would help bring about the "golden days" of Philippine revolutionary movement.

It is now possible to return to the proposed conceptual argument to assess how it may help understand this early period in the revolutionary movement's history. As demonstrated in reviewing the genesis of the movement, it was the timely confluence of two processes that explains best the formation of the CPP and the NPA. One was the mobilizing capacity of a small group of young political activists – fascinated with Mao's Cultural Revolution and his revolutionary model – to articulate and to "nationalize" what seemed to many as the "most advanced and most scientific" revolutionary knowledge at the time. Interestingly, the clash with the older leaders of the PKP came around the interpretation of the past, what had to be learned from it, and how such political experiences needed to be reviewed and corrected in order to cope with the changing times. The opposing views also had to do with how to integrate what appeared as the revolutionary knowledge and strategy of the day.

At the same time, there were very auspicious sociopolitical conditions at play that made revolutionary activism an attractive proposition. Marcos' insatiable ambitions to become the "supreme" cacique, the America's willingness and acquiescence to let him declare Martial Law, and the growing radicalization of a whole generation of student activists all played a critical role in helping the nascent Maoist revolutionary movement understand that it could seize the momentum of popular

[43] These new guerrillas were mostly urban activists coming from universities in contrast with the HMB [*Hukbong Mapagpalaya ng Bayan or* People's Liberation Army], which recruited primarily from the peasantry. As Nemenzo first pointed out, this social origin turned out to be an asset for the NPA in generating mass support: "the 'bourgeois education' of some NPA soldiers enabled them to play a role that the HMB never performed. NPA units were welcomed by the peasants because they were not there only to fight. They also taught the peasant new agriculture skills, herbal medicine, acupuncture, makeshift irrigation and so forth. More effectively than the local government and field agencies of national ministries, the NPA administered justice, maintained peace and order, organized small economic projects, ran adult education classes and, in the stable guerrilla fronts, even implemented a revolutionary land reform programme" (Nemenzo 1984a: 81).

[44] According to Chapman (1987: 81) "cadres struggling in Tarlac and Isabela became instant heroes and more than one street parade featured shouts of 'Dante for President'." Filipino writer Ruben Canoy made similar observation, pointing out that "[D]uring the first week of February 1971, students barricaded themselves inside the University of the Philippines, and proclaimed the area a 'mini-republic' – the Diliman Commune. Leftist wags put up signs naming the campus as 'Stalin University' and over Abelardo Hall they painted the legend: 'Dante Hall', Commander Dante then being the commander-in-chief of the communist New People's Army" (Canoy 1984: 2).

[45] As Sison (1989: 63) recalls, "[T] he mass actions of 1970–72 in Manila and throughout the country stimulated a proliferation of mass organizations and yielded a large number of militant mass activists and party cadres who volunteered to join the party and the NPA in the countryside."

dissatisfaction with the present regime. China's interest to spread revolution in Third-World nations was also an opportunity that helped the CPP portray itself beyond what was still an incipient movement – and in many ways a collection of revolutionary amateurs – into a much larger revolutionary wave. Without such favorable political conditions, good organizing skills, and a capacity to frame reality and demonstrate the "logic" and "necessity" of revolution, it is doubtful that these early revolutionaries equipped with their Marxist-Leninist-Maoist ideas could have succeeded in making an armed revolution an attractive avenue for social change.

15.4 The Constitution of a Collection Action Repertoire

By declaring Martial Law in 1972, Marcos sought to ensure the continuity and survival of his political regime, made up of himself, his wife, their cronies, and the military (Anderson 1988; Hutchcroft 1998: 110–142; Tiglao 1988: 41–50). Following its declaration, Marcos skillfully worked on a series of measures, including referenda to strengthen his legitimacy and solidify his control over civil society (Kang 1982; Rolando 1979: 85–112; Valdes 1989: 245–257). These mechanisms expanded the power of the executive branch, namely, its concentration in Marcos' hands. Another important development brought about by Martial Law was the dramatic expansion of the military and its increasing participation in the ruling coalition.[46] To guarantee the military's loyalty, Marcos "favoured officers to manage properties confiscated from his enemies, public corporations, townships, and so forth."[47]

Marcos used repression extensively to demobilize legal popular organizations and coerce potential political contenders.[48] Using the "communist threat," Marcos managed to crush almost completely all the political opposition. Within days of declaring Martial Law, about 30,000 individuals were detained: "very few were communists advocating the violent overthrow of the government."[49] In fact, "the majority

[46] As David Wurfel described, "[D]uring the 1960s, Philippine Force levels hovered around 35,000, including army, navy, air force and constabulary (Wurfel 1977). By 1971, the figure had climbed to 53,000. But by 1974, the armed forces neared the 100,000 mark, and by 1976 were over 113,000" (1986: 140). For his part, Gary Hawes has noted that while the Armed Forces became larger, "its role in maintaining civil order and opportunities to participate directly and indirectly in the economy were all vastly enhanced, and soldiers' pay was increased" (Hawes 1987: 40). See also Hernandez (1979) and Youngblood (1993: 40–47).

[47] Anderson (1988: 23) also pointed out that as a result of such treatment, "The upper-echelon officers came to live in a style to which only the oligarchy had hitherto been accustomed." For a short description of these takeovers especially those of the Lopez Clan, see Fox Butterfield (1978). "Marcos is Said to Strip Wealth of Major Foes," *International Herald Tribune*, (January 21–22).

[48] Marcos' strategy included disarming private armies that were often working for the landed oligarchy and in many instances his political enemies (Anderson 1988: 22).

[49] Journalist William Chapman (1987: 96) placed the figures even higher stating that "the government ultimately admitted that perhaps as many as 50,000 people were seized in the early years of martial law."

of those in prison were Filipinos who expressed their opposition to Marcos in democratic ways" (Bonner 1987: 112).[50]

15.4.1 Reactivating Urban-Based Organizing

Mass arrests, widespread repression, and a growing realization that Marcos had his own interests in mind in the so-called new society combined to make the revolutionary alternative quite attractive by the mid-1970s.[51] This was particularly true for an increasingly large section of the middle classes who at first had welcomed a "restoration" of law and order. At the same time, the party showed considerable creativity and adaptability to adjust to the changing context.[52] It also revealed a capacity for self-criticism and self-assessment. In a key document, *Our Urgent Tasks*, released in June 1976 as a result of discussions held during the third plenum, the central committee stated:

> The fascist rule cannot be used as the main reason for the slow growth of the party. The strictures of this tyrannical rule has been more than compensated for by the deep-going hatred and growing resistance of the broad masses of the people. [...] It is admitted that the period of one year after the first year of martial rule and before their [Manila-based national bureaus] dissolution in July 1974 constituted a big delay which unduly restricted the disposition of good cadres for various regional Party organizations eager and ready to get them.[53]

Within 2 years, legal mass organizations began to resume open protest activities.[54] One key factor for the resurgence of these open protests was the role of the Preparatory

[50] See also Wurfel (1988: 116) and Seekins (1993: 52). The partial list of detainees compiled by the Armed Forces of the Philippines and issued on September 25, 1972, showed a heterogeneous collection of individuals, a senator, several congressman, governors, academics, journalists, and also political activists. See "List of Detainees" (Camp Crame, Quezon City: Headquarters Service Battalion, Armed Forces of the Philippines, September 25, 1972).

[51] Martial Law contributed to the radicalization of a number of organizations and former reformist student leaders. The best-known case is Edgar Jopson, Jr., former chairperson of the National Union of Students of the Philippines (NUSP) who joined the CPP after Martial Law and became a leading cadre in the CPP. For a detailed account of Jopson's radicalization, see Pimentel (1989: 109–167).

[52] Even the Intelligence Service of the Armed Forces of the Philippines recognized this adaptive capacity on the part of the CPP. In its "Foreword" of Vol. III of its four-volume collection entitled the Reestablished Communist Party of the Philippines that reviews the Martial Law period, it is stated, "A potent factor in the phenomenal growth and endurance of the Philippine communist movement has been its notable adaptability to circumstances. It is an adaptability that has been wielded with increasing sophistication over the years, which speaks rather well of the insurgents' effective exploitation of the so-called objective conditions of society" (Armed Forces of the Philippines 1989: i).

[53] Communist Party of the Philippines, Central Committee (1976: 11).

[54] For example, around 1974, the SDK (*Samahang Demokratiko ng Kabataan*) released a document on the legal organizing under Martial Law. The document pointed out the need to adjust to the new conditions but also emphasized the importance to reactivate and launch open social protest (Samahang Demokratiko ng Kabataan 1974).

Commission of the National Democratic Front (NDF). Seven months after the declaration of Martial Law, the NDF was established on April 24, 1973.[55] Initially, it tried with relative success to enlist the members of the various organizations which were part of the MDP, banned under Martial Law.[56]

When it was formed, the NDF encompassed several sectoral organizations: *Kapisanan ng mga Gurong Makabayan* (KAGUMA or Association of Patriotic Teachers), *Kabataang Makabayan* (KM or Patriotic Youth), *Katipunan ng mga Samahang Manggagawa* (KASAMA or Federation of Labor Union), *Makabayang Kilusan ng Bagong Kababaihan* (MAKIBAKA or Free Movement of New Women), *Pambansang Katipunan ng mga Magbubukid* (PKM or National Association of Peasants), and the Christians for National Liberation (CNL) (Pimentel 1989: 177). CNL had been organized 2 months before on February 17, 1972, as a legal organization of priests, ministers, sisters, and religious activists, some coming from the Student Christian Movement (SCM) and Chi Rho.[57] As Felipe recalls more than 20 years later:

> Now that we are trying to recover our history, we have become very conscious that CNL was a product of the development of the Church people but especially of its involvement with the farmers with the Free Farmer's Federation. [...] Christians radicalized through their involvement with social movements. The Student Christian Movement was also a source of radicalization via the integration with farmers and urban poor. These Christian were radicalized and came to accept the ND [National Democratic] analysis and ND project but instead of joining the existing ND Christian Movement for a Democratic Philippines,

---

[55] See Rocamora (1978: 2–6). As the International Office of the NDF would explain in 1983, "In November 1972, the NDF PrepCom came out with the first issue of Liberation, its official organ. On April 24, 1973, the NDF PrepCom proclaimed its Ten-Point Program" (National Democratic Front of the Philippines 1983: 2).

[56] The initial preparatory commission of the NDF included church radicals and members of Movement for Democratic Philippines (MDP). The preparatory commission was the organization that Sison "envisioned to become the umbrella body for different groups opposed to Marcos" that would "band together under CPP leadership" (Abinales 1992: 34). See also Sison (1989: 77).

[57] A document entitled "Orientation of Our Political Work in the Church Sector" (Draft) traces the origins of CNL back to the First Quarter Storm: "[T]he full impact of the first quarter storm became felt in the mainstream of church activists only in 1971. One reaction is the formation of the Social Democratic Front headed by Manglapus, which advocated what was termed as 'middle way' between the present oppression and the 'future communist oppression'. Others started opening to the ND line. The first Christian group to organizationally adapt the national democratic line was the SCM-turned-KKKP [Student Christian Movement – Kilusang Khi Rho ng Pilipinas] in May 1971. The Kilusang Khi Rho ng Pilipinas adapted the ND line on a national scale. Many organizations remained basically reformist but became open to discussion on the ND line" (Communist Party of the Philippines n.d.: 17). This story was confirmed in various interviews: author's interview with "Otavalo," Manila, February 28, 1995; author's interview with "Fr. Paulo," Manila, March 21, 1995; and author's interview with "Felipe," Manila, March 7, 1995.

they decided to put up their own organization as Christians in order to maintain their Christian identity and Christian inspiration. They set up CNL.[58]

The Church played a courageous and determining role in initially protecting and later mobilizing urban poor communities. During the early days of Martial Law, there were quite a number of urban poor communities that were targeted for demolition. As "Otavalo" points out:

> There were a lot of demolitions especially in ZOTO [Zone One Tondo Organization]. We were involved in community work in these neighborhoods. [...]. From September 1972 to 1973, we were forming U.G [Underground] cells in the convents and parishes. In 1973, [...] we organized in Santa Cruz, the forum of the Concerned Christians [...]. On the legal ground, we established the Philippine Ecumenical Council for Community Organizations which had a training program in ZOTO. At this time, ZOTO was expanding with about 25,000 families.[59]

Initially timid, by 1975 there would be some clear acts of defiance, especially among the urban youth, workers, and urban poor who had become disenchanted with Marcos corruption, illicit operations, and cronyism. Again, the Church workers and community organizers played an important role:

> At this time [1973–74], I applied as Community Organizer in Magsaysay Village [urban poor community]. I was not suited for UG work. I had to identify a place to print *Filipinas* [CNL official publication] and also organized discussion groups. It was an exciting time. As community organizer, I worked with Father J.J. Coquio, one Italian group, Father Elasi and Father Francis who were all later deported. The framework on how to work above ground during Martial Law with the Fathers of Missions Abroad came from CNL.[60]

The Church continued to a take a lead role in organizing above ground social mobilization until the late 1970s. However, this was not without tension with the underground level.[61] Key institutions were established such as PEACE (Philippine Ecumenical Action for Community Development), NASSA (National

---

[58] Interview with "Felipe," March 7, 1995. As the statement released by the Provisional National Executive Committee of the Christians for National Liberation and published in Liberation around the time of the Pope John Paul II visit explained, the historical roots of CNL can be traced back to the Vatican II Council: "The reforms initiated by the Vatican II Council, which had been convoked by a predecessor, Pope John XXIII, stirred the Roman Catholic Church in the Philippines from its apathy on many social questions. The liberalization process helped us to make our liturgy relevant to our needs and culture" (Christians for National Liberation 1981).

[59] Interview with "Otavalo," Manila, February 28, 1995.

[60] Interview with "Otavalo," February 28, 1995. As David Wurfel (1988: 17) noted, "the Catholic Church has provided the most effective leadership for mass discontent against the martial law regime."

[61] As a statement issued by CNL revealed, there seemed to have been a tendency within certain sectors of CNL to place an emphasis on Church institutions: "In strengthening their position while undertaking the manifold tasks of supporting the basic movements, the revolutionary elements in the Churches and their allies in the sector cannot expect to draw strength from the vaunted power of Church institutions or religious personalities with connections in high places. There are some national democrats who still have not grasped the nature of Church institutions and who rely too much on institutional support" (Christians for National Liberation [n.d.]: 4).

Secretariat for Social Action, Justice and Peace) created by the Catholic Bishops' Conference of the Philippines (CBCP), and the Church Labor Center (CLC). As Otavalo (a CNL leading member at the time) adds, "The BCC-CO [Basic Christian Community – Community Organization] and the Pastoral Institute were also organized" during the same period.[62] The role of the women religious congregations was quite important at the time:

> The religious nuns' humanitarian vocation has led them into the political arena. The nuns have been haunting the dictatorship, ever since fascist suppression intensified. It was their zeal that brought the world's attention to the tortures, abuses, and barbarous crimes of the Marcos military minions against the Filipino people. They have formed themselves into task forces to assist not only the political detainees but also the workers in their seminars and symposia as well as their strikes, the urban poor in the struggle for decent living and livelihood, the peasants in cases of land grabbing, and the minorities in their right to live in their ancestral abode. The nuns have made available their religious houses, institutions and facilities for these purposes. Their gray, white, and black habits in strikes and mass demonstrations have often boosted the morale of the participants. (CNL n.d.)

15.4.2 A New Momentum and the Resurgence of Open Mass Movements

By 1978, it had become clear for increasingly large segments of the population, including segments of the Philippine bourgeoisie and nationalist elite, that Martial Law was evolving into a patrimonial regime centered around the Marcos couple and their retinue of cronies.[63] These failures and abuses of the Marcos administration were becoming altogether quite obvious by the late 1970s. With growing social discontent, the revolutionary movement became increasingly acceptable to middle forces, including the large segment of Church workers. These would be important assets for expansion in urban areas.[64]

The resurgence of the legal and open mass protest was for many the most significant event of the second half of the 1970s. After three years of relative paralysis and "organizing quietly," the first open mass protests were organized in 1975 (Rocamora 1978: 8). There were more than 50 strikes launched between 1975 and 1976, and for the first time, there were mass demonstrations in the streets of Manila.

---

[62] Interview with "Otavalo," February 28, 1995. See also Youngblood (1993: 81–86). The Armed Forces of the Philippines also became increasingly wary of radicalism in the Church by the late 1970s. In 1979, Galileo Kintanar, a member of the AFP, published in the *Quarterly National Security Review* an article entitled "Contemporary Religious Radicalism in the Philippines" in which he stated that "Considering the subversive thrust of the religious radicals, the State cannot but act in a firm and determined manner. National security considerations demand but [sic] these religious radicals be identified and the object of punitive measures" (Kintanar 1979).

[63] See Hutchcroft (1998: 110–142), Shalom (1986: 171–176), and Schirmer and Shalom (1987: 175–178).

[64] For the Church sector, see Youngblood (1993: 65–100). On the "middle-forces," see Pimentel (1989: 171–181). See also Timberman (1991: 98–116) and Wurfel (1988: 124–127).

This was largely a product of the underground work conducted by party cadres in the various NDF mass organizations and sectoral organizations.[65] The strike most remembered was "La Tondeña," the first industrial strike that signaled the emergence of a new wave of mobilization.[66] Women's increased participation in mass movement and factory organizing was also associated with that first strike:

> Mass actions exploded in 1975, kicked off by the strike of the workers of La Tondeña Distillery. Filipino women joined the man in demanding for the repeal of the ban on strikes and, later as the mass actions progressed, in denouncing the worsening economic conditions and the loss of democratic rights.[67]

Along with a rise in worker's protest, the student and youth sector once again became militant.

15.4.3 Occupying a Greater Political Space on the Left

Marcos' controlled and facade election of 1978 election helped fuel support for the CPP as more and more people felt that electoral struggles were pointless and that violence might be the only remedy. As Wurfel (1988: 133) has observed, "[T]he effort

[65] The renewed militancy in mass movement extended beyond Manila. The Western Visayas Regional Committee's summing-up document stated that by 1979, there was a surge in the urban mobilization. See Communist Party of the Philippines, Regional Committee – Western Visayas (1981).

[66] A member of the Manila-Rizal Committee at the time provided an interesting description of the resurgence of the legal mass movement: "After the declaration of Martial Law, the masses were just being prudent. There was some kind of state of fear among the people because it was difficult to strike or organize marches in the street. The only mass actions were those organized by underground groups who would suddenly come out in the Plaza: all of sudden, a strike leader would bring out a megaphone and call people for an assembly, then there would be two or three speakers sloganeering and then a rapid dispersal. Lightning rallies were massive. We made a breakthrough in December 1975, when there was a US dignitary here. I think it was Nixon who visited Manila and at that time, there was the case of La Tondeña. In November, we had spontaneous strikes in about 300 factories. So, we decided to hold a rally right at the gates of Malacañang or Mendiola, because we were sure that the military wouldn't touch the strikers and the marchers and thought we will maximize the situation. And that was a breakthrough. We were able to gather about 5,500 workers, most of them workers and urban poor" (author's interview with Byron, Manila, September 7, 1995). Stories about the resurgence in open mass protest were recounted in various books, for example, Pimentel (1989: 152–167) and Wurfel (1988: 16).

[67] "Filipino Women in the Struggle Against Martial Law" (circa 1977: 2). This particular document is especially interesting because it goes on detailing specific labor actions undertaken by women during these years: "The garment workers of Gelmart Industries, Inc. (an American firm that manufactures garments for export) strongly resisted management's busting of their union activities. […] The women workers of Royal Undergarments (a factory manufacturing women's undergarments for export) proved they are capable of organizing and running their own affairs […] The women workers of Jack and Jill (a candy and confectionary factory) made use of effective tactics. […] The wives of the workers of Engineering Equipment Inc. (a construction firm that exports materials and workers) actively lent support to the workers' strike. Many middle-aged, the women boosted the morale of their men by joining the picket line, some even with their kids and daughters in tow […]" ("Filipino Women in the Struggle Against Martial Law," (circa 1977), unpublished document: 2–3).

at legitimation backfired. Some of the more radical candidates went underground, and the net effect was further to polarize the Philippine political scene, strengthening the Left in relation to the moderate opposition."[68] With the surrender of the PKP leadership in 1974 after its violent internal split that led to the formation of the MLG (Marxist-Leninist Group), the CPP was also able to become relatively hegemonic within the more militant and left-leaning opposition.[69] Gradually, the CPP-NPA-NDF was becoming increasingly attractive to a broad range of disgruntled social sectors.

For example, it was around that time that Horacio Morales – a well-recognized public servant, awarded for his government service, and executive vice-president of the Development Academy of the Philippines – defected to the NPA.[70] In his statement announcing that he was joining the NPA, Morales stated, "For almost ten years, I have been an official in the reactionary government, serving the Marcos regime and all that it stands for, serving a ruling system that has brought so much suffering and misery to the broad masses of the Filipino people" (Horacio 1977: 1). The statement was released on December 26, 1977, that evening he was going to be given one of the Philippine "Ten Outstanding Young Men" (TOYM) award. As Jones has written, "[I]nstead he had a message read on his behalf announcing his defection to the National Democratic Front" (Jones 1989: 146). While its purpose was clearly propaganda, it is notable that there was no mention of the CPP, but instead it was the NDF and its program that were emphasized.[71] The other important point in that letter was Morales' call to other civil servants to join in the struggle against the Marcos dictatorship. The significance of Morale's letter goes beyond his own defection; it marked the beginning of a period where the movement would rapidly expand and become increasingly capable of forming what CPP cadres called "broad legal alliances" (referred to as BLAs).[72]

---

[68] Wurfel even quotes a former senator who in May 1978 stated that in fact Marcos was driving "the people to radicalism" (*Philippine Liberation Courier* 1978, quoted in Wurfel, 1988: 133).Rocamora (1978: 6) makes a similar argument writing "Throughout most of the last 6 years of martial law, therefore, national democratic forces have had no serious ideological or organizational rivals in the resistance."

[69] Francisco Nemenzo, a founding member of the MLG and former leading cadre of PKP, has written that when the PKP leadership decided to support Martial Law, it created a major internal crisis with the party: "[T]he official analysis of martial law provoked another wave of splits, more threatening to party authority than the one in 1967. The internal debates became so acrimonious that the leadership resorted to the familiar Stalinist technique of conflict-resolution; namely, to kidnap, torture and execute dissenters after forcing them to sign false confessions" (Nemenzo 1984a: 85). Once the internal purge was completed, the PKP went on to negotiate a reconciliation process with the Marcos regime that included its legalization.

[70] Author's interview with Horacio "Boy" Morales, Manila, November 8, 1995.

[71] In his letter, Morales wrote, "[T]hus, I have decided to join the National Democratic Front and take part in the armed revolution against the Marcos dictatorship and all it serves. I see that this evil regime must be overthrown and destroyed. I see that the national democratic program is the correct, real and lasting answer to our people's deepest needs and highest aspirations. In its ten-point program, the National Democratic Front calls for the replacement of the present dictatorship with a coalition government of a national democratic form" (Morales 1977: 2).

[72] Author's interview with "Maude," Manila, June 7, 1995, and with "Otavalo," Manila, February 28, 1995.

Thus, the late 1970s were an important period because the importance of the urban work began to be emphasized by various cadres within the party. Legal mass organizations began to emerge in urban areas and urban poor and community-organizing work was also becoming increasingly important. In the urban areas, the other important breakthrough was the ongoing work around the National United Front and its efforts to reach out to other political formations and allies.

15.4.4 Organizing Social Movements: Maximizing Openings in the Political Opportunity Structures: Building Broad Legal Alliances (BLAs)

When it was established in 1981, the National Campaign for Mass Movement encompassed various mechanisms (bureaus and secretariats) responsible for sectoral mass movement (trade unions, teachers, women, youth, and students). Several broad coalitions were successfully organized in the early 1980s in response to the political conjuncture in an attempt to gather increasing momentum and broader alliances.[73] In fact, while there were breakthroughs with the workers' sector, the youth and student movement also began recovering. The recovery and expansion of the student-and-youth sector began with a clearer orientation, a broad movement for mass organizing, the Democratic Reforms Movements, clear objectives and targets (prioritization of schools), and a well-defined orientation for "Step-by-Step Organizing among the Ranks of the Student-Youth."[74]

As early as 1981, building BLAs – a tactic designed to reach out to other political opposition groups and potential allies – began mobilizing a significant amount of energy within the CPP. Another important development of the period was the emergence of many legal institutions and the establishment of legal development projects. This started in the late 1970s and was mostly spearheaded by the Church sector. As "Joey" noted these "became the forerunners of the present NGOs."[75] One of the big advantages of these institutions and projects is that they brought resources and connections to the movement. The revolutionary movement had a policy of centralization of resources. Initially, policies on centralization were quite flexible:

> It took time before the 60–40 became a rule. They were just starting to come in small amounts compared to the bigger amounts of later years. That is why the sharing was rather flexible. It depended on the projects. With these new resources, more efforts could be expended to organizing and many other activities. I think that at the time, it was even the main source of funding for the army for a period of time, late 1970s and during the 1980s.

---

[73] The People's Assembly on the Pope's Arrival (PAPA) and the Alliance of Citizens Toward Independence, Oneness and Nationalism (ACTION) are two examples of these types of coalition established in reaction to political opportunities. See PAPA, "Friday the 13th: Another Victory for the People's Struggle," (February 14, 1981) and ACTION, "The Marcos US State Visit: National Betrayal and Mendicancy," (September 28, 1982). Planning of large mass movement campaigns also became increasingly sophisticated (Communist Party of the Philippines 1983).

[74] "The Democratic Reforms Movement" (circa 1982), unpublished document.

[75] Author's interview with "Joey," Manila, July 15, 1995.

> At first, it was the legal project that would be the number one source. Taxation would come second. Yet, taxation could only be done in certain areas in Mindanao and Luzon, not in Southern Tagalog or Central Luzon. At the same time, looking back, it started something negative, a negative trend and that is over-dependence and reliance on foreign funding, so the funding agencies became a Vatican or Mecca of some sorts. The people have to make annual trips and pilgrimage and all these reports, all these credible realities.[76]

In the early 1980s, the international solidarity network was quite optimistic given the 1979 Nicaraguan revolution and to a lesser extent the Iranian revolution the same year. The Philippines along with El Salvador were perceived by many as next in line.[77] By the early 1980s, the Philippine revolutionary movement could see itself part of a broad range of revolutionary movements:

> The struggles and victories of other revolutionary peoples, such as the Nicaraguan, Salvadoran, and Guatemalan peoples in Central America, the Maubere people in East Timor, the Palestinian people in the Middle East, the Namibian, South African, and Sahrawi peoples in Africa, are an added reason for revolutionary optimism.[78]

What it meant in terms of tactics for the CPP was to polarize the growing sense of disgust toward the Marcos regime and create a two-pole situation between Marcos and his cronies versus the Filipino people as embodied in the National Democratic Movement, which represented the "only alternative": "The principal conflict is now between the people, on the one hand, and US imperialism and the Marcos clique of comprador big capitalists, big landlords and big bureaucrats, on the other."[79] The murder of Benigno Aquino brought about an important surge of discontent and mass mobilization. Most obvious in urban centers, this new wave of mobilization brought in a spectrum of sectors including middle classes, professionals, business people, and an increasingly larger segment of the economic elite disgruntled with both the political and economic state of affairs. It also led to the formation of broad legal coalitions opposing Marcos and demanding justice:

> By the time of the funeral, the coalition that organized the August 25 march had been formalized into the Justice for Aquino, Justice for All [...] On September 9, a procession and mass to commemorate the end of the mourning period turned into a march by 30,000 and the first explicitly anti-Marcos mass action following the murder. Over the next few days, smaller demonstrations of 10,000 or more were held in various parts of the city and suburbs. The demonstration by well-dressed business people at Manila's financial district in Makati on September 16, received the wide international media attention. [...] All of these mass actions culminated in the half-million strong rally on September 21, 1983, commemorating the eleventh anniversary of the declaration of Martial Law and 30 days after the Aquino's murder. (Rocamora 1983: 14)[80]

---

[76] Author's interview with "Santiago" [date and place withheld for anonymity reasons].

[77] At the end of the decade, parallels between the two revolutionary movements would be made. See "The Philippines and El Salvador," 1990, *Midweek*, 5 (18): 32–34.

[78] National Democratic Front of the Philippines (1983: 5).

[79] Communist Party of the Philippines (1983: 12).

[80] According to a position paper released by the "Students Leaders' Forum," the September 21 sit-down demonstration at Mendiola turned out to be quite violent: "In the ensuing violence between military and paramilitary units on one hand, and students and citizens from nearby communities on the other, at least 11 people, including a policeman, a fireman and a marine were killed" (Students Leaders' Forum 1983: 1).

Benigno Aquino's assassination widened significantly the political opposition to Marcos[81]:

> By the millions, people poured onto the streets, marching for hours in the hot sun and cold rain. Day after day, they came braving Marcos' threats and police bullets. Workers in worn clothes, nuns in billowy habits, students in T-shirts, business executives in coat and tie. (Rocamora 1983: 1)

This resulted in a multiplication of alliances and the formation of an increasing large number of organizations.[82] In August 1983, the party began experimenting with a growing number of alliances. The growing opposition generated by the assassination placed the CPP in front of key dilemmas on how to interact with the growing reformist opposition. As Rocamora wrote:

> The new situation also imposed heavy new heavy responsibilities on the NDF. As an organization with the support of a broad stratum of Philippine society that includes peasants, students, workers, religious and middle class professionals, the NDF has to lead in the struggle for unity within the opposition. At the same time, the NDF has to make sure that new elements in the opposition do not compromise principles paid for with years struggle. (Rocamora 1983: 18)

In October 1983, the central committee produced an important document entitled "Overthrow the U.S.-Marcos Fascist Dictatorship" (Communist Party of the Philippines 1983). Presented as an "urgent message" to the Filipino people, the document sought to rally as many sources of support as possible.[83] As "Joey" recalls, the document:

> Laid down the analysis of the situation and the tactics of this period. To sum up the content of the document: one, there was a recognition that that a new situation had came about and this situation was pregnant with certain possibilities like hastening the revolutionary process. [...] Another one was the broadening of the anti-dictatorship front, new allies were appearing and the older ones were becoming more militant. [...] I think another major

[81] As Cristina Del Carmen writes, "According to the NDF assessment, the Aquino assassination was the crucial event that pushed the polarization of the country. By murdering Aquino, Marcos has totally isolated himself the elite opposition will move away from its vain hopes of reconciling with Marcos and towards greater unity with the mass movement against dictatorship. The NDF stands poised on a period of rapid expansion" (Del Carmen 1983: 29).

[82] Writing in 1984, Rosenberg also noted the expanding rate of broad legal alliances following Aquino's assassination: "Within a week of the assassination, the loose coalition of mourners was formalized in an umbrella organization, 'Justice for Aquino, Justice for All', headed by former Senator Lorenzo Tañada. [...] The demonstrations quickly became more explicitly anti-government. On September 21, 1983, the 11th anniversary of the declaration of martial law, half a million Filipinos attended a rally in Manila to denounce the Marcos government. Sponsor of the rally established another political coalition, the Nationalist Alliance for Justice, Freedom, and Democracy, which included a wide spectrum of opposition groups" (Rosenberg 1984: 25).

[83] The document entitled "Overthrow the U.S.-Marcos Fascist Dictatorship, Establish a Revolutionary Coalition Government!" was signed by Central Committee on October 7, 1983, and published in *Ang Bayan* (1983a.b). It eventually became part of the basic mass course and a primer produced in Tagalog by Higmasik (Central Luzon group responsible for the Party publication) in December 1983 entitled "Tungkol sa Diktadurang US-Marcos."

> content – there was (sic) so many points – [...] the third was, the importance given to expand international solidarity work, now that the fight against the dictatorship had been broadened.[84]

Written following the "standardized structure" of a CPP manifesto, the document initially reviewed the "national situation" asserting the favorable conditions for a dramatic expansion of the revolution given the growing disenchantment with the Marcos dictatorship and the economic crisis. The document emphasized that the assassination of Aquino had created fertile ground for expansion.[85] Carefully crafted to identify potential allies as well as pinpoint enemies, the document recognized the growing radicalization across many sectors of society and the potential for mass mobilization and alliance building.[86] Respecting existing predetermined class categorization, the documents identified those that could be reached and organized. Aside from the usual workers, peasant masses, and the urban petty bourgeoisie – professionals, teachers, doctors, students, and youth – the Central Committee also invited segments of the national bourgeoisie to join in overthrowing the Marcos regime.

As the "new" opposition was becoming increasingly significant, traditional political parties were aware of the potentialities of achieving greater strength and began initiating various alliances. One of the early ones was United Democratic Opposition (UNIDO) which brought together nationalists, civil libertarians, and sectoral and regional political forces, including the *Nacionalista* Party, the Liberal Party, *Lakas ng Bayan*, *Pilipino* Democratic Party, National Union for Liberation, Mindanao Alliance, *Bicol Saro*, the Interim National Assembly Association, *Kabataang Pilipino*, and Women's Organization for Nationalism (Rocamora 1982: 6). Both party-led legal mass organizations and various BLA projects would be attempted. Writing barely 2 months after Aquino's assassination, Rocamora was optimistic that the CPP–NDF would be able to seize this upsurge in political protest:

> In the future, the role of the elite opposition will depend on its ability to move away from its vain hopes for reconciliation with Marcos and toward greater unity with the mass movement against the dictatorship. By murdering Aquino, Marcos has totally isolated himself. With one bullet, he has pushed the polarization of the country further than it has traveled in the last few years. The NDF stands poised on a period of rapid expansion. (Rocamora 1983: 22)[87]

[84] Author's interview with "Joey," Manila, July 15, 1995.

[85] Communist Party of the Philippines (1983: 1).

[86] New forms of protest were developing and broader ranges of social sectors were now involved in protest, as the document noted: "Very striking has been the presence of whole families and clans, including children, at the mass actions. And there have been any number of ways by which the people have expressed their protest. Aside from the marches and rallies, there have been picketing of the big commercial and service establishments owned by the Marcos clique, boycott of newspapers owned and controlled by the clique, letters to the editors, telephone calls to live radio programs, publication, reproduction and dissemination of manifestos and other propaganda materials, sticking of posters in public places, painting of slogans on walls, and such other activities as indoor rallies, symposiums and convocations. The 'noise barrage' has become an effective weapon in rattling the enemy, as has been confetti thrown out of high-rise buildings" (Communist Party of the Philippines 1983: 2).

[87] For an illustration of such call for unity, see "Only Unity and Struggle Against Tyranny Will Vindicate the Death of Our 'Martyrs'," *Liberation* (August 30, 1983).

Following, Aquino's assassination, broad coalition efforts started with JAJA (Justice for Aquino, Justice for All). JAJA proved to be successful as a broader formation that included many liberal bourgeois and bourgeois reformists and those not identified with the party. Aquino's assassination happened while there were efforts at broadening the Nationalist Alliance for Justice, Freedom, and Democracy to make it more inclusive. However, while non-NDF personalities were joining, such as Jose Diokno, Homobono Adaza, Butz Aquino, Salvador Laurel, and Eva Estrada-Kalaw, there were tensions in terms of whom and which factions would control the leadership.[88] As time passed, it was also becoming clear that other opposition forces were making efforts toward some form of unity. As Robert Youngblood reported:

> A number of indicators marked the intensification of efforts towards unity within the opposition over the past two years. In January 1984, for instance, former President Diosdado Macapagal, together with former senators Lorenzo Tañada and Jose Diokno, signed a unity "Compact," while in April 1984, Tañada and Diokno among others, signed a unity agreement in Hong Kong with Raul Manglapus, head of the US-based Movement for Free Philippines (MFP), and former senator Jovito Salonga, who at the time was still in political exile in the United States. Moreover, in December 1984, Salonga and Eva Estrada Kalaw, both of who head major divisions with the Liberal Party, forged an agreement in Los Angeles, California, aimed at unifying all factions of the party, and in January 1985, Salonga returned to the Philippines with the stated purpose of helping to unify the opposition. (Youngblood 1985: 227)

15.4.5 The BAYAN Attempt at Broad Coalitions

During this period, the party began to work for the creation of a broad coalition that would incorporate both CPP-influenced mass organizations and progressive personalities. The BAYAN alliance was conceived directly by the CPP as a broad alliance of the different opposition groups and individuals, including organizations such as Diokno's Kaakbay and Butz Aquino's ATOM (August Twenty-One Movement). As a key member of the United Front Commission remembers:

> BAYAN was a major UFC [United Front Commission] project, which sought to put together all sectoral movements, and was initially responsible to capture all forms of opposition. It sought to attract Diokno and BAYAN was to be used if Diokno was going to run against Marcos. As conceptualized Marcos was different things to different forces.[89]

---

[88] "Otavalo" remembered that in 1983 "we tried once again to organize broad legal alliances (BLA) as united front group which comprised Jose "Pepe" Diokno (a Liberal Democrat), anti-Marcos reactionaries, etc. We wanted it to be a nationalist alliance, which would involve Sarmiento, Guingona, Arroyo and Diokno. We first organized JAJA in 1984 and CORD (Coalition for the Restauration of Democracy) for the 1984 election" (author's interview with "Otavalo," Manila, February 28, 1995).

[89] Author's interview with "Elena," Manila, March 2, 1995. As "Alfonso" explained, "we knew that Pepe Diokno was not a communist or that he would not become a communist, but we wanted him because he had a lot of prestige" (interview, April 16, 1998). For his part, "Otavalo" remembers how Salas directly supervised the BAYAN initiative: "[A]fter the 1984 election, we started to work on the BAYAN project which sought to comprehensively address the political and electoral issues. The BAYAN project was directly under Bilog Salas' supervision" (author's interview with "Otavalo," Manila, February 28, 1995).

As can be seen, the BAYAN project was part of the effort by the party to establish "the political center and the backbone of the open mass movement."[90] While understanding clearly the favorable opening that existed in the political opportunity structure (POS), what the revolutionary movement was struggling with was the operationalization of the united front congruent with its overall strategic framework.

The BAYAN (*Bagong Alyansang Makabayan* or New Nationalist Alliance) project however proved to be a failure in terms of uniting most of the anti-Marcos opposition under a single banner. As in previous alliance projects, it appeared that the party's determination to control the leadership of the new formation backfired:

> For example, when what's this [BAYAN] was formed, when there was its inaugural meeting, some walked out. There were those who attended, but did not want to join BAYAN. They thought that we wanted to get the majority position in every decisive position. They observed that we wanted to get those. [...] Bilog [Salas] was in touch with comrades in the NUFC (National United Front Commission) to the minute details. For example, the secretary general's position should be ours. We should make sure that we would get it. The Chairmanship, we should ensure that we got it or somebody very reliable. [....] The national democratic forces already had this reputation of grabbing everything.[91]

By 1983, the party also decided to enhance its legal peasant struggle and establish a national peasant federation, the *Kilusang Magbubukid ng Pilipinas* (KMP, Peasant Movement of the Philippines). The legal peasant movement was seen as another methodology to help prepare guerrilla zones and assist in strengthening the mass movement. There was also recognition that the legal mass movement could assist the NPA in the process of opening new areas and conducting social investigation. KMP was seen as another component of the mass movement in particular for the antifeudal struggles since it would push for land reform.

15.4.6 A Revolution in Progress

By 1985, the revolutionary movement claimed that its guerrilla army included 6,834 NPA full-time armed combatants and 16,000 militia.[92] The CPP/NPA controlled about 18% of all barangays (the smallest administrative entities in the Philippines,

[90] Interviews with "Elena," Manila, March 2, 1995.

[91] Author's interview with "Alfonso," April 16, 1998. The story about the BAYAN debacle was recounted a number of times in several interviews (author's interviews with "Maude," Manila, June 21, 1995; "Santana," Manila, April 21, 1996; and "Elena," Manila, March 2, 1995).

[92] A different figure could be obtained if one would include all NPA personnel included support staff (medical, liaison, and finance), front committee personnel, and the Propaganda Organizing Team. Such aggregation would bring up the number of NPA members to 12,205.

Table 15.1 Various indicators of the Communist Party of the Philippines' strength by 1985

High-power rifles (HPR)	6,800	Full-time armed combatants (total)	6,849
		Companies	2,059
		Guerrilla units	3,264
		Platoons	950
		Squads	255
		Southern Luzon[a]	321
Revolutionary forces (minus POTs)	7,200	Guerrilla front: provinces	61
Propaganda and organizing teams (POTs)	6,000+	Cities/towns	723
Companies guerrilla units (GU)	26	Municipalities	10,173
Platoons guerrilla units (PGU)	38	District party organizations	146
Squad guerrilla units (SGU)	17	Section party organizations	441
Squad armed partisan units (APU) (Combatants)	116 (928)	Organized mass base	457,000
Partisan teams (Combatants)	155 (465)	General mass base	6.5 millions
Militia	16,000 (est.)		

Source: Communist Party of the Philippines, untitled [9th Plenum minutes] (1985: 79 and 100–101)
[a]Southern Luzon was counted separately

the equivalent of villages) and was present in 61 provinces out of a total of 73.[93] The CPP was also reaching record high membership.[94] Table 15.1 provides a series of indicators on the party's situation by the time the 9th Plenum began.

15.5 The 1985 Election Boycott Decision and the EDSA Uprising

After the announcement of the upcoming election by Marcos, the CPP executive committee decided not to convene an emergency politburo meeting or a special meeting of key cadres. Because the party had just completed a long Plenum, executive committee members decided not to reconvene or organize a meeting of the politburo. Instead, they decided that the position of the CPP would be to call for a

[93] Communist Party of the Philippines (1985).

[94] The total number of NPA fighters also became the source of an internal quarrel. Apparently, Salas authorized the publication in *Ang Bayan* of a certain figures regarding the total number of NPA: "He placed the number at 20,000. There was a big quarrel and a big fight within the Central Committee because one, it violated the guerrilla principle that you must always let the enemy underestimate you and number 2, it was not true. […] In 1985, we were around 7,000 plus with high power rifles and we had additional one or two thousands auxiliary forces armed with different kinds of weapons from garands […] You know some people were assisting, joining, marching with NPA units with no arms at all. […] When you measure a fighting strength, it should be in terms of the high-powered rifle strength. And by the way, the high-powered is not you know, so high-powered, it's M-16. The peak was in 1987. In 1987, we did not depart so much from the 1985 figure, because at the time Luzon and Visayas were picking up and Mindanao was going down, so it somehow canceled each other. So, I suspect it was around 8,000. We didn't really have a very reliable and accurate estimate" (author's interview with "Joey," Manila, July 1, 1995).

boycott of the election. The decision was taken after a long discussion and a tight vote, with three in favor of the boycott and two against. The decision would become all the more controversial since some politburo members demanded an immediate meeting because many members were still in Manila. For many, this was a strategic and fundamental mistake which largely contributed to the isolation of the party during the Aquino regime (1986–1992).

15.5.1 NGOs and NGOism

By the late 1980s, the contention within the revolutionary movement revolved around the role of NGOs and socioeconomic work in the revolutionary movement. NGOs were not new to the revolutionary movement, but their numbers began increasing rapidly post-EDSA.[95] There seemed to be two different trends at work. One was an attempt to seize the opportunity provided by all the funding agencies and funds that started to flow into the Philippines. The other was that NGOs working in development work became a way for many cadres to remain part of the movement while at the same time having a legal status and enjoying some of the benefits of the greater open political space. It is likely that there was some foot dragging and quiet resistance in this process. As Sison recalls, the party had started looking at NGOs in the 1970s:

> The first time the idea of tapping the NGOs was proposed in 1971. The party did not take it seriously but it was kept in mind. It was in 76 when there was a serious consideration. It was in 76 that three groups prepared, draft project proposals. You see, people and all projects were ready made. The revolutionary movement created the mass base already. The first writers of the project proposals were laughing when they were making the project proposals because, you know, the terminology of the funding agencies was such. [...] Well, they were for good things like certain projects. There's some benefit for the people, but you know, you could see the frame. Crumbs were being made available for the 3rd world NGOs, while the multinationals earned [...] profits.[96]

Sison also saw NGOs as a competing pole for activists. Reviewing the environmental movements, he argues:

> The worst destroyers of the environment, the worst polluters were the ones who had the initiative to do this business of funding the NGOs for the environmental cause. [...] Young people who would otherwise go to the Communist Party would be attracted to these things. But you know, environmentalism in the Philippines was pushed only slightly in the late 70s but in the 80s it made breakthroughs, especially when parties were built in Europe and many of the leftist elements were known to green parties.[97]

---

[95] EDSA refers to the massive popular gathering in support to the coup launched by Juan Ponce Enrile and General Fidel Ramos on February 22, 1986, following Marcos electoral fraud. The gathering took place on the Epifanio De Los Santos Avenue (EDSA). It is now remembered as the EDSA revolt. It was this massive mobilization combined with diplomatic pressure from the United States that led the Marcoses to leave the country.

[96] Author's interview with Sison, Utrecht, April 20, 1998.

[97] Ibid.

Finally, while NGOs represented an appealing source of funding, they were also a potential source of corruption, all the more attractive in a period of demoralization like after EDSA.

15.6 The Dilemma of Open Social Movement Organizing and NGO Development Work

By the late 1990s, the tendency toward a growing bureaucratization of the revolutionary movement organization with an expanded set of legal organizations was becoming more significant. In fact, the creation of a form of "revolutionary apparatchiks" in the organization could be noted.[98] Two well-placed insiders of the CPP, Sison and "Joey" – a leading cadre who found himself at the opposite side of a major debate in the 1990s (the "rectification campaign") – had similar observations about alarming trends that could be observed within the party after EDSA. For Sison, the funds brought about by the expanding numbers of party-led or party-controlled NGOs had a negative impact on the mass movement:

> Because of the extra funds from mass campaigns would come from certain NGOs. It would be first you have a meeting of organizations with access to NGOs. Like bosses, "Oh, how many will you bring?" [...] Then, "how much do you need?" That affected the concept of mass campaign. Mass campaign is a result of solid organizing. Of course, you fly high in mass campaign because you make sweeping propaganda but that is to encourage more people to be organized the solid way. But then so many premiums were being put on being a "big boss" on the top. You know, you have the alliance professionals, united front professionals. And you absorb more and more cadres into your offices. Then, you don't have enough cadres doing solid organizing at the grassroots. So even in the legal mass work, there was an undermining, not yet noticed, undermining then the actual contraction becoming obvious.[99]

For "Joey," the greater availability of funds made mass organizers less self-reliant and increasingly dependent on funding to organize mobilization. This trend became increasingly acute in the second half of the 1980s:

---

[98] For example, according to a cadre, who spent time with the executive committee in the mid-1980s, the thinking of leading cadre was to live in Manila and oftentimes in a large house. For example, before his arrest Salas, his wife, and his in-laws were living in a rented house in a well-to-do subdivision. This was the safe house of the executive committee. "It was a big house in BF Parañaque [one of Manila's wealthy suburbs]. One would think a wealthy person is inside because it was a big house and sometimes 2 to 3 cars parked in front [...]. That was still the time, when the party leadership was becoming very bureaucratic and frivolous. [...] We were isolated. It was like one big enterprise where privileges are institutionalized. [...] So, largely it [leadership] became more and more isolated from ordinary life of the Filipinos, especially the poor, especially if for example, you are housed in Manila. You have TV sets, you have good computers, you're riding cars, then you're quite privileged to eat in expensive restaurants because that would be safe and isolated, then the intelligence people would least suspect you to meet and you are quite free to do other things. [...] In fact, when I joined that bureaucratic set-up, I also started enjoying those times, those amenities" (author's interview with "Joey," Manila, February 17, 1996).

[99] Author's interview with Sison, Utrecht, April 20, 1998.

> It became worse after EDSA. Some district party organizations will tell you, we have no money so we cannot mobilize. If you send us you know 5,000 pesos, we can only mobilize 200. Now, if you send us 10,000 pesos, we mobilize like 500. To the point that it became some sort of, you know, another source of funding for some district operational expenses. In the same manner that legal institutions and legal projects were dealing with funding agencies. For example, they overshot their mobilization expenses. [...] Let us say for instance, "OK, give us 20,000 pesos to mobilize at least 3,000 people." But they are whispering around 15,000 pesos or 10,000 pesos, and then the 5,000 pesos would be spent for operation expenses, for other things. Then, mild cases of corruption started to appear.[100]

15.7 The National Mass Campaign Conference and People's Caucus

In April 1990, a national mass campaign conference was held. The mood of the meeting was quite optimistic following the December 1989 coup d'état attempt and the assessment of the politburo meeting. Its overall call was "cultivate the seeds of the new political situation." The assessment was that there were splits within the ruling classes "because the Aquino regime was losing its popular appeal compared to previous years, the Cory magic (Corazon 'Cory' Aquino) was waning fast."[101] At the same time, militancy seemed on the rise. In 1989, there had been a renewed militancy within the workers' movement. The teachers had also organized a national strike; the youth and students were more militant and even the government employees. However, for "Joey," a leading cadre of the politburo, the meeting fell short in terms of defining a strategy to maximize the existing political opportunities, and enhance the possibilities of the urban mass movement. At the time, a campaign to combine peasant and socioeconomic activities was conceived:

> One element was that there was a new gathering of forces with Congress for a People's Agrarian Reform (CPAR) that would heighten and broaden the criticism towards the Aquino regime's handling of the land reform issue. So there was a broad coalition that was formed to push [...] for better land reform measure and a faster implementation. So, one of the major flashpoints that we identified for a possible upsurge was the land reform issue. There were other issues, economic [...] oil price hike, something on oil price hike and then another

---

[100] Author's interview with "Joey," Manila, July 1, 1995. The problem of finance was a complex one because many full-time cadres had dependents that were often taken care of by relatives. As a Visayas Commission Cadre recalls, it was an issue in Samar: "In Samar, life in the barrio was extremely difficult and that was one factor why the armed struggle grew rapidly there. And then, there were cases where some cadres whose family on their own strived hard to put up small income-generating projects. These were criticized because they should be collectivized not family-based. [...] So, they even came to the point of something like confiscation. [...] The family was able to procure a chainsaw. It was confiscated by the party to collectivize the chainsaw. So, there was resentment, and actually, the cadre affected was a member of the Regional Organizing Committee and he ran amok. He killed leading regional cadres. About two or three were killed. [...] That happened in 1989" (author's interview with "Byron," Manila, September 13, 1995).

[101] Author's interview with "Joey," Manila, March 9, 1996.

> one the US bases issue. Yeah, [we wanted] to prepare several major campaigns for that and that would help sow the seeds for a new political upsurge. It sounded good at that time.[102]

The dominant concept was to take advantage of the lack of governance of the Aquino regime, divisions within the ruling elite, and the military to produce an upsurge that could possibly lead to an uprising. At the time, an EDSA scenario was entertained, as the amended Sison's 1989 CPP Anniversary Statement ("Carry Out Rectification, Further Strengthen the Party and Intensify the People's Revolutionary Struggle") mentioned wherein the ND movement would become a junior player in a coalition government.[103] At that time, the NUFC was also relatively successful once again in organizing broad coalitions. There were a series of initiatives to dialogue with other political blocs to form broad coalitions. At the time, one major coalition project was the People's Caucus initiative. What the party sought to do was to come up with a large multi-issue coalition. The agreement was to revitalize the alliance after almost a 2-year lull.

Since Aquino assumed power, the party had only be able to "manage issue-based alliance" like the Freedom from Debt Coalition, the Coalition for Nuclear-Free Philippines, the Labor Advisory and Consultative Council (LACC), the CPAR, and also, although with a more minimal role, the Peace Conference. Except for the latter, where the party placed fewer efforts, all the others "were prospering at the time."[104] In early 1990, cadres who were members of the National Mass Campaign Conference felt that there was a momentum to come up with something broader. As "Joey" points out, "[T]there was a good timing in 1990 when all these things were happening, the crisis of governance, the economic crisis, [...] from this dynamism, it led to the formation of the People's Caucus."[105]

With the impulse of the party, the People's Caucus gathered the support of other political formation and movements, the Pop. Dem. (Popular Democrats), BISIG (*Bukluran sa Ikauunlad ng Sosyalistang Isip at Gawa* – Federation for the Advancement of Socialist Thought and Praxis, an independent socialist coalition that included personalities associated with the MLG, Marxist-Leninist Group, independent Marxists, and left-social democrats), PKP, and several individual personalities perceived as nationalist and progressive. According to "Joey," the People's Caucus seemed to successfully rally together the protest around the oil price hike. The suggestion by the Manila-Rizal Committee (MR) was to launch a political-military strike that would have a military component in order to paralyze Manila. The National Organizing Commission agreed with the proposal, along with the Central Luzon and the Southern Tagalog region. There was divergence though related to the scale and scope of the military component, in that case, the burning of

---

[102] Ibid.

[103] Communist Party of the Philippines, Central Committee (1990: 21–22).

[104] Ibid.

[105] Author's interview with "Joey," Manila, March 9, 1996.

buses to paralyze traffic within and around Manila. The timing was important because the People's Strike had to be launched prior to the oil price hike.

> However, the launching was late. And Manila-Rizal Committee (MR) which had a big say in this thing because they had the larger mass base was more inclined toward developing a wage fight. A People's Strike is worker centered instead of a general protest against the oil price hike. So, we could not do anything anymore around the oil price hike because the momentum was gone in the general protest. We shifted to the issue of wages. That lessened the level of possible spontaneity that this protest might generate.[106]

As it turned out, on the day of the People's Strike, each region had a different understanding of the extent to which bus burning should be carried out; no quota or precise guidelines had been established. They also had different motivations:

> Like for instance, the CL [Central Luzon] group, was very interested in burning these buses of those who were refusing taxation. So, it was a good occasion to retaliate. MR was more on the intent to paralyze transportation. So, they identified a few choke points, and in those areas, they would burn buses. So, that was what happened. There was the People's Caucus, there was the build-up and then the buses, so many buses burned. [...] It was good that the democratic space was broad enough and the legality of the various organizations was established, that was why the mass movement was able to overcome, to endure the stress.[107]

At the time, the regional mass campaign committees, the MR Committee, and "Joey" had a clear rationale for the bus burning:

> We came to the idea that it was impossible really to stage a People's Strike in Manila without introducing an element of violence. That was the theory. So, we must employ an element of violence to paralyze it. So, we have to employ limited violence. And that was in the form of burning of the buses or puncturing them or barricading them in the streets. Actually, it was really a combination. There were several buses and vehicles that were not burned, but they were stopped and they were barricaded in the streets. However, there were many burned in Central Luzon, and Southern Tagalog, so it was magnified [by the media].[108]

After the first day of People's Strike, there was a meeting of the command body, and that night it received a telegram from the top leadership ordering a stop to the strike and bus burning. Looking back, "Joey" said that "in the overall political equation," the movement really lost. It also created a "tremendous setback" for the People's Caucus. As it turned out, political allies were furious because they felt that they had been betrayed, as they did not know that there would be some violence. In practice, it meant the end of the People's Caucus[109]; the National United Front cadres who had organized the alliances were also quite angry because they were as surprised as

---

[106] Ibid.

[107] Ibid.

[108] Ibid. "Patrick" from MR also made the same point: "The number of bus to be burned was in relation only to be able to paralyze" (author's interview with "Patrick," Manila, May 20, 1996).

[109] Author's interview with "Joey," Manila, March 10, 1996. "Patrick" also suggests that "the real problems with the bus burning were not so much with the workers but more with the middle classes that reacted quite negatively" (author's interview with "Patrick," Manila, May 20, 1996).

the allies, not having "been privy" to prior discussions and plans and felt that they had been used. There were even more complications because it was the partisan unit, the Alex Boncayo Brigade (the armed partisan unit), that was seen as burning the buses, and not a spontaneous mass action:

> That really heightened the matter and we really went beyond the policy, because the policy of what was acceptable at this stage was for a growing mass spontaneous action, people will burn buses, no problem. We could defend it if the media attacked it. But it would be another thing if military units will be employed to burn buses. Now that would imply something more. That would put a new factor in the equation and that was more serious. [...] It really went beyond the existing policy with regards to the proper employment of military forces in political mass struggles.[110]

15.7.1 The September Thesis

In 1990, the National Peasant Secretariat prepared a document entitled *The September Thesis*. The document basically argued for a greater role for the legal peasant movement. In the past, the peasant movement had been primarily defined in relation to the building of guerrilla zones with a limited role for its legal mass activities.[111] *The September Thesis* was in line with the thinking within the National Mass Campaign Committee and advocated for a greater role in sustaining mass campaigns with the possibility of supporting an uprising. It also argued that the socioeconomic context in the plain areas had changed significantly with the greater intrusion of capital and capitalist relations and therefore required a rethinking in the strategy of collective action of the peasant sector.[112] As "Salvador" explains, *The September 1990 Thesis* was:

> A sum-up document of the 1990/91 experiences. It was observed that there was a reduction in the number of armed operations. At the same time, we were experiencing a recovery process in the White Plains [unorganized areas]. This was pushed for not only because of the National Peasant Secretariat but also because of the support of the National Campaign Committee. We were pushing for an alliance-type formation. This meant concretely that we were organizing peasant formation not as KMP but using different names. We were also trying to combine NGO work with PO [People's Organization] organizers and party organizers. We were even able to get the "traditional organizations" to join the protest.[113]

[110] Author's interview with "Joey," Manila, March 10, 1996.

[111] See "Our Urgent Tasks" (Communist Party of the Philippines, Central Committee 1976).

[112] Similarly to the Manila-Rizal Committee and the National Organizing Commission, early in the 1990, the NPS organized a series of studies on other countries' revolutionary experiences as well as various theories of social change (author's interview with "Salvador," April 4, 1996, and "Otavalo," Manila, February 28, 1995). At the same time, as pointed out by Joey, in the early 1990s, there was not per se a clear ideological opposition; it was more "formless" and mixed with "disgust and dissatisfaction with the party paradigms. [...] There were loose ideas and loose discussions, un-theoretical and with little consistency" (author's interview with "Joey" April 6, 1996). At the same time, the quest for new ideas was present in many party organs, including several regional commissions.

[113] Author's interview with "Salvador," Manila, February 23, 1995.

As the same leading cadre of the National Peasant Secretariat (NPS) recalls, "From 1989 to 1992, the National Peasant Commission took the initiative of deploying cadres in the region to strengthen the legal organizing and put a greater emphasis on organizing in the plains."[114] As "Penelope," a peasant organizing cadre, recalls: "In 1991, we started with the open peasant movement. [...] We would let the peasants/farmers identified local issues and defined the national issues."[115] In fact, the experimentation with alternative ways of organizing peasants had begun the year before. The impetus for such organizing was to begin recovery of areas that were lost as the result of the decline in the revolutionary movement and the massive military counter-insurgency operations or areas affected by the anti-infiltration campaign. Not surprisingly, this organizing was ongoing in Southern Tagalog and Mindanao but also in many other places where farmers previously organized had been affected by military operations.

15.8 The End of a Cycle of Mobilization: The Dilemma of Bureaucratization and Institutionalization

As the movement expanded in the early 1980s, new tendencies began to emerge that would characterize much of the next 10 years. One was an increasing bureaucratization of the movement, and the other was a greater institutionalization of the various components as revealed earlier with the setting up of many new party structures. Both the bureaucratization and the institutionalization of the movement meant that an increasingly important number of cadres were removed from direct organizing work. But it also meant that higher organs were busy receiving reports, assessments, and summing up while trying to respond to a rapidly changing political situation. At the same time, a dependency on external funding was gradually emerging.

By 1983, recruitment and expansion of membership did not seem to be a problem, and the mass movement was picking up its own dynamism, and it was becoming possible to imagine "post-Marcos" scenarios. Aquino's assassination also affected American support to the Marcos regime. The United States had started to exert pressure for some reforms toward a greater political opening. The Americans were increasingly wary that the Philippines might develop into a new Iran or Nicaragua. The growing concerns by the American over the stability of the Marcos regime and the ongoing exploration of the CPP to establish friendly relations with other foreign governments indicated that the Philippine revolution was no longer a homegrown story. Between 1983 and 1985, the core leadership of the CPP (the executive committee and the politburo) exerted less centralized control on territorial and sectoral commissions, except on certain commissions, such as the National United Front Commission especially after the assassination of former Senator Benigno Aquino. In fact, the urban work (legal and illegal), mass movement organization, and united front tactics

[114] Ibid.

[115] Author's interview with "Penelope," Manila, March 4, 1995.

took on significantly greater importance and monopolized a lot of energy on the part of the core leadership. The setting up of what the party called BLAs consumed much of the energy. Yet, it would be this area of work where the lack of conceptual tools and analysis would be felt the most and would eventually create inertia at the time when the political context was rapidly evolving with a wide range of political opportunities.

The review of this intense period showed that the rapid growth of the movement created dilemmas for the conduct of the revolution which had become not only a nationwide affair but also complex and unwieldy to manage. The CPP underground now included a vast range of units, bureaus, departments, and secretariats, many connected to hundreds of institutions, legal mass movement organizations, and trade unions. There were new dilemmas with the management of such a growing movement and the complexification of structure and units which meant that more and more cadres were busy with management and administration work rather than organizing or acquiring a better sense of the overall development of the movement.

The boycott decision of the snap 1986 presidential election – later described by the CPP politburo as a tactical blunder – marked a turning point in the party's history because it resulted in the first widespread questioning of the party's leadership. The post-EDSA period had seen a multiplication of the number of legal organization, many of them are NGOs. Funds brought in by these NGOs created an attitude of patron-client with mass movement organizations, the latter relying on funds from the former for mobilizing. This created a tendency to depend on funds to organize. The management of this burgeoning of legal institutions had also direct human resource costs since it meant removing cadres involved in mass organizing and having them manage projects, preparing reports, etc.

Subtler was the change in perspective that this work was providing. While leading cadres were operating underground (clandestinely), party members working within legal organizations were developing a different understanding of political reality and gradually felt that the "center" (i.e., party leadership) had become out of touch with the changes. This tendency became more pronounced in the late 1980s when there was some questioning of the capacity of the party leadership to provide adequate analysis. Moreover, people working legally were likely to talk across lines with less concern about the compartmentalization of information, making the movement more vulnerable to arrests, which were numerous during those years. Within three years (1989–1992), the revolutionary movement experienced its greatest swing from pluralist explorations to renewed orthodoxy. This swing was not without cost. Starting in 1992, the CPP began fragmenting into a series of small political blocs leaving its orthodox core exposed but equipped and determined to fight back.

Although the revolutionary movement implosion might have appeared as surprising to the broad Filipino public, the seeds of discontent had been sown for quite some time. The difficult 1986–1989 period had allowed certain dynamics to unfold, the leadership had been weakened, and the greater institutionalization of the movement had created a substantial section of urban-based NGOs and legal institutions, bureaucrats, and legal mass movement organizers who were very attuned to what was happening in the rest of the world. They were also interfaced with international solidarity network volunteers who probably shared and discussed the trajectory of other revolutionary movements, including developments within the socialist bloc, the movement for democratization in China, and the Tiananmen Square massacre.

The CPP-led armed revolution has successfully survived and reasserted its ideological and organizational integrity after the 1992–1994 "Great Schism." By 1997, after 5 years of rectification, Sison felt the CPP had recovered a mass-base equivalent to what it had in 1983. The CPP revolutionary movement is still in 2012 the most consolidated and institutionalized bloc within the militant left. Despite such cohesion and a presence nationwide, it is difficult to assess the extent to which it constitutes a moving force within the broad Philippine political life.

There are two other reasons why one would expect the CPP revolution to persist for some time. The first is biographic availability, meaning that there are many potential recruits, mostly in rural areas where the CPP has focused its effort since the beginning of its "Second Rectification Campaign." While the first generation of CPP cadres came from the student movement, there is now a recognition that the largest number of members and guerrilla fighters is from peasant and worker (urban poor) origins. As "Alfonso," a veteran of the movement explained in 1998:

> Those whom we attract to the party and the people's army are primarily the masses of workers and peasants. Of course, the petite bourgeoisie, we need them in our ranks. Even what Jo [Sison] said, we need comrades who have education. High school and those who have gone to college, if possible.[116]

Assuming that there is some form of replenishing of cadres and that political opportunities continue to arise, the CPP revolution will persist. At the same time, the incapacity of the splintering groups of the CPP to act in a united way or develop a compelling political project has made it easier for the party to continue claiming some form of historical relevance.

References

Abinales, P. (1984). *Building the parliament of the streets: The birth, hegemony, and crisis of the Philippine student movement.* Unpublished mimeograph. Diliman: University of the Philippines.

Abinales, P. (1988). *Radicals and activists: Birth, hegemony and crisis of the Philippines student movement.* Unpublished mimeograph. Diliman: University of the Philippines.

Abinales, P. (1992). Jose Maria Sison and the Philippine revolution: A critique of an interface. *Kasarinlan: A Philippine Quarterly of Third World Studies, 8*(1), 7–81.

Abinales, P. N. (Ed.). (1996). *The revolution falters: The left in the Philippine politics after 1986* (Southeast Asia Program Series No.15, Southeast Asia Program Publications). Ithaca: Cornell University.

Agoncillo, T. (1967). Introduction to the first edition. In J. M. Sison (Eds.), *Struggle for national democracy.* Manila: Amado V. Hernandez Foundation.

Alvarez, S. (1992). *The Katipunan and the revolution: Memoirs of a general* (Translated into English by P. C. Malay). Quezon City: Ateneo de Manila University Press.

[116] "Alfonso," interview with author, Utrecht, April 16, 1998

Anderson, B. (1988). Cacique democracy in the Philippines: Origins and dreams. *New Left Review, 169*, 3–33.
Ang Bayan. (January 1983a). Workers' strikes: The regime never learns. *Ang Bayan, XIV*(13), 7–8.
Ang Bayan. (January 1983b). Red fighters get in shape for intensified warfare. *Ang Bayan, XIV*(13), 4–5.
Ang Bayan. (1970). *On the January 26th demonstration* (Special Release) *Ang Bayan*.
Armed Forces of the Philippines, Intelligence Service. (1989). *The reestablished communist party of the Philippines* (Vol. I-IV). Quezon City: Armed Forces of the Philippines.
Bonner, R. (1987). *Waltzing with a dictator: The Marcoses and the making of American policy*. New York: Times Book.
Butterfield, F. (1978, January 21–22). Marcos is said to strip wealth of major foes, *International Herald Tribune*.
Canoy, R. (1984). *The counterfeit revolution: The Philippines from martial law to the Aquino assassination*. Manila: Philippine Editions.
Caouette, D. (2011). Caciquisme, capitalisme de connivence et oligarchie: Les travers de l'État philippin contemporain. In D. Bach & M. Gazibo (Eds.), *État et néopatrimonialisme: Génèse et trajectoires contemporaines*. Ottawa: University of Ottawa Press.
Chapman, W. (1987). *Inside the Philippine revolution: The new people's army and its struggle for power*. New York: W.W. Norton.
Christians for National Liberation (CNL), Provisional National Executive Committee. (1981, February). CNL renew revolutionary pledge. *Liberation, IX*(2).
Christians for National Liberation. (n.d.). Unite with the masses against the U.S.-Marcos dictatorship & struggle for national freedom and democracy! (December 10th, 1979). *Dare to struggle, dare to win*. Mansfield Depot: Philippine Research Center.
Clarke, G. (1998). *The politics of NGOs in South-East Asia: Participation and protest in the Philippines*. London: Routledge.
Communist Party of the Philippines, Central Committee. (1983, October). Overthrow the U.S.-Marcos fascist dictatorship, establish a revolutionary coalition government! (Signed by Central Committee on October 7, 1983). *Ang Bayan, 15*(8).
Communist Party of the Philippines, Central Committee. (1976). Our urgent tasks. *Rebolusyon, I*(1), 1–33.
Communist Party of the Philippines, Central Committee. (1985). *Untitled* [9th Plenum Minutes], (Mimeographed).
Communist Party of the Philippines, Central Committee. (1990). Carry out rectification, further strengthen the party and intensify the people's revolutionary struggle. *Rebolusyon, I*(1), 5–22.
Communist Party of the Philippines, Regional Committee – Western Visayas. (1981). *Isang Dekadang Pagpupunayagi sa Rebolusyonaryong Pakikibaka sa Kanlurang Kabisayan*. Unpublished document, p. 22.
Communist Party of the Philippines. (n.d.). *Orientation of our political work in the church sector*. Unpublished Document.
Del Carmen, C. (1983, December 14). The NDF: The problem is public acceptability, *Who*, 28–29.
Fox, J. (1994). The difficult transition from clientelism to citizenship: Lessons from Mexico. *World Politics, 46*(2), 151–184.
Guerrero, A., & Dante, B. (1970, February 8). *Turn grief into revolutionary courage and militant unity for national democracy*. Unpublished Document.
Hawes, G. (1987). *The Philippine state and the Marcos regime: The politics of export*. Ithaca: Cornell University Press.
Hernandez, C. (1979). *The extent of civilian control of the military in the Philippines: 1946–1976*. Doctoral dissertation, State University of New York, Buffalo.
Hilhorst, D. (2003). *The real world of NGOs: Discourses, diversity and development*. London: Zed Books.
Hutchcroft, P. (1998). *Booty capitalism: The politics of banking in the Philippines*. Quezon City: Ateneo de Manila University Press.
Joaquin, N. (1988). *The Aquinos of Tarlac: An essay on history as three generations*. Manila: Solar Publishing Corporation.

Jones, G. (1989). *Red revolution: Inside the Philippine Guerilla movement*. Boulder: Westview Press.
Kabataang Makabayan – KM. (1970a, January 28). Continue the revolutionary anti-fascist struggle. *Mimeographed Statement.*
Kabataang Makabayan – KM. (1970b, March 17). Ibunsod Ang Malawakang Pakikibaka Laban sa Imperyalismong Amerikano, Katutubong Piyudalismo at Burokrata-Kapitalismo! *Mimeographed Statement.*
Kang, T. H. (1982). *The uses and abuses of crisis government in the Philippines*. Doctoral dissertation, New York University, New York.
Karl, T. L., & Schmitter, P. (1991). Modes of transition in Latin America, southern and eastern Europe. *International Social Science Journal, 128*, 269–284.
Kintanar, G. C. (1979, June). Contemporary religious radicalism in the Philippines. *Quarterly National Security Review of the National Defense College of the Philippines* (mimeographed).
Kitschelt, H. (1992). Political regime change: Structure and process-driven explanations? *American Political Science Review, 86*(4), 1028–1034.
Lacaba, J. (1982). *Days of disquiet, nights of rage: The first quarter storm and related events*. Manila: Salinlahi Publishing House.
Lachica, E. (1971). *Huk: Philippine Agrarian Society in revolt*. Manila: Solidaridad Publishing House.
Makabayan, K., & Secretariat, N. (1965). *Kabataang Makabayan handbook: Documents of the first National Congress*. Manila: Progressive Publications.
Malay, A. (1984). Some random reflections on Marxism and Maoism in the Philippines. In Third World Studies Centre (Ed.), *Marxism in the Philippines: Marx centennial lectures*. Quezon City: Third World Studies Center.
Morales, H. (1977, December 26). *Statement of Horacio Morales Jr., 1977 TOYM awardee for government service, executive vice president of the development academy of the Philippines.*
National Democratic Front of the Philippines, International Office. (1983, March–April). NDF celebrates 10th anniversary. *NDF Updates – Philippines* III (3).
Nemenzo, F. (1984a). Rectification process in the Philippine communist movement. In J.-J. Lim & S. Vani (Eds.), *Armed communist movements in southeast Asia* (pp. 69–101). Singapore: Institute of Southeast Asian Studies.
Nemenzo, F. (1984b, November). *An irrepressible revolution: The decline and resurgence of the Philippines communist movement*. Paper presented at the Work in Progress Seminar, Research School of Pacific Studies. Canberra: Australia National University.
Peter, V. N. (1970). *Revolution and Chinese foreign policy: Peking's support for wars of national liberation*. Berkeley: University of California Press.
Pimentel, B. (1989). *The unusual journey of Edgar Jopson*. Quezon City: Ken Inc.
Putnam, R. (1993). *Making democracy work: Civic traditions in modern Italy*. Princeton: Princeton University Press.
Putzel, J. (1995). Managing the 'Main Force': The communist party and the peasantry in the Philippines. *Journal of Peasant Studies, 22*(4), 645–671.
Quimpo, N. G. (2008). *Contested democracy and the left in the Philippines after Marcos*. New Haven: Yale University Southeast Asia Studies.
Rocamora, J. (1978). The united front in the Philippines. *Southeast Asia Chronicle, 62*, 2–6.
Rocamora, J. (1982). Turning point: The NDF takes the lead. *The Philippines in the 80s – From Normalization to Polarization Southeast Asia Chronicle, 83*, 1–7.
Rocamora, J. (1983, October). The Philippines after Aquino, after Marcos? In C. Barbara & R. Joel, (Eds.), *The Philippines after Aquino, after Marcos* (pp. 1–22). Analysis and News Clippings compiled by Philippine Support Committee and Southeast Asia Resource Center, Manila/Washington, DC.
Rolando, D. C. (1979). Constitutionality and judicial politics. In D. Rosenberg (Ed.), *Marcos and martial law in the Philippines*. Ithaca: Cornell University Press.
Rosenberg, D. (1984). Communism in the Philippines. *Problem of Communism, 33*(September–October), 24–46.
Rutten, R. (Ed.). (2008). *Brokering a revolution: Cadres in a Philippine insurgency*. Quezon City: Ateneo de Manila University Press.

Samahang Demokratiko ng Kabataan. (1974). *Hinggil sa Legal ng Pakikibaka*. Unpublished Document.

Samahang Demokratiko ng Kabataan (SDK). (circa 1974). Hinggil sa Legal ng Pakikibaka (mimeographed).

Saulo, A. (1990). *Communism in the Philippines: An introduction*. Manila: Ateneo de Manila University Press.

Schirmer, D., & Shalom, S. R. (Eds.). (1987). *The Philippines reader: A history of colonialism, neocolonialism, dictatorship and resistance*. Quezon City: Ken Inc.

Seekins, D. (1993). Historical setting. In R. Dolan (Ed.), *Philippines: A country study* (4th ed.). Washington, DC: Department of the Army.

Shalom, S. R. (1986). *The United States and the Philippines: A study of neocolonialism*. Quezon City: New Day Publishers.

Sison, J. M. (1967a). *Struggle for national democracy*. Quezon City: Progressive Publications.

Sison, J. M. (1967b). Report to the second national congress. In K. Makabayang (Ed.), *Kabataang Makabayan: Documents of the second National Congress*. Manila: Kabataang Makabayan.

Sison, J. M. (1972). *Struggle for national democracy* (Newth ed.). Manila: Amado V Hernandez Memorial Foundation.

Sison, J. M. (1979). *Philippine society and revolution* (4th ed.). Oakland: International Association of Filipino Patriots.

Sison, J. M. (with Rainer, W.). (1989). *The Philippine revolution: The leader's view*. New York: Crane Russak.

Starner, F. (1970, October 17). Whose bullet, whose blood? *Far Eastern Economic Review*, 23–30.

Student Power Assembly. (1969). *The Diliman Declaration, General Declaration of the Student Power Assembly of the Philippines* (Approved on March 9th, 1969). Unpublished Mimeograph.

Students Leaders' Forum (SLF). (1983, September 30). *On the September 21 and 23 demonstrations: Position paper*. Unpublished Document.

Tarrow, S. (1998 [1994]). *Power in movement: Social movements and contentious politics*. Cambridge: Cambridge University Press.

Tiglao, R. (1988). The consolidation of the dictatorship. In A. J.-D. Dios, P. B. Daroy, & L. Kalaw-Tirol (Eds.), *Dictatorship and revolution: Roots of people's power*. Manila: Conspectus Foundation.

Timberman, D. (1991). *A changeless land: Continuity and change in Philippine politics*. Singapore: Institute of Southeast Asia Studies.

Valdes, J. A. (1989). *National security, the dual state and the rule of exception: A study of the strategocratic political system*. Doctoral dissertation, Erasmus Universiteit Rotterdam, Rotterdam.

Weekley, K. (1996a), *From vanguard to rearguard: The communist party of the Philippines, 1968–1993*. Doctoral dissertation, University of Sidney, Camperdown.

Weekley, K. (1996b). From vanguard to rearguard: The theoretical roots of the crisis in the communist party of the Philippines. In P. Abinales (Ed.), *The revolution falters: The left in the Philippine politics after 1986* (pp. 28–59). Ithaca: Cornell University.

Weekley, K. (2001). *The communist party of the Philippines 1968–1993: A story of its theory and practice*. Quezon City: University of the Philippines Press.

Wurfel, D. (1977). Martial law in the Philippines: The methods of regime survival. *Pacific Affairs, 50*(1), 5–30.

Wurfel, D. (1988). *Filipino politics: Development and decay*. Quezon City: Ateneo de Manila University Press.

Youngblood, R. (1985). The Philippines in 1985: A continuing crisis of confidence. In Institute of Southeast Asian Studies (Ed.), *Southeast Asian affairs 1986*. Singapore: Institute of Southeast Asian Studies.

Youngblood, R. (1993). *Marcos against the church: Economic development and political repression in the Philippines*. Quezon City: New Day Publishers.

Part IV
Commentary

Chapter 16
What Do Social Scientists Do When They Do Comparative Work?

Lilian Mathieu

16.1 Comparative Work in Social Sciences and Studies in Contentious Politics

From its beginning, comparative work has stood at the core of social sciences methodology. As early as 1895, Émile Durkheim claimed that because sociology cannot use experimental methods, it has to rely on comparisons in order not only to describe but also to explain social facts. According to him, "comparative sociology is not a particular branch of sociology; it is sociology as such, when it ceases to be purely descriptive and aims to report the facts" (Durkheim 1987 [1895]: 137).[1] Another great social science founder, Max Weber, based his impressive economic history of world religions on comparisons between them (Protestantism, Ancient Judaism, Confucianism, etc.); his own sociological methodology is based on comparisons as it aims to make differences appear between an analytical ideal-type and a given empirical reality. For his part, Marc Bloch called comparison a "divining rod" for the historian (Bloch 1995 [1928]: 101), and his metaphor can certainly be extended to all social sciences.

Of course, the study of contentious politics was not immune to this methodological trend, and some major empirical and theoretical contributions to this field come from comparative research. Milestones in the study of revolutions like Barrington Moore's *Social Origins of Dictatorship and Democracy* (Moore 1966) and Theda Skocpol's *States and Social Revolutions* (Skocpol 1979) compare different countries in order to reveal revolutions' structural and political preconditions and dynamics. Comparing similar social movements in various countries has become the usual,

[1] Author's translation.

L. Mathieu (✉)
Centre National de la Recherche Scientifique, Centre Max Weber, Ecole normale supérieure de Lyon, 15 parvis Descartes, 69007 Lyon, France
e-mail: lilian.mathieu@ens-lyon.fr

B. Andreosso-O'Callaghan and F. Royall (eds.), *Economic and Political Change in Asia and Europe: Social Movement Analyses*, DOI 10.1007/978-94-007-4653-4_16,

and heuristic, way to reveal how and why they succeed or fail, institutionalize or radicalize, and develop or fade away. The political process theory, and its main concept of political opportunity structure, owes part of its success to its usefulness for comparative work, as it helps to identify, in each country under study, the institutional structures that open or close ways for protest. Decisive contributions to this theory, like Kitschelt's (1986) and Kriesi et al. (1995), are based on comparative studies that have shown that social movements have more opportunities to develop and succeed when they face an "open" or "weak" political opportunity structure but have no choice but to radicalize when a "strong" state remains closed to their grievances. However, one can focus on the movement side and compare different mobilizations within a sole national context. For example, this is what Touraine and his colleagues did when they compared different French movements (ecologist, regionalist, feminist, student, etc.) at the end of the 1970s in order to identify the one that would replace the allegedly declining workers' movement (Touraine 1982).

During his career, Charles Tilly advocated the use of comparisons in the study of contentious politics. In his methodological book entitled *Big Structures, Large Processes, Huge Comparisons* (Tilly 1984), he distinguished four ways to use comparison, which he called (a) individualizing comparison (where the point is to contrast cases in order to grasp their peculiarities), (b) universalizing comparison (which aims to establish that every instance of a phenomenon follows the same rule), (c) variation-finding comparison (which aims to establish a principle of variation in the character or intensity of a phenomenon by examining systematic differences between instances), and (d) encompassing comparison (which places different instances within a system, on the way to explaining their characteristic as a function of their varying relationships to the system as a whole) (Tilly 1984: 82–83). Many researchers have since followed his path, and comparison is nowadays recognized as a major scientific tool. But if the development and the standardization of comparative methodology in the study of social movements is a positive sign of scientific maturity, the other side of the coin is that it is also quite often taken for granted. In other words, social scientists know that they have to be comparative but at the risk of forgetting why they have to do comparative work, what they compare, and what is needed to complete a convincing and fruitful comparative study. Sometimes, the result is not a comparison but a juxtaposition of (more often national) case studies – in the same book or journal – that have little relationship with each other. When the chapters or articles are based on a well-conducted case study, they can be valuable in themselves, but their general input for sociological analysis may remain weak.

The problem, here, is not only that the so-called comparison is in fact a juxtaposition but also that the various cases are deemed comparable a priori, without even a minimal examination. When a social scientist decides to compare a particular movement (e.g., the pro-abortion movement) in a series of countries, he/she presupposes that such a movement exists and that abortion is a worthy cause in each country. This will probably be the case, and one can be confident that he/she will find a movement advocating women's reproductive rights in the country under investigation. But that movement will be very different, for example, in a country where abortion has long been a rather consensual issue (e.g., England) and in another where it has long been a hotly debated issue, revealing major political, ideological, or religious cleavages within society (e.g., Poland). It is not clear that the terms "movement" and "abortion" have the same meaning in two such countries and, as a consequence, that they can be easily "compared."

Given that this concluding chapter focuses above all on methodological issues, I would like to take the liberty of drawing my examples and references from contexts other than those of Asia or Europe. The words of caution and the criticisms that I lodge below against some of the liberal uses of comparative studies should not be viewed as expressions of reservation toward comparative approaches and studies. This volume shows quite clearly the benefits of doing comparative research given that it focuses on the extremely varied social and political realities between and across Europe and Asia. Comparative analyses are extremely useful analytical tools in the social sciences.

16.2 The Risks of Obvious Comparisons

One of the main risks researchers face is the implicit belief that there is a stable reality behind each term, a reality that one can locate everywhere and every time this term (or its translation) is used. In other words, terms like "social movement," "ecology," "antiracism," or "feminism" are supposed to designate the same reality wherever and whenever they are used. A feminist movement, for example, in a particular place and at a particular time, may be deemed to have essential traits in common with another movement, also called "feminist," in another place or at another time. These common traits can be summed up in a sociological definition that opens the way for bringing near and comparing the various phenomena that correspond to it. If a feminist movement is defined as a collective action led by women who advocate women's rights and who fight against male domination, it is possible to include as such early twentieth century suffragist mobilizations and early twenty-first-century "riot grrrl" punk bands.[2] The comparison between the two is not invalid and would surely be interesting. Its main result would probably be that both movements have a quite different conception of what "feminism" means, of the path women's emancipation should follow, and of the political means feminists should mobilize.

In other words, the same word "feminist" has a very different meaning depending upon whether it describes the suffragist or the riot grrrl movements, despite both claiming to fight for women's emancipation and both fitting in the above-stated definition.[3] Using the same word leads to misunderstanding of the fact that it is not

[2] Riot grrrl punk bands appeared in the American northwest during the early 1990s and developed a feminist and "queer" subculture with songs and fanzines that address problems pertinent to young white middle-class women such as sexual abuse, harassment, and body image (Moore and Roberts 2009: 284–288).

[3] Since the development of queer theory, which inspired some riot grrrl bands, the very definition of what a woman "is" has quite changed; if both movements fight for women's rights, they do not even deal with the same "women."

the same feminism and, maybe, that those groups are separated more by differences than by what they have in common. The danger here is what philosopher Ludwig Wittgenstein called *substantialism*, which he described as looking for a common substance behind the use of the same substantive (Wittgenstein 1958). Substantialism, to put it differently, is too confident in words; it believes that words "stick" to reality, that there cannot be any gap or displacement between a word and the reality it designates, or that the same word can only designate a unique reality (and not different realities). A good way to avoid this danger is to give a robust definition to the words – what social scientists call concepts – that are used in the analysis: whether they fit or not within the definition of what a feminist movement is, various women's collective actions will (or will not) be labelled as such and will (or will not) be considered available for comparison. Two opposite dangers, already stressed over 20 years ago by Giovanni Sartori (1991), then appear. The first is the temptation to provide a definition that is so large and so general that it encompasses almost everything, and the second is to define the phenomena under study in such precise and restricted ways that only very few occurrences can be compared.

The feminist example I chose to state my point is extreme and a little outrageous. Most sociologists are aware of these dangers and rely on perfectly working definitions that avoid both the perils of over-generalization and over-restriction and that are able to keep away from anachronism or confusion. Nevertheless, constant vigilance is needed in order to avoid inadvertent substantialism. This is especially the case in social movements' studies where analysts share a common conceptual vocabulary that has widely developed since the 1970s but whose meaning has sometimes become unclear. Notions like resources, repertoire, advocacy, conscience constituents, campaigns, social movement organization, frame alignment, and political opportunity structure, to quote just a few, are now in use internationally. But it is not always clear that all these concepts fit correctly with the social realities they intend to analyze, as there can be major differences between the first empirical case for which a concept has been elaborated and the subsequent cases for which it is used. The concept of "new social movement" (Melucci 1980), for example, has been helpful to specify and study movements with common traits (such as the post-materialist values and the rise of an educated middle-class constituency) that appeared and developed in western post-industrialized democracies during the 1970s; but it is not clear that it can offer the same insights for the analysis of movements (even with seemingly similar traits) that later appeared and/or in other political or cultural contexts (e.g., in post-communist or third-world countries). To sum up, the German feminist movement of the 1970s is surely a "new social movement," but it is doubtful that its contemporary Cuban or Kenyan counterparts can be considered as such.

Many of the concepts and notions social movement analysts use have been designed by American researchers who first studied American movements. They have proven very helpful in analyzing mobilizations in other countries but at the risk of missing some of their peculiarities. An interest group, for example, is a common and legitimate form of political action in the United States, but it has a rather stigmatizing label in France where the notion refers to illegitimate and undercover pressure on political elites. The economic vocabulary of "movement entrepreneurs" (McCarthy and Zald 1977) may well correspond to the American reality, where cultural tools frequently refer to markets and firms (Lamont and Thévenot 2000), but it is more a metaphor in many other countries where the individualistic and capitalist world view is less prevalent. Social movements can take a variety of forms – more or less formal and stable – and uniformly calling them "social movement organizations" misses this point. In France, it is not unimportant if a movement adopts the form of a stable and official "association" or if it chooses to remain a "collective," for example, an informal and leaderless gathering of individuals and groups that punctually unite to express some grievances and organize a few public actions.

There are different ways to avoid these difficulties. The first may be to renounce starting research with a robust and stable definition and study instead the way actors define themselves, why they identify with a movement's tradition or distance themselves from it, and how they cope with the various labels that others (competing movements, political authorities, the media, the general public, countermovements, and social scientists) may try to impose upon them. By so doing, the researcher can understand the practical constraints and dilemmas the actors face and how they try to overcome them. Many stigmatized groups, for example, challenge the dominant and pejorative views the "normal world" shares about them and promote a destigmatized, self-elaborated identity – like when a gay identity is opposed to the medical vocabulary of homosexuality or when unemployed people prefer to refer to themselves as "people who are deprived of jobs" (*privés d'emploi*) in order to stress that it is the economic system, and not their alleged laziness, that is responsible for their situation (Giugni 2008a, b). Some groups try to transform the stigma by referring to it with pride (Goffman 1963), while others try to escape it. Movements that think that "feminist" or "gay and lesbian" are old-fashioned labels, for example, use periphrases or new identities (like "gender equality" or "queer") in order to appear "modern."[4] Others may try to overcome a stigma and get recognition by identifying with a wider legitimate tradition (as some contemporary Turkish Muslim organizations try to do by joining a human rights advocacy transnational network).[5] Missing this point is to ignore an important part of social movement activity.

A second way is to reconstruct carefully the historical, political, social, and cultural context in which the studied movement takes place. This means that the movement cannot be taken at face value; its context of emergence, its own historical development, the resonance of its grievances within the population…have to be taken into account in order to differentiate it from (apparently) similar movements in other countries. I have already referred to the example of pro-choice movements in England and Poland. Despite sharing the same goals (making abortion legal and widely available to women), these movements do not share the same grievances,

[4] See Gamson (1995) for a study of the sometimes difficult relationships between older "gay and lesbian" and newer "queer" movements in the United States.

[5] This example is taken from Emre Öngün's doctoral dissertation on the transnationalization of Turkish social movements (Öngün 2008).

and they do not face the same opposition. Even the word "movement" may not have the same meaning in each country, as the Polish movement will certainly need to be more resolute than its more consensual and institutionalized English counterpart. The same could be said about antiracist movements in countries that have historically hosted migrants (like France) and others where immigration is a recent phenomenon (like Spain). The migration theme has not the same history, the same meaning, and the same resonance in both countries. All this means that a comparative study cannot be a superficial overview of apparently similar phenomena in various countries but needs a detailed – and often long and laborious – approach. Otherwise, the risk is the mingling of formal and superficial similarities with real identities. The risk becomes all the more apparent when the objective is to compare phenomena derived from historical processes and that belong to extremely varied cultural contexts, as in the cases outlined in this volume.

16.3 What to Compare?

Researchers face another perilous temptation: to pre-construct their objects in order to make them "comparable." They may fear that their objects will be "too different" to legitimize their comparison, so they may restrict them to a limited set of variables or issues. If in a given country the feminist movement addresses a wide range of issues (unequal pay between women and men, rape, prostitution, abortion, etc.) whereas in another country feminists focus mainly on abortion, only this topic will be compared and the comparison will miss a major difference between the two national movements. A similar problem may appear at the methodological level. A series of collective action frames, for example, is established before the fieldwork, and the researcher's goal is to identify which frame is applicable to each national movement. The risk then is to miss frames that were not planned and to disregard the fact that what is apparently the same frame has in fact different meanings in different countries. By so doing, social scientists run the risk of eroding the differences between the various phenomena they plan to compare. The problem then is that little is left for analysis after the phenomenon has been reduced to a standardized analytical grid and that only minor variations can be identified in the end process. What is paradoxically forgotten here is that differences between the objects (e.g., between pro-choice movements in a series of countries) are not a methodological problem but rather the main purpose of the analysis. Comparison is not intended to ward off differences but rather to identify and to explain them.

The difficulty, here, is not in the exercise of constructing comparable objects prior to comparison. On the contrary, this is a necessary step in order to be sure that the comparison is under control and is not a furtive or a hazardous linking between heterogeneous realities that have little to do with each other. The difficulty rather lies in an anxious desire to over-control the comparison. By being afraid of not being rigorous enough, the researcher may define his or her object in such a restricted way that the studied cases are made homogeneous before the comparison takes place, and little room is left therefore for scientific discovery. There is no definite answer to this difficulty, but a methodological equilibrium needs to be found: cases must be rigorously constructed in order to be compared but in a way flexible enough to leave open the possibility of finding unexpected results.

It may be possible to avoid some of these problems by adopting another kind of comparison. Instead of comparing formally similar objects (e.g., movements with the seemingly same agenda in different countries), it may be useful to compare objects that have little in common.[6] Instead of comparing pro-choice movements in England, France, Spain, Italy, and Poland, why not compare pro-choice and pro-life movements? Or even more, why not compare a progressive and legitimate movement with a marginal religious sect? They surely are very different kinds of movements or groupings. Their goals, constituencies, organization, and resources are heterogeneous and probably opposite on many points but, despite these undeniable differences, as collectives or organizations they probably face some similar problems: recruiting constituents, making their position heard, mobilizing resources, coping with managerial issues, etc. Comparing them would not mean assimilating them but rather looking at how groups with different values and confronted with analogous organizational issues find different or similar responses. Such a comparison would lead to a more general understanding of the role that values play in collective action or of the set of organizational forms available in our societies than a comparison between too similar objects (How can we be sure that the findings resulting from the comparison of five national pro-choice movements are available for other kinds of movements?). Despite the fact that it may at first seem not legitimate or strange, "comparing the incomparable," as French historian Marcel Détienne (2010) puts it, is more ambitious and can offer more generalized findings.

Here again, the terms of the comparison must be rigorously controlled in order to avoid a superficial and hazardous assimilation. A pro-choice movement is certainly not a religious sect. But, despite all that differentiate them, they may face similar practical problems and (perhaps, if the study finally shows it) find similar responses that do (or do not) directly depend on their goals or ideology. What Détienne calls the "dissonance test" (*épreuve de la dissonance*) is a precious analytical tool here. It forces the researcher to contextualize the objects of study in order to make apparent what are the real (and not the superficial or formal) common points or significant differences between them and what makes sense of them. One well-known Europe-Asia comparison can illustrate this point. Reinhard Bendix's evaluation of German Junkers' and Japanese samurais' attitudes toward their respective countries' industrialization and political modernization during the nineteenth century is a good example of such heuristic connections. Despite shared positions in their countries' class structures, they adopted opposite positions toward industrialization and political modernization, as the Junkers resisted them while the Samurais supported them

[6] This may be considered as following Wittgenstein's warning against "a main cause of philosophical disease – a one-sided diet: one nourishes one's thinking with only one kind of example" (Wittgenstein 2001 [1953]: 593).

(Bendix 1964). The identification of these differences then helps to find their explanation in the peculiarities of each national historical and cultural context. This way of using comparison is what makes social sciences closer to experimental methods.

If comparison leads to the identification of common traits, the question remains of their status. The risk then is of over-generalizing the findings: if a researcher identifies the same trait in a wide series of movements, he/she can be tempted to proclaim a general law of contentious politics from which no contentious phenomenon can ever escape. Crane Brinton's (1965) classic theory of revolutions is a good example of such an error in asserting that all revolutions necessarily follow the same stages (old regime, moderate revolutionary regime, reign of terror, "Thermidor" period). But the same problem can be found in the sequential analysis of democratic transitions – such as the one elaborated by O'Donnell et al. (1986) – that try to identify their successive stages (from the liberalization of the authoritarian regime to the consolidation of a new democracy).[7]

Wittgenstein's philosophy can once again be useful against a new difficulty of substantialism: there is no essence of social movements (or of any social fact) governed by an immutable set of generic "laws." The common traits the comparative methodology is able to identify can be seen as what Wittgenstein calls "family resemblances" (2001 [1953]: § 66–67) such as in a family where nobody has exactly the same face but whose members may, for some, have the same nose and for others, the same ears or hair; thus, various social movements may share some common points (a collective action repertoire, a bureaucratic organization, a set of contentious frames, etc.), but not all social movements share the same set of definitional criteria.

16.4 How Concepts Can Help Control Comparisons: The Mechanism and Process Example

Hopefully, renouncing identifying general and immutable laws of phenomena like social movements, revolutions, or democratic transitions does not mean that social scientists have to renounce producing rigorous accounts of social reality. It is possible to construct concepts and theories that help to compare and analyze social phenomena while avoiding the various risks – substantialism and anachronism being the more frequent among them – which I have stressed so far. I will end this chapter by presenting and discussing one recent theoretical model that helps to avoid these dangers by focusing on family resemblances rather than on substantive identities.

This theoretical framework was set up by McAdam et al. in *Dynamics of Contention* (2001) – and completed by Tilly and Tarrow in *Contentious Politics* (2007) – in which they invite social scientists to identify mechanisms within processes. They define

[7] See Dobry (2000) for an elaboration of this critique.

mechanisms as "a delimited class of events that alter relations among specified sets of elements in identical or closely similar ways over a variety of situations" (McAdam et al. 2001: 24) and processes as "regular combinations and sequences of mechanisms that produce similar (generally more complex and contingent) transformations of those elements" (Tilly and Tarrow 2007: 29). Brokerage, polarization, boundary activation, certification, diffusion, repression, etc., are such mechanisms that can be found within processes like globalization, radicalization, scale shift, identity shift, or institutionalization. Any kind of process does not need the presence of the same mechanisms, and different combinations of mechanisms can be found in the same process. Polarization, for example, may happen when a movement radicalizes but not necessarily, and there are some identity shift processes that can be explained by a certification mechanism and others that cannot be so explained.

What is proposed here is not a general theory that would submit every contentious episode to the same analytic framework but a conceptual tool kit that helps the researcher to identify what is common, despite all that differentiate them, between different phenomena (social movements, revolutions, political crises, civil wars, etc.) in various historical and geographical contexts.[8] The same mechanism or process can be located in very different settings; for example, brokerage (defined as the "production of a new connection between previously unconnected or weakly connected sites" [Tilly and Tarrow 2007: 215]) can be at work at a small scale during a limited and short-lived factory strike (e.g., when workers from two different workshops join in action) and during a major political crisis (like when French workers coalesced with agitating students in May 1968). The concept does not suggest that a localized strike is the same thing as a major political crisis or that there is a common essence uniting the two. It points to the fact that there is a "family resemblance" between them and that both can be studied with the same concept. Once again, comparing what seems at first incomparable may be more heuristic than comparing too-close realities.

Such an approach is useful for comparative studies as it can prevent substantialism at two levels. First, it does not consider that phenomena like social movements, revolutions, political crisis, and so on are radically different realities that have nothing to do with each other and that need their own specific analytical models. Second, it helps to identify similarities between different cases but without abusive assimilation. It also encourages researchers to locate and explain cases that may appear as exceptions (e.g., why communist regimes collapsed in 1989 in Eastern Europe but not in China despite the students' vigorous mobilization), and as such helps to deepen the analysis of a given kind of phenomenon.

This theoretical framework also has limits and shortcomings. The concepts designate relevant mechanisms but hardly explain what is at work within them and leave little place for actors' agency and subjectivity (Mathieu 2004). It is not, of course, the only (nor even the main) available tool kit for the comparative study

[8] That is what the authors demonstrate when they illustrate their theoretical framework with cases chosen in very different settings (e.g., in democratic and authoritarian regimes).

of social protest. But it was worth mentioning because the way the authors have defined their concepts and the kind of knowledge these analytic tools help to produce avoid some of the main sociological problems that comparative studies face.

Although this chapter may have sounded critical toward the way some social scientists use comparison, its aim was not to invalidate comparative methods. On the contrary, it aims to restore the undeniable and irreplaceable heuristic vocation of comparison by recalling some of the basic methodological rules that researchers should follow in order to make their results rigorous and convincing. To tell the truth, most social scientists are perfectly aware of these methodological precautions and produce insightful comparative studies. But it may be worth recalling them against the inevitable trend to the standardization of social sciences methods.

References

Bendix, R. (1964). Preconditions and development: A comparison of Japan and Germany. In R. Bendix (Ed.), *Nation-building and citizenship*. New York: Wiley.

Bloch, M. (1995 [1928]). *Histoire et historiens*. Paris: Armand Colin.

Brinton, C. (1965). *The Anatomy of revolution*. New York: Vintage Books.

Detienne, M. (2010). *Comparing the incomparable*. Stanford: Stanford University Press.

Dobry, M. (Ed.). (2000). *Democratic and capitalist transitions in eastern Europe. Lessons for the social sciences*. Dordrecht: Kluwer.

Durkheim, É. (1987 [1895]). *Les Règles de la méthode sociologique*. Paris: Presses Universitaires de France.

Gamson, J. (1995). Must identity movement self-destruct? A queer dilemma. *Social Problems, 42*(3), 390–407.

Giugni, M. (Ed.) (2008a). The contentious politics of European unemployment: An Introduction. *Mobilization*, Special issue, *13*(3).

Giugni, M. (2008b). Welfare states, political opportunities, and the mobilization of the unemployed: A cross-national analysis. *Mobilization special issue: The Contentious politics of European Unemployment, 13*(3), 297–310.

Goffman, E. (1963). *Stigma: Notes on the management of spoiled identity*. Englewood Cliffs: Prentice Hall.

Kitschelt, H. (1986). Political opportunity structures and political protest: Anti-nuclear movements in four democracies. *British Journal of Political Science, 16*, 57–85.

Kriesi, H., Koopmans, R., Duyvendak, J., & Giugni, M. (1995). *New social movements in western Europe: A comparative analysis*. London: UCL Press.

Lamont, M., & Thévenot, L. (Eds.). (2000). *Rethinking comparative cultural sociology*. Cambridge: Cambridge University Press.

Mathieu, L. (2004). Des mouvements sociaux à la politique contestataire: Les voies tâtonnantes d'un renouvellement de perspective. *Revue Française de Sociologie, 45*(3), 561–580.

McAdam, D., Tarrow, S., & Tilly, C. (2001). *Dynamics of contention*. Cambridge: Cambridge University Press.

McCarthy, J., & Zald, M. (1977). Resource mobilization and social movements: A partial theory. *The American Journal of Sociology, 82*(6), 1212–1241.

Melucci, A. (1980). The new social movements: A theoretical approach. *Social Science Information, 19*(2), 217–218.

Moore, B. (1966). *Social origins of dictatorship and democracy*. Boston: Beacon.

Moore, R., & Roberts, M. (2009). Do it yourself mobilization: Punk and social movements. *Mobilization, 14*(3), 273–291.

O'Donnell, G., Schmitter, P., & Whitebread, L. (Eds.). (1986). *Transition from authoritarian rule*. Baltimore: John Hopkins University Press.

Öngün, E. (2008). Action collective transnationale et contraintes de l'espace national. Enquête sur les formes de l'engagement en Turquie dans le contexte de "l'européanisation" (Doctoral Dissertation, Institut d'études politiques d'Aix-en-Provence, France). *Doctoral Dissertation in Political Science*.

Sartori, G. (1991). Comparing and miscomparing. *Journal of Theoretical Politics, 3*(3), 243–257.

Skocpol, T. (1979). *States and social revolutions*. Cambridge: Cambridge University Press.

Tilly, C. (1984). *Big structures, large processes, huge comparisons*. New York: Russell Sage Foundation.

Tilly, C., & Tarrow, S. (2007). *Contentious politics*. New York: Paradigm Publishers.

Touraine, A. (Ed.). (1982). *Mouvements sociaux d'aujourd'hui*. Paris: Les Éditions ouvrières.

Wittgenstein, L. (1958). *The blue and brown books*. Oxford: Oxford University Press.

Wittgenstein, L. (2001 [1953]). *Philosophical investigations*. Oxford: Blackwell Publishing.

About the Authors

Bernadette Andreosso-O'Callaghan is a Jean Monnet Professor of Economic Integration and Director of the Euro-Asia Centre and of the Centre for European Studies at the University of Limerick, Ireland. She has published in the area of economic integration, Asia and the EU compared. A recent publication includes *Current Issues in Economic Integration* (Ashgate, 2010 – with M. Bruna Zolin).

Dominique Caouette is an Associate Professor in the Department of Political Science at the Université de Montréal, where he has taught international relations and Southeast Asian politics since 2004. His works have been published in *Kasarinlan: A Philippine Quarterly of Third World Studies*, *Pacific Focus, Geography Compass*, *Canadian Journal of Development Studies*, and *Possibles* as well as book chapters recently published in *L'Altermondialisme: Forums sociaux, résistances et nouvelle culture politique* (Éditions Écosociété, 2010), *La Politique internationale en question* (Presses de l'Université de Montréal, 2009), *L'Aide canadienne au développement* (Presses de l'Université de Montréal, 2008), *La Politique en question* (Presses de l'Université de Montréal, 2008), and *L'État des citoyennetés* (Presses de l'Université de Montréal, 2007). Recently he coedited with Pascale Dufour and Dominique Masson, *Solidarities Beyond Borders: Transnationalizing Women's Movement* (UBC Press, 2010), and with Sarah Turner, *Agrarian Angst and Rural Resistance in Contemporary Southeast Asia* (Routledge, 2009).

Didier Chabanet is a Marie Curie Fellow at the European University Institute in Florence, Italy. He is also a Senior Research Fellow at the Triangle Research Center of the École Normale Supérieure de Lyon, France (Lettres et Sciences Humaines). He is a well-known international scholar in the field of collective action, social exclusion, and poor people movements. Recent publications in this area include *The Mobilization of the Unemployed in Europe* (Palgrave, 2011 – edited with Jean Faniel) and *Collective Action and European Democracy* (Rowman and Littlefield, 2008 – with Richard Balme).

Pascale Dufour is an Associate Professor in the Department of Political Science at the Université de Montréal and Director of the Center of Research on Politics and

B. Andreosso-O'Callaghan and F. Royall (eds.), *Economic and Political Change in Asia and Europe: Social Movement Analyses*, DOI 10.1007/978-94-007-4653-4,

Social Development (www.cpds.umontreal.ca). She focuses on collective action and social movements in comparative perspective, especially in the context of globalization. Her work has been published in *French Politics*, *Canadian Journal of Political Science*, *Canadian Journal of Sociology*, *Mobilization*, and *Social Science Quarterly*. A recent book includes *Solidarities Beyond Borders: Transnationalizing Women's Movements* (UBC Press, 2010 – with Dominique Masson and Dominique Caouette). Her emerging research examines practices of local social forums in Québec and France.

Jean Faniel is a Researcher at the Centre de Recherche et d'Information Socio-politiques, in Brussels. His 2006 doctorate (Université Libre de Bruxelles, Belgium) analyzed the relationship between Belgian trade unions and the unemployed. He has published numerous articles on Belgian trade unions and the mobilizations of the unemployed in Europe. Recent publications include "L'Europe du chômage" (*Politique européenne*, Vol. 21, 2007 – edited with Didier Chabanet), *En mouvement: Perspectives pour le syndicat de demain* (CG/Amsab/ASP, 2009 – with Corinne Gobin, Carl Devos, and Kurt Vandaele), and *The Mobilization of the Unemployed in Europe* (Palgrave, 2011 – edited with Didier Chabanet).

Marco Giugni is a Professor at the Department of Political Science and International Relations and Director of the Institute of Social and Political Research (RESOP) at the University of Geneva, Switzerland. His research interests include social movements and collective action, immigration and ethnic relations, and unemployment and social exclusion.

Birgit Häse is the Director of the Centre for East Asian Studies at Technische Universität Dresden, Germany. She has published on issues of identity and nation building, gender, literature, and film with a regional focus on Greater China. A recent publication includes *Eroberungen aus dem Archiv – Beiträge zu den Kulturen Ostasiens* (Memories from the Archives: On East Asian Cultures) (Harrassowitz, 2009 – edited with Carsten Storm).

Christian Lahusen is a Professor of Sociology at the University of Siegen (Germany). His research interests include political sociology and European studies. He has published books and numerous articles on political interest representation and social movements, on political contentions in the field of labor market and social policies, and on protests by the unemployed.

Jasmine Lorenzini is a Doctoral Student at the Department of Political Science and International Relations and research assistant at the Institute of Social and Political Research at the University of Geneva, Switzerland. Her thesis analyzes the political integration of young long-term unemployed in Geneva and in other European cities.

Lilian Mathieu is the Director of Research at the Centre National de la Recherche Scientifique (France) and currently at the Centre Max Weber of the École Normale Supérieure de Lyon, France.

Michiaki Okuyama is a Professor at Nanzan University and Permanent Research Fellow at the Nanzan Institute for Religion and Culture in Nagoya, Japan. His works in English include "Camouflage and Epiphany: The Discovery of the Sacred in Mircea Eliade and Ōe Kenzaburō," in Bryan Rennie (ed.), *International Eliade* (SUNY, 2007); and "Religious Problems in Contemporary Japanese Society: Two Cases after the Aum Shinrikyo Affair," in Titus Hjelm (ed.), *Religion and Social Problems* (Routledge, 2010). He has served on the editorial board for an international journal *Religion* (Routledge, 2011) and as an internal adviser for *the Japanese Journal of Religious Studies* (1998).

Matt Perry is a Reader in Labor History at the University of Newcastle. He is an editor of the *Labour History Review*. He has published widely on the unemployed movements in Britain and France.

Anne-Cécile Renouard is a Research Scholar in political science at the University of Strasbourg (France).

Frédéric Royall is a Senior Lecturer in French Studies at the University of Limerick (Ireland) and has published extensively in the area of contemporary French and Irish politics and society.

Carsten Storm is Associate Professor at the Faculty for East Asian Studies at Ruhr University Bochum, Germany. He focuses on issues of culture, identity, historicity, and authenticity in China and Taiwan. Recent publications include *Imagining History: Identity, Historicity, Resistance, and Authenticity in Chinese Historical Novels* (Harrassowitz, 2010) and several articles in journals. He is also coeditor of *The Margins of Becoming: Identity and Culture in Taiwan*, (Harrassowitz, 2007 – with Mark Harrison) and *Eroberungen aus dem Archiv – Beiträge zu den Kulturen Ostasiens* [Memories from the Archives: On East Asian Cultures] (Harrassowitz, 2009 – with Birgit Haese).

M. Bruna Zolin is a Professor of Commodity Markets and Economics of Rural Development at Ca' Foscari University, Venice, Italy. She has published mainly in the areas of agricultural markets and rural development policies. Her latest publication in the field of economic integration between Asia and Europe includes *Current Issues in Economic Integration* (Ashgate, 2010 – with Bernadette Andreosso-O'Callaghan).

References

Anderson, B. (1996). Elections and participation in three Southeast Asian Countries. In R. Taylor (Ed.), *The politics of elections in Southeast Asia*. Cambridge: Cambridge University Press.

Asian Development Bank. (2000). *Annual report*. Manilla: Asian Development Bank.

Association de Recherches et d'Études du Mouvement Ouvrier de la Région de Saint-Nazaire. (1983). *Saint-Nazaire et le Mouvement Ouvrier de 1920 à 1939*. Saint-Nazaire: Aremors.

Béroud, S., & Bouffartigue, P. (2009). *Quand le travail se précarise, quelles résistances collectives?* Paris: La Dispute.

Chabanet, D., & Royall, F. (2010). *Mobilising against Marginalisation in Europe*. Newcastle: Cambridge Scholars Publishing.

Commission of the European Communities. (2009). *Sixth progress report on economic and social cohesion* (COM 2009 295 final). Brussels: Report from the European Parliament and Council

Communist Party of the Philippines, Central Committee (1983). Overthrow the U.S.-Marcos Fascist dictatorship, establish a revolutionary coalition government!, (Signed by Central Committee on October 7th), *Ang Bayan*, 15(8). [Chapter 15].

Croucher, R. (1987). *We refuse to starve in silence: A history of the NUWM, 1920–46*. London: Lawrence and Wishart.

Croucher, R. (1995). Divisions in the movement: The NUWM and its rivals in comparative perspective. In G. Andrews, N. Fishman, & K. Morgan (Eds.), *Opening the books: Essays on the social and cultural history of the British communist party*. London: Pluto Press.

Croucher, R. (2008). History of unemployed movements. *Labour History Review, 73*(1), 1–18.

Davies, S. (1992). The membership of the national unemployed workers' movement, 1923–1938. *Labour History Review, 57*(1), 29–36.

della Porta, D. (2005). Démocratie en mouvement: Les manifestants du Forum social européen, des liens aux réseaux. *Politix, 17*(68), 49–79.

Evans, N. (1999). South Wales has been roused as never before: Marching against the means test, 1934–1936. In D. Howell & K. Morgan (Eds.), *Crime, protest and police in modern British society*. Cardiff: University of Wales Press.

Frank, A. G., & Fuentes, M. (1990). Civil democracy, social movements in world history. In S. Amin, G. Arrighi, A. G. Frank, & I. Wallerstein (Eds.), *Transforming the revolution: Social movements and the world-system*. New York: Monthly Review Press.

Harmer, H. (1989). The failure of the communists: The national unemployment workers movement 1921–39: A disappointing success. In A. Thorpe (Ed.), *The failure of political extremism in interwar Britain*. Exeter: University of Exeter.

Harris, J. (1972). *Unemployment and politics: A study in English social policy, 1886–1914*. Oxford: Clarendon Press.

Harrison, R. (1978). New light on the police and the hunger marchers. *Bulletin – Society for the Study of Labour History, 37*, 17–49.

B. Andreosso-O'Callaghan and F. Royall (eds.), *Economic and Political Change in Asia and Europe: Social Movement Analyses*, DOI 10.1007/978-94-007-4653-4,

Hayburn, R. (1972). The police and the hunger marches. *International Review of Social History, 17*(2), 625–644.

Hobson, B. (Ed.). (2003). *Recognition struggles and social movements: Contested identities, agency and power*. New York: Cambridge University Press.

Kourchid, O. (1999). Les mouvements de chômeurs en France. 1919–1935. Historiographie selon la Vie Ouvrière. In *Images et Mouvements du Siècle* (Les Raisins de la Colère, Vol. 2). Paris: France-Progrès.

Kriesi, H. (1995). The political opportunity structure of new social movements: Its impact on their mobilization. In J. Craig Jenkins & Klandermans Bert (Eds.), *The politics of social protest*. Minneapolis: University of Minnesota Press.

Miller, F. (1976). The unemployment policy of the national government, 1931–36. *Historical Journal, 19*, 453–476.

Miller, F. (1979). The British unemployment assistance crisis of 1935. *Journal of Contemporary History, 14*, 329–352.

Reiss, M. (2008). Circulars, surveys and support: Trades councils and the marches of 1936. *Labour History Review, 73*(1), 89–112.

Stevenson, J. (1979). The police and the 1932 hunger march. *Bulletin – Society for the Study of Labour History, 38*, 24–27.

Tanner, J. (2008). The only fighting element of the working class? Unemployed activism and protest in Sheffield, 1919–24. *Labour History Review, 73*(1), 133–144.

Tarrow, S. (1996). States and opportunities: The political structuring of social movements. In D. McAdam, J. McCarthy, & M. Zald (Eds.), *Comparative perspectives on social movements: Political opportunities, mobilizing structures, and cultural framings*. Cambridge: Cambridge University Press.

Tartakowsky, D. (2000). Syndicats et mobilisations de chômeurs dans les années trente. *Cahiers de Ressy, 3–4*, 16–21.

Tilly, C. (1984). Les origines du répertoire de l'action collective contemporaine en France et en Grande-Bretagne. *Vingtième Siècle, 4*, 89–108.

Tilly, C. (1995). *Popular contention in Great Britain, 1758–1834*. Cambridge: Harvard University Press.

Tilly, C. (1997). Parliamentarization of popular contention in Great Britain, 1758–1834. *Theory and Society, 26*, 245–273.

Traugott, M. (Ed.). (1995). *Repertoires and cycles of collective action*. Durham: Duke University Press.

Ward, S. (2008). The means test and the unemployed in South Wales and North-East of England, 1931–39. *Labour History Review, 73*(1), 113–132.

Index

B. Andreosso-O'Callaghan and F. Royall (eds.), *Economic and Political Change in Asia and Europe: Social Movement Analyses*, DOI 10.1007/978-94-007-4653-4,

Printed by Printforce, the Netherlands